T0138673

Introduction to
Certificateless Cryptography

Introduction to Certificateless Cryptography

Hu Xiong
Zhen Qin
Athanasios V. Vasilakos

CRC Press
Taylor & Francis Group
Boca Raton   London   New York

CRC Press is an imprint of the
Taylor & Francis Group, an **Informa** business

CRC Press
Taylor & Francis Group
6000 Broken Sound Parkway NW, Suite 300
Boca Raton, FL 33487-2742

Printed on acid-free paper
Version Date: 20160622

International Standard Book Number-13: 978-1-4822-4860-9 (Hardback)

Library of Congress Cataloging-in-Publication Data

Names: Xiong, Hu, author. | Qin, Zhen, 1982- author. | Vasilakos, Athanasios, author.
Title: Introduction to certificateless cryptography / Hu Xiong, Zhen Qin, and Athanasios V. Vasilakos.
Description: Boca Raton : Taylor & Francis, a CRC title, part of the Taylor & Francis imprint, a member of the Taylor & Francis Group, the academic division of T&F Informa, plc, [2017] | Includes bibliographical references and index.
Identifiers: LCCN 2016016910 | ISBN 9781482248609 (hardcover : acid-free paper)
Subjects: LCSH: Public key infrastructure (Computer security) | Public key cryptography. | Identification. | Data encryption (Computer science) | Computer networks--Security measures.
Classification: LCC QA76.9.A25 X75 2017 | DDC 005.8/2--dc23
LC record available at https://lccn.loc.gov/2016016910

Visit the Taylor & Francis Web site at
http://www.taylorandfrancis.com

and the CRC Press Web site at
http://www.crcpress.com

Printed and bound in the United States of America by Publishers Graphics, LLC on sustainably sourced paper.

Contents

SECTION II CL-PKC without Random Oracles

CHAPTER 3 ▪ CLE Secure in the Standard Model 59

SECTION IV   Applications, Extensions, and Related Paradigms

CHAPTER 8 ▪ Applications of CL-PKC   171

Section V   **Future Directions**

List of Figures

List of Tables

Preface

The public-key cryptography (PKC) revolution introduced by Diffie and Hellman in 1976 enables an entity (the sender) to securely send a message to another entity (the receiver) without requiring a preexisting shared secret key or any online interaction between these two entities. Different from symmetric cryptography, a pair of keys is involved in PKC to achieve the above-mentioned function such that a public key is widely published, while a corresponding private key is kept secret by the user himself/herself. A central problem for PKC is to ensure the connection between a particular public key and the user's identity. The traditional approach to address this problem is to rely on a public-key infrastructure (PKI), in which digital certificates are issued by one or more certificate authorities (CAs) to connect a user to the corresponding public key. Bearing the costly certificate management in mind, identity-based public-key cryptography (ID-PKC) was invented by Shamir to ease the certificate management in the sense that the user's public key can be derived directly from the user's publicly known information (e.g., an email address or cell phone number). Despite avoiding the need for a certificate in ID-PKC, a fully trusted third party, called a private key generator (PKG), is required to initially set up the system and calculate the private key for other entities. The fact that the PKG generates the private keys for the users in the system creates an inherent *key escrow* problem in ID-PKC.

In 2003, a new paradigm named certificateless public-key cryptography (CL-PKC) was presented by Al-Riyami and Paterson to retain the merits of ID-PKC (no PKI is needed) and traditional PKI (there is no key escrow) simultaneously. Similar to ID-PKC, each user in CL-PKC has a public known identity and a matching secret key calculated by a semitrusted third-party dubbed the key-generation center (KGC). In this way, digital certificates in the traditional PKI are eliminated in CL-PKC. Moreover, each user in CL-PKC also owns a public/private key pair generated by himself/herself, as in the traditional PKI. Thus, CL-PKC does not suffer from the key escrow problem since a user's private key is not available to the KGC. With its unique characteristic, CL-PKC has emerged as a distinct research area almost from scratch and now attracts many researchers and engineers from across the world. However, the only way to learn about CL-PKC until now has been to read scattered papers in this area, which makes the topic inaccessible to most people. The goal of this book is to give as complete a picture of CL-PKC by assimilating the existing literatures in a self-contained and consistent volume, while remaining accessible. Such a task is beyond the scope of research papers and survey papers, where the former only focus on narrow topics with nonstandard techniques and the latter in nature address at most a small number of major topics at a high level. Our intent is to cover all the important CL-PKC schemes that have been presented to date. Considering that the research work in this field is still actively continuing, this is only a snapshot of this topic in motion rather than the final word about it.

As for the partitioning of research areas into chapters, this book generally alternates between the "functional organization" and "academic organization" approaches. On the one hand, some chapters are organized according to the functions of interest to readers. For instance, all applications of CL-PKC schemes in different environments are

TABLE P.1 Hierarchical Levels of CL-PKC

Perspectives	
Future directions	Chapter 11
Applications and Extensions	
Applications of CL-PKC	Chapter 8
Extensions of CL-PKC	Chapter 9
Comparisons	
Comparisons with competitive paradigms	Chapter 10
Cryptographic functions	
Encryption	Chapters 3, 6, and 7
Signature	Chapters 4, 6, and 7
Key agreement	Chapters 6 and 7
Foundations	
Mathematical concepts and properties	Chapter 2
The random oracle model	Chapter 5
Motivation	
Avoiding key escrow	Chapter 1

addressed in one chapter. On the other hand, all schemes based on the same concept (i.e., certificateless encryption schemes paired with provable security in the standard model) might be covered in one chapter. We depict the hierarchical structure around which this book is organized in Table P.1 and believe that partitioning in this manner is certainly reasonable. Furthermore, one novelty of this book depends on the fact that it provides a rigorous treatment of CL-PKC in an accessible manner appropriate for beginners. To avoid obscuring the nature of this subject, security proofs of some important schemes, especially with some novel techniques, are selected and analyzed in detail. Many more schemes are presented without any formal proof, and in some cases only an intuitive description of the security reduction is offered.

Acknowledgments

This project would not have been accomplished successfully without the help, guidance, and support of many people. Despite the possibility of overlooking anyone, we would like to list the names of our supporters here.

First of all, we are thankful to CRC Press, especially Richard O'Hanley, for his enthusiasm and patience with the project due to the fact that the writing of this book took almost a year and a half (and included missing several deadlines).

We are also deeply indebted to Prof. Qianhong Wu, Dr. Fagen Li, and Ms. Jennifer Batamuliza, who read original drafts and provided us with constructive feedback and insightful suggestions.

Furthermore, we thank the moral support and understanding of our (respective) wives and children during the time spent on this book.

The financial support from the National Natural Science Foundation of China under grants #61003230, #61370026, and #61300191, the Open Funds from State Key Laboratory of Cryptology and Key Lab of Information Network Security under grant #C14608, the Fundamental Research Funds for the Central Universities under grant #ZYGX2013J073, and the Applied Basic Research Program of Sichuan Province under grant #2014JY0041 are also greatly appreciated.

Needless to say, any errors and omissions in the book are totally our own responsibility and we would greatly appreciate feedback about them from the readers. Thus, please send your comments to xionghu.uestc@gmail.com and put "Introduction to Certificateless Cryptography" in the subject line.

Hu Xiong and Zhen Qin
University of Electronic Science and Technology of China

Athanasios V. Vasilakos
Lulea University of Technology
December, 2015

List of Abbreviations

CA	Certificate authority	ICA	Identity certifying authority
CB-PKC	Certificate-based public-key cryptography	ID-PKC	Identity-based public-key cryptography
CL-AKA	Certificateless authenticated key agreement	KGC	Key-generation center
CL-PKC	Certificateless public-key cryptography	PKG	Private key generator
CLE	Certificateless encryption	PKI	Public-key infrastructure
CLS	Certificateless signature	SGC-PKC	Self-generated certificate public-key cryptography

I

Setting the Stage

CHAPTER 1

Avoiding Key Escrow

1.1 A BRIEF INTRODUCTION TO SYMMETRIC CRYPTOGRAPHY

Cryptography is an interdisciplinary field concerning sensitive digital data storage, transmission, and sharing [1]. Two basic functions of cryptography are to preserve the privacy of communication between two entities in different geographic locations and to provide authentication of one entity to another. The former function can be provided with symmetric-key encryption where the cryptographic keys for decryption of ciphertext may be identical to or easily derived from the keys for encryption of plaintext. In practice, the encryption/decryption keys represent a shared secret between the sender and the receiver that can be used to maintain secure communication over public channels [2]. The requirement that a shared secret key should be distributed through a secure channel between a sender and a receiver from being eavesdropped or modified is usually considered the main drawback of symmetric-key cryptography. Making matters worse, the management of the cryptographic keys has become a challenge when the number of communicating parties in the system increases. Concretely, the total number of secret keys in the system with n independent parties is $\binom{n}{2}$ and each participant has to maintain $n-1$ secret keys since a secret key is required for each pair of parties in system. Furthermore, it is difficult to design digital signatures with nonrepudiation and public verifiability in symmetric-key cryptography [3]. There were no solutions to the key predistribution problem and digital signatures until the revolutionary idea of public-key cryptography (PKC) was put forward over 40 years ago. An overview of symmetric-key cryptography is depicted in Figure 1.1.

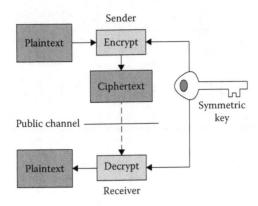

Figure 1.1 Symmetric-key cryptography where a single key is adopted for encryption and decryption.

1.2 SETTING OF ASYMMETRIC PKC

In 1976, the notion of PKC was initially introduced by Diffie and Hellman [4] to eliminate the need for secure key distribution channels and supply the counterpart of a handwritten signature in the electronic world [5]. The distinguishing feature of PKC is due to the fact that the key used to encrypt a message is different from the key used to decrypt it. In the environment of PKC, each user owns a pair of cryptographic keys: a public key and a corresponding private key. The public key is widely published, whereas the private key is kept secret by its proprietor. Although the public key and the private key are related mathematically, the system parameters will be chosen such that the private key is either impossible or prohibitively expensive to be obtained from the public key. Meanwhile, the secret channel between the sender and the receiver to share secret information is also eliminated since only public keys are involved in all communication while no private key is ever shared or transmitted. An overview of PKC is shown in Figure 1.2.

With the advent of PKC, the notion of a digital signature, a cryptographic analog of handwritten signatures, has also emerged [3,6]. A valid digital signature allows a sender to "certify" a message in such a way that any verifier can believe that the message was indeed originated from a known sender (authentication); the sender cannot deny having sent the message (nonrepudiation) and that the message has

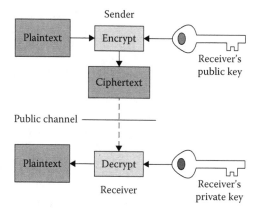

Figure 1.2 An overview of public-key cryptography (PKC).

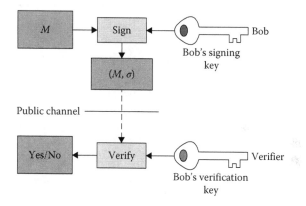

Figure 1.3 An overview of a digital signature.

not been modified in transit (integrity). The digital signature has been widely applied in the fields of software distribution, military affairs, financial transactions, and in other cases where the authenticity of a digital message or document is required. An overview of the digital signature is shown in Figure 1.3.

1.2.1 Traditional PKC

However, the issue of how to trust a public key should be addressed before PKC is brought into practice due to the fact that the public key of the user is usually a type of random string. The typical approach to guarantee the authenticity of a public key in traditional PKC is to use a public-key infrastructure (PKI), in which one or more certificate authorities (CAs) issue certificates to bind a user and its corresponding public key.

To obtain a certificate, the user submits his or her public key to the CA, who then performs the necessary (physical) verification and determines the identity of the target user. After such checking, the CA issues a digital signature (which is regarded as the digital certificate) on the public key of this user. Before a public key is employed in an encryption (in the encryption algorithm) or a verification (in the signing algorithm) operation, the certificate of the public key issued by the CA should be verified under the public key of the CA. In this way, the cost caused by certificate management such as creation, transmission, verification, and revocation of the certificate in traditional PKI is considered to be cumbersome [7].

1.2.2 Identity-Based PKC

Taking the heavy certificate management overhead into account, identity-based public-key cryptography (ID-PKC) was introduced by Shamir [8] to ease the certificate management problem in traditional PKI. It is challenging to construct efficient ID-based encryption schemes and only the concrete instantiation of an ID-based signature scheme has been proposed in [8]. The construction of efficient ID-based encryption remained an open problem for many years until the pairing-based and quadratic residues-based constructions were presented independently by Boneh–Franklin [9] and Cocks [10] in 2001. In ID-PKC, the public key of a user can be easily calculated from some publicly known identity information of the user, for example, a social security number, street address, email address, or telephone number. In this way, ID-PKC can eliminate the need for certificate management in the traditional PKI. A trusted third party, called the private key generator (PKG), is involved to initialize the system by generating the public parameters and computing private keys for all users according to their identities in ID-PKC. The PKG first publishes a "master" public key along with the system parameters and retains the corresponding master secret key. Any party can compute a user's public key corresponding to its identity by incorporating the master public key, system parameter, and identity value. As for the corresponding private key, the party authorized to use the identity first contacts the PKG, which in turn generates the private key based on the master private key and the identity and sends the private key to the requested user via a secure channel. With the property that anyone can encrypt messages (or verify signatures) with no prior distribution of keys between individual participants, ID-PKC receives a lot of attention from the industry and academic community [11,12]. A central problem with the use of ID-PKC is the inherent key escrow problem of a user's private key, that is to say, the PKG equipped with the knowledge of master secret key can compute any user's private key. Consequently, a malicious PKG can decrypt any ciphertext or forge a signature on any message on behalf of any user in the system without being detected. Thanks to this inborn problem, ID-PKC is considered to be suitable only for closed groups or private networks [8]. Therefore, it is desirable to eliminate key escrow in the ID-PKC setting to make it more applicable in the real world. An overview of ID-PKC is shown in Figure 1.4.

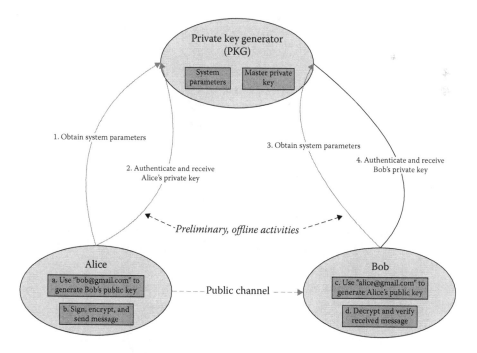

Figure 1.4 An overview of identity-based PKC.

1.3   WHY SHOULD I CARE ABOUT CERTIFICATELESS PKC

Extensive research efforts have been taken to deal with the key escrow problem without sacrificing the merits of the certificate-free property in the ID-PKC setting [9,13–16]. First of all, the basic idea of threshold cryptography was adopted by [9,13] to reduce the trust on the single PKG by distributing the master secret key among multiple PKGs. In a typical (n,t)-distributed PKG suggested by [9,13], the master key is shared among n PKG entities such that only $t(1 \leq t \leq n)$ or more entities can recover the master key, while a set of PKG entities of size $t - 1$ or smaller cannot extract the master secret key. In order to obtain his or her valid secret key, a user have to go to at least t PKG entities, prove his or her identity to each of them, and get a private key component. Further, it is burdensome to maintain multiple independent PKG entities in a commercial setting since these entities have to be jointly managed by several companies.

After that, the key escrow problem was considered by Goyal [14] and Goyal et al. [15] in a weaker threat model in the sense that a malicious PKG sells off a decryption key for any identity to make money. In other words, someone may bribe the PKG to obtain a private key (different from the one derived by the genuine user) for some targeted identity. Therefore, it is natural to assume that the malicious PKG should be penalized once this decryption key is discovered at a later stage by the genuine user. According to [14,15], an exponential number of valid decryption keys can be generated for each identity in the ID-PKC setting. Every user is involved in the private key-generation process to derive one decryption key corresponding to his or her identity from the PKG, while the PKG does not know which key this user has obtained. If another decryption key for the same identity has been computed and sold by the PKG, then this key will be different from the one got by the genuine user with nonnegligible probability, and simultaneous occurrence of two distinct decryption keys per identity is regarded as cryptographic proof of malicious behavior by the PKG. It is obvious that the approach in [14,15] can only partially solve the key escrow problem because the malicious PKG can still keep on decrypting or signing on behalf of each user in the system by itself.

By stripping the function of identity authentication from the traditional PKG, another approach was proposed by Chow [16] to mitigate the key escrow problem in ID-PKC. Different from the traditional ID-PKC, two independent authorities, that is, the identity certifying authority (ICA) and the PKG, will be involved in the secret key-generation process such that the ICA is responsible for authenticating the validity of a user's identity and the PKG can issue a private key to this user after the successful authentication between the user and the ICA. In this manner, it is impossible for the PKG to determine the identity involved in the key-generation process and hence the PKG does not know which private key should be generated by giving a ciphertext. However, the assumption in this approach is too strong to be accepted by the public since the PKG can decrypt any ciphertext if it is stored or transferred along with the corresponding identity.

Observing that all of the above-mentioned approaches cannot solve the key escrow problem satisfactorily, it is fair to say that it is interesting and challenging to defeat the malicious PKG effectively in the ID-PKC environment. By incorporating the merits of traditional PKC and ID-PKC simultaneously, the notion of certificateless public-key cryptography (CL-PKC), which is orthogonal to [9,13–16], was initially introduced in 2003 by Al-Riyami and Paterson [17]. Similar to ID-PKC, CL-PKC relies on the existence of a semitrusted key-generation center (KGC) that initially sets up the system and issues the partial private key to the user according to user's identity by using the master secret key. Meanwhile, a user public/private key pair is also calculated by the user itself. The full private key of a user, which is needed to perform the decryption or signing operation, consists of the partial private key and the user private key. Due to the fact that the KGC cannot access the user private key owned by the user itself, the key escrow problem has been removed in CL-PKC while preserving the *certificate-free* nature of the system. Obviously, CL-PKC can avoid the heavy overhead of certificate management in traditional PKC as well as the key escrow problem in ID-PKC altogether.[a] Since the introduction of CL-PKC, many concrete constructions, security models, and applications in this field have been proposed and revisited including certificateless encryption (CLE) [18], certificateless signature (CLS)

---

[a]One disadvantage of CL-PKC is that entire public key can no longer be obtained from only the identity information. In contrast to ID-PKC, two pieces of information, such as (1) the receiver's user public key and (2) the identity, are needed in order to encrypt a message to the receiver. In this way, the user public key should be transferred to the sender before the encryption operation has been performed. It is remarkable that CLS and CL-AKA do not suffer from this drawback since the user public key can be transferred or stored along with the signature or the authentication message.

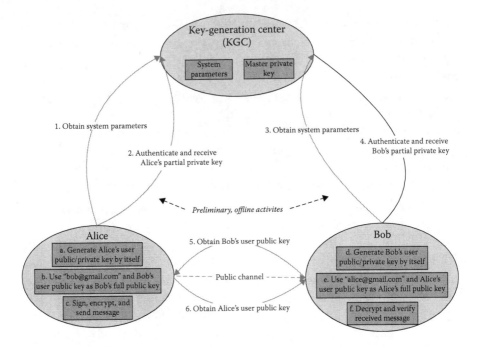

Figure 1.5 An overview of certificateless PKC.

[19,20], and certificateless authenticated key agreement (CL-AKA) [21] during the last decade. An overview of CL-PKC is depicted in Figure 1.5.

In view of the fruitful achievements in CL-PKC [22–30], it would be interesting and urgent to make this topic accessible to more people, such as graduate students, researchers, and engineers in the field of applied cryptography and information security. However, the only way to learn about CL-PKC until now has been to read scattering academic papers. Fortunately, this book will bridge this gap and make this paradigm more attainable. Different from the other books currently on the market, a rigorous treatment (definitions, precise assumptions, concrete and generic constructions, rigorous proofs of security, extensions, comparison with relative primitives, application scenarios, and future directions) of CL-PKC will be offered in a comprehensible manner. For a beginning graduate student, our book provides a comprehensive and state-of-the-art overview for a quick introduction in the field of CL-PKC. This monograph can also serve experienced security engineers or researchers in a unified framework to structure and organize their knowledge in this field. This should inevitably result in identification of new directions for CL-PKC research and better understanding of this primitive.

1.4   PLAN OF THE BOOK

Technical discussion starts from Chapter 2 and the current monograph consists of the following sections.

- **Part I—Setting the Stage.** This part, which is of preliminary nature, provides the importance of CL-PKC and necessary mathematical background needed in the following parts in which we discuss CL-PKC algorithms. The basic mathematical concepts and properties are not intended to be encyclopedic but rather are provided such that the reader can get some feel about how CL-PKC schemes can actually be constructed.

- **Part II—CL-PKC without Random Oracles.** Parts II and III of the book cover concrete and generic constructions of CL-PKC schemes such as the CLE, CLS, and CL-AKA schemes. Part II focuses on schemes where the security of these schemes can be proven without relying on the "random oracle" model. This part begins with concrete CLE schemes based on bilinear pairings. Next, generic constructions based on the existing traditional public-key encryption and identity-based encryption schemes are presented. Finally, some CLS schemes secure in the standard model built upon bilinear maps are shown.

- **Part III—CL-PKC in the Random Oracle Models.** The CLE and CLS schemes discussed in Part II are, generally speaking, regarded as impractical to use when performance is taken into account. Instead, the schemes with security proofs in the random oracle model are more efficient and widely used. Following a short introduction to the random oracle model, we discuss the concrete CLE scheme, CLS scheme, and CL-AKA protocol in this setting, and the efficient pairing of free CL-PKC constructions.

- **Part IV—Applications, Extensions, and Related Primitives.** This part summarizes the possible applications of CL-PKC in the area of onion routing [22], wireless body area networks [24], and

cloud computing [25,28]; investigates their relationships with the
certificate-based public-key cryptosystem (CB-PKC) [31] and self-
generated-certificate public-key cryptography (SGC-PKC) [32];
and describes the extension of CL-PKC schemes.

- **Part V—Future Directions.** In this part, some interesting
  directions for future research have been suggested from a number
  of perspectives such as efficient constructions with formal security
  proofs, extensions, and applications.

CHAPTER 2

Foundations

2.1 INTRODUCTION

The purpose of this chapter is to offer a brief review of all of the necessary cryptographic concepts needed in the following chapters. We start with mathematical background and the associated hard problems. The other aspect of this chapter is some facts regarding classical symmetric cryptography and the public-key cryptosystem. Finally, a concise description of provable security will be presented in the remainder of this chapter. We remark that this introduction is by no means exhaustive such that the approaches used to speed-up pairing computations or select suitable parameters of an elliptic curve is really beyond the scope of this book.

2.2 MATHEMATICAL CONCEPTS AND PROPERTIES

2.2.1 Concepts from Number Theory

2.2.1.1 Primes and Divisibility

Let $\mathbb{Z}$ be the set of integers. We say that a divides b (denoted as $a \mid b$) if there exists an integer c satisfying $ac = b$ for $a, b, c \in_R \mathbb{Z}$. If a does not divide b, we write $a \nmid b$. Despite this definition making sense even when one or more of these integers is negative or zero, we are only interested in the case when a, b, c are all positive. A direct observation is that if $a|b$ and $a|c$, then $a|(xb + yc)$ for any $x, y \in_R \mathbb{Z}$.

If $a|b$ and a is positive, a is regarded as a divisor or factor of b. Furthermore a is also called a *nontrivial* factor of b when $a \notin \{1, b\}$. A positive integer $p(> 1)$ is considered *prime* if it has no nontrivial factors; that is, it has only two divisors: 1 and p itself. A positive integer greater than 1 is called *composite* if this integer is not a prime number. It is the convention that "1" is neither prime nor composite.

According to the fundamental theorem of arithmetic, every integer greater than 1 can be expressed *uniquely* as a product of primes. Namely, any positive integer $n > 1$ can be written as $n = \prod_i p_i^{e_i}$ such that $\{p_i\}$ are distinct primes and $e_i \geq 1$ for all i; furthermore, the $\{p_i\}$ and $\{e_i\}$ are uniquely determined up to ordering.

Proposition 2.1 *Let a and b be two integers and $b > 0$. Then there exist unique integers q, r satisfying $a = qb + r$ and $0 \leq r < b$.*

c is known as the *greatest common divisor* of two nonnegative integers a, b (written as $\gcd(a, b)$) if c is the largest integer satisfying $c|a$ and $c|b$. It is noted that $\gcd(0, 0)$ is not defined, whereas $\gcd(b, 0) = \gcd(0, b) = b$. The notion of greatest common divisor also makes sense when either or both of a, b are negative but we will never need this; therefore, when we write $\gcd(a, b)$, we always assume that $a, b \geq 0$. Note that if p is prime, then $\gcd(a, p)$ is either equal to 1 or p. a and b are called as *relatively prime* if $\gcd(a, b) = 1$.

Proposition 2.2 *Let a, b be two positive integers. Then there exist $x, y \in \mathbb{Z}$ such that $ax + by = \gcd(a, b)$. Furthermore, $\gcd(a, b)$ is the smallest positive integer that can be expressed in this manner.*

Proof 2.1 *Let I denote the set $\{ax + by\}$, where x, y are chosen from $\mathbb{Z}$. Note that I certainly contains some positive integers since at least $a, b \in I$ such that $a = a \times 1 + b \times 0$ and $b = a \times 0 + b \times 1$. Let d denote the smallest positive integer in I. We claim that $d = \gcd(a, b)$ due to the fact that d can be represented as $d = ax + by$ for some $x, y \in \mathbb{Z}$ (recall that $d \in I$). In addition, to show that $d = \gcd(a, b)$, we must show that $d|a$ and $d|b$, and that d is the largest integer with this property. In fact, we can show that d divides every element in I. To prove this, take arbitrary $c \in I$ such that $c = ax' + by'$ with $x', y' \in \mathbb{Z}$. According to Proposition 2.1, we have $c = qd + r$ where q and r are integers and $0 \leq r < d$. Then*

$$r = c - qd = ax' + by' - q(ax + by) = (x' - qx)a + (y' - qy)b \in I$$

There is a contradiction between $r \neq 0$ and the choice of d as the smallest positive integer in I. Thus, it is obvious that $r = 0$ and hence $d|c$.

Since both a and b are elements in I, the above shows that $d|a$ and $d|b$. Suppose there exists $d' > d$ such that $d'|a$ and $d'|b$. Then $d'|ax+by$; since the latter is equal to d, this means $d'|d$, which is impossible if d' is larger than d. It is concluded that d is the largest integer dividing both a and b, and hence $d = \gcd(a, b)$.

Given a and b, the Euclidean algorithm *can be used to compute* $\gcd(a, b)$ *in polynomial time. The* extended Euclidean algorithm *can be used to compute the coefficients* x, y *(as in Proposition 2.2) in polynomial time as well. Interested readers can refer to [33] for more details.*

Proposition 2.3 *If* $c|ab$ *and* $\gcd(a, c) = 1$, *then* $c|b$. *In particular, if* p *is prime and* $p|ab$, *then either* $p|a$ *or* $p|b$.

Proof 2.2 *It is easy to observe that* $c \times \alpha = ab$ *for some integer* α *since* $c|ab$. *From* $\gcd(a, c) = 1$, *then, according to the previous proposition, there exist integers* x, y *such that* $1 = ax + cy$. *Multiplying both sides by* b, *we obtain*

$$b = axb + cyb = abx + cyb = c \times \alpha x + cyb = c \cdot (\alpha x + yb)$$

Since $(\alpha x + yb)$ *is an integer, it follows that* $c|b$.

The second part of this proposition follows from the fact that if $p \nmid a$, *then* $\gcd(a, p) = 1$.

Proposition 2.4 *If* $p|N$, $q|N$, *and* $\gcd(p, q) = 1$, *then* $pq|N$.

Proof 2.3 *We can see* $p\alpha = N$, $q\beta = N$ *from* $p|N$ *and* $q|N$, *and obtain* $1 = px + qy$ *from Proposition 2.2, where* α, β, x, y *are all integers. Multiplying both sides of the last equation by* N, *we obtain*

$$N = pxN + qyN = pxq\beta + qyp\alpha = pq(x\beta + y\alpha)$$

Thus, $pq|N$.

2.2.1.2 Modular Arithmetic

Let a, b, N be integers with $N > 1$. Let $[a \bmod N]$ denote the remainder of $a \in \mathbb{Z}$ upon division by N. In more detail: according to Proposition 2.1, there exist unique q, r such that $a = qN + r$ and $0 \le r < N$, and $[a \bmod N]$ is defined as this remainder r. Namely, $0 \le [a \bmod N] < N$. The process of mapping a to $[a \bmod N]$ is called *reduction modulo* N.

a and b are regarded as congruent modulo N (written as $a = b \bmod N$) if $[a \bmod N] = [b \bmod N]$, that is to say, the remainder when a is divided by N is equivalent to the remainder when b is divided by N. In this manner, $a = b \bmod N$ if and only if $N|(a - b)$. Note that $a = [b \bmod N]$ implies $a = b \bmod N$, but not vice versa. For example, $36 = 18 \bmod 18$ but $36 \neq [18 \bmod 18] = 0$.

We remark that congruence modulo N is an equivalence relation: that is, it is reflexive ($a = a \bmod N$ for all a), symmetric ($a = b \bmod N$ implies $b = a \bmod N$), and transitive (if $a = b \bmod N$ and $b = c \bmod N$ then $a = c \bmod N$). Congruence modulo N also obeys the standard rules of arithmetic with respect to addition, subtraction, and multiplication; so if $a = a' \bmod N$ and $b = b' \bmod N$, then $(a + b) = (a' + b') \bmod N$ and $ab = a'b' \bmod N$. Thus, the calculations of congruence modulo N can be simplified by "reducing and then adding/multiplying" instead of "adding/multiplying and then reducing."

Example 2.1 Let us compute $[3193015 \times 590702 \bmod 100]$. *Since $3193015 = 15 \bmod 100$ and $590702 = 2 \bmod 100$, we have*

$$3193015 \times 590702 = [3193015 \bmod 100] \cdot [590702 \bmod 100] \bmod 100$$
$$= 15 \times 2 = 30 \bmod 100$$

The cost of the alternate approach to derive the answer (namely, computing the product 3193015×590702 and then reducing the answer modulo 100) is much more expensive.

As opposed to addition, subtraction, and multiplication, the division operation in congruence modulo N has not been defined. That is to say, if $a = a' \bmod N$ and $b = b' \bmod N$, then it is not necessarily true that $a/b = a'/b' \bmod N$; in fact, the expression "$a/b \bmod N$" is not, in general, defined well. As a specific example related to division, $ab = cb \bmod N$ does not necessarily imply that $a = c \bmod N$.

Example 2.2 *Take $N = 12$. Then $3 \times 3 = 9 = 3 \times 7 \bmod 12$, but $3 \neq 7 \bmod 24$.*

However, a meaningful notion of division has also been defined for congruence modulo N. If for a given integer a there exists an integer a^{-1} such that $a \times a^{-1} = 1 \bmod N$, a^{-1} is viewed as a (multiplicative) inverse of a modulo N and a is considered as invertible modulo N. It is obvious to observe that if α is a multiplicative inverse of a modulo N, then so is $[\alpha \bmod N]$; furthermore, if α' is another multiplicative inverse, then $[\alpha \bmod N] = [\alpha' \bmod N]$. We can simply let a^{-1} denote the unique multiplicative inverse of a that lies in the range $\{0, \ldots, N-1\}$ if a is invertible.

In this way, division by a modulo N is defined as multiplication by a^{-1} modulo N if a is invertible modulo N (i.e., c/a is defined as $c \times a^{-1} \bmod N$). We stress that division by a is only defined when a is invertible. If $c \times a = b \times a \bmod N$ and a is invertible, then we may divide each side of the equation by a (or, equivalently, multiply each side by a^{-1}) to obtain

$$(c \times a) \times a^{-1} = (b \times a) \times a^{-1} \bmod N \Rightarrow c = b \bmod N$$

We see that in this case, division works "as expected" by adopting the idea of invertible integers. The natural question is that which integers are invertible modulo a given modulus N? To answer this question fully, Proposition 2.2 is used in the following proposition:

Proposition 2.5 *Let a, N be integers with $N > 1$. Then a is invertible modulo if and only if $\gcd(a, N) = 1$.*

Proof 2.4 *Assume a is invertible modulo N, and let b denote its inverse. It is evident that $a \neq 0$ since $0 \times b = 0 \bmod N$ regardless of the value of b. Since $a \times b = 1 \bmod N$, the definition of congruence modulo N implies that $a \times b - 1 = \alpha \times N$ for some $\alpha \in \mathbb{Z}$. Equivalently, $b \times a - \alpha \times N = 1$. According to Proposition 2.2, this implies $\gcd(a, N) = 1$.*

Conversely, if $\gcd(a, N) = 1$, then according to Proposition 2.2, there exist integers x, y such that $ax + Ny = 1$. Reducing each side of this equation modulo N gives $ax = 1 \bmod N$, and it is easy to see that x is a multiplicative inverse of a.

Example 2.3 *Let $N = 13$ and $a = 10$. Then $10 \times 4 + (-3) \times 13 = 1$, and so $4 = [4 \bmod 13]$ is the inverse of 10. One can verify that $10 \times 4 = 1 \bmod 13$.*

2.2.2 Concepts from Abstract Algebra

2.2.2.1 Group Theory

Assume $\mathbb{G}$ is a set. A *binary operation* $\circ$ defined over the set $\mathbb{G}$ (written as $g \circ h$ if $g, h \in \mathbb{G}$) is simply a function that takes as input two elements of $\mathbb{G}$ and outputs another element in the set $\mathbb{G}$. The formal definition of a *group* is described as follows.

Definition 2.1 *A group is a set $\mathbb{G}$ pairing with a binary operation $\circ$ such that:*

Closure Law: *For all $g, h \in \mathbb{G}$, the result of $g \circ h$ still remains in the set $\mathbb{G}$.*

Identity Law: *There exists an identity (ID) element $e \in \mathbb{G}$ such that for all $g \in \mathbb{G}$, $e \circ g = g = g \circ e$.*

Inverse Law: *For all $g \in \mathbb{G}$, there exists an element $h \in \mathbb{G}$ such that $g \circ h = e = h \circ g$. Such an h is called an inverse element of g.*

Associative Law: *For all $g_1, g_2, g_3 \in \mathbb{G}$, $(g_1 \circ g_2) \circ g_3 = g_1 \circ (g_2 \circ g_3)$.*

In this way, the set $\mathbb{G}$ along with the binary operation $\circ$ is defined as a group. When the set $\mathbb{G}$ has a finite number of elements, $(\mathbb{G}, \circ)$ is viewed as a finite group and $|\mathbb{G}|$ denotes the order of the group, that is, the number of elements in $\mathbb{G}$.

If $g \circ h = h \circ g$ for all $g, h \in \mathbb{G}$, this group is called an abelian group or commutative group. In this book, we will always deal with finite and abelian (commutative) groups.

If $(\mathbb{G}, \circ)$ is a group, a set $\mathbb{H} \subseteq \mathbb{G}$ pairing with the operation $\circ$ is called a subgroup of $(\mathbb{G}, \circ)$ if the set $\mathbb{H}$ forms a group under the involved operation $\circ$. To check that $(\mathbb{H}, \circ)$ is a subgroup, we need to verify closure, existence of ID and inverses, and associativity according to Definition 2.1. (In fact, associativity is inherited automatically from the group $(\mathbb{G}, \circ)$.) Every group $(\mathbb{G}, \circ)$ always has the trivial subgroups $(\mathbb{G}, \circ)$ and $(-e", \circ)$. $(\mathbb{H}, \circ)$ is called a *strict* subgroup of $(\mathbb{G}, \circ)$ if $\mathbb{H} \neq \mathbb{G}$.

Associativity implies that the notation of the long expression $g_1 \circ g_2 \circ \cdots \circ g_n$ without parentheses is unambiguous since it does not matter in what order we perform the operation $\circ$.

It is easy to see that the ID element in a group $(\mathbb{G}, \circ)$ is *unique*, and thus we can therefore refer to the ID element of a group. One can also demonstrate that each element g of a group has a unique inverse element.

In general, the abstract notation $\circ$ will not be used to denote the group operation directly. Either the *additive* notation or the *multiplicative* notation will be used instead depending on the involved group.

When additive notation has been adopted, the group operation applied to two elements g, h in the group is denoted as $g + h$; the ID element is denoted as "0," and the inverse element of g is denoted as $-g$. When multiplicative notation has been employed, the group operation applied to g, h in the group is denoted as $g \times h$ or simply gh; the ID element is denoted as "1," and the inverse element of g is denoted as g^{-1}. As in the case of multiplication modulo N, we also define division by g as multiplication by g^{-1} (i.e., $[(h/g) \bmod N]$ is defined as $[(h \times g^{-1}) \bmod N]$). Finally, we remark that this does not imply that the group operation corresponds to the addition or multiplication operation for integers. Instead, this merely serves as a useful general notation.

Example 2.4 *A set may be formed as a group under one operation, but not another operation. For example, the set of integers $\mathbb{Z}$ forms an abelian group under the addition operation: the ID element is "0," and every integer g has inverse ID $-g$. On the other hand, it does not form a group under multiplication operation since, for example, the multiplicative inverse of the integer "0" does not make sense.*

Example 2.5 *The set of complex numbers $\mathbb{C}$ is not a group under multiplication, since "0" does not have a multiplicative inverse. The set of nonzero complex numbers, however, is an abelian group under multiplication with ID "1."*

Example 2.6 *Let $N \geq 2$ be an integer. The set $\{0, \ldots, N-1\}$ with respect to addition modulo N is an abelian group of order N: closure is obvious; associativity and commutativity follow from the fact that the integers satisfy these properties; the ID element is 0; and since $a + (N - a) = 0 \bmod N$, it follows that the inverse element of any element a is $[(N - a) \bmod N]$. We denote this group by $(\mathbb{Z}_N, +)$. (Occasionally, the notion $\mathbb{Z}_N$ will also be used to denote the set $\{0, \ldots, N-1\}$ without involving any particular operation.)*

The "cancellation law" for groups has been demonstrated in the following lemma.

Lemma 2.1 *Let $(\mathbb{G}, \times)$ be a group and $a, b, c \in \mathbb{G}$. If $a \times c = b \times c$, then $a = b$. In particular, if $a \times c = c$, then a is the ID element in $\mathbb{G}$.*

Proof 2.5 *We know* $a \times c = b \times c$. *Multiplying both sides by the unique inverse element* c^{-1} *of the element* c, *we obtain* $a = b$. *In detail:*

$$a = a \times 1 = a \times (c \times c^{-1}) = (a \times c) \times c^{-1} = (b \times c) \times c^{-1}$$
$$= b \times (c \times c^{-1}) = b \times 1 = b$$

Group Exponentiation   It is often useful to be able to describe the group operation applied n times to a fixed element g, where n is a positive integer. As for the additive operation, we demonstrate this as $n \cdot g$ or ng; that is,

$$ng = n \cdot g \stackrel{\text{def}}{=} \underbrace{g + \ldots + g}_{n \;\; \text{times}}$$

Note that n is an *integer*, while g is a *group element*. So ng does not represent the group operation applied to n and g (indeed, we are working in a group where the group operation is written additively). However, the operation "behaves fortunately as it should"; for example, if $g \in \mathbb{G}$ and n, n' are integers, then $(ng) + (n'g) = (n + n')g, n(n'g) = (nn')g$, and $1 \cdot g = g$. In an *abelian* group $\mathbb{G}$ with $g, h \in \mathbb{G}$, $(ng) + (nh) = n(g + h)$.

As for the multiplicative operation, we demonstrate application of the group operation n times to an element g by g^n. That is,

$$g^n \stackrel{\text{def}}{=} \underbrace{g \times \ldots \times g}_{n \;\; \text{times}}$$

The familiar rules of exponentiation follow: $g^n \times g^{n'} = g^{n+n'}$, $(g^n)^{n'} = g^{nn'}$, and $g^1 = g$. Also, if $\mathbb{G}$ is a commutative group and $g, h \in \mathbb{G}$, then $g^n \cdot h^n = (gh)^n$.

The above notation can be extended to the case when n is zero or a negative integer in the natural way. Generally, we leave g^r undefined if r is not an integer. As for additive operation, we have $0 \cdot g \stackrel{\text{def}}{=} 0$ and $(-n) \cdot g \stackrel{\text{def}}{=} n \cdot (-g)$ such that n is a positive integer. (Note that in the equation "$0 \cdot g = 0$" the "0" on the left-hand side is the integer 0 while the "0" on the right-hand side is the identity element in the group.) As one would expect, it can be shown that $(-n) \cdot g = -(ng)$. As for multiplicative notation, $g^0 \stackrel{\text{def}}{=} 1$ and $g^{-n} \stackrel{\text{def}}{=} (g^{-1})^n$. Again, as expected, one can show that $g^{-n} = (g^n)^{-1}$.

Theorem 2.1 *If* $(\mathbb{G}, \times)$ *is a finite group with the order* $m = |\mathbb{G}|$, *then for any element* $g \in \mathbb{G}$, $g^m = 1$.

Proof 2.6 *We prove the theorem only for the commutative group* $(\mathbb{G}, \times)$ *(although it holds for any finite group). Fix arbitrary* $g \in \mathbb{G}$, *and let* $g_1, \ldots, g_m$ *be the elements of* $\mathbb{G}$. *We claim that*

$$g_1 \times g_2 \times \ldots \times g_m = (g \times g_1) \times (g \times g_2) \times \ldots \times (g \times g_m)$$

It is noted that $g \times g_i = g \times g_j$ *implies* $g_i = g_j$ *according to the cancellation law shown in Lemma 2.1. Thus the* m *elements in parentheses on the right-hand side of the displayed equation are pairwise different from each other. By considering that there are exactly* m *elements in* $\mathbb{G}$, *the* m *elements being multiplied together on the right-hand side are simply all elements of* $\mathbb{G}$ *in some permuted order. The order in which all elements of the group are multiplied does not matter due to the fact that the group* $(\mathbb{G}, \times)$ *is commutative, and thus the result of the right-hand side is identical to the result of the left-hand side.*

Fueled by the fact that $(\mathbb{G}, \times)$ *is commutative, all occurrences of the element* g *can be pulled out and we can obtain*

$$g_1 \times g_2 \times \ldots \times g_m = (g \times g_1) \times (g \times g_2) \times \ldots \times (g \times g_m)$$
$$= g^m \times (g_1 \times g_2 \times \ldots \times g_m)$$

Once again by the cancellation law in the group, it is obvious that $g^m = 1$.

Corollary 2.1 *If* $(\mathbb{G}, \times)$ *is a finite group with order* $m = |\mathbb{G}| > 1$, *then for any element* $g \in \mathbb{G}$ *and any integer* i, $g^i = g^{[i \bmod m]}$.

Proof 2.7 *According to Proposition 2.1,* i *can be expressed as* $qm + r$, *where* q, r *are integers and* r *can be demonstrated as* $[i \bmod m]$. *By Theorem 2.1,*

$$g^i = g^{qm+r} = g^{qm} \times g^r = 1^q \times g^r = g^r$$

holds.

Example 2.7 *As for the additive operation, the above corollary means that if* g *is an element in a group with order* m, *then* $i \cdot g = [i \bmod m] \cdot g$. *As an example, consider the group* $\mathbb{Z}_{25}$ *of order* $m = 25$, *and take* $g = 13$. *The corollary can be instantiated as*

$$303 \cdot 13 = [303 \bmod 15] \cdot 13 = 3 \cdot 13 = 13 + 13 + 13 = 39 = 14 \bmod 25$$

Corollary 2.2 *Let $(\mathbb{G}, \times)$ be a finite group with order $m = |\mathbb{G}| > 1$. Let $e > 0$ be an integer, and define the function $f_e : \mathbb{G} \to \mathbb{G}$ by $f_e(g) = g^e$. If $\gcd(e, m) = 1$, then f_e is a permutation. Furthermore, if $d = [e^{-1} \bmod m]$, then f_d is the inverse of f_e.*

Proof 2.8 *According to Proposition 2.5, e is invertible modulo m due to the fact that $\gcd(e, m) = 1$. To show that f_d is the inverse of f_e, for any $g \in \mathbb{G}$, we have*

$$f_d(f_e(g)) = f_d(g^e) = (g^e)^d = g^{ed} = g^{[ed \bmod m]} = g^1 = g$$

2.2.2.2 Group $(\mathbb{Z}_N^*, \times)$

As mentioned before, the set $\mathbb{Z}_N = \{0, \dots, N - 1\}$ pairing with the addition operation modulo N can be regarded as a group. One natural problem is that whether the set $\{0, \dots, N - 1\}$ associated with the multiplication operation modulo N can be viewed as a group or not. It is obvious that "1" can be considered the identity element for multiplication modulo N. However, not every element in this set is invertible in relation to multiplication modulo N; for example, the multiplicative inverse element of "0" obviously does not make sense. What makes matters worse: if $N = 8$, then the elements "2," "4," and "6" are not invertible when exhaustively trying every possible element in $\{0, \dots, 7\}$. Thus, it is necessary to identify which elements in $\{0, \dots, N - 1\}$ are invertible modulo N. Depending on Proposition 2.5, the element $a \in \{0, \dots, N-1\}$ is invertible if and only if $\gcd(a, N) = 1$. It is also easy to observe that the inverse element of a resides in the range $\{0, \dots, N - 1\}$. This results in the definition of the following set for $N > 1$:

$$\mathbb{Z}_N^* \overset{\text{def}}{=} \{a \in \{1, \dots, N - 1\} | \gcd(a, N) = 1\}$$

In other words, $\mathbb{Z}_N^*$ includes integers in the set $\{1, \dots, N - 1\}$ that are relatively prime to N.

Based on the discussion above, the identity element and inverse element associated with each element can be found in $\mathbb{Z}_N^*$. Furthermore, the commutativity and associativity features inherit from $\mathbb{Z}_N$ directly. To discuss the feature of closure, let $a, b \in \mathbb{Z}_N^*$ and $c = [a \times b \bmod N]$, and then assume $c \notin \mathbb{Z}_N^*$. This implies that $\gcd(c, N) \neq 1$, and so a prime p exists such that $p|N$ and $p|c$. From $c = [a \times b \bmod N]$, we see that $a \times b = qN + c$ for some integer q, and thus $p|a \times b$.

Based on Proposition 2.3, we obtain $p|a$ or $p|b$; this contradicts either $\gcd(a, N) = 1$ or $\gcd(b, N) = 1$ (recall that $a, b \in \mathbb{Z}_N^*$). In short, the set $\mathbb{Z}_N^*$ with respect to the multiplication operation modulo N forms a group.

Proposition 2.6 $\mathbb{Z}_N^*$ *is a commutative group pairing with the multiplication operation modulo N when $N > 1$ is an integer.*

Let $\phi(N)$ denote the order of the group $(\mathbb{Z}_N^*, \times)$ such that $\phi(N)(\overset{\text{def}}{=} |\mathbb{Z}_N^*|)$ and ϕ is called the *Euler phi function*. To compute the value of $\phi(N)$, we first consider the case when N is prime, that is $N = p$. In this case, all elements in $\{1, \dots, p-1\}$ are relatively prime to p, and so $\phi(p) = |\mathbb{Z}_p^*| = p - 1$. We then consider the case $N = p \times q$ such that p, q are distinct primes. We see that either $p|a$ or $q|a$ if an integer $a \in \{1, \dots, N-1\}$ is not relatively prime to N. Note that a cannot be divided by both p and q simultaneously since this would imply $pq|a$ and contradict $a < N(= p \times q)$. The elements in $\{1, \dots, N-1\}$ that can be divided by p are exactly the $(q-1)$ elements $p, 2p, 3p, \dots, (q-1)p$, and the elements that can be divided by q are exactly the $(p-1)$ elements $q, 2q, \dots, (p-1)q$. Thus, the number of elements that are divisible by neither p nor q is therefore given by

$$N - 1 - (q-1) - (p-1) = p \times q - p - q + 1 = (p-1)(q-1)$$

That is to say, $\phi(N) = (p-1)(q-1)$ when N is the product of two distinct primes p and q.

Theorem 2.2 *Let $N = \prod_i p_i^{e_i}$, where the $\{p_i\}$ are distinct primes and $e_i \geq 1$. Then $\phi(N) = N \times \prod_i (1 - \frac{1}{p_i - 1})$.*

Example 2.8 *Take $N = 24 = 3 \cdot 2^3$. Then $\mathbb{Z}_{24}^* = \{1, 5, 7, 11, 13, 17, 19, 23\}$ and $|\mathbb{Z}_N^*| = 8 = 24 \times (1 - \frac{1}{2}) \times (1 - \frac{1}{3}) = \phi(24)$. The inverse identity of 5 in $\mathbb{Z}_N^*$ is 5 itself, since $5 \times 5 = 25 = 1 \bmod 24$.*

Until now, the set $\mathbb{Z}_N^*$ under the multiplication operation modulo N has been shown to be a group with order $\phi(N)$. According to Theorem 2.1, we get the following theorem directly:

Theorem 2.3 *Take arbitrary $N > 1$ and $a \in \mathbb{Z}_N^*$. Then we obtain*

$$a^{\phi(N)} = 1 \bmod N$$

For the specific case when $N = p$ is prime and $a \in \{1, \ldots, p-1\}$, we have

$$a^{p-1} = 1 \bmod p$$

By Corollary 2.2, we obtain the following theorem easily:

Theorem 2.4 *Let $N > 1$ be an integer. For integer $e > 0$, we define $f_e : \mathbb{Z}_N^* \to \mathbb{Z}_N^*$ as $f_e(x) = x^e \bmod N$. If e is relatively prime to $\phi(N)$, then f_e is a permutation. Moreover, if $d = [e^{-1} \bmod \phi(N)]$, then f_d is the inverse of f_e.*

Group Isomorphisms

Definition 2.2 *A function $f : \mathbb{G} \to \mathbb{H}$ is said to be an isomorphism from a group $(\mathbb{G}, \circ_\mathbb{G})$ to another group $(\mathbb{H}, \circ_\mathbb{H})$ if (1) f is a bijective mapping and (2) for all $g_1, g_2 \in \mathbb{G}$ we have $f(g_1 \circ_\mathbb{G} g_2) = f(g_1) \circ_\mathbb{H} f(g_2)$. If these properties hold, then we say the group $(\mathbb{G}, \circ_\mathbb{G})$ and the group $(\mathbb{H}, \circ_\mathbb{H})$ are isomorphic and write this as $\mathbb{G} \cong \mathbb{H}$.*

An isomorphism from a group to another group provides an alternate and equivalent approach to think about the structure of groups. For example, if the group $(\mathbb{G}, \circ_\mathbb{G})$ is finite and $\mathbb{G} \cong \mathbb{H}$, then the group $(\mathbb{H}, \circ_\mathbb{H})$ must be finite and have the same order as $\mathbb{G}$. Also, if there exists an isomorphism f from a group $(\mathbb{G}, \circ_\mathbb{G})$ to another group $(\mathbb{H}, \circ_\mathbb{H})$, then f^{-1} is an isomorphism from $(\mathbb{H}, \circ_\mathbb{H})$ to $(\mathbb{G}, \circ_\mathbb{G})$.

Example 2.9 *The bijective mapping f where $f(n) = 2n$ is an isomorphism from the group $(\mathbb{Z}, +)$ to the group $(\mathbb{Z}_{2n}, +)$ because $f(a + b) = 2(a + b) = 2a + 2b = f(a) + f(b)$, where $\mathbb{Z}_{2n}$ denotes the set of even integers and $+$ is the addition operation for the integers.*

Example 2.10 *The bijective mapping f where $f(n) = 3^n$ is an isomorphism from the group $(\mathbb{Z}_6, +)$ to the group $(\mathbb{Z}_7^*, \times)$, where $+$ and $\times$ denote the addition operation modulo 6 and the multiplication operation modulo 7. On the one hand, $3^0 = 1$, $3^1 = 3$, $3^2 = 2$, $3^3 = 6$, $3^4 = 4$, and $3^5 = 5$. On the other hand, $f(2 + 3) = 3^{(2+3)} = 3^2 \times 3^3 = f(2) \times f(3)$.*

2.2.2.3 Chinese Remainder Theorem

Theorem 2.5 *Let $n_1, n_2, \ldots, n_k$ be integers that are pairwise relatively prime, that is, $\gcd(n_i, n_j) = 1$ for $i \neq j$. Then there exists a unique* *solution modulo the product* $n = n_1 \times n_2 \times \ldots \times n_k$ *to the following system of congruences:*

$$x \equiv a_1 \quad (\text{mod } n_1)$$
$$x \equiv a_2 \quad (\text{mod } n_2)$$
$$\vdots$$
$$x \equiv a_k \quad (\text{mod } n_k)$$

The solution to the system of congruences shown in Theorem 2.5 can be calculated as

$$x = \sum_{i=1}^{k} a_i N_i M_i \text{ mod } n \qquad (2.1)$$

where

$$N_i = \frac{n}{n_i}$$

and

$$M_i = N_i^{-1} \text{ mod } n_i$$

The solution can also be represented in a slightly different way which makes it easier to understand. Namely, we can rewrite Equation 2.1 as

$$x = \sum_{i=1}^{k} a_i \cdot e_i \text{ mod } n$$

such that

$$e_i \equiv \begin{cases} 1 & (\text{mod } n_i) \\ 0 & (\text{mod } n_j), j \neq i \end{cases}$$

So the solution of the Chinese remainder theory can be regarded essentially as an integer version of Lagrange interpolation, where a polynomial is created according to k points by calculating a similar set of coefficients that are either 0 or 1 and thus enforcing the desired behavior at the given points.

Example 2.11 *Consider the following system of congruences:*

$$x \equiv 2 \quad (\text{mod } 3) = a_1 \quad (\text{mod } n_1)$$
$$x \equiv 3 \quad (\text{mod } 5) = a_2 \quad (\text{mod } n_2)$$
$$x \equiv 2 \quad (\text{mod } 7) = a_3 \quad (\text{mod } n_3)$$

According to the solution of the Chinese remainder theorem, we see that

$$n = n_1 \times n_2 \times n_3 = 3 \times 5 \times 7 = 105$$

$$N_1 = \frac{n}{n_1} = \frac{105}{3} = 35$$

$$N_2 = \frac{n}{n_2} = \frac{105}{5} = 21$$

$$N_3 = \frac{n}{n_3} = \frac{105}{7} = 15$$

$$M_1 = N_1^{-1} \bmod n_1 = 2^{-1} \bmod 3 = 2$$

$$M_2 = N_2^{-1} \bmod n_2 = 3^{-1} \bmod 5 = 1$$

$$M_3 = N_3^{-1} \bmod n_3 = 2^{-1} \bmod 7 = 1$$

so that

$$x = (a_1 \times N_1 \times M_1 + a_2 \times N_2 \times M_2 + a_3 \times N_3 \times M_3) \bmod 105$$
$$= (2 \times 35 \times 2 + 3 \times 21 \times 1 + 2 \times 15 \times 1) \bmod 105$$
$$= 23 \bmod 105$$

In this example, we can also think of the solution as finding integers e_1, e_2, and e_3 such that

$$x = (2 \times e_1 + 3 \times e_2 + 2 \times e_3) \bmod 105$$

$$e_1 = 70 \equiv \begin{cases} 70 & (\bmod\ 3) \\ 0 & (\bmod\ 5) \\ 0 & (\bmod\ 7) \end{cases}$$

$$e_2 = 21 \equiv \begin{cases} 0 & (\bmod\ 3) \\ 21 & (\bmod\ 5) \\ 0 & (\bmod\ 7) \end{cases}$$

and

$$e_3 = 15 \equiv \begin{cases} 0 & (\bmod\ 3) \\ 0 & (\bmod\ 5) \\ 15 & (\bmod\ 7) \end{cases}$$

2.2.2.4 Cyclic Groups and Generators

Let $(\mathbb{G}, \times)$ be a finite group with order m. For arbitrary $g \in \mathbb{G}$, consider the set

$$\langle g \rangle \overset{\text{def}}{=} \{g^0, g^1, \ldots\}$$

According to Theorem 2.1, $g^m = 1$. If $i \leq m$ denotes the smallest positive integer for which $g^i = 1$, then the above sequence repeats after i terms (i.e., $g^i = g^0$, $g^{i+1} = g^1$, ..., $g^{2i} = g^0$, etc.), and so

$$\langle g \rangle = \{g^0, \ldots, g^{i-1}\}$$

It is obvious to see that $\langle g \rangle$ contains exactly i elements since if $g^j = g^k$ with $0 \leq j < k < i$, then $g^{k-j} \neq 1$ thanks to the choice of i.

It is easy to observe that $(\langle g \rangle, \times)$ can be regarded as a subgroup of $(\mathbb{G}, \times)$, which is generated by the element g. If the order of the subgroup $(\langle g \rangle, \times)$ is i, then i is called the *order* of element g.

Definition 2.3 *If $(\mathbb{G}, \times)$ is a finite group and g is randomly chosen from $\mathbb{G}$, then the order of element g is defined as the smallest positive integer i such that $g^i = 1$.*

Proposition 2.7 *If $\mathbb{G}$ is a finite group, and $g \in \mathbb{G}$ is an element with order i, then for any integer x, we have $g^x = g^{[x \bmod i]}$.*

Proof 2.9 *The proof of this proposition is similar to the proof of Corollary 2.1 and thus we omit it here.*

Proposition 2.8 *If $\mathbb{G}$ is a finite group and $g \in \mathbb{G}$ is an element with order i, then $g^x = g^y$ if and only if $x = y \bmod i$.*

Proof 2.10 *If $x = y \bmod i$, then $[x \bmod i] = [y \bmod i]$ and according to the previous proposition, we directly have*

$$g^x = g^{[x \bmod i]} = g^{[y \bmod i]} = g^y$$

On the other hand, from $g^x = g^y$, we can easily obtain $g^{x'} = g^{y'}$ from the previous proposition, where $x' = [x \bmod i]$ and $y' = [y \bmod i]$. We in turn get $g^{x'}(g^{y'})^{-1} = g^{x'-y'} = 1$. If $x' \neq y'$, the difference $x' - y'$ is then a nonzero integer smaller than i since both x' and y' are smaller than i. There is a contradiction between the fact that i is the order of element g and the fact that $x' - y'$ is a nonzero integer smaller than i. Therefore, we obtain $x = y'$ directly.

The identity element of any group $(\mathbb{G}, \circ)$, which has order 1, can generate the group $(\langle e \rangle, \circ)$. Furthermore, the identity element is known as the only element with order 1. On the other hand, if an element $g \in \mathbb{G}$ of order m (where m denotes the order of the group $(\mathbb{G}, \circ)$) can be found, then $\langle g \rangle = \mathbb{G}$. In other words, $\mathbb{G}$ can be generated by the element g and considered a cyclic group. Here, g is called a generator of $\mathbb{G}$. (Different from the identity element, a cyclic group may have multiple generators.) If g is a generator of a cyclic group $(\mathbb{G}, \circ)$, then, by definition, every element $h \in \mathbb{G}$ can be derived by computing g^x for some $x \in \{0, \ldots, m-1\}$.

Proposition 2.9 *Let $(\mathbb{G}, \circ)$ be a finite group with order m, and the element $g \in \mathbb{G}$ features with the order i. Then $i|m$.*

Proof 2.11 *By Theorem 2.1, $g^m = 1$. According to Proposition 2.7, we have $g^m = g^{[m \bmod i]}$ when element g features with the order i. If $i \nmid m$, then $i' \stackrel{\text{def}}{=} [m \bmod i]$ is a nonzero integer smaller than i such that $g^{i'} = 1$. This contradicts the fact that i is the order of the element g.*

Corollary 2.3 *If $(\mathbb{G}, \circ)$ is a group with prime order p, then this group is cyclic. Furthermore, all elements of $\mathbb{G}$ other than the identity element are generators of $(\mathbb{G}, \circ)$.*

Proof 2.12 *Based on Proposition 2.9, the only possible orders of elements in the group $(\mathbb{G}, \circ)$ are 1 and p. Only the identity element features with the order 1, and so all other elements are order p and can generate the original group.*

In addition to the groups of prime order, the additive group $\mathbb{Z}_N$, for $N > 1$, provides another example of a cyclic group, whereas the element 1 offers the function of generator.

Theorem 2.6 *If p is prime, then $(\mathbb{Z}_p^*, \times)$ forms a cyclic group.*

The proof of this theorem is outside the scope of this book and the interested reader can refer to [34] for more details.

Example 2.12 *Consider the group $(\mathbb{Z}_{11}^*, \times)$, which is cyclic by the previous theorem. We have $\langle 10 \rangle = \{1, 10\}$, and so 10 is not a generator. However,*

$$\langle 2 \rangle = \{1, 2, 4, 8, 5, 10, 9, 7, 3, 6\} = \mathbb{Z}_{11}^*$$

and so 2 is a generator of $\mathbb{Z}_{11}^*$.

Given a cyclic group $\mathbb{G}$ with order q, we can represent this group by a generator $g \in \mathbb{G}$ as $\mathbb{G} = \{g^0, g^1, \ldots, g^{q-1}\}$. In other words, each element $h \in \mathbb{G}$ can be expressed as $h = g^x$ such that $x \in \mathbb{Z}_q$. Correspondingly, x is called the discrete logarithm of h with respect to the generator g such that $x = \log_g h$. Noted that the logarithms in this case are regarded as "discrete" because these logarithm values range over a finite range, as opposed to "standard" logarithms from calculus whose values are within an infinite set.

The discrete logarithm problem in a cyclic group $\mathbb{G}$ with respect to a given generator g is to calculate x such that $g^x = h$ with the input of a random element $h \in \mathbb{G}$. Formally speaking, $\mathcal{G}$ is a polynomial-time algorithm with the input 1^n to output a cyclic group $\mathbb{G}$ with order q and a generator $g \in \mathbb{G}$. In addition, the group operation in $\mathbb{G}$ is required to be computed efficiently (i.e., in time polynomial in n). Consider the following experiment between a given algorithm $\mathcal{A}$ and the algorithm $\mathcal{G}$:

The discrete logarithm experiment $\mathsf{DLog}_{\mathcal{A},\mathcal{G}}(n)$

1. Given the parameter n, the algorithm $\mathcal{G}$ outputs $(\mathbb{G}, q, g)$, where $\mathbb{G}$ denotes a cyclic group with order q and g is a generator of $\mathbb{G}$ such that $||q|| = n$.

2. Choose $h \leftarrow \mathbb{G}$ at random.

3. Given $\{\mathbb{G}, q, g, h\}$, the task of $\mathcal{A}$ is to output $x \in \mathbb{Z}_q$.

4. This experiment outputs 1 if $g^x = h$, and 0 otherwise.

Definition 2.4 *The discrete logarithm problem is said to be hard relative to the algorithm $\mathcal{G}$ if for all probabilistic, polynomial-time algorithms $\mathcal{A}$, the probability $\Pr[\mathsf{DLog}_{\mathcal{A},\mathcal{G}}(n) = 1]$ is negligible.*

By way of example, groups of the form $\mathbb{Z}_p^*$, where p is a prime number, offer one family of cyclic groups in which the discrete logarithm problem is believed to be hard [5,34].

2.2.3 Elliptic-Curve Groups

Different from $\mathbb{Z}_p^*$, another interesting class of groups widely used in cryptographic applications is those consisting of points on elliptic curves. Despite elliptic-curve groups being very crucial in practical construction of cryptographic primitives, our treatment of such groups in this book is rather minimal and sacrifices generality in favor of simplicity. The basic reason for this approach is due to the fact that most cryptographic primitives based on elliptic-curve groups can be understood and investigated by treating the underlying group in a completely generic manner without involving any particular group used to instantiate the primitive. Namely, cryptographic primitives can be built on arbitrary cyclic groups, and the security of these schemes can be proved as long as the related computational problem in the underlying group is believed to be hard no matter how the group is actually instantiated. Therefore, the mathematical background needed for a deeper understanding of elliptic-curve groups is beyond the scope of this book. Interested readers can refer to [35] for more details.

Define $\mathbb{Z}_p$ as $\{0, \ldots, p-1\}$ for $p \geq 5$ is a prime. Despite the fact that the elliptic curves can be defined over arbitrary (finite or infinite) fields, only the cases such that $p \neq 2$ or 3 are taken into consideration to eliminate the additional complications. The elliptic curve E over $\mathbb{Z}_p$ represents the set of points (x, y) defined by the equation $y^2 = x^3 + ax + b \bmod p$ with $a, b \in_R \mathbb{Z}_p$, and with the discriminant $4a^3 + 27b^2 \neq 0 \bmod p$ (this condition ensures that the equation $x^3 + ax + b = 0 \bmod p$ has no repeated roots). This set of points on $\mathbb{Z}_p$ along with a distinguished point $\mathcal{O}$ at infinity $\{(x, y) \mid x, y \in \mathbb{Z}_p \wedge E(x, y) = 0\} \cup \{\mathcal{O}\}$ outline the curve E. The elements of the set $E(\mathbb{Z}_p)$ are called the points on the elliptic curve E defined by $y^2 = x^3 + ax + b \bmod p$, and $\mathcal{O}$ is called the "point at infinity."

Example 2.13 *An element $y \in \mathbb{Z}_p^*$ is called a quadratic residue modulo p if there exists an $x \in \mathbb{Z}_p^*$ such that $x^2 = y \bmod p$; while x is regarded as a square root of y in this case. According to [33], every quadratic residue modulo p has exactly two square roots for $p > 2$ is prime.*

Let $f(x)$ be a function such that $f = x^3 + x + 6$ and consider the curve $E : y^2 = f(x) \bmod 11$. Each value of x for which $f(x)$ is a quadratic residue modulo 11 yields two points on the curve; a value of x for which $f(x) = 0 \bmod 11$ gives one point on the curve $E(\mathbb{Z}_{11})$. The points on the curve $E(\mathbb{Z}_{11})$ (shown in Table 2.1) can be identified and explained as follows:

- $f(0) = 6 \bmod 11$, a quadratic nonresidue modulo 11.

- $f(1) = 8 \bmod 11$, a quadratic nonresidue modulo 11.

TABLE 2.1   Points on the Elliptic Curve $y^2 \equiv x^3 + x + 6$ mod 11

x	0	1	2	3	4	5	6	7	8	9	10
$x^3 + x + 6$ mod 11	6	8	5	3	8	4	8	4	9	7	4
Quadratic residue or nonresidue modulo 11?	×	×	✓	✓	×	✓	×	✓	✓	×	✓
y			4	5		2		2	3		2
			7	6		9		9	8		9

- $f(2) = 5$ mod 11, a quadratic residue modulo 11 with square roots 4 and 7. This yields the points $(2,4),(2,7) \in E(\mathbb{Z}_{11})$.

- $f(3) = 3$ mod 11, a quadratic residue modulo 11 with square roots 5 and 6. This yields the points $(3,5),(3,6) \in E(\mathbb{Z}_{11})$.

- $f(4) = 8$ mod 11, a quadratic nonresidue modulo 11.

- $f(5) = 4$ mod 11, a quadratic residue modulo 11 with square roots 2 and 9. This yields the points $(5,2),(5,9) \in E(\mathbb{Z}_{11})$.

- $f(6) = 8$ mod 11, a quadratic nonresidue modulo 11.

- $f(7) = 4$ mod 11, a quadratic residue modulo 11 with square roots 2 and 9. This yields the points $(7,2),(7,9) \in E(\mathbb{Z}_{11})$.

- $f(8) = 9$ mod 11, a quadratic residue modulo 11 with square roots 3 and 8. This yields the points $(8,3),(8,8) \in E(\mathbb{Z}_{11})$.

- $f(9) = 7$ mod 11, a quadratic nonresidue modulo 11.

- $f(10) = 4$ mod 11, a quadratic residue modulo 11 with square roots 2 and 9. This yields the points $(10,2),(10,9) \in E(\mathbb{Z}_{11})$.

Including the point $\mathcal{O}$ at infinity, there are seven points in $E(\mathbb{Z}_{11})$.

A common approach to conceptualize $E(\mathbb{Z}_p)$ intuitively is to observe the graph with equation $y^2 = x^3 + ax + b$ over the real numbers (rather than the equation $y^2 = x^3 + ax + b$ mod p) as in Figure 2.1. Despite this figure not corresponding exactly to $E(\mathbb{Z}_p)$ because $E(\mathbb{Z}_p)$ consists of only a finite number of points (recall that $\mathbb{Z}_p$ is a finite set), while there are an infinite number of solutions to the same equation over the real numbers, the picture offers insightful intuition. In such a figure, the point at infinity $\mathcal{O}$ can be viewed as sitting at the top of the y-axis and lying on every vertical line.

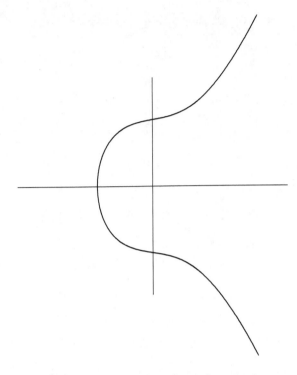

Figure 2.1 Graph of the elliptic curve $y^2 = x^3 + x + 6$ such that $\triangle > 0$.

Observations from Figure 2.2 demonstrate that every line intersecting with the elliptic curve $E(\mathbb{Z}_p)$ intersects this curve in exactly three points. When the elliptic line is tangent to the curve at the point P, the point P is counted twice, and the point $\mathcal{O}$ is also counted (when the line is vertical). A binary operation (called "addition") can be defined from this fact and denoted by "+" on points of $E(\mathbb{Z}_p)$ as follows:

- The point $\mathcal{O}$ is defined as the identity element such that $P + \mathcal{O} = \mathcal{O} + P = P$ for all $P \in E(\mathbb{Z}_p)$.

- We obtain

$$P_1 + P_2 + P_3 = \mathcal{O} \tag{2.2}$$

when P_1, P_2, P_3 are colinear points on E. (Note that the ordering of P_1, P_2, P_3 has been disregarded in the sense that the addition operation is commutative for all points and associative for colinear points.)

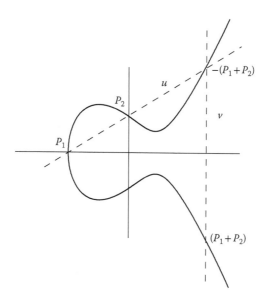

Figure 2.2 Addition operations on points on an elliptic curve.

Negation. For a point P, the negation of P is defined as the point $-P$ such that $P + (-P) = \mathcal{O}$. If $P = \mathcal{O}$, it is easy to see that $-P = \mathcal{O}$. Otherwise, due to the fact that $P + (-P) + \mathcal{O} = (P + (-P)) + \mathcal{O} = \mathcal{O} + \mathcal{O} = \mathcal{O}$ and from Equation 2.2, it is evident that the negation of P corresponds to the third point on the line passing through P and $\mathcal{O}$ or, in other words, the vertical line passing through P . According to Figure 2.2, $-P$ is simply the reflection of P in the x-axis; that is, if $P = (x, y)$, then $-P = -(x, y) = (x, -y)$.

Addition of points. To evaluate the sum $P_1 + P_2$ for two arbitrary points $P_1, P_2 \neq \mathcal{O}$ on the elliptic curve E, we can draw the line through P_1, P_2 (if $P_1 = P_2$, then draw the line tangent to E at P_1) and identify the third point of intersection P_3 of this line with the curve E. From Equation 2.2, we can directly derive $P_1 + P_2 = -P_3$. If $P_3 = \mathcal{O}$, then $P_1 + P_2 = -\mathcal{O} = \mathcal{O}$. Otherwise, if the third point of intersection of the line through P_1 and P_2 is the point $P_3 = (x, y) \neq \mathcal{O}$, then

$$P_1 + P_2 = -P_3 = (x, -y)$$

It is straightforward but tedious to carry out the addition law concretely. Assume $P_1 = (x_1, y_1)$ and $P_2 = (x_2, y_2)$ are two points in $E(\mathbb{Z}_p)$ with $P_1, P_2 \neq \mathcal{O}$ and E is represented by the equation

$y^2 = x^3 + ax + b \bmod p$. The slope of the line through these points can be computed as

$$
\lambda = \begin{cases} \frac{y_2 - y_1}{x_2 - x_1} \bmod p, & P_1 \neq P_2 \\ \frac{3x_1^2 + a}{2y_1} \bmod p, & P_1 = P_2 \end{cases}
$$

The line passing through P_1 and P_2 can be outlined by the equation

$$
y = \lambda \cdot (x - x_1) + y_1 \bmod p \tag{2.3}
$$

To find the third point of intersection of this line with E, substitute Equation 2.3 into $y^2 = x^3 + ax + b \bmod p$ to obtain

$$
\left(\lambda \cdot (x - x_1) + y_1 \right)^2 = x^3 + ax + b \bmod p
$$

The values of x that satisfy this equation are x_1, x_2, and $[\lambda^2 - x_1 - x_2 \bmod p]$. The first two solutions correspond to the original points P_1 and P_2, while the third is the x-coordinate of the third point of intersection P_3. The y-value corresponding to this third value of x is $y = [\lambda \cdot (x - x_1) + y_1 \bmod p]$. That is, $P_3 = (x_3, y_3)$ where

$$
x_3 = (\lambda^2 - x_1 - x_2) \bmod p, \qquad y_3 = [\lambda \cdot (x_1 - x_3) - y_1] \bmod p
$$

It is straightforward that the set of points $E(\mathbb{Z}_p)$ pairing with the addition law defined above form an abelian group. All the necessary properties have almost been shown: closure under the addition law depends on the fact (the proof is omitted due to space limits) that any line intersecting E intersects this curve at exactly three points; $\mathcal{O}$ serves as the identity element; the inverse element of each point on $E(\mathbb{Z}_p)$ can also be found in $E(\mathbb{Z}_p)$; and commutativity of addition law rests on Equation 2.2. The final property to verify is associativity, which the interested reader can check themselves with tedious calculation.

According to Table 2.1, there are seven points in the set $E(\mathbb{Z}_{11})$ with the curve $E : y^2 = x^3 + x + 6 \bmod 11$ such that:

$$
E(\mathbb{Z}_{11}) = \{\mathcal{O}, (2,4), (2,7), (3,5), (3,6), (5,2), (5,9), (7,2), (7,9), (8,3),
$$
$$
(8,8), (10,2), (10,9)\}
$$

Suppose $P = (2,7)$, $2P = P + P$ can be computed as follows: First, the slope of the line can be calculated as follows:

$$
\lambda = \frac{3 \times 2^2 + 1}{2 \times 7} \bmod 11 = \frac{2}{3} \bmod 11 = 8
$$

After that, we obtain

$$x_3 = (8^2 - 2 - 2) \bmod 11 = 5$$
$$y_3 = [8 \times (2 - 5) - 7] \bmod 11 = 2$$

Therefore, $2P = (5, 2)$. Similarly, we can also get $3P = (8, 3)$, $4P = (10, 2)$, $5P = (3, 6)$, $6P = (7, 9)$, $7P = (7, 2)$, $8P = (3, 5)$, $9P = (10, 9)$, $10P = (8, 8)$, $11P = (5, 9)$, $12P = (2, 4)$, $13P = \mathcal{O}$.

It is easy to see that $E(\mathbb{Z}_{11})$ along with the addition operation forms a commutative group with the generator $P = (2, 7)$.

Similar to $\mathbb{Z}_p^*$, elliptic-curve groups provide another family of cyclic groups in which the discrete logarithm problem is believed to be hard [35].

2.2.4 Bilinear Pairing

Let $\mathbb{G}$ be a cyclic multiplicative group with generator g and prime order p and $\mathbb{G}_T$ be another multiplicative cyclic group of the same order p. A bilinear pairing refers to a map $\hat{e} : \mathbb{G} \times \mathbb{G} \to \mathbb{G}_T$ with the following properties:

1. Bilinearity: For all $g_1, g_2 \in \mathbb{G}$, and $a, b \in \mathbb{Z}_p^*$, $\hat{e}(g_1^a, g_2^b) = \hat{e}(g_1, g_2)^{ab}$.

2. Nondegeneracy: There exist $g_1, g_2 \in \mathbb{G}$ such that $\hat{e}(g_1, g_2) \neq 1_{\mathbb{G}_T}$.

3. Computability: For all $g_1, g_2 \in \mathbb{G}$, there is an efficient algorithm to compute $\hat{e}(g_1, g_2)$.

The modified Weil pairing [9] or Tate pairing [36] defined on the elliptic curves can be adopted to implement such an admissible bilinear map.

2.3 PUBLIC-KEY CRYPTOGRAPHY

The discussion thus far has been very general. We now show some concrete examples of public-key encryption and signature schemes in the traditional PKI and identity-based public-key cryptography (ID-PKC) settings, respectively. As mentioned in [1], public-key encryption enables two parties to communicate with each other securely without any shared secret information in advance. Let us call the sender Alice and the receiver Bob. Bob first selects the key pair (pk_B, sk_B) and sends the public key pk_B to Alice over any channel but keeps the private key sk_B secure and secret. Before sending the sensitive message m to Bob, Alice generates the ciphertext c by performing the encryption algorithm $c = \mathsf{Enc}_{pk_B}(m)$ under Bob's public key. To recover the message m, Bob decrypts the ciphertext c by carrying out the inverse decryption $\mathsf{Dec}_{sk_B}(c)$ with his own private key sk_B. According to [3], a digital signature allows a user to generate a signature on the given message with secret key sk in such a way that any other party who knows this user's corresponding public key pk can ensure that the message indeed originated from this user and has not been altered in any way. Let us call the sender Alice and the receiver Bob. The sender Alice first generates a public/secret key pair (pk_A, sk_A), and then distributes pk_A in some reliable way to the other users in the system while keeping sk_A secret. When the message m originated from Alice needs to be authenticated, Alice can generate a digital signature σ on the message m using her private key sk_A; the pair (m, σ) will be then sent. Anyone who knows the public key pk_A can verify the authenticity of m by checking whether $\mathsf{Vrfy}_{pk}(m, \sigma) \stackrel{?}{=} 1$ or not. In this section, we have chosen to focus on the most well-known and longstanding public-key primitives.

Observing that all existing constructions of public-key encryption and signature schemes are proven secure under some assumptions associated with the hardness of solving some mathematical problems, the number-theoretic hard problems related to these constructions have been first reviewed here.

Definition 2.5 *(RSA Problem) Let $N = p \times q$, where p and q are two distinct odd prime numbers. Let e be a random prime number such that $\gcd(e, (p-1) \times (q-1)) = 1$, and let $\mathbb{G}$ be a cyclic subgroup of Z_N^*. Given (N, e) and $y \in \mathbb{G}$, the RSA problem consists of finding $z \in Z_N$ such that $y = z^e$.*

Definition 2.6 *(Discrete Logarithm (DL) Problem) Let $\mathbb{G}$ be a finite cyclic group and g be a generator of $\mathbb{G}$. Given a random element $h \in \mathbb{G}$, the DL problem consists of computing the exponent x such that $h = g^x$.*

Definition 2.7 *(Weil–Diffie–Hellman (WDH) Problem) Given a generator P of $\mathbb{G}$ and a triple $< aP, bP, cP >$ for random $a, b, c \in \mathbb{Z}_p^*$, the WDH problem is to compute $\hat{e}(P, P)^{abc} \in \mathbb{G}_T$.*

Definition 2.8 *(Decision Diffie–Hellman (DDH) Problem) Given a generator P of $\mathbb{G}$ and a tuple $< aP, bP, cP >$ for $a, b, c \in \mathbb{Z}_p^*$, the DDH problem is to decide whether $c \stackrel{?}{=} ab \bmod q$ holds or not.*

Definition 2.9 *(Computational Diffie–Hellman (CDH) Problem) Given a generator P of $\mathbb{G}$ and a tuple $< aP, bP >$ for $a, b \in \mathbb{Z}_p^*$, the CDH problem is to compute abP.*

2.3.1 Public-Key Encryption Algorithms

2.3.1.1 Framework of Public-Key Encryption

Definition 2.10 *A public-key encryption scheme (see Figure 2.3) consists of the following three algorithms:*

1. *Gen: Given a security parameter 1^n, this algorithm outputs a pair of public and secret keys $(\mathsf{pk}, \mathsf{sk})$.*

2. *Enc: With an input public key pk and a message m from some underlying plaintext space, this algorithm outputs a ciphertext c, which can be denoted as $c \leftarrow \mathsf{Enc}_{\mathsf{pk}}(m)$.*

3. *Dec: With an input private key sk and a ciphertext c, this algorithm outputs a message m or a special symbol $\perp$ to denote failure, which can be written as $m = \mathsf{Dec}_{\mathsf{sk}}(c)$.*

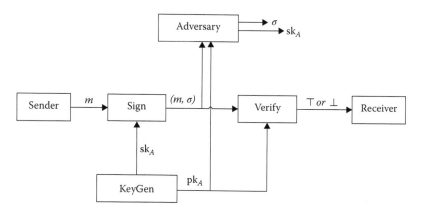

Figure 2.3 An overview of public-key encryption.

We make the consistency constraint that for every n, every $(\mathsf{pk}, \mathsf{sk})$ generated by $\mathsf{Gen}(1^n)$, every message m in the appropriate underlying plaintext space, and $c = \mathsf{Enc}_{\mathsf{pk}}(m)$, $\mathsf{Dec}_{\mathsf{sk}}(c) = m$.

2.3.1.2 RSA Encryption Scheme

The RSA encryption scheme [6] is the most widely used public-key encryption scheme and its security depends on the intractability of the RSA problem. Concretely, the RSA encryption scheme consists of the following three algorithms:

Gen: To create the public key and the corresponding secret key, the following steps are performed:

1. Randomly choose two prime numbers p and q such that $|p| \approx |q|$;
2. Compute $N = p \times q$;
3. Compute $\phi(N) = (p - 1) \times (q - 1)$;
4. Randomly choose an integer $e < \phi(N)$ such that $\gcd(e, \phi(N)) = 1$, and compute the integer d such that $e \times d \equiv 1 \bmod \phi(N)$;
5. Publish (N, e) as the public key, and keep d as the corresponding private key. Note that p, q and $\phi(N)$ will be destroyed safely.

Enc: Before sending a sensitive message $m < N$, the sender creates the ciphertext $c = m^e \bmod N$. (Note that the plaintext message space is in fact $\mathbb{Z}_N^*$.)

Dec: To decrypt the ciphertext c, the corresponding receiver computes $m = c^d \bmod N$.

2.3.1.3 ElGamal Encryption Scheme

The ElGamal encryption scheme [37] is constructed based on the DL problem. Concretely, the ElGamal encryption scheme consists of the following three algorithms:

Gen: To create the public key and the corresponding secret key, the following steps are performed:

1. Choose a random multiplicative generator g of $\mathbb{Z}_p^*$ such that p is a random prime number

2. Pick a random number $1 \le x \le p-2$ as the private key

3. Compute the corresponding public key by $y = g^x (\mathrm{mod}\ p)$

4. Publish (p, g, y) as the public key, and keep x as the corresponding private key

Enc: Before sending a sensitive message $m \in \mathbb{Z}_p^*$, the sender picks $1 \le k \le p-2$ and computes the ciphertext as follows:

$$c_1 = g^k (\mathrm{mod}\ p), \quad c_2 = y^k (\mathrm{mod}\ p)$$

Dec: To decrypt the ciphertext (c_1, c_2), the following steps are performed:

$$m = c_2 / c_1^x (\mathrm{mod}\ p)$$

2.3.1.4 Framework of ID-Based Encryption Scheme

Definition 2.11 *An ID-based encryption scheme (see Figure 2.4) consists of the following three algorithms:*

Setup: *With an input security parameter k, this algorithm is performed by the PKG to create the system parameters* params *and the master secret key* master-key *such that* params *will be distributed to all users in the system and* master-key *will be kept secret by the PKG itself.*

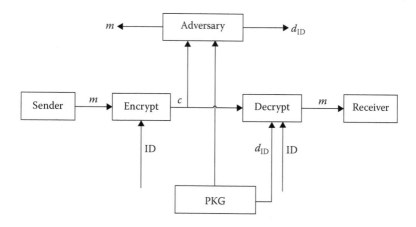

Figure 2.4 An overview of identity (ID)-based encryption.

Extract: *With input* params, master-key, *and an arbitrary identity* ID ∈ $\{0,1\}^*$, *this algorithm is performed by the PKG to generate a private key d_{ID}. After that, d_{ID} will be sent to the corresponding user secretly.*

Enc: *With input* params, ID, *and* m, *this algorithm outputs a ciphertext* c.

Dec: *With input* params, ID, c, *and the corresponding private key d_{ID}, this algorithm recovers* m.

2.3.1.5 Boneh–Franklin IBE

The first practical identity-based encryption scheme was constructed by Boneh and Franklin [9] based on bilinear pairings and its security depends on the WDH problem. First the basic Boneh–Franklin IBE scheme, which is not secure against an adaptive chosen ciphertext attack (CCA),[a] is presented. The only reason for describing the basic scheme is to improve the readability of the full scheme. After that, the full scheme extends the basic scheme to achieve security against an adaptive CCA.

Boneh–Franklin IBE (Basic Scheme) Concretely, the basic Boneh–Franklin IBE scheme consists of the following four algorithms:

Setup: The algorithm works as follows:

1. Let $\hat{e} : \mathbb{G} \times \mathbb{G} \to \mathbb{G}_T$ be a symmetric bilinear pairing defined in Section 2.2.4.

2. Pick a random $s \in \mathbb{Z}_q^*$ and set $P_{\text{pub}} = sP$.

3. Choose two cryptographic hash functions $H_1 : \{0,1\}^* \to \mathbb{G}^*$ and $H_2 : \mathbb{G}_T \to \{0,1\}^n$.

The system parameters params $= \{P, P_{\text{pub}}, H_1, H_2\}$ are published to everyone in the system, while master-key $s \in \mathbb{Z}_q^*$ is kept secret by the PKG.

---

[a]The details on adaptive chosen ciphertext attack can be found in Section 2.4.

Extract: With an input string $\mathsf{ID} \in \{0,1\}^*$, this algorithm is performed by the PKG as follows:

1. Compute $d_{\mathsf{ID}} = s \cdot H_1(\mathsf{ID})$ as the private key associated with the identity ID.

2. Send d_{ID} to the user ID secretly.

Encrypt: To encrypt m under the public key ID, r is chosen from $\mathbb{Z}_q^*$ and the ciphertext is generated as follows:

$$c = \langle rP, m \oplus H_2(g_{\mathsf{ID}}^r) \rangle, \text{ where } g_{\mathsf{ID}} = \hat{e}(H_1(\mathsf{ID}), P_{\mathrm{pub}}) \in \mathbb{G}_T$$

Decrypt: Given a ciphertext $c = \langle U, V \rangle$ encrypted using the public key ID, the plaintext message can be recovered as follows:

$$V \oplus H_2(\hat{e}(d_{\mathsf{ID}}, U)) = m$$

Boneh–Franklin IBE (Full Scheme) Concretely, the full Boneh–Franklin IBE scheme consists of the following four algorithms:

Setup, Extract: The algorithms are the same as those in the above basic scheme. In addition, two additional hash functions $H_3 : \{0,1\}^n \times \{0,1\}^n \to \mathbb{Z}_q^*$ and $H_4 : \{0,1\}^n \to \{0,1\}^n$ are required.

Encrypt: To encrypt m under the public key ID, choose a random $\gamma \in \{0,1\}^n$, set $r = H_3(\gamma, m)$, and generate the ciphertext as follows:

$$C = \langle rP, \gamma \oplus H_2(g_{\mathsf{ID}}^r), m \oplus H_4(\gamma) \rangle, \text{ where } g_{\mathsf{ID}} = \hat{e}(H_1(\mathsf{ID}), P_{\mathrm{pub}})$$

Decrypt: Let $\langle U, V, W \rangle$ be a ciphertext encrypted using the public key ID. Given a ciphertext $c = \langle U, V, W \rangle$ encrypted using the public key ID, the plaintext message can be recovered as follows:

1. Compute $V \oplus H_2(\hat{e}(d_{\mathsf{ID}}, U)) = \gamma$.

2. Compute $W \oplus H_4(\gamma) = m$.

3. Set $r = H_3(\gamma, m)$. Test that $U = rP$. If not, reject the ciphertext.

4. Output m.

2.3.2 Signature Algorithms

2.3.2.1 Framework of Digital Signature

Definition 2.12 *A signature scheme (see Figure 2.5) consists of the following three algorithms:*

Gen: *Given a security parameter 1^n, this algorithm outputs a public and secret key pair (pk, sk).*

Sign: *With an input private key sk and a message m from some underlying message space, this algorithm outputs a signature σ, which can be written as $\sigma \leftarrow \mathsf{Sign}_{sk}(m)$.*

Verify: *With an input public key pk, a message m, and a signature σ, this algorithm returns 1 for accept or 0 for reject.*

We make the consistency constraint that for every n, every (pk, sk) generated by **Gen**, *and every message m, it holds that*

$$\mathsf{Verify}_{pk}(m, \mathsf{Sign}_{sk}(m)) = 1$$

2.3.2.2 RSA Signature Scheme

The RSA cryptosystems [6] may be used to provide both encryption and digital signature. The RSA digital signature is described as follows:

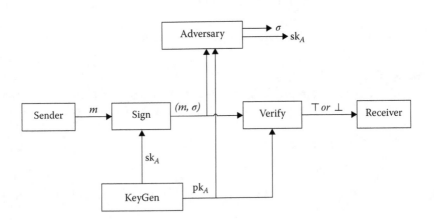

Figure 2.5 An overview of a digital signature.

Gen: To create the public key and the corresponding secret key, the following steps are performed:

1. Randomly choose two prime numbers p and q such that $|p| \approx |q|$;
2. Compute $N = p \times q$;
3. Compute $\phi(N) = (p-1) \times (q-1)$;
4. Randomly choose an integer $e < \phi(N)$ such that $\gcd(e, \phi(N)) = 1$, and compute the integer d such that $e \times d \equiv 1 \bmod \phi(N)$;
5. Publish (N, e) as the public key, and keep d as the corresponding private key. Noted that p, q, and $\phi(N)$ will be destroyed safely.

Sign: To create a signature of message $m \in \mathbb{Z}_N^*$, the signer creates $\sigma = m^d \bmod N$.

Verify: Given a message–signature pair (m, s), this algorithm outputs 1 if $m = \sigma^e \bmod N$, and returns 0 otherwise.

2.3.2.3 ElGamal Signature Scheme

The ElGamal cryptosystems [6] may be used to provide both encryption and digital signature. The ElGamal digital signature is described as follows:

Gen: To create the public key and the corresponding secret key, the following steps are performed:

1. Choose a random multiplicative generator g of $\mathbb{Z}_p^*$ such that p is a random prime number
2. Pick a random number $1 \leq x \leq p-2$ as the private key
3. Compute the corresponding public key by $y = g^x (\bmod\ p)$
4. Publish (p, g, y) as the public key, and keep x as the corresponding private key

Sign: To create a signature of message $m \in \mathbb{Z}_p^*$, the signer picks a random number $1 \leq k \leq p-2$ and generates a signature (r, s) such that

$$r = g^k (\bmod p), \quad s = k^{-1}(m - x \times r)(\bmod p - 1)$$

Verify: Given a message–signature pair $(m, (r, s))$, this algorithm outputs 1 if $y^r \times r^s = g^m (\text{mod } p)$, and returns 0 otherwise.

2.3.2.4 Schnorr Signature Scheme

Many variations of the basic ElGamal signature scheme have been proposed and the Schnorr signature scheme [38] is one well-known variant. The ElGamal digital signature is described as follows:

Gen: The system parameters are generated as follows:

1. Choose two prime numbers p and q such that $q|p-1$
2. Choose an element $g \in \mathbb{Z}_p^*$ of order q
3. Select a cryptographic hash function $H : \{0,1\}^* \to \mathbb{Z}_q$
4. Select a random number $x \in_R \mathbb{Z}_q$ as the secret key and compute $y = g^{-x}(\text{mod } p)$ as the public key. Publish (p, q, g, y, H) as the public key and keep x as the corresponding secret key

The parameters (p, q, g, H) are publicized for use by system-wide users.

Sign: To create a signature on message $m \in \{0,1\}^*$, the signer picks a random number k from $\mathbb{Z}_q$ at random and computes a signature such that $r = g^k (\text{mod } p)$, $e = H(m||r)$, and $s = k + x \times e (\text{mod } q)$.

Verify: Given a message–signature pair $(m, (e, s))$, this algorithm outputs 1 if $r' = g^s \times y^e (\text{mod } p)$ and $e' = H(m||r')$, and returns 0 otherwise.

2.3.2.5 Digital Signature Standard

In 1991, a digital signature algorithm (DSA) was presented by the U.S. National Institute of Standards and Technology (NIST), and it was later called the Digital Signature Standard (DSS) [39] by the U.S. Federal Information Processing Standard (FIPS 186). DSS is regarded as the first digital signature scheme recognized by the U.S. government and is described as follows.

Gen: The system parameters are generated as follows:

1. Select a prime number q such that $2^{159} < q < 2^{160}$.

2. Choose t such that $0 \le t \le 8$, and select a prime number p, where $2^{511+64t} < p < 2^{512+64t}$ and $q|(p-1)$.

3. Select a generator g of the unique cyclic group with order q in $\mathbb{Z}_p^*$.

   (a) Select an element $h \in \mathbb{Z}_p^*$ and compute $g = h^{(p-1)/q}$ mod p.

   (b) If $g = 1$, then go to previous step.

4. Select a random integer x such that $1 \le x \le q - 1$ and compute $y = g^x \mod p$.

5. (p, q, g, y) is published as the public key, while x is kept secret as the private key of the corresponding user.

Sign: To create a signature on message $m \in \{0,1\}^*$, the following steps are performed:

1. Select a random secret integer k such that $0 < k < q$.

2. Compute $r = (g^k \mod p) \mod q$.

3. Compute $k^{-1} \mod q$.

4. Compute $s = k^{-1}\{h(m) + xr\} \mod q$.

5. (r, s) is returned as the signature on the message m.

Verify: Given a message–signature pair $(m, (r, s))$, the following steps are performed to check the validity of the signature:

1. Compute $u_1 = s^{-1} \cdot h(m) \mod q$ and $u_2 = r \cdot s^{-1} \mod q$.

2. Output 1 if $r = (g^{u_1} y^{u_2} \mod p) \mod q$ and return 0 otherwise.

2.3.2.6   Framework of ID-Based Signature Scheme

Definition 2.13 *An ID-based encryption scheme (see Figure 2.6) consists of the following three algorithms:*

Setup: With an input security parameter k, this algorithm is performed by the PKG to create the system parameters **params** and the master secret key **master-key** such that **params** will be distributed to all users in the system and **master-key** will be kept secret by PKG itself.

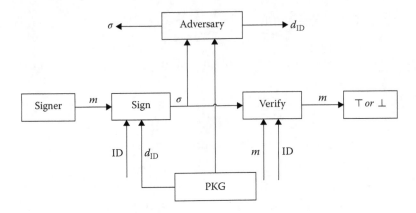

Figure 2.6 An overview of an ID-based signature.

Extract: With input params, master-key, and an arbitrary identity ID ∈ {0,1}*, this algorithm is performed by the PKG to generate a private key d_{ID}. After that, d_{ID} will be sent to the corresponding user secretly.

Sign: Given a message m, an identity ID, a private key d_{ID}, and params, this algorithm generates the signature σ on the message m under the identity ID.

Verify: Given a signature σ, a message m, an identity ID, and params, this algorithm returns 1 for accept or 0 for reject.

2.3.2.7   Cha–Cheon Identity-Based Signature

Inspired by [9], an ID-based signature scheme has been proposed by Cha and Cheon [40] using gap Diffie–Hellman (GDH) groups, where the GDH group is a cyclic group, and the CDH problem is hard but the DDH problem is easy. Cha–Cheon's identity-based signature (IBS) scheme is described as follows:

Setup: Let $\hat{e} : \mathbb{G} \times \mathbb{G} \to \mathbb{G}_T$ be a symmetric bilinear pairing defined in Section 2.2.4. Choose a generator P from the group $\mathbb{G}$, pick a random $s \in \mathbb{Z}_p^*$, set $P_{\text{pub}} = sP$, and choose cryptographic hash functions $H_1 : \{0,1\}^* \times G \to \mathbb{Z}_p^*$ and $H_2 : \{0,1\}^* \to \mathbb{G}$. The system parameter $(P, P_{\text{pub}}, H_1, H_2)$ is published, while the master secret key s is kept secret by the PKG.

Extract: Given an identity ID, this algorithm computes $d_{\text{ID}} = sH_2(\text{ID})$ and sends it to the user associated with identity ID secretly.

Sign: Given a secret key d_{ID} and a message m, pick a random number $r \in \mathbb{Z}_p^*$ and output a signature $\sigma = (U, V)$ such that $U = rH_2(\text{ID})$, $h = H_1(m, U)$, and $V = (r + h)d_{\text{ID}}$.

Verify: To verify a signature $\sigma = (U, V)$ on a message m under an identity ID, this algorithm outputs 1 if $\hat{e}(U + hH_2(\text{ID}), P_{\text{pub}}) = \hat{e}(P, V)$, and returns 0 otherwise, where $h = H_1(m, U)$.

2.3.2.8 Bellare–Namprempre–Neven IBS

Bellare et al. [41] proposed the first pairing-free IBS scheme based on the DL problems. Bellare–Neven–Namprempre's IBS scheme is described as follows:

Setup: Generate an elliptic curve E over a finite field $\mathbb{Z}_p$, a prime q dividing the number of points on E, and a curve point P of order q, and pick a random $x \in \mathbb{Z}_q^*$ and compute $P_{\text{pub}} = xP$. Choose two cryptographic hash functions $H_1, H_2 : \{0, 1\}^* \to \mathbb{Z}_p$. $\langle \mathbb{Z}_p, E, q, P, P_{\text{pub}}, H_1, H_2 \rangle$ is published as the system parameter and x is kept secret as the master secret key by the PKG.

Extract: Given an identity ID, the PKG picks a random $r \in \mathbb{Z}_q^*$ and computes $R = rP$, $c = H_1(\text{ID}, R)$, and $s = r + cx \bmod q$. (R, s) is sent to the user associated with ID secretly.

Sign: Given a secret key pair (R, s) associated with ID and a message m, pick a random $t \in \mathbb{Z}_q^*$ and compute $T = tP$, $h = H_2(\text{ID}, m, R, T)$ and

$$z = t + hs \bmod q$$

The resulting signature is $\sigma = (R, T, z)$.

Verify: To verify a signature $\sigma = (R, T, z)$ of a message m for an identity ID, compute $h = H_2(\text{ID}, m, R, T)$ and $c = H_1(\text{ID}, R)$ and check whether

$$zP = T + h(R + cP_{\text{pub}})$$

holds or not.

2.4 PROVABLE SECURITY

Provable security, which involves the exact definitions, precise assumptions, and rigorous security proof of cryptographic primitives, is regarded as the methodology unavoidable in designing, analyzing, and evaluating new primitives [42–44]. The basic reason for the necessity of provable security originates from the fact that the security of a cryptographic primitive cannot be checked in the same way that software is typically checked. Without a proof that no adversary with enough computational resources can break the primitive, we can only depend on our intuition about the security of the mentioned primitive. Unfortunately, history has already demonstrated that intuition in cryptography and information security is disastrous in the sense that countless examples of unproven schemes or schemes only with a heuristic security proof were broken (sometime immediately or sometimes years after being published or deployed).

Instead of indiscreetly assuming a given cryptographic primitive is secure, provable security assumes that some mathematical problem is hard to solve, and then aims to prove that the given primitive is secure provided this assumption. Concretely, the proof proceeds by presenting an explicit reduction showing how to construct an efficient algorithm C that succeeds in solving certain computational tasks that were assumed to be hard from any efficient adversary $\mathcal{A}$ that succeeds in breaking the primitive with nonnegligible probability. The steps of such a proof can be outlined at a high level as follows.

We first assume that some mathematical problem X cannot be solved by any polynomial-time algorithm except with negligible probability. To prove that some cryptographic primitive Π is secure, the following steps are performed.

Initial: Assume an efficient adversary $\mathcal{A}$ attempts to attack the cryptographic primitive Π and denote $\mathcal{A}$'s success probability by ε.

1. An efficient algorithm C is constructed by employing adversary $\mathcal{A}$ as a subroutine to solve problem X. Given an instance of some input of mathematical problem X, the algorithm C will simulate an execution of Π for the adversary $\mathcal{A}$ such that:

   a. The view of $\mathcal{A}$ when it is invoked as a subroutine by C should be identical to the view of $\mathcal{A}$ when it interacts with the real primitive Π itself.

b. Furthermore, if $\mathcal{A}$ succeeds in breaking the execution of Π which is being simulated by $\mathcal{C}$, this should enable $\mathcal{C}$ to solve the given instance of X with inverse polynomial probability $\frac{1}{p}$.

2. From Step 1, it is obvious that if ε is not negligible, then the problem X can be solved by $\mathcal{C}$ with nonnegligible probability $\frac{\varepsilon}{p}$, which contradicts the initial assumption. Therefore, we conclude that, given the assumption associated with X, no efficient algorithm $\mathcal{A}$ can succeed with nonnegligible probability ε; in other words, Π is proven to be computationally secure formally.

2.4.1 Public-Key Encryption

As for the security model of public-key encryption, we begin our definitional treatment by considering the case of an eavesdropping adversary who observes a single ciphertext that it wishes to crack. In other words, the eavesdropping adversary does not have any further interaction with the sender or the receiver after receiving a (single) ciphertext. Intuitively speaking, the security model for public-key encryption is depicted by the definition of indistinguishability. Particularly, consider an experiment $\mathsf{PubK}^{\mathrm{eav}}_{\mathcal{A},\Pi}(n)$ between an eavesdropping adversary $\mathcal{A}$ and a corresponding simulator/challenger $\mathcal{C}$ in which $\mathcal{A}$ outputs two messages m_0 and m_1 with equal length, and in turn is given an encryption of one of these messages randomly chosen by $\mathcal{C}$ using a randomly generated key. According to the definition of indistinguishability, a public-key encryption scheme Π is said to be secure if, in this experiment, no adversary $\mathcal{A}$ can distinguish which message is encrypted better than a naive guess. We now give the formal definition of $\mathsf{PubK}^{\mathrm{eav}}_{\mathcal{A},\Pi}(n)$ as follows.

Given a public-key encryption scheme $\Pi = (\mathsf{Gen}, \mathsf{Enc}, \mathsf{Dec})$ and an adversary $\mathcal{A}$, the eavesdropping experiment $\mathsf{PubK}^{\mathrm{eav}}_{\mathcal{A},\Pi}(n)$ is defined as follows:

1. The algorithm $\mathsf{Gen}(1^n)$ is performed by $\mathcal{C}$ to calculate keys (pk, sk).

2. After receiving the public key pk, $\mathcal{A}$ outputs a pair of messages (m_0, m_1) such that $|m_0| = |m_1|$.

3. After receiving (m_0, m_1), C chooses a random bit $b \leftarrow \{0, 1\}$ and sends to A a ciphertext $c \leftarrow \mathsf{Enc}_{pk}(m_b)$. Here, c is called the challenge ciphertext.

4. After receiving c, A outputs a bit b' and wins the experiment if $b' = b$.

Definition 2.14 *A public-key encryption scheme* $\Pi = (\mathsf{Gen}, \mathsf{Enc}, \mathsf{Dec})$ *is regarded to achieve indistinguishability against an eavesdropper if for all probabilistic, polynomial-time adversaries* A*, the advantage of* A *in the eavesdropping experiment* $\mathsf{PubK}_{A,\Pi}^{eav}(n)$*, defined as* $\mathsf{Adv}_{\Pi}^{ind\text{-}eav}(A) = |2Pr[b' = b] - 1|$*, is negligible.*

2.4.1.1   Security against Chosen-Plaintext Attacks

In view of the fact that a relatively weak attacker who only passively eavesdrops on the communication has been modeled in the eavesdropping experiment, a more powerful type of adversarial attacker who is allowed to query encryptions of multiple messages in an adaptive manner should be considered to simulate the attacker's capabilities in the real world. Thus, a chosen-plaintext attack (CPA) has been defined to enable the adversary A to interact freely with an encryption oracle to encrypt messages of A's choice.

Specifically, consider the following experiment defined for public-key encryption scheme $\Pi = (\mathsf{Gen}, \mathsf{Enc}, \mathsf{Dec})$; the CPA indistinguishability experiment $\mathsf{PubK}_{A,\Pi}^{cpa}(n)$ between the adversary A who can mount a CPA and a corresponding simulator/challenger C is defined as follows:

Initial: The algorithm $\mathsf{Gen}(1^n)$ is performed by C to calculate keys (pk, sk).

Phase 1: After receiving the public key pk, A issues a sequence of queries to the oracle $\mathsf{Enc}_{pk}(\cdot)$ adaptively.

Challenge: After deciding Phase 1 is over, A outputs a pair of messages (m_0, m_1) with equal length. C now chooses a random bit $b \leftarrow \{0, 1\}$ and sends to A a ciphertext $c \leftarrow \mathsf{Enc}_{pk}(m_b)$. Here, c is called the challenge ciphertext.

Phase 2: The adversary A now issues a second sequence of queries to the oracle $\mathsf{Enc}_{pk}(\cdot)$ adaptively again as in Phase 1.

Guess: After receiving c, A outputs a bit b' and wins the experiment if $b' = b$.

Definition 2.15 *A public-key encryption scheme* $\Pi = (\mathsf{Gen}, \mathsf{Enc}, \mathsf{Dec})$ *is regarded to achieve indistinguishability against CPAs if for all probabilistic, polynomial-time adversaries* $\mathcal{A}$, *the advantage of* $\mathcal{A}$ *in the experiment* $\mathsf{PubK}_{\mathcal{A},\Pi}^{\mathrm{cpa}}(n)$, *defined as* $\mathsf{Adv}_{\Pi}^{\mathrm{ind\text{-}cpa}}(\mathcal{A}) = |2Pr[b' = b] - 1|$, *is negligible.*

2.4.1.2 Security against Chosen-Ciphertext Attacks

To strengthen the adversary's capabilities further, a third type of adversary, who is more powerful than the former two types of adversaries and can mount a CCA [45,46], should be taken into consideration. In this attack model, the adversary is not only allowed to encrypt any messages of its choice as in the CPA model, but is also enabled to decrypt any ciphertexts of its choice. Therefore, the chosen-ciphertext attack is regarded as the most powerful attack associated with public-key encryption so far.

Specifically, consider the following experiment defined for public-key encryption scheme $\Pi = (\mathsf{Gen}, \mathsf{Enc}, \mathsf{Dec})$; the CCA indistinguishability experiment $\mathsf{PubK}_{\mathcal{A},\Pi}^{\mathrm{cca}}(n)$ (shown in Figure 2.7) between the adversary $\mathcal{A}$ who can mount a chosen-ciphertext attack and a corresponding simulator/challenger $\mathcal{C}$ is defined as follows.

Initial: The algorithm $\mathsf{Gen}(1^n)$ is performed by $\mathcal{C}$ to calculate keys (pk, sk).

Phase 1: After receiving the public key pk, $\mathcal{A}$ issues a sequence of queries to the encryption oracle $\mathsf{Enc}_{pk}(\cdot)$ and the decryption oracle $\mathsf{Dec}_{sk}(\cdot)$ adaptively.

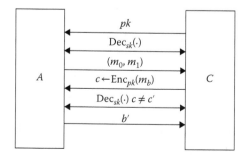

Figure 2.7 CCA experiment $\mathsf{PubK}_{\mathcal{A},\Pi}^{\mathrm{cca}}(n)$ for public-key encryption.

Challenge: After the deciding Phase 1 is over, $\mathcal{A}$ outputs a pair of messages (m_0, m_1) with equal length. $\mathcal{C}$ now chooses a random bit $b \leftarrow \{0, 1\}$ and sends to $\mathcal{A}$ a ciphertext $c \leftarrow \mathsf{Enc}_{pk}(m_b)$. Here, c is called the challenge ciphertext.

Phase 2: After receiving c, $\mathcal{A}$ now issues a second sequence of queries to the oracles $\mathsf{Enc}_{pk}(\cdot)$ and $\mathsf{Dec}_{sk}(\cdot)$ adaptively again as in Phase 1 with the restriction that the challenged ciphertext cannot be queried to the decryption oracle.

Guess: $\mathcal{A}$ outputs a bit b' and wins the experiment if $b' = b$.

Definition 2.16 *A public-key encryption scheme* $\Pi = (\mathsf{Gen}, \mathsf{Enc}, \mathsf{Dec})$ *is regarded to achieve indistinguishability against chosen-ciphertext attacks if for all probabilistic, polynomial-time adversaries* $\mathcal{A}$, *the advantage of* $\mathcal{A}$ *in the experiment* $\mathsf{PubK}^{cca}_{\mathcal{A}, \Pi}(n)$, *defined as* $\mathsf{Adv}^{ind\text{-}cca}_{\Pi}(\mathcal{A}) = |2Pr[b' = b] - 1|$, *is negligible.*

2.4.2 ID-Based Encryption

Different from the public-key encryption in the traditional public-key infrastructure (PKI), the definition of chosen-ciphertext security must be strengthened a bit in ID-PKC due to the fact that the attacker might already own the private keys of users $ID_1, \ldots, ID_n$ of her choice when she attacks another public key ID. To ensure the security of the encryption scheme in the ID-based environment [9], the definition of chosen-ciphertext security must enable the attacker to obtain the private key associated with any identity of his or her choice (other than the challenged public key ID being attacked).

2.4.2.1 Security against Chosen-Ciphertext-and-Identity Attacks

Specifically, consider the following experiment defined for ID-based encryption scheme $\Pi = (\mathsf{Setup}, \mathsf{Extract}, \mathsf{Encrypt}, \mathsf{Decrypt})$; the CCA indistinguishability experiment $\mathsf{IBE}^{cca,cida}_{\mathcal{A}, \Pi}(n)$ (shown in Figure 2.8) between the adversary $\mathcal{A}$ who can mount the chosen-ciphertext attack and a corresponding simulator/challenger $\mathcal{C}$ is defined as follows:

Initial: The algorithm Setup is performed by the challenger $\mathcal{C}$ to generate the system parameters params, which will be forwarded to the adversary $\mathcal{A}$.

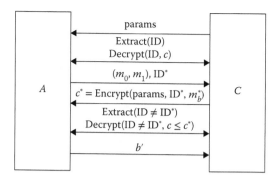

Figure 2.8   CCA experiment $\text{IBE}_{\mathcal{A},\Pi}^{\text{cca,cida}}(n)$ for ID-based encryption.

Phase 1: $\mathcal{A}$ can perform a polynomially bounded number of queries in an adaptive manner as follows:

- Upon receiving an identity ID_i, $\mathcal{C}$ runs private key extraction oracle $\text{Extract}(\cdot)$ on ID_i and forwards the associated private key to $\mathcal{A}$.
- Upon receiving a tuple (ID_i, c_i), $\mathcal{C}$ runs decryption oracle $\text{Decrypt}(\cdot)$ on (ID_i, c_i), and sends the result to $\mathcal{A}$.

Challenge: After deciding Phase 1 is over, the adversary submits two plaintexts (m_0, m_1) with equal length and an identity ID^* to $\mathcal{C}$ such that the identity ID^* must not have been sent to the private key extraction oracle $\text{Extract}(\cdot)$ in Phase 1. After receiving (m_0, m_1), $\mathcal{C}$ selects a random bit $b \in \{0,1\}$, sets $c = \text{Encrypt}(\text{params}, \text{ID}^*, m_b)$, and forwards c to the adversary as the challenge ciphertext.

Phase 2: This is identical to Phase 1 with the restriction that

- $\mathcal{A}$ must not have sent ID^* to the private key extraction oracle $\text{Extract}(\cdot)$.
- $\mathcal{A}$ must not have sent (ID^*, c) to the decryption oracle $\text{Decrypt}(\cdot)$.

Guess: $\mathcal{A}$ outputs a bit b' and wins the experiment if $b' = b$.

Definition 2.17 *An ID-based encryption scheme* $\Pi = (\text{Setup, Extract,}$ $\text{Encrypt, Decrypt})$ *is regarded to achieve indistinguishability against chosen-ciphertext attacks if for all probabilistic, polynomial-time adversaries* $\mathcal{A}$, *the advantage of* $\mathcal{A}$ *in the experiment* $\text{IBE}_{\mathcal{A},\Pi}^{\text{cca,cida}}(n)$, *defined as* $\text{Adv}_{\Pi}^{\text{ind-cca-ibe}}(\mathcal{A}) = |2Pr[b' = b] - 1|$, *is negligible.*

2.4.3 Digital Signature

To capture the adversary's power in the digital signature, a security property called existential unforgeability against a chosen-message attack [47] should be achieved; existential unforgeability means that the adversary should not be able to generate a valid signature on any message, and the chosen-message attack means that the adversary is able to obtain signatures on any messages it wishes during its attack. We now give the formal definition of existential unforgeability against a chosen-message attack as follows.

2.4.3.1 Security against Chosen-Message Attacks

Let Π = (Gen, Sign, Verify) be a signature scheme, and consider the following experiment Sig-forge$_{\mathcal{A},\Pi}^{\text{cma}}(n)$ (shown in Figure 2.9) between an adversary $\mathcal{A}$ and a corresponding challenger/simulator $\mathcal{C}$ as follows:

Initial: The algorithm Gen is run by $\mathcal{C}$ to obtain keys (pk, sk) such that the public key pk is forwarded to the adversary $\mathcal{A}$, whereas the private key sk is kept secret by $\mathcal{C}$ itself.

Attack: After receiving the public key pk, $\mathcal{A}$ is given access to the signing oracle Sign$_{sk}(\cdot)$, which returns a signature Sign$_{sk}(m)$ for any message m of $\mathcal{A}$'s choice.

Forgery: $\mathcal{A}$ outputs a message and signature pair (m^*, σ^*). $\mathcal{A}$ wins this experiment if Verify$_{pk}(m^*, \sigma^*) = 1$ with the restriction that σ^* has not been queried to the oracle Sign$_{sk}(\cdot)$.

Definition 2.18 *A signature scheme* Π = (Gen, Sign, Vrfy) *is said to achieve existentially unforgeability under an adaptive chosen-message*

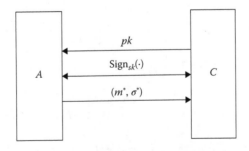

Figure 2.9 Unforgeability experiment Sig-forge$_{\mathcal{A},\Pi}^{\text{cma}}(n)$ for signatures.

attack if for all probabilistic polynomial-time adversaries $\mathcal{A}$, the advantage of $\mathcal{A}$ winning the experiment Sig-forge$_{\mathcal{A},\Pi}^{\text{cma}}(n)$ *is negligible.*

2.4.4 ID-Based Signature

The security model of existential unforgeability under an adaptive chosen-message attack in the traditional PKI can be extended to the identity-based environment naturally [40,41]. We now give the formal definition of existential unforgeability against a chosen-message attack for the ID-based signature as follows.

2.4.4.1 Security against Chosen-Message-and-Identity Attacks

Let Π = (Setup, Extract, Sign, Verify) be a signature scheme, and consider the following experiment IBS-forge$_{\mathcal{A},\Pi}^{\text{cma,cida}}(n)$ (shown in Figure 2.10) between an adversary $\mathcal{A}$ and a corresponding challenger/simulator $\mathcal{C}$ as follows:

Initial: The algorithm Setup is performed by the challenger $\mathcal{C}$ to generate the system parameters params, which will be forwarded to the adversary $\mathcal{A}$.

Attack: $\mathcal{A}$ can perform a polynomially bounded number of queries in an adaptive manner as follows:

- Upon receiving an identity ID_i, $\mathcal{C}$ runs private key extraction oracle Extract($\cdot$) on ID_i and forwards the associated private key to $\mathcal{A}$.
- Upon receiving a tuple (ID, m), $\mathcal{C}$ runs signing oracle Sign($\cdot$) on (ID, m) and forwards the result to $\mathcal{A}$.

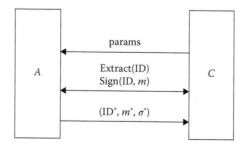

Figure 2.10 Unforgeability experiment IBS-forge$_{\mathcal{A},\Pi}^{\text{cma,cida}}(n)$ for ID-based signatures.

Forgery: $\mathcal{A}$ outputs a message m^*, an identity ID^*, and a signature σ^*. $\mathcal{A}$ is said to succeed in the experiment $\mathsf{IBS\text{-}forge}_{\mathcal{A},\Pi}^{\mathsf{cma,cida}}(n)$ if the following requirements are satisfied:

1. $\mathsf{Verify}(\mathsf{params}, \mathsf{ID}^*, m^*, \sigma^*) = 1$.

2. ID^* has not been queried to the private key extraction oracle $\mathsf{Extract}(\cdot)$.

3. (ID^*, m^*) has not been queried to the signing oracle $\mathsf{Sign}(\cdot)$.

Definition 2.19 *An ID-based signature scheme* $\Pi = (\mathsf{Setup}, \mathsf{Extract}, \mathsf{Sign}, \mathsf{Verify})$ *is said to achieve existentially unforgeability under an adaptive chosen-message attack if for all probabilistic polynomial-time adversaries* $\mathcal{A}$, *the advantage of* $\mathcal{A}$ *winning the experiment* $\mathsf{IBS\text{-}forge}_{\mathcal{A},\Pi}^{\mathsf{cma,cida}}(n)$ *is negligible.*

II

CL-PKC without Random Oracles

CHAPTER 3

CLE Secure in the Standard Model

3.1 INTRODUCTION

Our objective in this chapter is to present certificateless encryption (CLE) schemes that can be proven secure without relying on the random oracle model (a brief introduction to the random oracle model will be presented in Chapter 5). This part begins with the formal definitions of CLE schemes followed by the examination and ranking of existing security models according to the adversaries' capabilities. Next, we concisely survey the state of the art of CLE schemes so far. Finally, some concrete pairing-based CLE schemes and generic CLE schemes secure in the standard model are shown.

3.2 MODELING CERTIFICATELESS PUBLIC-KEY ENCRYPTION SCHEMES

3.2.1 Al-Riyami and Paterson Formulation

The framework of the CLE scheme (see Figure 3.1), which was initially defined by Al-Riyami and Paterson [17], and Al-Riyami [48], consists of the following seven algorithms:

Setup: On input of a security parameter 1^k, this algorithm is usually performed by the key-generation center (KGC) to generate the public system parameters **params** and the corresponding master secret key **master-key**.

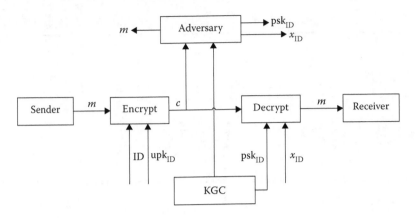

Figure 3.1 An overview of certificateless encryption.

Extract-Partial-Private-Key: On input of the master secret key master-key, the public system parameters params, and an identity ID, ∈ $\{0, 1\}^*$, this algorithm is usually performed by the KGC to generate the user's partial private key psk_{ID}. Noted that this algorithm is performed by the KGC once for each user, and the partial private key psk_{ID} is distributed to the corresponding user via a secure channel.

Set-Secret-Value: On input of the public system parameters params and a user's identity ID, this algorithm is run by the user himself/herself to generate a user secret value x_{ID}.

Set-Private-Key: On input of the public system parameters params, a user's partial private key psk_{ID}, and a user's secret value x_{ID}, this algorithm is run by the user himself/herself to generate the full user private key usk_{ID}.

Set-Public-Key: On input of the public system parameters params and a user's secret value x_{ID}, this algorithm is usually carried out by the user himself/herself to generate a user public key upk_{ID}.

Encrypt: On input of the public system parameters params, a user's identity ID, a user's public key upk_{ID}, and a message m, this algorithm can be run by any entity to generate the ciphertext c.

Decrypt: On input of the public system parameters params, a user's secret key usk_{ID}, and a ciphertext c, this algorithm can be executed by the user to return either a message m or the error symbol ⊥ demonstrating a decryption error.

Similar to the traditional public-key encryption (PKE) scheme and identity-based encryption (IBE) scheme, a CLE scheme enables any entity to encrypt a message for an intended receiver only with publicly available information. However, different from the traditional PKE scheme, the necessity of public-key certificates is eliminated since the key-replacement adversary, who distributes a false public key upk_{ID} for an identity ID, still cannot perform the decryption operation on the ciphertext encrypted under the false user public key without the partial private key psk_{ID}. On the other hand, distinct from the IBE scheme, a CLE scheme solves the key escrow problem such that a honest-but-curious KGC cannot calculate the full private key since the secret value x_{ID} associated with that user's public key upk_{ID} will not be disclosed to anyone other than the user himself/herself.

3.2.2 Equivalence to the Original Seven-Algorithm Framework

A natural observation on the aforementioned framework is that the Set-Private-Key algorithm can be removed directly since the function of user secret key usk_{ID} can be achieved by adopting the secret value x_{ID} and partial private key psk_{ID} together. In this way, the Decrypt algorithm is defined by taking the secret value x_{ID} and partial private key psk_{ID} as input. Therefore, the formulation given by Al-Riyami and Paterson can be simplified with the equivalent function as follows:

Setup

Extract-Partial-Private-Key

Set-Secret-Value

Set-Public-Key

Encrypt

Decrypt

Furthermore, this framework can be further simplified by incorporating the Set-Secret-Value and Set-Public-Key algorithms as one single Set-User-Keys algorithm defined as follows [18,49]:

Set-User-Keys: On input of the master public key mpk and a user's identity ID, this algorithm is run to output a public/private key pair (upk_{ID}, usk_{ID}).

In this way, a more versatile framework of CLE, in which a scheme consists of only five algorithms, is given as follows [50]:

Setup

Extract-Partial-Private-Key

Set-User-Keys

Encrypt

Decrypt

3.2.3 Baek, Safavi-Naini, and Susilo's Framework

To construct a pairing-free CLE scheme, Baek et al. [51] further simplified the formulation given by Al-Riyami and Paterson. In Baek et al.'s framework, a user public key can only be calculated after a partial private key has been derived. Specifically, the partial private key in Baek et al.'s model consists of not only a partial private key (used to generate the full private key) but also a partial public key (used to generate the full public key). In other words, a slight change has been made to the Set-Public-Key algorithm:

Set-Public-Key: On input of the master public key mpk, a user's partial private key psk_{ID}, and secret value x_{ID}, this algorithm is performed to output a user public key upk_{ID} associated with this user.

Different from Al-Riyami and Paterson's original formulation, Baek et al.'s framework does not allow an entity to distribute a public key upk_{ID} before receiving the partial private key psk_{ID} from the KGC, and therefore cannot obtain messages to be encrypted "into the future." It should be noted that, under this framework, the functions of the Set-Secret-Value, Set-Public-Key, and Set-Private-Key algorithms can also be provided by a single Set-User-Keys algorithm defined as follows:

Set-User-Keys: On input of the master public key mpk, a user's identity ID, and a partial private key psk_{ID}, this algorithm is run to output a public/private key pair (upk_{ID}, usk_{ID}).

Similar to the Al-Riyami and Paterson formulation, the framework of CLE can also be simplified to involve only five algorithms as follows:

Setup

Extract-Partial-Private-Key

Set-User-Keys

Encrypt

Decrypt

It is also noted that the concept of a secret value has been removed in this framework, which incurs some modifications of the corresponding security models.

3.3 SECURITY DEFINITIONS FOR CERTIFICATELESS PUBLIC-KEY ENCRYPTION SCHEMES

Due to the lack of public-key authentication (e.g., in the form of a digital certificate) in certificateless public-key cryptography (CL-PKC), it is natural to suppose that the adversary can replace anyone's public key of his/her choice. To capture the attack in this way, adversaries who can replace the public key of any user of their choice are called type I adversaries in [17,48]. It is obvious that a secure certificateless scheme must feature the property that it is infeasible for a type I adversary to gain nothing useful under the false public-key chosen by himself/herself. Furthermore, an assumption that must be made in CL-PKC is that the KGC never mounts a public-key replacement attack to a target user because of the fact that the KGC equipped with the partial private key could impersonate any user without being detected by generating a user private/public key pair and then replacing the original public key with the false one. However, the KGC, also known as a type II adversary in [17,48], can undoubtedly engage in other adversarial activities such as eavesdropping on ciphertexts and making decryption queries. In this way, the assumption is reasonable since the level of trust in the KGC in CL-PKC is identical to the trust in a certificate authority (CA) in a traditional public-key infrastructure (PKI).

3.3.1 General Security Model

Combining the formulation of CLE and security models of encryption schemes in traditional PKC and ID-PKC, the security of a CLE scheme is defined by two (very similar) games between a challenger $\mathcal{C}$ and an adversary $\mathcal{A}_1$ or $\mathcal{A}_2$. Adversary $\mathcal{A}_1$ models attacks where an adversary other than the KGC replaces the user's public key $\mathsf{upk}_{\mathsf{ID}}$. However, the partial private key $\mathsf{psk}_{\mathsf{ID}}$ cannot be accessed by $\mathcal{A}_1$. Adversary $\mathcal{A}_2$ models the malicious-but-passive KGC who owns the master secret key but cannot perform the public-key replacement attack on the target user. In both cases, an attacker $\mathcal{A} = (\mathcal{A}_1, \mathcal{A}_2)$ attempts to break the chosen ciphertext attack (CCA) security of the CLE scheme similar to the security model for traditional PKE and IBE. The general security game between $\mathcal{A}$ and the challenger $\mathcal{C}$ is depicted as follows:

Initial: The challenger/simulator $\mathcal{C}$ generates the public system parameters **params** and the corresponding master secret key **master-key** by performing the Setup algorithm. $\mathcal{C}$ keeps **master-key** secret and publishes **params**. It is noted that **master-key** will be given to type II adversary $\mathcal{A}_2$.

Phase 1: A type I or II adversary $\mathcal{A}$ can adaptively access certain oracles (depicted subsequently).

Challenge: After deciding phase 1 is over, $\mathcal{A}$ outputs an identity ID^* and two messages (m_0, m_1) with equal length. Now, $\mathcal{C}$ randomly chooses a bit $b \in \{0, 1\}$ and computes the challenge ciphertext $c^* = \mathsf{Encrypt}(\mathsf{params}, \mathsf{ID}^*, \mathsf{upk}_{\mathsf{ID}^*}, m_b)$ under the current public key $\mathsf{upk}_{\mathsf{ID}}^*$. When the user public key $\mathsf{upk}_{\mathsf{ID}}^*$ has not been created yet, $\mathcal{C}$ generates a public key $\mathsf{upk}_{\mathsf{ID}}^*$ associated with identity ID^* by executing the Set-Secret-Value and Set-Public-Key algorithms.

Phase 2: Now, $\mathcal{A}$ can adaptively access certain oracles (depicted subsequently) similar to Phase 1.

Guess: On input of c^*, $\mathcal{A}$ terminates the security game by outputting a guess b' for b, and $\mathcal{A}$ is said to win the aforementioned game if $b = b'$.

It now remains to define the oracles that $\mathcal{A}$ may have access to in the security game. It is noted that type II adversary $\mathcal{A}_2$ does not need to access **Partial-Private-Key-Extract** oracle to derive partial private keys since **master-key** has already been given to $\mathcal{A}_2$.

Create-User: This oracle takes as input an identity ID $\in \{0,1\}^*$; if ID has already been created, nothing will be performed by this oracle. Otherwise, the oracle obtains the partial private key $\mathsf{psk}_{\mathsf{ID}}$, the user secret value x_{ID}, and the user public key $\mathsf{upk}_{\mathsf{ID}}$ by performing the Extract-Partial-Private-Key, Set-Secret-Value, and Set-Public-Key algorithms, respectively. It then stores $(ID, \mathsf{upk}_{\mathsf{ID}}, x_{\mathsf{ID}}, \mathsf{psk}_{\mathsf{ID}})$ into a list $\mathcal{L}$. In both cases, $\mathsf{upk}_{\mathsf{ID}}$ is returned to the adversary.

Public-Key-Replace: This oracle captures the attacker's capability to dupe a legitimate sender to use an invalid public key. On input of a query on (ID, $\mathsf{upk}'_{\mathsf{ID}}$), this oracle replaces the user ID's original public key with $\mathsf{upk}'_{\mathsf{ID}}$ and updates the corresponding item in the list $\mathcal{L}$. It is noted that the secret value used to generate $\mathsf{upk}'_{\mathsf{ID}}$ is not required to be provided by the adversary [20].

Partial-Private-Key-Extract: On input of a query on the identity ID, this oracle searches the list $\mathcal{L}$ and returns the corresponding partial private key $\mathsf{psk}_{\mathsf{ID}}$ by performing the Extract-Partial-Private-Key algorithm.

Secret-Value-Extract: On input of a query on the identity ID, this oracle searches the list $\mathcal{L}$ and returns the corresponding secret value x_{ID} by performing the Set-Secret-Value algorithm.

As we have mentioned, an adaptively chosen ciphertext adversary could not only encrypt any messages of its choice but also decrypt any ciphertexts of its choice. Thus, in addition to the above oracles, a **Decrypt** oracle should also be accessed by the adversaries. However, there is a debate about how to define the **Decrypt** oracle precisely [17,48,49,52–61]. Specifically, this **Decrypt** oracle will be different depending on the adversaries's capability that will be depicted as follows.[a]

Normal-Decrypt [48,52,55,61]: On input of an identity ID and a ciphertext c generated by $\mathsf{Encrypt}(m, \mathsf{params}, \mathsf{upk}_{\mathsf{ID}}, \mathsf{ID})$ such that $\mathsf{upk}_{\mathsf{ID}}$ can only be the user ID's original public-key, this oracle responds with the resulting plaintext by performing the decryption algorithm with the support of the partial private key and the original user secret value.

---

[a]The nomenclature for these different oracles is borrowed from [18,20].

Strong-Decrypt [18,53,56–58,60]: On input of an identity ID and a ciphertext c generated by $\mathsf{Encrypt}(m, \mathsf{params}, \mathsf{upk}'_{\mathsf{ID}}, \mathsf{ID})$ such that $\mathsf{upk}'_{\mathsf{ID}}$ could be the user ID's original public key or any valid public-key value chosen by the adversary, this oracle responds with the resulting plaintext by performing the decryption algorithm with the support of the partial private key and some information sv. When $\mathsf{upk}'_{\mathsf{ID}}$ is the replaced user public key, the adversary is required to provide the corresponding secret value sv which is used to calculate the $\mathsf{upk}'_{\mathsf{ID}}$ chosen by itself. Alternatively, the original secret value will be adopted in the decryption algorithm when $\mathsf{upk}'_{\mathsf{ID}}$ is the original user public key.

Super-Decrypt [17,51,59,62,63]: On input of an identity ID and a ciphertext c generated by $\mathsf{Encrypt}(m, \mathsf{params}, \mathsf{upk}'_{\mathsf{ID}}, \mathsf{ID})$ such that $\mathsf{upk}'_{\mathsf{ID}}$ could be the user ID's original public key or any valid public-key value chosen by the adversary, this oracle responds with the resulting plaintext by performing the decryption algorithm. When $\mathsf{upk}'_{\mathsf{ID}}$ is the replaced user public key chosen by the adversary, it is unnecessary for the adversary to provide the corresponding secret value which is used to produce the public key chosen by itself.

Definition 3.1 *A CLE scheme is said to be IND-CCA2 secure if there is no PPT adversary $\mathcal{A}$ which wins the IND-CCA2 game with a non-negligible advantage.*

3.3.2 Type I Attackers

In the CL-PKC environment, the type I adversary is modeled to capture the attacks mounted by a third-party attacker other than the KGC who can compromise the user secret key or replace the user's public key, but cannot compromise the master secret key nor get access to the user's partial private key. By considering the debates about the adversaries' capabilities, we categorized the type I attackers into three types, that is, the normal type I adversary, the strong type I adversary, and the super type I adversary, from the aspects of practice and theory.

3.3.2.1 Security against a Normal Type I Adversary

In this section, the first kind of type I adversary $\mathcal{A}_1$, named the normal type I adversary, is considered to capture the following attack scenarios:

1. $\mathcal{A}_1$ can access the **Normal-Decrypt** oracle described earlier on the ciphertext that is generated under the target user's identity ID and original user public key $\mathsf{upk_{ID}}$.

2. The target user's secret value x_{ID} and partial private key $\mathsf{psk_{ID}}$ will be kept secret.

3. The target user ID's public key can be replaced with $\mathsf{upk'_{ID}}$ by $\mathcal{A}_1$ of its choice. Furthermore, $\mathcal{A}_1$ can also generate the ciphertext associated with the target user under the identity ID and the replaced public key $\mathsf{upk'_{ID}}$.

Inspired by the CCA model [45,46], $\mathcal{A}_1$ may choose a ciphertext and obtain its corresponding decryption from the target user ID. Although $\mathcal{A}_1$ can replace the target user ID's public key with the $\mathsf{upk'_{ID}}$ of its choice and ask for decryptions of ciphertexts from the target user ID, we argue that, in most cases, it is unrealistic for an adversary $\mathcal{A}_1$ to dupe the target user ID into decrypting ciphertexts generated under a public key chosen by the adversary itself. In other words, the target user ID in the CLE environment cannot prevent his/her public key from being replaced. However, it would be a strong assumption that the target user ID decrypt the ciphertext that is generated under the replaced public key. On the other hand, either the secret value x_{ID} or the partial private key $\mathsf{psk_{ID}}$ of the target user cannot be accessed by the adversary $\mathcal{A}_1$.

The indistinguishability of a CLE scheme against a normal type I adaptively chosen ciphertext adversary $\mathcal{A}_1$ is defined as follows (shown in Figure 3.2):

Initial: The challenger/simulator $\mathcal{C}$ generates the public system parameters **params** and the corresponding master secret key **master-key** by performing the **Setup** algorithm.

Phase 1: $\mathcal{A}_1$ can adaptively access the **Create-User, Public-Key-Replace, Partial-Private-Key-Extract, Secret-Value-Extract**, and **Normal-Decrypt** oracles.

Challenge: After deciding phase 1 is over, $\mathcal{A}_1$ outputs a challenge identity ID^* and two messages (m_0, m_1) with equal length. Now, $\mathcal{C}$ randomly chooses a bit $b \in \{0, 1\}$ and computes the challenge ciphertext $c^* = \mathsf{Encrypt}(\mathsf{params}, \mathsf{ID}^*, \mathsf{upk_{ID}^*}, m_b)$ under the current public key $\mathsf{upk_{ID}^*}$.

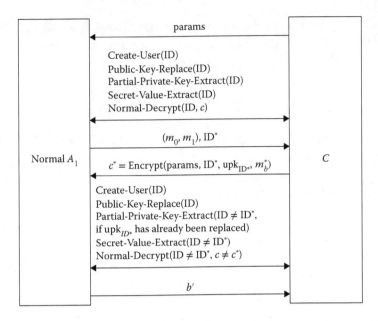

Figure 3.2 IND-CCA2-Normal-I experiment for certificateless encryption (CLE) scheme.

Phase 2: Now, $\mathcal{A}_1$ can adaptively access the **Create-User, Public-Key-Replace, Partial-Private-Key-Extract, Secret-Value-Extract**, and **Normal-Decrypt** oracles similar to phase 1 with the following restrictions:

- The secret value associated with the challenge identity ID^* cannot be extracted by $\mathcal{A}_1$ at any time.

- The partial private key associated with the challenge identity ID^* cannot be extracted by $\mathcal{A}_1$ if the corresponding user public key $\mathsf{upk}_{\mathsf{ID}^*}$ has already been replaced before the challenge identity ID was issued.

- If the public key of one user has already been replaced by $\mathcal{A}_1$, the secret value of this user cannot be extracted by $\mathcal{A}_1$.

- The challenge ciphertext c^* and the identity ID^* cannot be issued to the **Normal-Decrypt** oracle unless the user public key $\mathsf{upk}_{\mathsf{ID}^*}$ has already been replaced before the challenge identity was issued.

Guess: On input of c^*, $\mathcal{A}_1$ terminates the security game by outputting a guess b' for b, and $\mathcal{A}_1$ is said to win the preceding game if $b = b'$.

Definition 3.2 *A CLE scheme is said to achieve indistinguishability against a normal type I adaptively chosen ciphertext adversary if there is no PPT adversary $\mathcal{A}_1$ that wins the preceding IND-CCA2-Normal-I game with a nonnegligible advantage.*

3.3.2.2 Security against a Strong Type I Adversary

In this section, we enhance the attack capabilities of the adversary $\mathcal{A}_1$ and formalize the second type of $\mathcal{A}_1$, named the strong type I adversary, to capture the attack scenario where $\mathcal{A}_1$ can ask for decryptions of ciphertexts generated under the identity ID and user public key $\mathsf{upk}_{\mathsf{ID}}$ from the target user ID. Here $\mathsf{upk}_{\mathsf{ID}}$ could be any valid public-key value chosen by $\mathcal{A}_1$ or the user ID's original user public key. In the former case, the strong type I adversary $\mathcal{A}_1$ is required to provide the corresponding secret value that is used to calculate the public key chosen by itself.

The attack scenario described enables $\mathcal{A}_1$ to ask for the decryptions of ciphertexts from the target user ID using the secret value sv provided by $\mathcal{A}_1$ itself [18,53,56–58,60]. It is evident that a scheme secure against a strong type I adversary can also resist the attack mounted from a normal type I adversary. This kind of attack indicates that the target user ID will perform the decryption operation with his/her own partial private key and the secret value provided by $\mathcal{A}_1$. In other words, this scenario implies that the target user ID will intentionally do a favor for $\mathcal{A}_1$ to attack himself/herself. This assumption seems much stronger than the normal type I adversary in most situations.

The indistinguishability of a CLE scheme against a strong type I adaptively chosen ciphertext adversary $\mathcal{A}_1$ is defined as follows (shown in Figure 3.3):

*Initial***:** The challenger/simulator $\mathcal{C}$ generates the public system parameters **params** and the corresponding master secret key **master-key** by performing the **Setup** algorithm.

*Phase 1***:** $\mathcal{A}_1$ can adaptively access the **Create-User, Public-Key-Replace, Partial-Private-Key-Extract, Secret-Value-Extract**, and **Strong-Decrypt** oracles.

*Challenge***:** After deciding phase 1 is over, $\mathcal{A}_1$ outputs a challenge identity ID^* and two messages (m_0, m_1) with equal length. Now, $\mathcal{C}$ randomly chooses a bit $b \in \{0, 1\}$ and computes the challenge

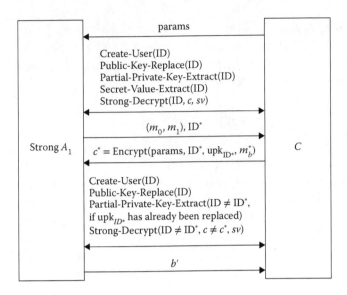

Figure 3.3 IND-CCA2-Strong-I experiment for CLE scheme.

ciphertext $c^* = \mathsf{Encrypt}(\mathsf{params}, \mathsf{ID}^*, \mathsf{upk}_{\mathsf{ID}^*}, m_b)$ under the current public key $\mathsf{upk}_{\mathsf{ID}}^*$.

Phase 2: Now, $\mathcal{A}_1$ can adaptively access the **Create-User, Public-Key-Replace, Partial-Private-Key-Extract, Secret-Value-Extract**, and **Strong-Decrypt** oracles similar to phase 1 with the following restrictions:

- The partial private key associated with the challenge identity ID^* cannot be extracted by $\mathcal{A}_1$ if the corresponding user public key $\mathsf{upk}_{\mathsf{ID}^*}$ has already been replaced before the challenge identity ID was issued.

- If the public key of one user has already been replaced by $\mathcal{A}_1$, the secret value of this user cannot be extracted by $\mathcal{A}_1$.

- The challenge ciphertext c^*, the identity ID^*, and the secret value sv provided by $\mathcal{A}_1$ cannot be issued to the **Strong-Decrypt** oracle.

Guess: On input of c^*, $\mathcal{A}_1$ terminates the security game by outputting a guess b' for b, and $\mathcal{A}_1$ is said to win the aforementioned game if $b = b'$.

Different from the security model defined in Section 3.3.2.1, the strong type I adversary $\mathcal{A}_1$ is allowed to derive the secret value of the target user ID^*, which implies that the secret value associated with current user public key $\mathsf{upk}_{\mathsf{ID}^*}$ might be leaked out.

Definition 3.3 *A CLE scheme is said to achieve indistinguishability against a strong type I adaptively chosen ciphertext adversary if there is no PPT adversary $\mathcal{A}_1$ that wins the aforementioned IND-CCA2-Strong-I game with a nonnegligible advantage.*

3.3.2.3 Security against a Super Type I Adversary

In this section, we formalize the third type of $\mathcal{A}_1$, named the super type I adversary, to capture the attack scenario where $\mathcal{A}_1$ can ask for decryptions of ciphertexts generated under the identity ID and user public key $\mathsf{upk}_{\mathsf{ID}}$ from the target user. Here $\mathsf{upk}_{\mathsf{ID}}$ could be any valid public-key value chosen by $\mathcal{A}_1$ or the target user's original user public key. In the former case, it is not necessary for the super type I adversary $\mathcal{A}_1$ to provide the corresponding secret value that is used to calculate the public key chosen by itself.

The attack scenario described above gives the adversary $\mathcal{A}_1$ as much power as possible such that the challenger is expected to correctly respond to decryption queries made on identities for which the adversary has replaced the public key. Furthermore, $\mathcal{A}_1$ is not required to provide the secret value sv associated with the public key chosen by itself. In this way, a black box knowledge exactor is assumed to exist implicitly such that the secret value associated with the public key chosen by $\mathcal{A}_1$ can be extracted from this black-box and used in the decryption oracle.[a] In fact, a super type I adversary is considered the strongest attacker so far even though it is still uncertain whether it reflects a realistic attack scenario. Undoubtedly, a CLE scheme that is secure in

---

[a]Generally speaking, a decryption oracle accessed by an adversary simulates the fact that the adversary can derive some information from a legitimate receiver about the decryptions of some ciphertexts. For instance, the legitimate receiver can be bribed to disclose the message himself/herself or the legitimate receiver's behavior after receiving a ciphertext can be observed and analyzed to deduce whether this ciphertext is a valid encryption of a particular message. Obviously, the situation where the receiver attempts to decrypt the ciphertext using the secret value corresponding to the replaced public key cannot happen. Therefore, this kind of decryption oracle which will accurately decrypt ciphertexts encrypted under the replaced public key gives the adversary more power than it would have in reality.

this kind of security model offers a higher security level than one that is secure in a strong or a normal type I security model.

The indistinguishability of a CLE scheme against a super type I adaptively chosen ciphertext adversary $\mathcal{A}_1$ is defined as follows (shown in Figure 3.4):

Initial: The challenger/simulator $\mathcal{C}$ generates the public system parameters **params** and the corresponding master secret key **master-key** by performing the Setup algorithm.

Phase 1: $\mathcal{A}_1$ can adaptively access the **Create-User, Public-Key-Replace, Partial-Private-Key-Extract, Secret-Value-Extract**, and **Super-Decrypt** oracles.

Challenge: After deciding phase 1 is over, $\mathcal{A}_1$ outputs a challenge identity ID^* and two messages (m_0, m_1) with equal length. Now, $\mathcal{C}$ randomly chooses a bit $b \in \{0, 1\}$ and computes the challenge ciphertext $c^* = \mathsf{Encrypt}(\mathsf{params}, \mathsf{ID}^*, \mathsf{upk}_{\mathsf{ID}^*}, m_b)$ under the current public key $\mathsf{upk}_{\mathsf{ID}}^*$.

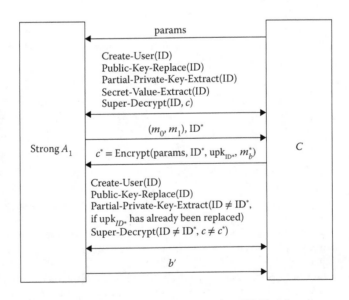

Figure 3.4 IND-CCA2-Super-I experiment for CLE scheme.

Phase 2: Now, $\mathcal{A}_1$ can adaptively access the **Create-User, Public-Key-Replace, Partial-Private-Key-Extract, Secret-Value-Extract**, and **Super-Decrypt** oracles similar to phase 1 with the following restrictions:

- The partial private key associated with the challenge identity ID^* cannot be extracted by $\mathcal{A}_1$ if the corresponding user public key $\mathsf{upk}_{\mathsf{ID}^*}$ has already been replaced before the challenge identity ID was issued.

- If the public key of one user has already been replaced by $\mathcal{A}_1$, the secret value of this user cannot be extracted by $\mathcal{A}_1$.

- The challenge ciphertext c^* and the identity ID^* cannot be issued to the **Super-Decrypt** oracle.

Guess: On input of c^*, $\mathcal{A}_1$ terminates the security game by outputting a guess b' for b, and $\mathcal{A}_1$ is said to win the aforementioned game if $b = b'$.

Definition 3.4 *A CLE scheme is said to achieve indistinguishability against a super type I adaptively chosen ciphertext adversary if there is no PPT adversary $\mathcal{A}_1$ which wins the aforementioned IND-CCA2-Super-I game with a nonnegligible advantage.*

3.3.3 Type II Attackers

In the CL-PKC environment, the type II adversary $\mathcal{A}_2$ simulates the KGC who owns the master secret key and might mount several attacks such as eavesdropping on ciphertexts and making decryption queries. By considering the debates about the adversaries' capabilities, we categorized the type II attackers into normal $\mathcal{A}_2$, strong $\mathcal{A}_2$, and super $\mathcal{A}_2$. However, the strong $\mathcal{A}_2$ is unnecessary to define particularly since this kind of adversary can win the security game trivially. Specifically, the **Strong-Decrypt** oracle can answer queries either by using the oracle **Normal-Decrypt** (then the oracle **Strong-Decrypt** is exactly identical to the oracle **Normal-Decrypt**) or by decrypting the ciphertexts using the corresponding secret value provided by the adversary. The basic reason for this depends on the fact that the type II adversary $\mathcal{A}_2$ owns the master secret key and can generate the partial private key for any user by itself.

Similar to Section 3.3.2.1, the indistinguishability of a CLE scheme against a normal (*resp.* super) type II adaptively chosen ciphertext adversary $\mathcal{A}_2$ is defined as follows (shown in Figure 3.5):

Initial: The challenger/simulator $\mathcal{C}$ executes the Setup algorithm and returns the public system parameters params and the master secret key master-key to $\mathcal{A}_2$.

Phase 1: $\mathcal{A}_2$ can adaptively access the **Create-User, Public-Key-Replace, Secret-Value-Extract**, and **Normal-Decrypt** (*resp.* **Super-Decrypt**) oracles.[a]

Challenge: After deciding phase 1 is over, $\mathcal{A}_2$ outputs a challenge identity ID^* and two messages (m_0, m_1) with equal length. Now, $\mathcal{C}$ randomly chooses a bit $b \in \{0, 1\}$ and computes the challenge ciphertext $c^* = \mathsf{Encrypt}(\mathsf{params}, \mathsf{ID}^*, \mathsf{upk}_{\mathsf{ID}^*}, m_b)$ under the current public key $\mathsf{upk}_{\mathsf{ID}}^*$.

Phase 2: Now, $\mathcal{A}_2$ can adaptively access the **Create-User, Public-Key-Replace, Partial-Private-Key-Extract, Secret-Value-**

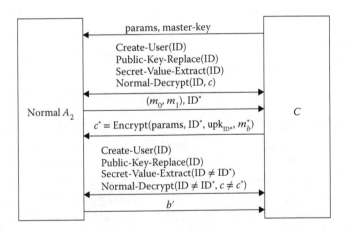

Figure 3.5 IND-CCA2-Normal-II experiment for CLE scheme.

---

[a]It is noted that the **Partial-Private-Key-Extract** oracle is no longer needed in this security game since $\mathcal{A}_2$ can generate the partial private key with the knowledge of the master secret key himself/herself.

Extract, and **Normal-Decrypt** (*resp.* **Super-Decrypt**) oracles similar to phase 1 with the following restrictions:

- The secret value associated with the challenge identity ID^* cannot be extracted by $\mathcal{A}_2$ at any time.
- If the public key of one user has already been replaced by $\mathcal{A}_2$, the secret value of this user cannot be extracted by $\mathcal{A}_2$.
- The challenge ciphertext c^* and the identity ID^* cannot be issued to the **Normal-Decrypt** (*resp.* **Super-Decrypt**) oracle.

Guess: On input of c^*, $\mathcal{A}_2$ terminates the security game by outputting a guess b' for b, and $\mathcal{A}_2$ is said to win the aforementioned game if $b = b'$.

Definition 3.5 *A CLE scheme is said to achieve indistinguishability against a normal type II adaptively chosen ciphertext adversary if there is no PPT adversary $\mathcal{A}_2$ that wins the aforementioned IND-CCA2-Normal-II game with a nonnegligible advantage.*

3.3.4 Malicious-but-Passive KGC Attacks

The introduction of CL-PKC is motivated by the desire to solve the key escrow problem in ID-PKC environments. In the security model defined for CLE, a defense against the type II adversary implies the elimination of the key escrow problem in the sense that the type II adversary (i.e., the malicious KGC) cannot decrypt the ciphertext on behalf of the user provided that the KGC would not actively extract the user secret value or replace the user public key. Taking the CLE paradigm as an example, the malicious KGC can only passively eavesdrop on the ciphertexts and attempt to decrypt them with the knowledge of the partial private key. This kind of KGC is termed a malicious-but-passive KGC in the rest of this book.[a] According to the observations shown in [62], the malicious-but-passive KGC formalized in [17,48,52–61] is assumed to perform the Setup algorithm honestly by calculating its master public/secret key and deleting any data used during this algorithm according to scheme

---

[a]Similar to CL-PKC, the malicious CA in a traditional PKI is also assumed not to issue new certificates associated with arbitrary public keys of its choice since the CA can impersonate any user easily in this way. With this assumption, users in CL-PKC invest the identical trust level in the KGC as they would in a CA in a traditional PKI.

specification. This does not necessarily reflect reality since the KGC is assumed to be originally benign, and after setting up the system, it suddenly becomes malicious and attempts to impersonate users. It is more natural if this malicious-but-passive KGC is considered to be malicious at the very beginning of the **Setup** algorithm. That is to say, the master public/private key pair along with the system-wide parameters can be generated maliciously by the KGC to mount the type II attack more easily in the later stage of the system. More specifically, the KGC can derive the user secret key after the user has published its own user public key if the KGC maliciously calculates its master public key, which is computationally indistinguishable from the one generated honestly according to the scheme specification.

To capture this new kind of type II attack, named the malicious-but-passive KGC attack, Au et al. [62] revisited the security models for a type II adversary and removed the assumption that the KGC has to calculate the system parameters along with the master key pair honestly. Combined with different **Decrypt** oracles, the security of the CLE schemes against a malicious-but-passive KGC attack is defined in the following games:

Initial: The challenger/simulator C executes A_2 on the security parameter k. A_2 returns a master public key mpk and the system parameters **params**. Note that A_2 cannot make any query at this stage with the exception that A_2 is enabled to access the specific random oracles of the underlying scheme at any stage of the game if the security analysis is performed under some model such as the random oracle model.

Phase 1: A_2 can adaptively access all oracles as in the game defined in Section 3.3.3. However, the **Create-User** oracle is modified as follows:

Create-User: This oracle takes not only an identity $ID \in \{0,1\}^*$ but also the user partial private key psk_{ID} as the input.[a] If the item associated with the identity ID has already been created, nothing is to be executed by the oracle. Otherwise, this oracle performs the algorithms **Set-Secret-Value** and **Set-Public-Key** to obtain the secret value x_{ID} and the public key upk_{ID}, respectively.

---

[a]In this way, it implies that the user secret value can be obtained by A_2 with the support of the user partial private key psk_{ID}.

Then this oracle inserts $(\mathsf{ID}, \mathsf{upk}_{\mathsf{ID}}, x_{\mathsf{ID}}, \mathsf{psk}_{\mathsf{ID}})$ to the list $\mathcal{L}$. In this case, ID is said to be created. In both cases, $\mathsf{upk}_{\mathsf{ID}}$ is returned.

Challenge: After deciding phase 1 is over, $\mathcal{A}_2$ outputs an identity ID^* and two messages (m_0, m_1) with equal length. Now, $\mathcal{C}$ randomly chooses a bit $b \in \{0, 1\}$ and computes the challenge ciphertext $c^* = \mathsf{Encrypt}(\mathsf{params}, \mathsf{ID}^*, \mathsf{upk}_{\mathsf{ID}^*}, m_b)$ under the current public key $\mathsf{upk}_{\mathsf{ID}}^*$. When user public key $\mathsf{upk}_{\mathsf{ID}}^*$ has not been created yet, $\mathcal{C}$ generates a public key $\mathsf{upk}_{\mathsf{ID}}^*$ associated with identity ID^* by executing the Set-Secret-Value and Set-Public-Key algorithms.

Phase 2: Now, $\mathcal{A}_2$ can adaptively access certain oracles similar to phase 1.

Guess: On input of c^*, $\mathcal{A}$ terminates the security game by outputting a guess b' for b, and $\mathcal{A}_2$ is said to win the aforementioned game if $b = b'$.

Definition 3.6 *A CLE scheme is said to achieve indistinguishability against a malicious but passive type II adaptively chosen ciphertext adversary if there is no PPT adversary $\mathcal{A}_2$ that wins the aforementioned security game with a nonnegligible advantage.*

3.4 SURVEYING CERTIFICATELESS PUBLIC-KEY ENCRYPTION SCHEMES

The state of the art of CLE schemes is surveyed and summarized in Table 3.1 by categorizing the existing literature according to different perspectives [18].

3.4.1 Concrete Constructions of CLE Schemes

Paired with the introduction and formal formation of certificateless encryption in [17,48], Al-Riyami and Paterson suggested the first concrete scheme based on bilinear pairing along with provable security. After that, a new concrete CLE scheme was presented and claimed to be more efficient than the original scheme in [52]. Unfortunately, the scheme in [52] was broken by Libert and Quisquater [59] later. Furthermore, Libert and Quisquater proposed an improved scheme based on a stronger computational assumption, that is, p-Bilinear Diffie–Hellman Inversion (p-BDHI) assumption. Subsequently, Cheng et al. [66] proposed two CLE schemes that are secure under the Bilinear

TABLE 3.1 Comparison of Existing CLE Schemes

Scheme	References	Style	Model	Type I model	Type II model	Broken?
Al-Riyami 1/Yum–Lee 1	[48,61]	Generic	SM	Normal type I	Normal type II	[59,64,65]
Al-Riyami 2	[48]	Generic	—	No proof given	No proof given	[18]
Al-Riyami 3	[48]	Generic	—	No proof given	No proof given	[64]
Al-Riyami–Paterson 1	[17,48]	Concrete	ROM	Super type I	Normal type II	
Al-Riyami–Paterson 2	[48,52]	Concrete	ROM	Super type I	Normal type II	[64]
Au et al.	[62]	Concrete	ROM	Super type I	Mal. super type II	?
Baek et al.	[51]	Concrete	ROM	Super type I	Normal type II	
Bentahar et al.	[53]	Generic	ROM	strong type I	Normal type II	
Cheng et al. 1	[66]	Generic	ROM	Super type I	Super type II	
Cheng et al. 2	[66]	Concrete	ROM	No decryption oracle	No decryption oracle	
Cheng et al. 3	[66]	Concrete	ROM	Super type Ia	Super type II	
Dent–Libert–Paterson 1	[54]	Generic	SM	Super type I	Super type II	
Dent–Libert–Paterson 2	[54]	Concrete	SM	Super type I	Super type II	
Dent	[18]	Generic	SM	strong type I	Mal. normal type II	
Lai–Kou 1	[63,67]	Concrete	ROM	Super type I	Normal type II	?
Lai–Kou 2	[63,67]	Concrete	ROM	Super type I	Normal type II	?
Lai et al.	[68]	Concrete	ROM	No decryption oracle	No decryption oracle	
Libert–Quisquater 1	[59]	Generic	ROM	Super type I	Normal type II	
Libert–Quisquater 2	[59]	Generic	ROM	Super type I	Normal type II	
Libert–Quisquater 3	[59]	Generic	ROM	Super type I	Normal type II	
Libert–Quisquater 4	[59]	Concrete	ROM	Super type I	Normal type II	
Liu–Au–Susilo	[60]	Concrete	SM	strong type I	Normal type II	

Huang–Wong 1	[56,58]	Generic	SM	Strong type I	Mal. normal type II
Huang–Wong 2	[57]	Generic	SM	Strong type I	Mal. normal type II
Huang–Wong 3	[57]	Generic	SM	Strong type I	Mal. normal type II
Hwang et al.	[69]	Concrete	SM	Strong type I	Mal. normal type II
Park et al. 1	[65]	Concrete	SM	No decryption oracle	No decryption oracle
Park et al. 2	[65]	Concrete	SM	Super type I	Super type II
Sun et al.	[70]	Concrete	ROM	Super type I	Normal type II
Sun–Li et al.	[71]	Concrete	ROM	Super type I	Normal type II
Sepahi et al.	[72]	Concrete	SM	Strong type I	Normal type II
Yang–Tan 1	[73]	Concrete	ROM	Super type I	Super type II
Yang–Tan 2	[73]	Concrete	ROM	Super type I	Super type II
Yum–Lee	[61]	Generic	SM	Strong type I	Normal type II [64,65]

Note: ROM: random oracle model; SM: standard model; Concrete: constructions with a full description; Generic: constructions based on other primitives; ?: unknown.

Diffie–Hellman (BDH) assumption. By adopting the twinning technique in [74], Sun and Li [71] presented a short-ciphertext CCA2 secure CLE under the BDH assumption.

The security proof of all these schemes are given in the random oracle model, which was initiated by Bellare and Rogaway [75] to give rigorous "proofs of security" for certain cryptographic primitives. However, the random oracle model has received a lot of criticism in the sense that some popular cryptosystems proved secure in the random oracle are shown to be insecure when the random oracle is instantiated by any real-world hashing functions [76–78]. Thus, it is desirable to design provably secure CLE schemes without random oracles. To eliminate the limitations of the random oracle model, Dent et al. [54] proposed a concrete CLE scheme based on Waters' IBE scheme [79] and Boyen et al.'s [80] hierarchical IBE scheme [80], and then proved the security of this scheme in the super type I and super type II models without resorting to random oracles. Independent of [54], Liu et al. [60] and Park et al. [65] proposed two secure concrete CLE schemes without random oracles, respectively. Furthermore, Liu et al. [60] identified the denial of decryption attacks[a] and suggested a new paradigm called self-generated-certificate public-key cryptography (SGC-PKC) to withstand the DoD attack by using the certificateless signature as a building block. Indeed the SGC-PKC involves a user issuing a certificate for the public key using the certificateless signature scheme and thus the certificate has been reintroduced in SGC-PKC. The only difference between the SGC-PKC and traditional PKC is that the certificate in SGC-PKC is generated by the user himself/herself while the certificate in PKI is calculated by a trusted CA. To resist the quantum attack, Sepahi et al. [72] obtained an efficient CCA-secure CLE scheme in the standard model from a lattice-based assumption.

---

[a]Suppose one user, named Alice, intends to send encrypted sensitive data to another user, named Bob. Alice needs to takes Bob's identity and corresponding user public key as input to perform the encryption operation. To deny Bob from decrypting the ciphertext, the adversary replaces Bob's user public key with any public key not belonging to Bob. Due to the lack of certificate in CL-PKC, Alice will perform the encryption algorithm using Bob's identity and a replaced public key. In this way, Bob cannot carry out the decryption operation to obtain the sensitive data, even though the adversary also cannot gain any secret information. This destructive attack, which is similar to a denial of service (DoS) attack, is called a denial of decryption (DoD) attack.

3.4.2 Generic Constructions of CLE Schemes

Soon after the introduction of CL-PKC, researchers turned their attention to the construction of a CLE scheme built from general primitives [48,53,61,66]. In this way, CLE can be constructed in a more general manner without involving any mathematic tools. The first approach to construct certificateless encryption schemes in this manner were given by Al-Riyami [48] and Yum and Lee [61] independently. The intuition was to build a CLE scheme by combining a general ID-based public-key encryption scheme with standard public-key encryption schemes. The user's public key would be the identity of the user and the public key in the PKE scheme. Correspondingly, the user's private key combines the user's identity-based private key (provided by the KGC as the partial private key) and the private key for the PKE scheme. After that, Yum and Lee [81] proposed a new generic CLE scheme similar to the schemes in [48,61]. Unfortunately, none of those naive constructions is secure [59,64] regarding the model defined in [17]. Libert and Quisquater [59] showed simple variants to remedy the pitfalls. Cheng et al. [66] proposed a general approach to build a CLE solution by integrating an identity-based encryption (IBE) scheme, a Diffie–Hellman-type key establishment algorithm, and a secure hash-function. Meanwhile, Park et al. [65] proved that all the known generic constructions of CLE schemes are not secure against CCA and also proposed two concrete CLE schemes that are provably secure against CCA without random oracles. One year later, Dent [18] presented a generic scheme that is secure against super type I and super type II attackers by combining certificateless encryption that is secure against attackers that make no decryption oracle queries, a PKE scheme, and a noninteractive zero-knowledge proof system.

Different from the first approach in [48,59,61,66,81], Bentahar et al. [53] extended the key encapsulation mechanism (KEM) into the certificateless public-key encryption (CL-PKE) environment and proposed a generic CL-KEM construction from any IBE scheme plus a special form of public-key encryption scheme. In [53], a CLE scheme is shown to be constructed by composing a certificateless KEM with a standard data encapsulation mechanism (DEM). This construction involves separating the encryption scheme into an asymmetric KEM part (which randomly generates a symmetric key K and an "encapsulation" of that key) and a symmetric DEM part (which encrypts a message under the symmetric key K). Subsequently, the relationship between ID-based key agreement protocols and certificateless KEM schemes is discussed by Fiore et al. [82,83]. In particular, they demonstrated a generic way to transform identity-based key agreement protocols to a certificateless KEM scheme. Later, Yang and Tan [73] displayed that directly applying this transformation results in an insecure CL-KEM scheme and gave a fix without extra computational cost. Huang and Wong [57] extended the concept of a certificateless KEM to a certificateless Tag-KEM by borrowing the idea of Abe et al. [84] in the public-key setting. The merit of Tag-KEMs rests on the fact that they can be composed with passively secure DEMs and still construct schemes that are secure against active attackers. Huang and Wong proposed a generic secure KEM and Tag-KEM that can be proven secure without depending on the random oracle methodology.

3.4.3 Pairing-Free Constructions

In spite of several advantages and rapid advances, the implementation of bilinear pairing is still regarded as expensive [85,86]. In order to eliminate the costly pairing operation, Baek et al. [51] presented a computation-friendly CLE scheme by relaxing the requirement that a user need not own a partial private key before generating a public key. However, a flaw has been found in their proof and thus the security of the scheme has to be viewed as unproven [87]. To resist the denial of decryption (DoD) attack mentioned in [60], Lai and Kou [63] and Lai et al. [67] weakened Baek et al.'s [51] scheme to enforce the Set-User-Keys algorithm to be performed before the Extract-Partial-Private-Key algorithm. Furthermore, Lai and Kou [63,67] presented a pairing-free self-generated-certificate public-key encryption scheme based on their modified CLE scheme along with an application in the key management and authentication system for ad hoc wireless networks. In view of the fact that the type I adversary defined in [51] is not enabled to replace the public key associated with the challenge identity, Sun et al. [70] reviewed the security model in [51] and proposed an improved scheme to solve this problem by incorporating the signing algorithm of the Schnorr signature scheme into the Extract-Partial-Private-Key algorithm and the corresponding verification algorithm into the Encrypt algorithm. Inspired by [82,83], Yang and Tan [73] presented a generic construction of a CLE scheme from an ID-based key agreement protocol and generated a new pairing-free CLE scheme by directly applying the transformation to the Fiore–Gennaro ID-based key agreement protocol [88]. Based on the RSA-based key agreement protocol [89], Lai et al. [68] presented an RSA-based CLE scheme and showed the security proof in the random oracle model. By considering the limitations in [63,67], Yan et al. [90] proposed a novel CLE scheme without the requirement that the Set-User-Keys algorithm must be performed before the Extract-Partial-Private-Key algorithm at the cost of increasing the computational overhead.

3.4.4 Constructions Secure against Malicious KGC Attacks

In addition to identifying the malicious-but-passive KGC attack, Au et al. [62] showed that the schemes proposed in [17] are vulnerable to malicious-but-passive KGC attacks. After that, they claimed that the generic encryption scheme proposed by Libert and Quisquater in [59] is secure against this kind of attack. Furthermore, Au et al. also asserted that a CLE scheme secure against an malicious-but-passive KGC attack can be constructed by applying the certificateless Fujisaki–Okamoto transform in [59] to a suitably random scheme that is secure against malicious type II attackers that do not make any decryption oracle queries. Unfortunately, Dent [18] showed that the certificateless Fujisaki–Okamoto transform is not secure against malicious type II attackers in general. In other words, it is concluded that the certificateless Fujisaki–Okamoto transform does not achieve security in the malicious type II model.

Huang and Wong [56] demonstrated that the CLE scheme in [60] is also insecure against the malicious-but-passive KGC attack and proposed a generic scheme by sequentially composing an IBE scheme and a PKE scheme in a manner similar to [48]. The only difference in [56] is that the sender is enforced to sign the ciphertext with a one-time signature (OTS) scheme where the corresponding verification key is attached to the plaintext. Huang and Wong [57,58] have also proposed a generic KEM and a Tag-KEM scheme that are proven secure in the malicious normal type II models. These constructions are similar to the scheme in [56] other than the fact that the signature scheme is replaced with a secure message authentication code. Therefore, significant performance improvement can be achieved and the resulting schemes are only slightly less efficient than the scheme in [53]. Following the approach in [57,58], Dent [18] proposed a secure CLE scheme by combining an IBE scheme and a PKE scheme in parallel using the techniques of Dodis and Katz [91]. The first concrete CLE scheme secure against malicious KGC attack in the standard model was also presented by Hwang et al. [69].

3.4.5 Extensions of CLE Schemes

By introducing a security-mediator (SEM) to perform a partial decryption operation for the user by request, Chow et al. [92] suggested a new paradigm called security-mediated certificateless encryption. Different from the traditional CLE scheme, the partial private key associated with the identity is securely given to the SEM instead of the user himself/herself, and the user owns only the user secret value in the security-mediated certificateless encryption scheme. In this way, each user's decryption request will be sent to the SEM, who in turn checks whether the user is revoked before it carries out the partial decryption operation. Chow et al. [92] also presented a concrete construction and a generic construction in the random oracle model and the standard model, respectively. After that, Chow et al. [93] extends the definition of a common security-mediated certificateless encryption scheme in [92] to a hierarchical security-mediated certificateless encryption scheme to support hierarchical identifiers. Furthermore, a timed-release encryption is also constructed from the hierarchical security-mediated certificateless encryption scheme. Recently, Seo et al. [25] proposed a paring-free security-mediated certificateless encryption scheme and applied this encryption scheme to secure the sharing of sensitive information in public clouds.

Proxy re-encryption [94] has been considered a promising candidate to secure data sharing in the public cloud by enabling the cloud to transform the ciphertext to legitimate recipients on behalf of the data owner and preserving data privacy from a semi-trusted cloud [95]. In 2010, Sur et al. [96] proposed the first CL-PRE scheme. Their scheme is based on Libert and Quisquater's [59] CL-PKE scheme and CCA security in the random oracle model. In 2012, based on the first CL-PKE scheme [17], Xu et al. [97] constructed a CPA-secure CL-PRE scheme, which was firstly introduced to cloud-based data-sharing scenarios. In 2013, Yang et al. [98] pointed out that both Sur et al.'s [96] and Xu et al.'s [97] schemes utilized costly bilinear pairings and demonstrated that Xu et al.'s scheme cannot provide ciphertext confidentiality. Then they fixed the security problem and firstly proposed two CL-PRE schemes without pairings, a CPA-secure CL-PRE scheme and a CCA-secure CL-PRE scheme, based on Baek et al.'s [51] CL-PKE scheme. Even though Yang et al.'s [98] scheme has high efficiency, two drawbacks of their scheme are that the construction of its first-level ciphertext may greatly consume resources and their security proof only holds under a weaker security model in which the type I adversary is not allowed to replace the public key associated with the challenge identity. Keeping these drawbacks in mind, Qin et al. [99] proposed a strongly secure CL-PRE scheme without bilinear pairing. This scheme is proven to be secure against an adaptive CCA under a stronger security model in which the type I adversary is allowed to replace the public key associated with the challenge identity.

Similar to traditional PKC and ID-PKC, it is natural to equip CL-PKC with revocation functionality to deal with the cases where the subscription of a user expires or the secret key of a user has been exposed. Until now, there was little literature on addressing the revocation problem in existing CLE schemes. As a solution to this problem for CL-PKC, Al-Riyami and Paterson [17] suggested that the CL-PKC construction may inherit the revocation mechanism in ID-PKC [9] such that users renew their private keys periodically to revoke users, and senders use the receivers' identities and user public key concatenated with the current time period. In [100], Tsai and Tseng formally defined the syntax and security notions of the revocable CLE scheme and proposed a concrete revocable CLE scheme based on bilinear pairing operations. However, the computation cost for the KGC at each time period is linear to the total number of users, and thus the revocation solution in [100] does not scale too well. Thus, Xiong and Qin [101] presented a CLE scheme with efficient revocation. Specifically, the revocation mechanism in [101] is highly scalable, which is especially suitable for large-scale networks, in the sense that the key-update overhead on the side of the KGC increased logarithmically in the number of users.

With confidentiality and non-repudiation features, the concept of signcryption originated by Zheng [102] in 1997 has found wide applications where both confidentiality and authentication are required. Compared with the traditional signature-then-encryption approach, signcryption enjoys a lower computational cost and communication overhead. As an extension of signcryption in the CL-PKC setting, Barbosa and Farshim [103] initialized the notion of certificateless signcryption (CL-SC) to gain the merits of CL-PKC and signcryption simultaneously. After that, several CL-SC schemes have also been proposed [104,105]. To remove the random oracles in the security proof of CL-SC, Liu et al. [106] proposed the first efficient and provably secure CL-SC scheme in the standard model by integrating the idea of certificateless signature [60,107] and certificateless encryption [18,69]. However, Liu et al.'s scheme has been shown to be insecure against the outsider attack [108] and the malicious-but-passive KGC attack [109], respectively. After that, Jin et al. [110] proposed an improvement to remedy the weakness in [60]. Unfortunately, Xiong [111] showed that Jin et al.'s CL-SC scheme still does not offer neither semantical security against CCA nor existential unforgeability against chosen message attacks once the malicious-but-passive KGC is considered. To remedy the security flaws in [110], Xiong showed a further improved CL-SC scheme secure in the standard model.

3.5 CONCRETE CONSTRUCTION

In this section, three representative CLE schemes, including two concrete constructions [54,69] and one general construction [58], are introduced.

3.5.1 Dent–Libert–Paterson CL-PKE

By applying the techniques from [80] to the two-level hierarchical extension of Waters' IBE scheme [79], Dent et al. [54] proposed the first concrete CLE scheme secure in the standard model. The authors claimed that this scheme doesn't intend to be secure against adversaries that maliciously generate system-wide parameters.

Setup: Let $\hat{e} : \mathbb{G}_1 \times \mathbb{G}_1 \rightarrow \mathbb{G}_2$ be the bilinear pairing, and $\mathbb{G}_1$ be a cyclic group with order p, and let g be a generator for the group $\mathbb{G}_1$. Compute $g_1 = g^\gamma$ for a random $\gamma \in \mathbb{Z}_p^*$, and pick a group element $g_2 \in \mathbb{G}$ randomly and vectors $(u', u_1, \ldots, u_n), (v', v_1, \ldots, v_n) \in \mathbb{G}^{n+1}$. We note that the following hash functions can be defined with these vectors:

$$F_u(\mathsf{ID}) = u' \prod_{i=1}^{n} u_j^{i_j} \qquad \text{and} \qquad F_v(w) = v' \prod_{i=1}^{n} v_j^{w_j}$$

where $\mathsf{ID} = i_1 i_2 \ldots i_n$ and $w = w_1 w_2 \ldots w_n$. We also select a collision-resistant (CR) hash function $H : \{0,1\}^* \to \{0,1\}^n$. The public parameters are

$$\mathsf{params} = (g, g_1, g_2, u', u_1, \ldots, u_n, v', v_1, \ldots, v_n)$$

and the master secret is $\mathsf{master\text{-}secret} = g_2^\gamma$.

Extract-Partial-Private-Key: Pick $r \in Z_p^*$ at random and return $\mathsf{psk}_{\mathsf{ID}} = (\mathsf{psk}_1, \mathsf{psk}_2) = (g^\gamma \cdot F_u(\mathsf{ID})^r, g^r)$.

Set-Secret-Value: Return a randomly chosen secret value $x_{\mathsf{ID}} \in \mathbb{Z}_p^*$.

Set-Public-Key: Return $\mathsf{upk}_{\mathsf{ID}} = (X, Y) = (g^{x_{\mathsf{ID}}}, g_1^{x_{\mathsf{ID}}})$.

Set-Private-Key: Parse $\mathsf{psk}_{\mathsf{ID}}$ into $(\mathsf{psk}_1, \mathsf{psk}_2)$, choose $r' \in \mathbb{Z}_p^*$, and set the private key to

$$\mathsf{sk}_{\mathsf{ID}} \leftarrow (s_1, s_2) = (\mathsf{psk}_1^{x_{\mathsf{ID}}} \cdot F_u(\mathsf{ID})^{r'}, \mathsf{psk}_2^{x_{\mathsf{ID}}} \cdot g^{r'}) = (g_2^{\gamma x_{\mathsf{ID}}} \cdot F_u(\mathsf{ID})^t, g^t)$$

with $t = r x_{\mathsf{ID}} + r'$.

Encrypt: To encrypt $m \in \mathbb{G}_T$, parse $\mathsf{upk}_{\mathsf{ID}}$ as (X, Y), then check that it has the right shape (i.e., $\hat{e}(X, g_1)/\hat{e}(g, Y) = 1_{\mathbb{G}_T}$). If so, choose $s \in \mathbb{Z}_p^*$ and compute

$$C = (C_0, C_1, C_2, C_3) \leftarrow (m \cdot e(Y, g_2)^s, g^s, F_u(\mathsf{ID})^s, F_v(w)^s)$$

where $w = H(C_0, C_1, C_2, \mathsf{ID}, \mathsf{upk}_{\mathsf{ID}})$.

Decrypt: Parse C as (C_0, C_1, C_2, C_3) and the private key $\mathsf{sk}_{\mathsf{ID}}$ as (s_1, s_2). Check that

$$\hat{e}(C_1, F_u(\mathsf{ID}) \cdot F_v(w)) = \hat{e}(g, C_2 \cdot C_3)$$

where $w = H(C_0, C_1, C_2, \mathsf{ID}, \mathsf{upk}_{\mathsf{ID}})$, and reject C if those conditions do not hold. Otherwise, return

$$m \leftarrow C_0 \cdot \frac{\hat{e}(C_2, s_2)}{\hat{e}(C_1, s_1)}$$

To check the completeness, we note that private keys (s_1, s_2) satisfy

$$\hat{e}(g, s_1) = \hat{e}(Y, g_2) \cdot \hat{e}(F_u(\mathsf{ID}), s_2) \text{ and so } \hat{e}(C_1, s_1) = \hat{e}(Y, g_2)^s \cdot \hat{e}(C_2, s_2)$$

3.5.2 Hwang–Liu–Chow CL-PKE

Similar to [54], Hwang et al. [69] proposed a concrete CLE scheme by applying the techniques of [80] to the two-level hierarchical extension of Waters' IBE [79] to achieve CCA security. Furthermore, a different **User-Key-Gen** algorithm is devised to resist the malicious KGC attack. It consists of the following algorithms:

Setup: Select a pairing $\hat{e} : \mathbb{G}_1 \times \mathbb{G}_1 \to \mathbb{G}_2$ where the order of $\mathbb{G}_1$ is p. Let g be a generator of $\mathbb{G}_1$. Randomly select $\alpha, \beta, \mu', \mu_1, \ldots, \mu_{n_u}, \nu', \nu_1, \ldots, \nu_{n_m}$ from $\mathbb{Z}_p^*$, and then compute $g_1 = g^{\alpha}$, $h = \hat{e}(g^{\alpha}, g^{\beta})$, $u' = g^{\mu'}$, $m' = g^{\nu'}$, $u_i = g^{\mu_i}$ for $i = 1, \ldots, n_u$, $m_i = g^{\nu_i}$ for $i = 1, \ldots, n_m$. Let $\mathbf{U} = (u_i)$, $\mathbf{M} = (m_i)$. Let $H : \{0,1\}^* \to \{0,1\}^n$ be a CR cryptographic hash function. The public parameters are $\mathsf{params} = \{\mathbb{G}_1, \mathbb{G}_2, \hat{e}, g, g_1, h, u', \mathbf{U}, m', \mathbf{M}, H\}$ and the master secret is $(\alpha, \beta, \mu', \mu_1, \ldots, \mu_{n_u}, \nu', \nu_1, \ldots, \nu_{n_m})$.

Extract-Partial-Private-Key: Let ID be a bit string of length n_u representing an identity and let $\mathsf{ID}[i]$ be the i-th bit of ID. Define $\mathcal{U} \subset \{1, \ldots, n_u\}$ to be the set of indices i such that $\mathsf{ID}[i] = 1$. To construct the partial secret key of identity ID, the KGC randomly picks $r_{\mathsf{ID}} \leftarrow_R \mathbb{Z}_p^*$ and computes:

$$\left(g_2^{\beta} \left(u' \prod_{i \in \mathcal{U}} u_i \right)^{r_{\mathsf{ID}}}, g^{r_{\mathsf{ID}}} \right) = (\mathsf{psk}_{\mathsf{ID},1}, \mathsf{psk}_{\mathsf{ID},2})$$

Set-User-Keys: An entity selects a secret value $x_{\mathsf{ID}} \leftarrow_R \mathbb{Z}_p^*$ and computes the user public key as $\mathsf{upk}_{\mathsf{ID}} = (X_{\mathsf{ID}}, \sigma_{\mathsf{ID}}) = (h^{x_{\mathsf{ID}}}, \sigma_{\mathsf{ID}})$, where σ_{ID} is the Schnorr OTS using x_{ID} as the signing key and $(h, X_{\mathsf{ID}} = h^{x_{\mathsf{ID}}})$ as the verification key. According to [69], the OTS can be generated by applying the technique of the Fiat–Shamir transform without random oracles as described in [112]. Then it randomly selects $r'_{\mathsf{ID}} \leftarrow_R \mathbb{Z}_p^*$ and computes its private key $\mathsf{usk}_{\mathsf{ID}}$ as

$$(\mathsf{usk}_{\mathsf{ID},1}, \mathsf{usk}_{\mathsf{ID},2}) = \left(\mathsf{psk}_{\mathsf{ID},1}^{x_{\mathsf{ID}}} \cdot \left(u' \prod_{i \in \mathcal{U}} u_i \right)^{r'_{\mathsf{ID}}}, \mathsf{psk}_{\mathsf{ID},2}^{x_{\mathsf{ID}}} \cdot g^{r'_{\mathsf{ID}}} \right)$$

$$= \left(g_1^{\beta x_{\mathsf{ID}}} \cdot \left(u' \prod_{i \in \mathcal{U}} u_i \right)^{r_{\mathsf{ID}} x_{\mathsf{ID}} + r'_{\mathsf{ID}}}, g^{r_{\mathsf{ID}} x_{\mathsf{ID}} + r'_{\mathsf{ID}}} \right)$$

Encrypt: To encrypt $m \in \mathbb{G}_T$, first check whether the public key X_{ID} is correctly formed, by checking whether σ_{ID} is a valid signature, using (h, X_{ID}) as the verification key. If not, output $\perp$ and abort the algorithm. Otherwise, select a value $s \leftarrow_R \mathbb{Z}_p^*$ and compute: (Let w be a n-bit string and w_i the i-th bit of w.)

$$C = (C_0, C_1, C_2, C_3) = \left(m \cdot (X_{\mathsf{ID}})^s, g^s, \left(u' \prod_{i \in \mathcal{U}} u_i \right)^s, \left(v' \prod_{j=1}^n v_j^{w_j} \right)^s \right)$$

where $w = H(C_0, C_1, C_2, \mathsf{ID}, \mathsf{upk}_{\mathsf{ID}}) \in \{0,1\}^n$.

Decrypt: Given a ciphertext $C = (C_0, C_1, C_2, C_3)$, check that

$$e\left(C_1, \left(u' \prod_{i \in \mathcal{U}} u_i \right) \cdot \left(v' \prod_{j=1}^n v_j^{w_j} \right) \right) = e(g, C_2 C_3)$$

where $w = H(C_0, C_1, C_2, \mathsf{ID}, \mathsf{upk}_{\mathsf{ID}}) \in \{0,1\}^n$. If not, output $\perp$. Otherwise, compute

$$m = C_0 \cdot e(C_2, \mathsf{usk}_{\mathsf{ID},2}) / e(C_1, \mathsf{usk}_{\mathsf{ID},1})$$

3.5.2.1 Security Analysis

In this part, the concrete construction described is proved to be secure against a malicious KGC under the following decisional bilinear Diffie–Hellman (DBDH) assumption, CR assumption, and OTS assumption in the standard model.

Definition 3.7 *Given two groups $\mathbb{G}_1$ and $\mathbb{G}_2$ of the same prime order p, a bilinear map $\hat{e} : \mathbb{G}_1 \times \mathbb{G}_1 \to \mathbb{G}_2$ and a generator g of $\mathbb{G}_1$, the DBDH problem in $(\mathbb{G}_1, \mathbb{G}_2, \hat{e})$ is to decide whether $Z = \hat{e}(g,g)^{abc}$ given (g, g^a, g^b, g^c) and an element $Z \in \mathbb{G}_2$. We define the advantage of a distinguisher against the BDDH problem like this:*

$$\begin{aligned} Adv(\mathcal{A}) \quad = \quad & |P_{a,b,c,\in_R \mathbb{Z}_p, Z \in_R \mathbb{G}_2}[1 \leftarrow \mathcal{A}(g^a, g^b, g^c, Z)] \\ & - P_{a,b,c,\in_R \mathbb{Z}_p}[1 \leftarrow \mathcal{A}(g^a, g^b, g^c, \hat{e}(g,g)^{abc})]| \end{aligned}$$

The advantage $\mathrm{Adv}(\mathcal{A})$ is assumed to be negligible.

Definition 3.8 *CR assumption: A hash function $H \leftarrow \mathcal{H}(k)$ is collision resistant if for all PPT algorithms $\mathcal{A}$ the advantage*

$$Adv_{\mathcal{A}}^{CR}(k) = \Pr[H(x) = H(y) \wedge x \neq y | (x,y) \leftarrow \mathcal{A}(1^k, H) \wedge H \leftarrow \mathcal{H}(k)]$$

is negligible as a function of the security parameter.

Definition 3.9 *OTS: A OTS scheme is existential unforgeable against a chosen-message attack if for all PPT algorithms $\mathcal{A}$ the advantage $\mathrm{Adv}A_{\mathcal{A}}^{OT}(k)$, which is*

$$\Pr[\mathsf{VF}(pk, m, \sigma) = 1 | (pk, sk) \leftarrow \mathsf{KG}(k) \wedge (m, \sigma) \leftarrow \mathcal{A}^{SGN(sk, m_q)}(pk)]$$

is negligible as a function of the security parameter, and if $m \neq m_q$, where KG, SGN, and VF are the key generation, signing, and verification algorithm of the OTS scheme, respectively. Note that the adversary can make at most one query to the signing oracle.

Theorem 3.1 *Let $\mathcal{A}_2$ be a type II adversary that makes at most q_d decryption queries, and q_{pk} public-key queries. Then we have*

$$Adv_{\mathcal{A}_2}^{CL} \leq 4q_{pk}q_d(n+1) \cdot Adv_{\mathcal{A}'}^{DBDH}(k) + q_{pk} \cdot Adv_{\mathcal{A}''}^{CR}(k)$$

where $\mathcal{A}'$ and $\mathcal{A}''$ are algorithms that run in approximately the same time as $\mathcal{A}_2$.

Proof 3.1 *The intuition behind Theorem 3.1 can be found in Figure 3.6. A sequence of modified attack games is defined in the proof. Each of the games operates on the same underlying probability space. The attacker attempts to distinguish a hidden bit b and eventually outputs a guess b', where the hidden bit b takes on identical values across all games, while some of the rules that define how a simulator responds to oracle queries may differ from game to game.*

We let S_i be the event that $b = b'$ in the game i and Adv_i denote the adversary's advantage in the game i. Then, $Adv_i = |\Pr[S_i] - 1/2|$. We start from game 1 and show from the definition of game i for $i > 1$ that $|\Pr[S_i] - 1/2|$ is negligible if and only if $|\Pr[S_{i-1}] - 1/2|$ is negligible. Let E be an event that can occur during the execution of the adversary and that is independent of S_i (i.e., $\Pr[S_i|E] = \Pr[S_i]$). Let game $i + 1$ be the attack environment that is identical to game i unless E occurs. If E does not occur, the adversary will choose the same bit that it

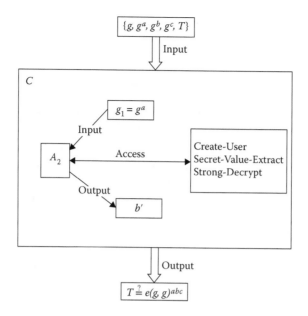

Figure 3.6   Intuition for Theorem 3.1.

did in game i (i.e., $\Pr[S_{i+1}|\neg E] = \Pr[S_i|\neg E] = \Pr[S_i]$). Otherwise, it outputs a random bit b' (i.e., $\Pr[S_{i+1}|E] - 1/2$). Then we have

$$
\begin{aligned}
\left|\Pr[S_{i+1}] - 1/2\right| &= \left|\Pr[S_{i+1}|E]\Pr[E] + \Pr[S_{i+1}|\neg E]\Pr[\neg E] - 1/2\right| \\
&= \left|\Pr[E]/2 + \Pr[S_i|\neg E]\Pr[\neg E] - 1/2\right| \\
&= \left|(1 - \Pr[\neg E])/2 + \Pr[S_i]\Pr[\neg E] - 1/2\right| \\
&= \Pr[\neg E]\left|\left|\Pr[S_i] - 1/2\right|\right.
\end{aligned}
$$

Therefore, $Adv_{i+1} = \Pr[\neg E] \cdot Adv_i$.

Game 1. This game is identical to the original attack environment. A type II adversary $\mathcal{A}_2$ first outputs (mpk, msk) to the simulator $\mathcal{B}$ and interacts with $\mathcal{B}$. It issues up to q_{pk}, q_{sk}, and q_d queries to **Create-User, Secret-Value-Extract**, and **Strong-Decrypt**, respectively. We define the following sets:

1. $\mathsf{pk_L} = \{\mathsf{ID}_1, \ldots, \mathsf{ID}_{q_{pk}}\}$: the set of identities queried for the **Create-User** oracle.

2. $\mathsf{sk_L} = \{\mathsf{ID}'_1, \ldots, \mathsf{ID}'_{q_{sk}}\}$: the set of identities queried for the **Secret-Value-Extract** oracle.

3. $\mathsf{D_w} = \{w_1, \ldots, w_{q_d}\}$: the set of strings $w_j = H(C_0, C_1, C_2, \mathsf{ID}_j, pk_j)$ involved in **Strong-Decrypt** queries.

$\mathcal{A}_2$ selects a target identity/public-key pair $(\mathsf{ID}^*, pk_{\mathsf{ID}^*})$ with two equal length messages m_0, m_1, where $\mathsf{ID}^* \notin \mathsf{sk_L}$, and sends them to $\mathcal{C}$. It is given $C^* = (C_0^*, C_1^*, C_2^*, C_3^*)$ as the challenge ciphertext. At this time, we denote $w^* = H(C_0^*, C_1^*, C_2^*, \mathsf{ID}^*, pk_{\mathsf{ID}^*})$ and $w^* \notin \mathsf{D_w}$.

Game 2. In this game, $\mathcal{C}$ first selects an identity ID_i in pk_L at random. Let g^a, g^b be random elements such that a, b are unknown to $\mathcal{C}$. Then, it sets X_{ID_i} by $e(g^a, g^b)^{\alpha\beta}$. At this time, x_{ID_i} is regarded as ab because $h = e(g^\alpha, g^\beta)$. π_{ID_i} can be simulated in the same way as in the signing oracle of the OTS. It also picks $\kappa \in \{0, \ldots, n\}$ and lets τ be an integer such that $\tau(n+1) < p$. In addition, it randomly selects vectors $(x', x_1, \ldots, x_n)$ in $\mathbb{Z}_\tau$ and $(y', y_1, \ldots, y_n)$ in $\mathbb{Z}_p$ and sets

$$v' = (g^a)^{x' - \kappa\tau} g^{y'}, \qquad v_j = (g^a)^{x_j} g^{y_j} \quad \text{for} \quad 1 \leq j \leq n$$

If $\mathcal{A}_2$ does not select ID_i as a target identity (namely, $\mathsf{ID}_i \neq \mathsf{ID}^*$), then $\mathcal{C}$ aborts. Therefore, $Adv_2 = \frac{1}{q_{pk}} Adv_1$.

Game 3. This game is identical to game 2 except that $\mathcal{C}$ halts if the attacker submits a decryption query $(C, \mathsf{ID}, pk_{\mathsf{ID}})$ for a well-formed ciphertext $C = (C_0, C_1, C_2, C_3)$, where w is either equal to the same value as a previously submitted ciphertext or w is equal to w^* in the post-challenge phase. For such a legal decryption query, we have $C \neq C^*$ or $(\mathsf{ID}, pk_{\mathsf{ID}}) \neq (\mathsf{ID}^*, pk_{\mathsf{ID}^*})$. In either case, this implies a collision for H. Hence, we can construct an algorithm $\mathcal{A}''$ such that $|\Pr[S_2] - \Pr[S_3]| \leq Adv_{\mathcal{A}''}^{CR}(k)$.

Game 4. We define the following functions from the values of game 2:

$$J(w) = x' + \sum_{j=1}^n w_j x_j - \kappa\tau, \qquad K(w) = y' + \sum_{j=1}^n w_j y_j$$

taking as input an n-bit string $w = w_1 \ldots w_n$. Then $F_v(w) = v' \prod_{j=1}^n v_j^{w_j} = (g^a)^{J(w)} \cdot g^{K(w)}$.

Game 4 is the same as game 3 except that, after $\mathcal{A}_2$ outputs her guess b' for b, $\mathcal{C}$ checks whether $J(w^*) = 0 \bmod p$. If $J(w^*) \neq 0 \bmod p$, then $\mathcal{C}$ aborts and outputs a random bit b'. The event that $J(w^*) = 0 \bmod p$ happens by chance because $\mathcal{A}_2$ does not know information on all values $(x', x_1, \ldots, x_n, \kappa, \tau)$ to compute $J(w)$ at all. Actually, $\Pr[J(w^*) = 0 \bmod p] = \Pr[\kappa\tau = (x' + \sum_{j=1}^n w_j x_j)]$ since $(x' + \sum_{j=1}^n w_j x_j) < \tau(n+1)$, $\kappa\tau < \tau(n+1)$ and $\tau(n+1) < p$. Therefore,

$$\Pr[J(w^*) = 0 \bmod p] = \frac{1}{\tau(n+1)}$$

and $Adv_4 = \frac{1}{\tau(n+1)} Adv_3$.

Game 5. We modify the way the challenge ciphertext is constructed. $\mathcal{C}$ introduces a new variable $c \leftarrow \mathbb{Z}_p^*$ and $C_1^* = g^c$. It flips a coin b, and computes $C_0^* = m_b \cdot X_{\mathsf{ID}^*}^c$, $C_2^* = C_1^{*U_{\mathsf{ID}^*}} = (g^c)^{U_{\mathsf{ID}^*}}$, and $C_3^* = C_1^{*K(w^*)} = (g^c)^{K(w^*)}$, where $w^* = H(C_0^*, C_1^*, C_2^*, \mathsf{ID}^*, pk_{\mathsf{ID}^*})$ and $U_{\mathsf{ID}^*} = \sum_{i \in \mathcal{U}} \mu_j$. Clearly, $Adv_5 = Adv_4$.

Game 6. We change game 5 so that, after $\mathcal{A}_2$ outputs his or her guess b', $\mathcal{C}$ aborts and replaces $\mathcal{A}_2$'s output by a random bit b' if $J(w_\ell) = 0 \bmod \tau$ for some $w_\ell \in D_w$, where $\ell \in \{1, \ldots, q_d\}$. Since $\Pr[J(w) = 0 \bmod \tau] = 1/\tau$, $Adv_6 = (1 - \frac{1}{\tau})^{q_d} \cdot Adv_5 \geq (1 - \frac{q_d}{\tau}) \cdot Adv_5$ as $\Pr[J(w) = 0 \bmod \tau] = 1/\tau$. If we set $\tau = 2q_d$, then $Adv_6 \geq \frac{1}{2} Adv_5$.

Game 7. We effectively change the treatment of $\mathcal{A}_2$'s queries. For all **Create-User**, **Secret-Value-Extract**, and **Strong-Decrypt** queries not involving ID^*, $\mathcal{C}$ can respond to queries by running the algorithms Extract-Partial-Private-Key(mpk, msk, ID), Set-User-Keys(mpk, psk_{ID}), and Decrypt$(mpk, sk_{\mathsf{ID}}, C)$. In addition, it responds to all decryption queries involving ID^* as follows. When it receives decryption queries for a valid ciphertext (C_0, C_1, C_2, C_3) for ID^*, $\mathcal{C}$ aborts and outputs a random bit b' as in game 6 if $J(w) = 0 \bmod \tau$, Otherwise, $\mathcal{C}$ can extract m by computing

$$\omega \leftarrow H(C_0, C_1, C_2, \mathsf{ID}^*, pk_{\mathsf{ID}^*})$$
$$(g^a)^s \leftarrow (C_3/C_1^{K(\omega)})^{1/J(\omega)}$$
$$m \leftarrow C_0/e(g^{as}, g^b)^{\alpha\beta} = C_0/e(g^\alpha, g^\beta)^{abs} = C_0/X_{\mathsf{ID}^*}^s$$

Note that we can compute $(C_3/C_1^{K(\omega)})^{1/J(\omega)}$, since $J(\omega) \neq 0 \bmod p$ if $J(\omega) \neq 0 \bmod \tau$. We observe that $\mathcal{C}$ correctly answers $\mathcal{A}_2$'s queries as in game 6. This implies $Adv_7 = Adv_6$.

Game 8. We again alter the generation of the challenge ciphertext. For a variable c introduced in game 5, let $C_1^* = g^c$ and $Z = e(g^a, g^b)^c$. $\mathcal{C}$ retrieves values α, β, flips a coin b, and computes $C_0^* = m_b \cdot Z^{\alpha\beta}$, $C_2^* = (g^c)^{U_{ID^*}}$, and $C_3^* = (g^c)^{K(w^*)}$, where $w^* = H(C_0^*, C_1^*, C_2^*, \mathsf{ID}^*, pk_{\mathsf{ID}^*})$. We have $Adv_8 = Adv_7$.

Game 9. We again alter the challenge phase. This time, $\mathcal{C}$ "forgets" the value c and simply retains C_1^*. The challenge ciphertext is constructed as in game 8 but using a randomly chosen $Z \in \mathbb{G}_T$ this time. The whole simulation only depends on the values g^a, g^b, g^c and the simulator does not use a, b, c at all. Therefore, $|\Pr[S_8] - \Pr[S_9]| \leq Adv_{\mathcal{A}'}^{\text{DBDH}}(k)$ and $\Pr[S_9] = 1/2$:

$$Adv_6 = Adv_7 = Adv_8 \leq Adv_{\mathcal{A}'}^{\text{DBDH}}(k),$$
$$Adv_4 = Adv_5 \leq 2 \cdot Adv_6$$

Since $Adv_4 = Adv_3/(\tau(n+1))$ and $\tau = 2q_d$, we get

$$Adv_3 \leq 4q_d(n+1) \cdot Adv_{\mathcal{A}'}^{\text{DBDH}}(k),$$
$$Adv_2 \leq Adv_{\mathcal{A}''}^{\text{CR}}(k) + Adv_3 \leq 4q_d(n+1) \cdot Adv_{\mathcal{A}'}^{\text{DBDH}}(k) + Adv_{\mathcal{A}''}^{\text{CR}}(k)$$

In consequence, since $Adv_2 = 1/q_{pk} \cdot Adv_1$, we obtain

$$Adv_1 \leq 4q_{pk}q_d(n+1) \cdot Adv_{\mathcal{A}'}^{\text{DBDH}}(k) + q_{pk} \cdot Adv_{\mathcal{A}''}^{\text{CR}}(k)$$

Now we provide the security proof of our scheme against type I adversaries.

Theorem 3.2 *Let $\mathcal{A}_1$ be a type I adversary that makes at most q_d decryption queries. Then we have*

$$Adv_{\mathcal{A}_1}^{\text{CL}} \leq 4q_{pk}q_d(n+1) \cdot Adv_{\mathcal{A}'}^{\text{DBDH}}(k) + Adv_{\mathcal{A}''}^{\text{CR}}(k) + Adv_{\mathcal{A}_s}^{\text{OT}}(k)$$

where $\mathcal{A}'$, $\mathcal{A}''$, and $\mathcal{A}_s$ are algorithms that run in approximately the same time as $\mathcal{A}_1$.

Proof 3.2 *The intuition behind Theorem 3.1 can be found in Figure 3.7. The proof is done in a way similar to that of Theorem 3.1.*

Game 1. This game is identical to the original attack environment. $\mathcal{C}$ runs $\mathsf{Setup}(1^k)$ and outputs (mpk, msk). A type I adversary $\mathcal{A}_1$ is given mpk. Then it issues up to $q_{psk}, q_{pk}, q_{rpk}, q_{sk}$, and q_d queries to **Partial-Private-Key-Extract**, **Create-User**, **Public-Key-Replace**, **Secret-Value-Extract**, and **Normal-Decrypt**, respectively. We define the following sets:

1. $\mathsf{pk_L} = \{\mathsf{ID}_1, \dots, \mathsf{ID}_{q_{pk}}\}$: the set of identities queried for the **Create-User** oracle.

2. $\mathsf{rpk_L} = \{\mathsf{ID}_1, \dots, \mathsf{ID}_{q_{rpk}}\}$: the set of identities queried for the **Public-Key-Replace** oracle.

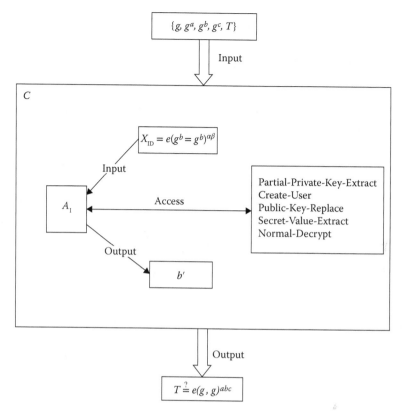

Figure 3.7 Intuition for Theorem 3.2.

3. $\mathsf{psk_L} = \{\mathsf{ID}_1', \ldots, \mathsf{ID}_{q_{psk}}'\}$: the set of identities queried for the **Partial-Private-Key-Extract** oracle.

4. $\mathsf{D_w} = \{\omega_1, \ldots, \omega_{q_d}\}$: the set of strings $\omega_j = H(C_0, C_1, C_2, \mathsf{ID}_j, pk_j)$ involved in **Normal-Decrypt** queries.

$\mathcal{A}_1$ selects a target identity/public-key pair $(\mathsf{ID}^*, pk_{\mathsf{ID}^*})$ with two equal length messages m_0, m_1, where $ID^* \in \mathsf{psk_L}$ or $ID^* \in \mathsf{rpk_L}$, and sends them to $\mathcal{C}$. It is given $C^* = (C_0^*, C_1^*, C_2^*, C_3^*)$ as the challenge ciphertext. At this time, we denote $\omega^* = H(C_0^*, C_1^*, C_2^*, \mathsf{ID}^*, pk_{\mathsf{ID}^*})$ and $\omega^* \in \mathsf{D_w}$.

Game 2. This game is identical to game 1, except some values of the mpk in the system parameters are replaced with following. Let g^a be a random element in $\mathbb{G}$ such that a is unknown to $\mathcal{C}$. It randomly selects $\beta \in \mathbb{Z}_p^*$, and sets $g_1 = g^a$, $h = (g^\alpha, g^\beta)$. In addition, it also picks

$\|_v \in \{0, \dots, n\}$ and lets τ_v be an integer such that $\tau_v(n+1) < p$. It randomly selects vectors $(x_v', x_{v,1}, \dots, x_{v,n})$ in $\mathbb{Z}_{\tau_v}$ and $(y_v', y_{v,1}, \dots, y_{v,n})$ in $\mathbb{Z}_p$ and sets:

$$v' = (g^a)^{x_v' - \|_v \tau_v} g^{y_v'}, \qquad v_j = (g^a)^{x_{v,j}} g^{y_{v,j}} \quad \text{for} \quad 1 \leq j \leq n$$

The replaced public key has the same distribution as the public key generated in the previous game. It should also contain a valid one-time signature π. Hence, we can construct an algorithm $\mathcal{A}_s$ such that $|\Pr[S_1] - \Pr[S_2]| \leq Adv_{\mathcal{A}_s}^{\text{OT}}(k)$. Note that $(\nu_1, \dots, \nu_n)$ and α of msk (which is regarded as a) are unknown to $\mathcal{C}$. However, it securely keeps other values $(\beta, \mu', \mu_1, \dots, \mu_n, \nu')$ of msk.

Game 3. In this game, $\mathcal{C}$ first selects an identity ID_i in $\mathsf{pk_L}$ at random. Let g^b be a random element in $\mathbb{G}$ such that b is unknown to $\mathcal{C}$. Then it sets X_{ID_i} by $e(g^a, g^{b\beta})$. At this time, x_{ID_i} is regarded as b because $h = e(g^a, g^\beta)$. We can see that $Adv_3 = Adv_2$.

Game 4. This game is identical to game 3 except that $\mathcal{C}$ halts if the attacker submits a decryption query $(C, \mathsf{ID}, pk_{\mathsf{ID}})$ for a well-formed ciphertext $C = (C_0, C_1, C_2, C_3)$, where w is either equal to the same value as a previously submitted ciphertext or w is equal to w^* in the post-challenge phase. For such a legal decryption query, we have $C \neq C^*$ or $(\mathsf{ID}, pk_{\mathsf{ID}}) \neq (\mathsf{ID}^*, pk_{\mathsf{ID}^*})$. In either case, this implies a collision for H. Hence, we can construct an algorithm $\mathcal{A}''$ such $|\Pr[S_3] - \Pr[S_4]| \leq Adv_{\mathcal{A}''}^{\text{CR}}(k)$.

Game 5. We define the following functions from the values of game 3:

$$J(w) = x' + \Sigma_{i=1}^n w_j x_j - \kappa\tau, \quad K(w) = y' + \Sigma_{j=1}^n w_j y_j$$

taking as input an n-bit string $w = w_1 \dots w_n$. Then $F_v(w) = v' \Pi_{j=1}^n v_j^{w_j} = (g^a)^{J(w)} \cdot g^{K(w)}$.

Game 5 is the same as game 4 except that, after $\mathcal{A}_1$ outputs her guess b' for b, $\mathcal{C}$ checks whether $J(w^*) = 0 \mod p$. If $J(w^*) \neq 0 \mod p$, then $\mathcal{C}$ aborts and outputs a random bit b'. The event that $J(w^*) \neq 0 \mod p$ happens by chance because $\mathcal{A}_1$ does not know information on all values $(x', x_1, \dots, x_n, \kappa, \tau)$ to compute $J(w)$ at all. Actually, $\Pr[J(w^*) = 0 \mod p] = \Pr[\kappa\tau = (x' + \Sigma_{j=1}^n w_j x_j)]$ since $(x' + \Sigma_{j=1}^n w_j x_j) < \tau(n+1)$, $\kappa\tau < \tau(n+1)$ and $\tau(n+1) < p$. Therefore,

$$\Pr[J(w^*) = 0 \mod p] = \frac{1}{\tau(n+1)}$$

and $Adv_5 = 1/\tau(n+1)Adv_4$.

Game 6. We modify the way the challenge ciphertext is constructed. $\mathcal{C}$ introduces a new variable $c \leftarrow \mathbb{Z}_p^*$ and $C_1^* = g^c$. It flips a coin b, and computes $C_0^* = m_b \cdot X_{\mathsf{ID}^*}^c$, $C_2^* = C_1^{*U_{\mathsf{ID}^*}} = (g^c)^{U_{\mathsf{ID}^*}}$, and $C_3^* = C_1^{*K(w^*)} = (g^c)^{K(w^*)}$, where $w^* = H(C_0^*, C_1^*, C_2^*, \mathsf{ID}^*, pk_{\mathsf{ID}^*})$ and $U_{\mathsf{ID}^*} = \sum_{i \in \mathcal{U}} \mu_j$. Clearly, $Adv_6 = Adv_5$.

Game 7. We change game 6 so that, after $\mathcal{A}_1$ outputs her guess b', $\mathcal{C}$ aborts and replaces $\mathcal{A}_1$'s output by a random bit b' if $J(w_\ell) = 0$ mod τ for some $w_\ell \in D_w$, where $\ell \in \{1, \dots, q_d\}$. Since $\Pr[J(w) = 0 \mod \tau] = 1/\tau$, $Adv_6 = (1 - \frac{1}{\tau})^{q_d} \cdot Adv_5 \geq (1 - \frac{q_d}{\tau}) \cdot Adv_5$ as $\Pr[J(w) = 0 \mod \tau] = 1/\tau$. If we set $\tau = 2q_d$, then $Adv_7 \geq \frac{1}{2} Adv_6$.

Game 8. We effectively change the treatment of $\mathcal{A}_1$'s queries. For all **Create-User, Secret-Value-Extract**, and **Normal-Decrypt** queries not involving ID^*, $\mathcal{C}$ can respond to queries by running the algorithms Extract-Partial-Private-Key$(mpk, \beta, \mathsf{ID})$ (only β in msk, instead of msk, is required to generate psk_{ID} for a queried ID), Set-User-Keys(mpk, psk_{ID}), and Decrypt$(mpk, sk_{\mathsf{ID}}, C)$. When it receives a public key replace query, it replaces a previously generated public key pk_{ID} for ID with a new one pk'_{ID}. If the decryption query involves an identity ID with a replaced public key, the corresponding private key x_{ID} is required to be supplied. Otherwise it aborts. In addition, it responds to all decryption queries involving ID^* as follows. When it receives decryption queries for a valid ciphertext (C_0, C_1, C_2, C_3) for ID^*, $\mathcal{C}$ aborts and outputs a random bit b' as in game 6 if $J(w) = 0 \mod \tau$, Otherwise, $\mathcal{C}$ can extract m by computing

$$w \leftarrow H(C_0, C_1, C_2, \mathsf{ID}^*, pk_{\mathsf{ID}^*}),$$
$$(g^a)^s \leftarrow (C_3/C_1^{K(w)})^{1/J(w)},$$
$$m \leftarrow C_0/e(g^{as}, B)^\beta = C_0/e(g^a, B^\beta)^s = C_0/X_{\mathsf{ID}^*}^s$$

where $B = g^b$ if $\mathsf{ID}^* \notin /\mathsf{rpk}_\mathsf{L}$ or $B = g^{x_{\mathsf{ID}^*}}$ otherwise, since x_{ID^*} should be given to the decryption oracle if $\mathsf{ID}^* \in \mathsf{rpk}_\mathsf{L}$. Note that we can compute $(C_3/C_1^{K(w)})^{1/J(w)}$, since $J(w) \neq 0 \mod p$ if $J(w) \neq 0 \mod \tau$. We observe that $\mathcal{C}$ correctly answers $\mathcal{A}_1$'s queries as in game 6. This implies $Adv_8 = Adv_7$.

Game 9. We again alter the generation of the challenge ciphertext. For a variable c introduced in game 5, let $C_1^* = g^c$ and $Z = e(g^a, g^b)^c$. $\mathcal{C}$ retrieves values α, β, flips a coin b, and computes $C_0^* = m_b \cdot Z^\beta$,

$C_2^* = (g^c)^{U_{ID^*}}$, and $C_3^* = (g^c)^{K(w^*)}$, where $w^* = H(C_0^*, C_1^*, C_2^*, \mathsf{ID}^*,$ $pk_{\mathsf{ID}^*})$. We have $Adv_9 = Adv_8$.

Game 10. We again alter the challenge phase. This time, $\mathcal{C}$ "forgets" the value c and simply retains C_1^*. The challenge ciphertext is constructed as in game 9 but using a randomly chosen $Z \in \mathbb{G}_T$ this time. The whole simulation only depends on the values g_a, g_b, g_c and the simulator does not use a, b, c at all. Therefore, $|\Pr[S_9] - \Pr[S_{10}]| \leq Adv_{\mathcal{A}'}^{\mathsf{DBDH}}(k)$ and $\Pr[S_{10}] = 1/2$.

$$Adv_7 = Adv_8 = Adv_9 \leq Adv_{\mathcal{A}'}^{\mathsf{DBDH}}(k)$$

$$Adv_5 = Adv_6 \leq 2 \cdot Adv_7$$

Since $Adv_5 = Adv_4/(\tau(n+1))$ and $\tau = 2q_d$, we get

$$Adv_4 \leq 4q_d(n+1) \cdot Adv_{\mathcal{A}'}^{\mathsf{DBDH}}(k)$$

$$Adv_3 \leq Adv_{\mathcal{A}''}^{\mathsf{CR}}(k) + Adv_4 \leq 4q_d(n+1) \cdot Adv_{\mathcal{A}'}^{\mathsf{DBDH}}(k) + Adv_{\mathcal{A}''}^{\mathsf{CR}}(k)$$

In consequence, since $Adv_3 = Adv_2$ and $Adv_1 \leq Adv_{\mathcal{A}_s}^{\mathsf{OT}}(k) + Adv_2$, we obtain

$$Adv_1 \leq 4q_d(n+1) \cdot Adv_{\mathcal{A}'}^{\mathsf{DBDH}}(k) + Adv_{\mathcal{A}''}^{\mathsf{CR}}(k) + Adv_{\mathcal{A}_s}^{\mathsf{OT}}(k)$$

3.5.3 Huang–Wong CL-PKE

In [58], Huang and Wong proposed a generic CLE scheme and showed that it is proven secure against the malicious-but-passive KGC attacks in the standard model.

Let IBE = (Setup, Extract, Encrypt, Decrypt) be an IND-ID-CCA2 secure IBE scheme, PKE = (Gen, Enc, Dec) an IND-CCA2 secure public-key encryption scheme, and S = (Gen, Sign, Verify) a strong OTS scheme. Based on these three primitives, a generic CLE scheme is shown in Figure 3.8. Similar to [61], this construction can be considered a sequential combination of public-key encryption and IBE. To resist the attack mounted by the malicious-but-passive KGC, this construction additionally involves a strong OTS that ensures the correctness of a ciphertext.

Theorem 3.3 *The CLE scheme described is type-I IND-ID-CCA2 secure, provided that the underlying IBE scheme is IND-ID-CCA2 secure, and the OTS scheme S is strongly unforgeable.*

• $(\text{params}, \text{master-key}) \leftarrow \text{Setup}(1^k) : (\text{params}, \text{master-key}) \leftarrow \text{IBE.Setup}(1^k)$
• $\text{psk}_{\text{ID}} \leftarrow \text{Extract-Partial-Private-Key}(\text{master-key}, \text{ID}) : \text{psk}_{\text{ID}} \leftarrow \text{IBE.Extract}(\text{master-key},$ $\text{ID})$
• $(\text{upk}_{\text{ID}}, \text{usk}_{\text{ID}}) \leftarrow \text{Set-User-Keys}(1^k, \text{params}) : (\text{upk}_{\text{ID}}, \text{usk}_{\text{ID}}) \leftarrow \text{PKE.KG}(1^k)$

• $c \leftarrow \text{Encrypt}(\text{params}, \text{upk}_{\text{ID}}, \text{ID}, m) :$	• $m \leftarrow \text{Decrypt}(\text{psk}_{\text{ID}}, \text{usk}_{\text{ID}}, \text{ID}, c) :$
$(vk, sk) \leftarrow \text{S.Gen}(1^k)$	parse c as (c_2, σ, vk).
$c_1 \leftarrow \text{IBE.Encrypt}(\text{params}, \text{ID}, m\|vk)$	if $\text{S.Verify}(vk, \sigma, c_2) = 0, m \leftarrow \perp; else :$
$c_2 \leftarrow \text{PKE.Enc}(\text{upk}_{\text{ID}}, c_1)$	$c_1 \leftarrow \text{PKE.Dec}(\text{usk}_{\text{ID}}, c_2)$
$\sigma \leftarrow \text{S.Sign}(sk, c_2)$	$m\|vk' \leftarrow \text{IBE.Dec}(\text{psk}_{\text{ID}}, \text{ID}, c_1)$
$c = (c_2, \sigma, vk)$	if $vk' \neq vk$, then $m \leftarrow \perp$

Figure 3.8 Description of the generic CLE scheme.

Proof 3.3 *To improve the readability of the proof, we first briefly show where the trick is intuitively. Since S is a strong OTS scheme, a PPT adversary cannot produce a valid forgery using the verification key in the challenge ciphertext with nonnegligible probability, so the adversary cannot gain any advantage by manipulating the challenge ciphertext. On the other hand, if an adversary breaks the type-I security of CLE, another algorithm can be easily constructed to break the IND-ID-CCA2 security of IBE. The detail of the security proof can be found in [58].*

Theorem 3.4 *The CLE scheme described is type-II IND-ID-CCA2 secure if the underlying public-key encryption scheme PKE is IND-CCA2 secure and the signature scheme S is strongly one-time unforgeable.*

Proof 3.4 *To improve the readability of the proof, we first briefly show where the trick is intuitively. Since the adversary knows the master secret key of IBE, the type-II security of CLE has to rely on the security of PKE. As a proof of type-I security, the OTS and the verification key embedded in the hidden plaintext ensures that the adversary cannot gain any advantage from manipulating the ciphertext. The detail of the security proof can be found in [58].*

CHAPTER 4

CLS Secure in the Standard Model

4.1 MODELING CERTIFICATELESS SIGNATURE (CLS) SCHEMES

In this section, we first review the original framework of the CLS schemes proposed in the seminar work [17]. Then we describe the simplified version equivalent to the original seven-algorithms framework [50,113].

4.1.1 Framework of CLS Schemes

According to the original definition in [17] (see Figure 4.1), a CLS scheme is defined by the following seven algorithms: Setup, Extract-Partial-Private-Key, Set-Secret-Value, Set-Private-Key, Set-Public-Key, Sign, and Verify. The description of each algorithm is as follows:

Setup: On input of a security parameter 1^k, this algorithm is usually performed by the key-generation center (KGC) to generate the public system parameters params and the corresponding master secret key master-key.

Extract-Partial-Private-Key: On input of the master secret key master-key, the public system parameters params, along with an identity $\mathsf{ID} \in \{0,1\}^*$, this algorithm is usually performed by the KGC to generate the user's partial private key $\mathsf{psk_{ID}}$. Note that this algorithm is performed by the KGC once for each user, and the partial private key $\mathsf{psk_{ID}}$ is distributed to the corresponding user via a secure channel.

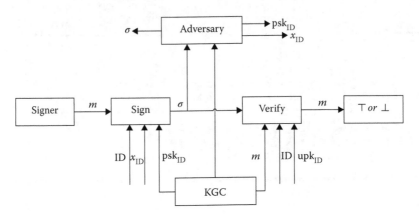

Figure 4.1 An overview of certificateless signature (CLS).

Set-Secret-Value: On input of the public system parameters params and a user's identity ID, this algorithm is run by the user himself/herself to generate a user secret value x_{ID}.

Set-Private-Key: On input of the public system parameters params, a user's partial private key psk_{ID}, and a user's secret value x_{ID}, this algorithm is run by the user himself/herself to generate the full user private key usk_{ID}.

Set-Public-Key: On input of the public system parameters params and a user's secret value x_{ID}, this algorithm is usually carried out by the user himself/herself to generate a user public key upk_{ID}.

Sign: On input of the public parameters params, an identity ID, the corresponding user private key usk_{ID}, and a message m to be signed, this algorithm outputs a CLS σ.

Verify: On input of the public parameters params, an identity ID, the corresponding user public key upk_{ID}, and a message/signature pair (m, σ), this algorithm outputs 1 if the signature is correct or 0 otherwise.

In general, the algorithms Setup and Partial-Private-Key-Extract are carried out by the KGC.

4.1.2   Equivalence to the Original Seven-Algorithm Framework

Similar to certificateless encryption (CLE), defined in Chapter 3, the framework of CLS can also be simplified such that the Set-Private-Key algorithm can be removed directly since the function of user secret key $\mathsf{usk}_{\mathsf{ID}}$ can be achieved by adopting the secret value x_{ID} and partial private key $\mathsf{psk}_{\mathsf{ID}}$ together [20,114]:

Setup

Extract-Partial-Private-Key

Set-Secret-Value

Set-Public-Key

Sign

Verify

According to [50], the framework can be further simplified by incorporating the Set-Secret-Value and Set-Public-Key algorithms as one single Set-User-Keys algorithm defined as follows:

Set-User-Keys: On input of the master public key mpk and a user's identity ID, this algorithm is run to output a public/private key pair $(\mathsf{upk}_{\mathsf{ID}}, \mathsf{usk}_{\mathsf{ID}})$.

In this way, a more versatile framework of CLS, in which a scheme consists of only five algorithms, is given as follows:

Setup

Extract-Partial-Private-Key

Set-User-Keys

Sign

Verify

4.2 SECURITY DEFINITIONS FOR CLS SCHEMES

Integrating the syntax of CLS and security models of signature schemes in traditional public-key cryptography (PKC) and identity-based public-key cryptography (ID-PKC), the security of a CLS scheme is defined by two (very similar) games between a challenger $\mathcal{C}$ and an adversary $\mathcal{A}_1$ or $\mathcal{A}_2$. Indeed, to capture the attack mounted by the adversaries who can replace the public key of any user of their choice, the type I adversary is defined [17,48]. In addition, the type II adversary has been modeled to capture the attacks where the attacker owns the master secret key but cannot replace the target user's public key [17,48].

4.2.1 Adversaries and Oracles

Similar to CLE, defined in Chapter 3, there are four oracles that can be accessed by both $\mathcal{A}_1$ and $\mathcal{A}_2$:

Create-User: This oracle takes as input an identity $\mathsf{ID} \in \{0,1\}^*$; if ID has already been created, nothing will be performed by this oracle. Otherwise, the oracle obtains the partial private key $\mathsf{psk}_{\mathsf{ID}}$, the user secret value x_{ID}, and the user public key $\mathsf{upk}_{\mathsf{ID}}$ by performing the Extract-Partial-Private-Key, Set-Secret-Value, and Set-Public-Key algorithms, respectively. It then stores $(ID, \mathsf{upk}_{\mathsf{ID}}, x_{\mathsf{ID}}, \mathsf{psk}_{\mathsf{ID}})$ in a list $\mathcal{L}$. In both cases, $\mathsf{upk}_{\mathsf{ID}}$ is returned to the adversary.

Public-Key-Replace: This oracle captures the attacker's capability to dupe a legitimate sender to use an invalid public key. On input of a query on $(\mathsf{ID}, \mathsf{upk}'_{\mathsf{ID}})$, this oracle replaces the user ID's original public key with $\mathsf{upk}'_{\mathsf{ID}}$ and updates the corresponding item in the list $\mathcal{L}$. It is noted that the secret value used to generate $\mathsf{upk}'_{\mathsf{ID}}$ is not required to be provided by the adversary [20].

Partial-Private-Key-Extract: On input of a query on the identity ID, this oracle searches the list $\mathcal{L}$ and returns the corresponding partial private key $\mathsf{psk}_{\mathsf{ID}}$ by performing the Extract-Partial-Private-Key algorithm.

Secret-Value-Extract: On input of a query on the identity ID, this oracle searches the list $\mathcal{L}$ and returns the corresponding secret value x_{ID} by performing the Set-Secret-Value algorithm.

According to the existential unforgeability under an adaptive chosen-message attack originally defined in [47], an adaptively chosen message adversary could obtain some message/signature pairs of its choice. Therefore, besides the above four oracles, a **Sign** oracle should be accessed by the adversaries. However, there is some debate about the **Sign** oracle in terms of its concrete attack power. In this way, adversaries are not only categorized by $\mathcal{A}_1$ and $\mathcal{A}_2$.

4.2.2   Type I Adversaries

4.2.2.1   Security against a Normal Type I Adversary

In this section, the first kind of type I adversary $\mathcal{A}_1$, named the normal type I adversary, is considered to capture the following attack scenarios:

1. $\mathcal{A}_1$ can obtain some message/signature pairs (m_i, σ_i) that are generated by the target user ID using this ID's secret value x_{ID} and partial private key psk_{ID}.

2. The target user's secret value x_{ID} and partial private key psk_{ID} will be kept secret.

3. The target user ID's public key can be replaced with upk'_{ID} by $\mathcal{A}_1$ of its choice. Furthermore, $\mathcal{A}_1$ can also dupe any third party to verify the signature under the identity ID and the replaced public key upk'_{ID}.

In reality, the adversary may be able to obtain the target user's valid signatures from eavesdropping on the intended receivers. These signatures are generated by the target user himself/herself using his/her own user secret value and partial private key. Although $\mathcal{A}_1$ can replace the target user ID's public key with a upk'_{ID} of its choice, it is unreasonable for the adversary $\mathcal{A}_1$ to get any signatures from ID such that the signatures are valid under the replaced public key upk'_{ID} in most cases. In other words, the target user ID in the CLE environment cannot prevent his/her public key from being replaced. However, it would be a strong assumption that the target user ID generates the valid signatures under the replaced public key. On the other hand, either the secret value x_{ID} or the partial private key psk_{ID} of the target user cannot be accessed by the adversary $\mathcal{A}_1$.

The existential unforgeability of a CLS scheme against a normal type I adaptively chosen message and chosen identity adversary $\mathcal{A}_1$ is defined by the following game (shown in Figure 4.2):

Initial: The challenger/simulator $\mathcal{C}$ generates the public system parameters **params** and the corresponding master secret key **master-key** by performing the **Setup** algorithm.

Attack: In this phase, $\mathcal{A}_1$ can adaptively access the **Create-User**, **Public-Key-Replace**, **Partial-Private-Key-Extract**,

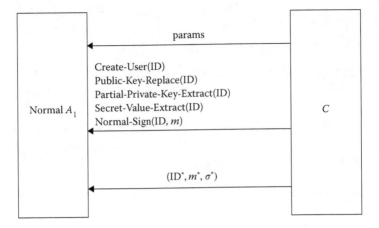

Figure 4.2 CMA-CIDA-Normal-I experiment for CLS scheme.

and **Secret-Value-Extract** oracles adaptively. In addition, $\mathcal{A}_1$ can also access the **Normal-Sign** oracle defined as follows:

Normal-Sign: On input of a query (ID, m), where ID represents the identity that has been created and m denotes the message to be signed, this oracle outputs a signature σ such that $1 \leftarrow$ $\mathsf{Verify}(m, \sigma, \mathsf{params}, \mathsf{ID}, \mathsf{upk}_{\mathsf{ID}})$.

Forgery: After the deciding *Attack* phase is over, $\mathcal{A}_1$ outputs a forgery $(m^*, \sigma^*, \mathsf{ID}^*)$, where $\mathsf{upk}_{\mathsf{ID}^*}$ denotes the current public key of the user ID^* in the list $\mathcal{L}$. $\mathcal{A}_1$ is regarded to win this game if the following requirements are satisfied:

- The item (ID^*, m^*) has never been submitted to the oracle **Normal-Sign**.
- The challenge identity ID^* has never been submitted to the **Partial-Private-KeyExtract** oracle or **Secret-Value-Extract** oracle.
- $1 \leftarrow \mathsf{Verify}(m, \sigma, \mathsf{params}, \mathsf{ID}^*, \mathsf{upk}_{\mathsf{ID}^*})$.

Definition 4.1 *A CLS scheme is said to achieve existential unforgeability against a normal type I adaptively chosen message and chosen identity adversary if there is no probabilistic polynomial time (PPT) adversary $\mathcal{A}_1$ that wins the above CMA-CIDA-Normal-I game with a nonnegligible advantage.*

4.2.2.2 Security against a Strong Type I Adversary

In this section, we enhance the attack power of the adversary $\mathcal{A}_1$ and formalize the second type of $\mathcal{A}_1$, named the strong type I adversary, to capture the attack scenario that $\mathcal{A}_1$ can obtain some message/signature pairs (m_i, σ_i) that are valid under the identity ID and user public key $\mathsf{upk}_{\mathsf{ID}}$. Here $\mathsf{upk}_{\mathsf{ID}}$ could be any valid public key value chosen by $\mathcal{A}_1$ or the user ID's original user public key. In the former case, the strong type I adversary $\mathcal{A}_1$ is required to provide the corresponding secret value which is used to calculate the public key chosen by itself.

The attack scenario described above enables $\mathcal{A}_1$ to obtain the target user ID's signatures which are generated using the secret value sv provided by itself. It is evident that a scheme secure against a strong type I adversary can also resist the attack mounted from a normal type I adversary. This kind of attack indicates that the target user ID will perform the signing operation with his/her own partial private key and the secret value provided by $\mathcal{A}_1$. In other words, this scenario implies that the target user ID will intentionally do a favor for $\mathcal{A}_1$ to attack himself/herself. This assumption seems much stronger than the normal type I adversary in most situations.

The existential unforgeability of a CLS scheme against a strong type I adaptively chosen message and chosen identity adversary $\mathcal{A}_1$ is defined by the following game similar to that defined in Section 4.2.2.1 (shown in Figure 4.3), with the only difference being that the strong type I adversary $\mathcal{A}_1$ can query a different sign oracle **Strong-Sign**:

Initial: The challenger/simulator $\mathcal{C}$ generates the public system parameters **params** and the corresponding master secret key **master-key** by performing the **Setup** algorithm.

Attack: In this phase, $\mathcal{A}_1$ can adaptively access the **Create-User**, **Public-Key-Replace**, **Partial-Private-Key-Extract**, and **Secret-Value-Extract** oracles adaptively. In addition, $\mathcal{A}_1$ can also access the **Strong-Sign** oracle defined as follows:

Strong-Sign: On input of a query (ID, m, sv) such that ID represents the identity that has been created, m denotes the message to be signed, and sv is some information sv, the oracle performs as follows:

1. If $sv = \perp$, this oracle carries out the signing algorithm with the ID's original secret value x_{ID} and partial private key

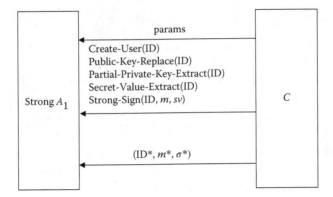

Figure 4.3 CMA-CIDA-Strong-I experiment for CLS scheme.

$\mathsf{psk}_{\mathsf{ID}}$ to generate the signature σ on this message. After that, the signature σ will be returned as the answer.

2. Otherwise, this oracle carries out the signing algorithm with the sv provided by $\mathcal{A}_1$ and ID's partial private key $\mathsf{psk}_{\mathsf{ID}}$ to generate the signature σ on this message. After that, the signature σ will be returned as the answer.

Forgery: After the deciding *Attack* phase is over, $\mathcal{A}_1$ outputs a forgery $(m^*, \sigma^*, \mathsf{ID}^*)$, where $\mathsf{upk}_{\mathsf{ID}^*}$ denotes the current public key of the user ID^* in the list $\mathcal{L}$. $\mathcal{A}_1$ is regarded to win this game if the following requirements are satisfied:

- The item (ID^*, m^*, sv) has never been submitted to the the the oracle **Strong-Sign**.

- The challenge identity ID^* has never been submitted to the **Partial-Private-KeyExtract** oracle.

- $1 \leftarrow \mathsf{Verify}(m, \sigma, \mathsf{params}, \mathsf{ID}^*, \mathsf{upk}_{\mathsf{ID}^*})$.

Different from the model defined in Section 4.2.2.1, $\mathcal{A}_1$ is allowed to derive the secret value associated with the target user ID^*, which mirrors the fact that x_{ID^*} might be leaked out.

Definition 4.2 *A CLS scheme is is said to achieve existential unforgeability against a strong type I adaptively chosen message and chosen identity adversary if there is no PPT adversary $\mathcal{A}_1$ that wins the above CMA-CIDA-Strong-I game with a nonnegligible advantage.*

4.2.2.3 Security against a Super Type I Adversary

In this section, we formalize the third type of $\mathcal{A}_1$, named the super type I adversary, to capture the attack scenario that $\mathcal{A}_1$ can obtain some message/signature pairs (m_i, σ_i) such that $1 \leftarrow$ Verify$(m_i, \sigma_i, \mathsf{params}, \mathsf{ID}, \mathsf{upk_{ID}})$ from the target user. Here $\mathsf{upk_{ID}}$ could be any valid public key value chosen by $\mathcal{A}_1$ or the target user's original user public key. In the former case, it is not necessary for the super type I adversary $\mathcal{A}_1$ to provide the corresponding secret value that is used to calculate the public key chosen by itself.

The attack scenario described above gives the adversary $\mathcal{A}_1$ as much power as possible such that the challenger is expected to correctly respond to signing queries made on identities for which the adversary has replaced the public key. Furthermore, $\mathcal{A}_1$ is not required to provide the secret value sv associated with the public key chosen by itself. In this way, a black-box knowledge extractor is assumed to have existed implicitly such that the secret value associated with the public key chosen by $\mathcal{A}_1$ can be extracted from this black box and used in the signing oracle.[a] In fact, the super type I adversary is considered the strongest attacker so far even though it is still uncertain whether it reflects a realistic attack scenario. Undoubtedly, a CLS scheme that is secure in this kind of security model offers a higher security level than one that is secure in a strong or a normal type I security model.

The existential unforgeability of a CLS scheme against a super type I adaptively chosen message and chosen identity adversary $\mathcal{A}_1$ is defined by the following game similar to that defined in Section 4.2.2.1 (shown in Figure 4.4), with the only difference being that the strong type I adversary $\mathcal{A}_1$ can query a different sign oracle **Super-Sign**:

Initial: The challenger/simulator $\mathcal{C}$ generates the public system parameters **params** and the corresponding master secret key **master-key** by performing the **Setup** algorithm.

---

[a]Generally speaking, a signing oracle accessed by an adversary implies that the adversary can obtain some valid message/signature pairs from a legitimate signer. For instance, the legitimate signer can be bribed to generate the signature on some given message by performing the signing algorithm according to the scheme specification. Obviously, the situation where the signer attempts to generate the signature using the secret value corresponding to the replaced public key cannot happen. Therefore, this kind of signing oracle that which will accurately generate the valid signature under the replaced public key gives the adversary more power than it would have in reality.

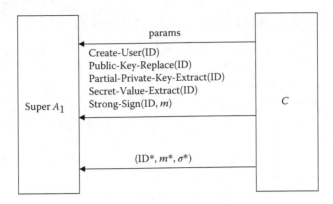

Figure 4.4 CMA-CIDA-Super-I experiment for CLS scheme.

Attack: In this phase, $\mathcal{A}_1$ can adaptively access the **Create-User**, **Public-Key-Replace**, **Partial-Private-Key-Extract**, and **Secret-Value-Extract** oracles adaptively. In addition, $\mathcal{A}_1$ can also access the **Super-Sign** oracle defined as follows:

Super-Sign: On input of a query (ID, m), this oracle returns a signature σ such that $1 \leftarrow \mathsf{Verify}(m, \sigma, \mathsf{params}, \mathsf{ID}, \mathsf{upk}_{\mathsf{ID}})$ and $\mathsf{upk}'_{\mathsf{ID}}$ could be the user ID's original public key or any valid public key value chosen by the adversary. When $\mathsf{upk}'_{\mathsf{ID}}$ is the replaced user public key chosen by the adversary, it is unnecessary for the adversary to provide the corresponding secret value that is used to produce the public key chosen by itself.

Forgery: After the deciding *Attack* phase is over, $\mathcal{A}_1$ outputs a forgery $(m^*, \sigma^*, \mathsf{ID}^*)$, where $\mathsf{upk}_{\mathsf{ID}^*}$ denotes the current public key of the user ID^* in the list $\mathcal{L}$. $\mathcal{A}_1$ is regarded to win this game if the following requirements are satisfied:

- The item (ID^*, m^*) has never been submitted to the oracle **Super-Sign**.
- The challenge identity ID^* has never been submitted to the **Partial-Private-Key-Extract** oracle.
- $1 \leftarrow \mathsf{Verify}(m, \sigma, \mathsf{params}, \mathsf{ID}^*, \mathsf{upk}_{\mathsf{ID}^*})$.

Definition 4.3 *A CLS scheme is said to achieve existential unforgeability against a strong type I adaptively chosen message and chosen identity adversary if there is no PPT adversary $\mathcal{A}_1$ that wins the above CMA-CIDA-Super-I game with a nonnegligible advantage.*

4.2.3 Type II Adversaries

In the certificateless public-key cryptography (CL-PKC) environment, the type II adversary $\mathcal{A}_2$ simulates the KGC that owns the master secret key and might mount several attacks such as eavesdropping on signatures and making signing queries. By considering the debates about the adversaries' capabilities, we categorized the type II attackers into normal $\mathcal{A}_2$, strong $\mathcal{A}_2$, and super $\mathcal{A}_2$. However, the strong $\mathcal{A}_2$ is unnecessary to define particularly since this kind of adversary can win the security game trivially. Specifically, the **Strong-Sign** oracle can answer queries either by using the oracle **Normal-Sign** (then the oracle **Strong-Sign** is exactly identical to the oracle **Normal-Sign**) or by generating the signatures using the corresponding secret value provided by the adversary. The basic reason for this depends on the fact that the type II adversary $\mathcal{A}_2$ owns the master secret key and can generate the partial private key for any user by itself.

Similar to Section 4.2.2.1, the existential unforgeability of a CLS scheme against a normal (*resp.* super) type II adaptively chosen message and chosen identity adversary $\mathcal{A}_2$ is defined as follows (shown in Figure 4.5):

***Initial*:** The challenger/simulator $\mathcal{C}$ executes the Setup algorithm and returns the public system parameters params and the master secret key master-key to $\mathcal{A}_2$.

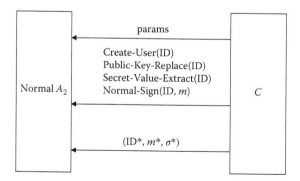

Figure 4.5 CMA-CIDA-Type-I experiment for CLS scheme.

Attack: In this phase, $\mathcal{A}_2$ can adaptively access the **Create-User**, **Public-Key-Replace**, **Secret-Value-Extract**, and **Normal-Sign** (*resp.* **Super-Sign**) oracles adaptively.[a]

Forgery: After the deciding *Attack* phase is over, $\mathcal{A}_2$ outputs a forgery $(m^*, \sigma^*, \mathsf{ID}^*)$, where $\mathsf{upk}_{\mathsf{ID}^*}$ denotes the current public key of the user ID^* in the list $\mathcal{L}$. $\mathcal{A}_2$ is regarded to win this game if the following requirements are satisfied:

- The item (ID^*, m^*) has never been submitted to the oracle **Normal-Sign** (*resp.* **Super-Sign**).
- The challenge identity ID^* has never been submitted to the **Secret-Value-Extract** oracle.
- $1 \leftarrow \mathsf{Verify}(m, \sigma, \mathsf{params}, \mathsf{ID}^*, \mathsf{upk}_{\mathsf{ID}^*})$. Here, $\mathsf{upk}_{\mathsf{ID}^*}$ denotes the original user public key associated with the user ID^*.

Definition 4.4 *A CLS scheme is said to achieve existential unforgeability against a type II adaptively chosen message and chosen identity adversary if there is no PPT adversary $\mathcal{A}_2$ that wins the above security game with a nonnegligible advantage.*

4.2.4 Malicious-but-Passive KGC Attack

According to [62], the malicious-but-passive KGC attack should also be considered in the CLS environment such that the master public/private key pair along with the system-wide parameters can be generated maliciously by the KGC to mount the type II attack more easily in the later stage of the system. Combined with different **Sign** oracles, the security of the CLS schemes against a malicious-but-passive KGC attack is defined in the following games:

Initial: The challenger/simulator $\mathcal{C}$ executes $\mathcal{A}_2$ on the security parameter k. $\mathcal{A}_2$ returns a master public key mpk and the system parameters params. Note that $\mathcal{A}_2$ cannot make any query at this stage with the exception that $\mathcal{A}_2$ is enabled to access the specific random oracles of the underlying scheme at any stage of the game if the security analysis is performed under some model such as the random oracle model.

---

[a]It is noted that the **Partial-Private-Key-Extract** oracle is no longer needed in this security game since $\mathcal{A}_2$ can generate the partial private key with the knowledge of the master secret key himself/herself.

Attack: $\mathcal{A}_2$ can adaptively access all oracles as in the game defined in Section 3.3.3. However, the **Create-User** oracle is modified as follows:

Create-User: This oracle takes not only an identity $\mathsf{ID} \in \{0,1\}^*$, but also the user partial private key $\mathsf{psk}_{\mathsf{ID}}$ as the input.[a] If the item associated with the identity ID has already been created, nothing is to be executed by the oracle. Otherwise, this oracle performs algorithms **Set-Secret-Value** and **Set-Public-Key** to obtain the secret value x_{ID} and the public key $\mathsf{upk}_{\mathsf{ID}}$, respectively. Then this oracle inserts $(\mathsf{ID}, \mathsf{upk}_{\mathsf{ID}}, x_{\mathsf{ID}}, \mathsf{psk}_{\mathsf{ID}})$ to the list $\mathcal{L}$. In this case, ID is said to be created. In both cases, $\mathsf{upk}_{\mathsf{ID}}$ is returned.

Forgery: Same as defined in Section 4.2.3.

Definition 4.5 *A CLS scheme is said to achieve existential unforgeability against a malicious-but-passive type II adaptively chosen message and chosen identity adversary if there is no PPT adversary $\mathcal{A}_2$ that wins the above security game with nonnegligible advantage.*

4.3 SURVEYING CLS SCHEMES

The state of the art of CLS schemes is surveyed and summarized in Table 4.1 by categorizing the existing literature according to different perspectives [20,114,115].

The first concrete CLS scheme was initially proposed based on the bilinear pairing in [17]. However, a formal security model for analyzing the scheme's security in terms of existential unforgeability was not given. Also, this original construction was found to be insecure against a type I adversary by Huang et al. [116]. Moreover, Huang et al. also proposed a modification to fix this problem and proved its security in the random oracle model. A generic approach to construct a CLS scheme was proposed by Yum and Lee [137]. However, Hu et al. [50,113] showed that the generic construction in [137] is insecure against the key replacement attack and suggested a fix in the standard model. Later, Zhang et al. [19] revisited the security model of CLS schemes in [19] and [116] and presented an improved security model along with a more efficient concrete CLS scheme. A new construction for CLS was introduced by Gorantla and Saxena [121] without providing formal proofs

---

[a]In this way, it implies that the user secret value can be obtained by $\mathcal{A}_2$ with the support of the user partial private key $\mathsf{psk}_{\mathsf{ID}}$

TABLE 4.1 Comparison of Existing Certificateless Signature Schemes

Scheme	References	Style	Model	Type I model	Type II model	Broken?
Al-Riyami and Paterson	[17]	Concrete	—	No formal proof	No formal proof	[62,116]
Choi et al.	[117]	Concrete	ROM	Strong type I	Strong type II	
Choi et al.	[118]	Concrete	ROM	Super type I	Super type II	[119]
Du and Wen	[120]	Concrete	ROM	Strong type I	Normal type II	[118]
Gorantla and Saxena	[121]	Concrete	-	No formal proof	No formal proof	[122]
Gong and Li	[123]	Concrete	-	Super type I	Super type II	
He et al.	[124]	Concrete	ROM	Normal type I	Normal type II	[125,126]
Hu et al.	[50,113]	Generic	ROM	Super type I	Strong type II	
Huang et al.	[116]	Concrete	ROM	Normal type I	Super type II	
Huang et al.-1	[20,114]	Concrete	ROM	Normal type I	Mal. super type II	
Huang et al.-2	[20,114]	Concrete	ROM	Super type I	Mal. super type II	
Liu et al.	[60]	Concrete	SM	Super type I	Normal type II	[62,107,114]
Tso et al.	[127,128]	Concrete	ROM	Normal type I	Mal. normal type II	
Tso et al.	[129]	Concrete	ROM	Super type I	Super type II	[119]
Xiong et al.	[107]	Concrete	SM	Normal type I	Normal type II	[130]
Yap et al.	[131]	Concrete	ROM	Normal type I	Super type II	[132,133]
Yu et al.	[134]	Concrete	SM	Normal type I	Normal type II	[135,136]
Yuan and Wang	[135]	Concrete	SM	Normal type I	Normal type II	
Yum and Lee	[137]	Generic	ROM	Normal type I	Normal type II	[50,113]
Zhang et al.	[19]	Concrete	ROM	Super type I	Mal. super type II	
Zhang and Zhang	[138]	Concrete	ROM	Super type I	Mal. super type II	
Zhang and Mao	[139]	Concrete	ROM	Normal type I	Normal type II	[140]

Note: ROM, random oracle model; SM, standard model; Concrete, constructions with a full description; Generic, constructions based on other primitives; ?, unknown.

and was shown to be insecure by Cao et al. [122]. Choi et al. [117] and Yap et al. [131] presented some efficient CLS schemes secure in the model defined in [116]. Due to the fact that the type I adversary has not been captured in this model, Yap et al's. [131] scheme is shown to be insecure against the key replacement attack by [132,133]. Castro and Dahab [141] discussed two inaccuracies found in the security proofs of CLS schemes and redefined the scope of application of the forking lemma in the CLS setting. Inspired by the survey for CLE schemes [18], Huang et al. [20,114] revisited the security models of CLS schemes and further classified the type I/II adversary into three types as mentioned in Section 4.2. Two novel concrete CLS schemes are also constructed in [20,114]. Their first CLS scheme is claimed to be secure against a normal type I adversary and a super type II adversary with a rather short signature length. The latter scheme is very efficient and regarded to be secure in the strongest security model where the type I/II adversary is a super adversary. Subsequently, Shim [142] showed that the first CLS scheme in [20,114] is indeed universally forgeable against strong or super type I adversaries that can replace users' public keys and obtain signatures under the replaced public keys. Zhang and Zhang [138] put forward a new CLS scheme secure against a super type I/II adversary, which is more efficient than the other CLS schemes achieving the same security level. On the other hand, the schemes in [17,116] are shown to secure the malicious-but-passive KGC attack by [62].

Due to the fact that transmitting even one bit of data consumes significantly more power than executing one 32-bit instruction [143], a short digital signature [20,144], which can offer a high security level at the cost of relatively short signature length, is always desirable in mobile devices with a short battery life such as portable digital assistants (PDAs), Radio frequency identification chips, sensors, and smart phones. It is natural to introduce the notion of short signatures into CL-PKC and design an efficient certificateless short signature with provable security. After the first concrete certificateless short signature given in [20,114], Du and Wen [120] proposed a short CLS scheme and claimed that their scheme is provably secure against a the strong type I and normal type II adversaries in the random oracle model. However, Choi et al. [118] showed that the short CLS scheme in [120] is insecure against a strong type I adversary and then proposed a new short CLS scheme secure against the super type I/II adversary. Based on the idea of Boneh et al.'s [144] short signature scheme, Tso et al. [127,128]

introduced an efficient short CLS scheme secure against a normal type I/II adversary. Later on, Tso et al. [129] gave another short CLS scheme and claimed that this scheme is secure against adversaries providing with super signing oracle. He et al. [146] proposed a new efficient certificateless short signature scheme and showed this scheme to be secure against both the super type I and the super type II adversaries. Recently, Du and Wen [119] showed that both Choi et al.'s [118] scheme and Tso et al.'s [129] scheme are vulnerable to strong type I adversaries, not to mention super type I adversaries.

Based on the idea in [41], He et al. [124] proposed a pairing-free CLS scheme and demonstrated that their scheme is provably secure in the random oracle model. However, Tian and Huang [125] and Tsai et al. [126] demonstrated that the scheme in [124] is insecure against a type II adversary. To remedy the problem, Tsai et al. [126] also proposed an improvement for security against normal type I/II adversaries. Furthermore, Gong and Li [123] proposed a novel CLS scheme without pairing and demonstrated that their scheme is secure against super type I/II adversaries. Independent of these works, Zhang and Mao [139] presented an RSA-based construction of a CLS scheme and showed that their scheme is provably secure in the random oracle model. However, He et al. [140] showed that the scheme in [139] is insecure against a type I adversary. After that, Sharma et al. [147] proposed an improved RSA-based CLS scheme and gave the formal security proof in the random oracle.

The first concrete CLS scheme in the standard model was proposed by Liu et al. [60]. Xiong et al. [107] and Huang and Wong [57] independently showed that the scheme in [60] is subject to the malicious-but-passive KGC attack [62]. Moreover, Xiong et al. [107] provided a countermeasure to resist the malicious-but-passive KGC attack. However, Shim and Lee [130] demonstrated that their scheme is in fact still insecure against the malicious-but-passive KGC attack. To overcome the security flaw in [60] and [107], Yu et al. [134] further proposed an improved CLS scheme that enjoys shorter system parameters and higher computational efficiency than the previous schemes. But Yuan and Wang [135] and Guan et al. [136] independently showed that Yu et al.'s [134] scheme is not secure against the key replacement attack and the malicious-but-passive KGC attack. Moreover, Yuan and Wang [135] further proposed an improved scheme that overcomes the security flaws without affecting the merits of the scheme in [134].

4.4 CONCRETE CONSTRUCTION

In this section, two representative concrete CLS schemes secure in the standard model [107,135] are introduced.

4.4.1 Xiong–Qin–Li's Scheme

Based on the idea from [60] and [148], Xiong et al. [107] proposed a concrete CLS scheme secure in the standard model. Although this scheme was shown to be vulnerable to the malicious-but-passive KGC attack [130], the intention of including this scheme is merely to offer a gentle introduction to the CLS scheme secure in the standard model.

4.4.1.1 Complexity Assumption

Definition 4.6 *Nonpairing-based generalized bilinear Diffie–Hellman (NGBDH) assumption. Given a group $\mathbb{G}$ of prime order p with generator g and elements $g^a, g^b \in \mathbb{G}$, where a, b are selected uniformly at random from $\mathbb{Z}_p^*$, the NGBDH problem in $\mathbb{G}$ is to output (g^{abc}, g^c). An adversary $\mathcal{A}$ has at least an ϵ advantage if*

$$Pr[\mathcal{A}(g, g^a, g^b) = (g^{abc}, g^c)] \geq \epsilon$$

We say that the (ϵ, t)-NGBDH assumption holds in a group G if no algorithm running in time at most t can solve the NGBDH problem in $\mathbb{G}$ with an advantage of at least ϵ.

Definition 4.7 *Many-DH assumption. Given a group $\mathbb{G}$ of prime order p with generator g and elements $g^a, g^b, g^c, g^{ab}, g^{ac}, g^{bc} \in \mathbb{G}$, where a, b, c are selected uniformly at random from $\mathbb{Z}_p^*$, the Many-DH problem in $\mathbb{G}$ is to output g^{abc}. An adversary $\mathcal{A}$ has at least an ϵ advantage if*

$$Pr[\mathcal{A}(g, g^a, g^b, g^c, g^{ab}, g^{ac}, g^{bc}) = g^{abc}] \geq \epsilon$$

We say that the (ϵ, t)-Many-DH assumption holds in a group G if no algorithm running in time at most t can solve the Many-DH problem in $\mathbb{G}$ with an advantage of at least ϵ.

4.4.1.2 Concrete Construction

Let $H_u : \{0,1\}^* \to \{0,1\}^{n_u}$ and $H_m : \{0,1\}^* \to \{0,1\}^{n_m}$ be two collision-resistant cryptographic hash functions for some $n_u, n_m \in \mathbb{Z}$.

They are used to create identities and messages of the desired length, respectively:

Setup: Select a pairing $\hat{e} : \mathbb{G}_1 \times \mathbb{G}_1 \rightarrow \mathbb{G}_2$, where the order of $\mathbb{G}_1$ is p. Let g be a generator of $\mathbb{G}_1$. Randomly select $\alpha \leftarrow_R \mathbb{Z}_p$, compute $g_1 = g^\alpha$, and pick $g_2 \leftarrow_R \mathbb{G}_1$. Also select randomly the following elements: $u', m' \leftarrow_R \mathbb{G}_1$, $u_i \leftarrow_R \mathbb{G}_1$ for $i = 1, \ldots, n_u$, $m_i \leftarrow_R \mathbb{G}_1$ for $i = 1, \ldots, n_m$. Let $\mathbf{U} = (u_i)$, $\mathbf{M} = (m_i)$. The public parameters are $(\mathbb{G}_1, \mathbb{G}_2, \hat{e}, g, g_1, g_2, u', \mathbf{U}, m', \mathbf{M})$ and the master secret is g_2^α.

Extract-Partial-Private-Key: Let u be a bit string of length n_u representing an identity and let $u[i]$ be the i-th bit of u. Define $\mathcal{U} \subset \{1, \ldots, n_u\}$ to be the set of indices i such that $u[i] = 1$. To construct the partial secret key of identity ID, the KGC randomly picks $r_u \leftarrow_R \mathbb{Z}_p$ and computes:

$$\left(g_2^\alpha \left(u' \prod_{i \in \mathcal{U}} u_i \right)^{r_u}, g^{r_u} \right) = (\mathsf{psk}^{(1)}, \mathsf{psk}^{(2)})$$

Set-User-Keys: User selects a secret value $x \leftarrow_R \mathbb{Z}_p$ as his/her secret key usk, and computes his/her public key as $\mathsf{upk} = \hat{e}(g_1, g_2)^x$.

Sign: To sign a message $m \in \{0,1\}^*$, the signer with identity ID, partial secret key $(\mathsf{psk}^{(1)}, \mathsf{psk}^{(2)})$, and secret key usk and compute $\mathsf{m} = H_m(m)$. Let $\mathsf{m}[i]$ be the i-th bit of m and let $\mathcal{M} \subset \{1, \ldots, n_m\}$ be the set of indices i such that $\mathsf{m}[i] = 1$. A signature of u on m is constructed by picking $r_\pi, r_m \leftarrow_R \mathbb{Z}_p$, and computing $U = u' \prod_{i \in \mathcal{U}} u_i$ and

$$\sigma = ((\mathsf{psk}^{(1)})^{\mathsf{usk}} (U)^{r_\pi} \left(m' \prod_{j \in \mathcal{M}} m_j \right)^{r_m}, (\mathsf{psk}^{(2)})^{\mathsf{usk}} g^{r_\pi}, g^{r_m})$$

$$= (V, R_\pi, R_m)$$

Verify: Given a signature $\sigma = (V, R_\pi, R_m)$ for an identity ID and public key upk on a message m, a verifier first computes $\mathsf{m} = H_m(m)$, $U = u' \prod_{i \in \mathcal{U}} u_i$ and checks whether $(\mathsf{upk})^p = 1_{\mathbb{G}_2}$ and $\hat{e}(V, g) = \mathsf{upk} \cdot \hat{e}(u' \prod_{i \in \mathcal{U}} u_i, R_\pi) \cdot \hat{e}(m' \prod_{j \in \mathcal{M}} m_j, R_m)$.

4.4.1.3 Security Analysis

Theorem 4.1 (*Type I Existential Unforgeability*). *The CLS scheme is (ϵ, t)-existential unforgeable against a type I adversary with an advantage of at most ϵ and runs in time at most t, assuming that the (ϵ', t')-NGBDH assumption holds in $\mathbb{G}_1$, where $\epsilon' \geq \epsilon/16(q_e + q_s)q_s(n_u + 1)(n_m + 1)$ and $t' = t + O((q_e n_u + q_s(n_u + n_m))\rho + (q_k + q_e + q_s)\tau)$, where q_e is the number of queries made to the oracle **Partial-Private-Key-Extract**, q_s the number of queries made to the **Sign** oracle, q_k the number of queries made to the oracles **Secret-Value-Extract** and **Create-User** altogether, and ρ and τ the time for a multiplication and an exponentiation in $\mathbb{G}_1$, respectively.*

Proof 4.1 *The intuition behind Theorem 4.1 can be found in Figure 4.6. The algorithm $\mathcal{C}$ will be given a group $\mathbb{G}_1$ of prime order p with generator g and elements $g^a, g^b \in \mathbb{G}_1$, where a, b are selected uniformly at random from $\mathbb{Z}_p^*$. To be able to use $\mathcal{A}_1$ to output (g^{abc}, g^c), $\mathcal{C}$ must be able to simulate a challenger for $\mathcal{A}_1$. Such a simulation can be created in the following way:*

Initial: *$\mathcal{C}$ sets $l_u = 2(q_e + q_s)$ and $l_m = 2q_s$ and randomly chooses two integers k_u and k_m, with $0 \leq k_u \leq n_u$ and $0 \leq k_m \leq n_m$. We will assume that $l_u(n_u + 1) < p$, and $l_m(n_m + 1) < p$ for the given values of $q_e, q_s, q_k, n_u,$ and n_m. The simulator then chooses an integer $x' \leftarrow_R \mathbb{Z}_{l_u}$ and a vector (x_i) of length n_u, with $x_i \leftarrow_R \mathbb{Z}_{l_u}$ for all i. Likewise, it chooses another integer $z' \leftarrow_R \mathbb{Z}_{l_m}$ and a vector (z_j) of length n_m, with $z_j \leftarrow_R \mathbb{Z}_{l_m}$ for all j. Lastly, $\mathcal{C}$ chooses two integers $y', w' \leftarrow_R \mathbb{Z}_p$ and two vectors, (y_i) and (w_j), of length n_u and n_m, respectively, with $y_i, w_j \leftarrow_R \mathbb{Z}_p$ for all i and j. Two pairs of functions are defined for an identity u and a message m, respectively:*

$$F(u) = x' + \sum_{i \in \mathcal{U}} x_i - l_u k_u \qquad J(u) = y' + \sum_{i \in \mathcal{U}} y_i$$

$$K(m) = z' + \sum_{j \in \mathcal{M}} z_j - l_m k_m \qquad L(m) = w' + \sum_{j \in \mathcal{M}} w_j$$

*$\mathcal{C}$ assigns $g_1 = g^a$, $g_2 = g^b$, $u' = g_2^{-l_u k_u + x'} g^{y'}$, $u_i = g_2^{x_i} g^{y_i}$ $(1 \leq i \leq n_u)$, $m' = g_2^{-l_m k_m + z'} g^{w'}$, and $m_j = g_2^{z_j} g^{w_j}$ $(1 \leq j \leq n_m)$, and the system parameters **params**$=(g_1, g_2, u', (u_i), m', (m_j))$ are sent to $\mathcal{A}_1$. Moreover, this assignment of parameters means that the master secret will be $g_2^{\alpha} = g_2^a = g^{ab}$ and we have the following equations:*

$$U = u' \prod_{i \in \mathcal{U}} u_i = g_2^{F(u)} g^{J(u)} \text{ and } m' \prod_{i \in \mathcal{M}} m_i = g_2^{K(m)} g^{L(m)}$$

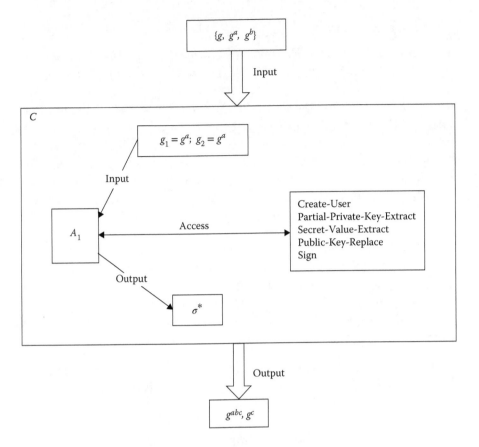

Figure 4.6 Intuition for Theorem 4.1.

Attack: *C simulates all oracles as follows:*

Create-User Oracle: On input of an identity ID and the user partial key psk_{ID}, *C looks up its list L to find the corresponding entry. If it does not exist, C runs the Set-User-Keys algorithm to generate a secret and public key pair. It then stores* $(ID, psk_{ID}, upk_{ID}, usk_{ID})$ *into a list L. In both cases,* upk_{ID} *is returned.*

Partial-Private-Key-Extract Oracle: Consider a query for the private key of an identity ID (C computes $u = H_u(ID)$*). C does not know the master secret, but assuming* $F(u) \neq 0 \bmod p$*, it can construct a private key by choosing* $r_u \leftarrow_R \mathbb{Z}_p$ *and computing* $(psk^{(1)}, psk^{(2)}) = (g_1^{-J(u)/F(u)} (u' \prod_{i \in U} u_i)^{r_u}, g_1^{-1/F(u)} g^{r_u})$. *It can* *be verified that defining* $(\mathsf{psk}^{(1)}, \mathsf{psk}^{(2)})$ *in this manner yields a valid user partial key of u assuming* $\tilde{r}_u = r_u - a/F(u)$, *since*

$$\mathsf{psk}^{(1)} = g_1^{-\frac{J(u)}{F(u)}} \left(u' \prod_{i \in U} u_i \right)^{r_u} = g_2^a \left(g_2^{F(u)} g^{J(u)} \right)^{-a/F(u)} \left(g_2^{F(u)} g^{J(u)} \right)^{r_u}$$

$$= g_2^a \left(g_2^{F(u)} g^{J(u)} \right)^{r_u - a/F(u)}$$

$$= g_2^a \left(u' \prod_{i \in U} u_i \right)^{\tilde{r}_u}$$

and $\mathsf{psk}^{(2)} = g_1^{-1/F(u)} g^{r_u} = g^{r_u - a/F(u)} = g^{\tilde{r}_u}$. *So all the private keys computed by* $\mathcal{C}$ *will be indistinguishable from the keys generated by a true challenger to* $\mathcal{A}_1$. *However, the above simulation will abort if* $F(u) = 0 \bmod p$. *Given the assumption* $l_u(n_u+1) < p$, *which implies that* $0 \le l_u k_u < p$ *and* $0 \le x' + \sum_{i \in U} x_i < p$, *it is easy to find that* $F(u) = 0 \bmod p$ *implies* $F(u) = 0 \bmod l_u$. *Therefore,* $F(u) \ne 0 \bmod l_u$ *implies* $F(u) \ne 0 \bmod p$.

Secret-Value-Extract *Oracle: Upon receiving a query for a public key of an identity* ID, $\mathcal{C}$ *looks up* $\mathcal{L}$ *to find the corresponding entry. If it does not exist,* $\mathcal{C}$ *runs* **Set-User-Keys** *to generate a secret and public key pair. It stores the key pair in* $\mathcal{L}$ *and returns the secret key* $\mathsf{usk}_{\mathsf{ID}}$.

Public-Key-Replace *Oracle: Upon receiving a query for a public key replace oracle request of an identity* ID, $\mathcal{C}$ *looks up* $\mathcal{L}$ *to replace the corresponding entry. If it does not exist,* $\mathcal{C}$ *creates a new entry for this identity.*

Sign *Oracle: Consider a query for a signature of* ID *on* m. $\mathcal{C}$ *first checks from* $\mathcal{L}$ *whether the public key of* ID *has been replaced or not. If it has been replaced, it aborts. Otherwise, it computes* $u = H_u(\mathsf{ID})$. *If* $F(u) \ne 0 \bmod l_u$, $\mathcal{C}$ *just constructs a partial secret key as in the* ***Partial-Private-Key-Extract*** *query, and then it checks from* $\mathcal{L}$ *whether the secret key of* ID *has been created or not. If it is not been created, then it runs the* ***Set-User-Keys*** *algorithm and stores the secret/public key pair in* $\mathcal{L}$. *If it has been created, it just uses the* ***Sign*** *algorithm to create a signature on* ID *and* m.

*If $F(u) = 0 \bmod l_u$, $\mathcal{C}$ will try to construct a signature in a similar way to the construction of a private key in a **Partial-Private-Key-Extract** query. Assume $K(m) \neq 0 \bmod l_m$. Using the argument mentioned above, it implies $K(m) \neq 0 \bmod p$ provided that $l_m(n_m + 1) < p$. The signature can be constructed by first picking $r_\pi, r_m \leftarrow_R \mathbb{Z}_p$, getting the secret key x from $\mathcal{L}$ (if it has not been created, run the **Set-User-Keys** algorithm first), and computing $\sigma = ((U)^{r_\pi} g_1^{-L(m)/K(m)x}(m' \prod_{j\in\mathcal{M}} m_j)^{r_m x}, g^{r_\pi}, g_1^{-1/K(m)} g^{r_m x}) = (g_2^{ax}(U)^{r_\pi}(m' \prod_{j\in\mathcal{M}} m_j)^{\tilde{r}_m}, g^{r_\pi}, g^{\tilde{r}_m})$, where $\tilde{r}_m = r_m x - a/K(m)x$. If $K(m) = 0 \bmod l_m$, the simulator will simply abort.*

The correctness can be shown as below:

$$
\begin{aligned}
V &= (U)^{r_\pi} g_1^{-\frac{L(m)}{K(m)}x}\left(m' \prod_{j\in\mathcal{M}} m_j\right)^{r_m x} \\
&= (U)^{r_\pi} g_1^{-\frac{L(m)}{K(m)}x}\left(g_2^{K(m)} g^{L(m)}\right)^{r_m x} \\
&= (U)^{r_\pi} g^{-\frac{axL(m)}{K(m)}}\left(g_2^{K(m)} g^{L(m)}\right)^{\frac{ax}{K(m)}} \\
&\quad \times \left(g_2^{K(m)} g^{L(m)}\right)^{-\frac{ax}{K(m)}}\left(g_2^{K(m)} g^{L(m)}\right)^{r_m x} \\
&= (U)^{r_\pi} g^{-\frac{axL(m)}{K(m)}} g^{abx} g^{\frac{axL(m)}{K(m)}}\left(g_2^{K(m)} g^{L(m)}\right)^{\tilde{r}_m} \\
&= (U)^{r_\pi} g_2^{ax}\left(m' \prod_{j\in\mathcal{M}} m_j\right)^{\tilde{r}_m}
\end{aligned}
$$

Forgery: *If $\mathcal{C}$ does not abort as a consequence of one of the queries above, $\mathcal{A}_1$ will, with a probability of at least ϵ, return an identity u^*, a message m^*, and valid forgery $\sigma_i^* = (V, R_\pi, R_m)$ on m^*. If $F(u^*) \neq 0 \bmod p$ or $K(m^*) \neq 0 \bmod p$, then $\mathcal{C}$ will abort. If, on the other hand, $F(u^*) = 0 \bmod p$ and $K(m^*) = 0 \bmod p$, $\mathcal{C}$ computes and outputs*

$$
\frac{V}{R_\pi^{J(u^*)} R_m^{L(m^*)}} = \frac{g_2^{ax}(U)^{r_\pi}(m' \prod_{k\in M} m_k)^{r_m}}{g^{J(u^*)r_\pi} g^{L(m^*)r_m}} = g^{abx}
$$

$\mathcal{C}$ outputs (g^{abx}, g^x) as the solution to the NGBDH problem instance.

Probability Analysis. For the simulation to complete without aborting, we require the following conditions to be fulfilled:

1. All **Secret-Value-Extract** queries on an identity ID have $F(u) \neq 0 \bmod l_u$, where $u = H_u(ID)$.

2. All **Sign** queries (ID, m) will either have $F(u) \neq 0 \bmod l_u$ or $K(m) \neq 0 \bmod l_m$, where $m = H_m(m)$,

3. $F(u^*) = 0 \bmod l_u$ and $K(m^*) = 0 \bmod l_m$.

In order to make the analysis simpler, we will bound the probability of a subcase of this event. Let $u_1, \ldots, u_{q_I}$ be the identities appearing in either **Partial-Private-Key-Extract** oracle queries or **Sign** oracle queries not involving the challenge identity and let $m_1, \ldots, m_{q_M}$ be the messages in the sign queries involving the challenge identity u^*. Clearly, we will have $q_I \leq q_e + q_s$ and $q_M \leq q_s$. Define the events A_i, A^*, B_j, B^* as

$A_i : F(u_i) \neq 0 \bmod l_u$, where $i = 1, \ldots, q_I \quad A^* : F(u^*) = 0 \bmod p$
$B_j : K(m_j) \neq 0 \bmod l_m$, where $j = 1, \ldots, q_M \quad B^* : K(m^*) = 0 \bmod p$

The probability of C not aborting is $Pr[\text{not abort}] \geq Pr[(\bigwedge_{i=1}^{q_I} A_i \wedge A^*) \wedge (\bigwedge_{j=1}^{q_M} B_j \wedge B^*)]$. It is easy to see that the events $(\bigwedge_{i=1}^{q_I} A_i \wedge A^*)$ and $(\bigwedge_{j=1}^{q_M} B_j \wedge B^*)$ are independent.

The assumption $l_u(n_u + 1) < p$ implies that if $F(u) = 0 \bmod p$ then $F(u) = 0 \bmod l_u$. In addition, it also implies that if $F(u) = 0 \bmod l_u$, there will be a unique choice of k_u with $0 \leq k_u \leq n_u$ such that $F(u) = 0 \bmod p$. Since k_u, x' and vector (x_i) of length n_u are randomly chosen, we have

$$Pr[A^*] = Pr[F(u^*) = 0 \bmod p \wedge F(u^*) = 0 \bmod l_u]$$
$$= Pr[F(u^*) = 0 \bmod l_u]Pr[F(u^*) = 0 \bmod p | F(u^*) = 0 \bmod l_u]$$
$$= \frac{1}{l_u} \frac{1}{n_u + 1}$$

On the other hand, we have $Pr[\bigwedge_{i=1}^{q_I} A_i | A^*] = 1 - Pr[\bigvee_{i=1}^{q_I} \overline{A}_i | A^*] \geq 1 - \sum_{i=1}^{q_I} Pr[\overline{A}_i | A^*]$, where $\overline{A}_i$ denotes the event $F(u_i) = 0 \bmod l_u$.

If F is evaluated on two different identities, u_{i1} and u_{i2}, then the sums appearing in $F(u_{i1})$ and $F(u_{i2})$ will differ in at least one randomly chosen value, and the events $F(u_{i1}) = 0 \bmod l_u$ and $F(u_{i2}) =$

0 mod l_u will be independent. Also since the events A_i and A^* are independent for any i, we have $Pr\left[\overline{A_i}|A^*\right] = 1/l_u$. Hence , we have

$$Pr\left[\bigwedge_{i=1}^{q_I} A_i \wedge A^*\right] = Pr[A^*]Pr\left[\bigwedge_{i=1}^{q_I} A_i|A^*\right] \geq \frac{1}{l_u(n_u+1)}\left(1 - \frac{q_e+q_s}{l_u}\right)$$

and setting $l_u = 2(q_e+q_s)$ as in the simulation gives $Pr[\bigwedge_{i=1}^{q_I} A_i \wedge A^*] \geq 1/4(q_e+q_s)(n_u+1)$

A similar analysis for the sign queries gives the result $Pr[\overline{B_j}|B^*] \geq 1/4q_s(n_m+1)$ and we get that $Pr[not\ abort] \geq Pr[\overline{A_i}|A^*]Pr[\overline{B_j}|B^*] \geq 1/16(q_e+q_s)q_s(n_u+1)(n_m+1)$

If the simulation does not abort, $\mathcal{A}_1$ will produce a forged signature with probability at least ϵ. Thus $\mathcal{C}$ can solve for the NGBDH problem instance with probability $\epsilon' \geq \epsilon/16(q_e+q_s)q_s(n_u+1)(n_m+1)$.

The time complexity of $\mathcal{C}$ is dominated by the exponentiation and multiplication operations for large values of n_u and n_m performed in the partial secret key extraction and sign queries, There are $O(n_u)$ and $O(n_u+n_m)$ multiplications and $O(1)$ and $O(1)$ exponentiations in the partial secret key extraction and sign queries, respectively. There is $O(1)$ exponentiation in the public and secret key queries. The time complexity of $\mathcal{C}$ is $t + O((q_e n_u + q_s(n_u+n_m))\rho + (q_k + q_e + q_s)$.

Theorem 4.2 *(Type II Existential Unforgeability). The CLS scheme is (ϵ, t)-existential unforgeable against a type II adversary with an advantage of at most ϵ and runs in time at most t, assuming that the (ϵ', t')-Many-DH assumption holds in $\mathbb{G}_1$, where $\epsilon' \geq \epsilon/16(q_e+q_s)q_s q_k(n_u+1)(n_m+1)$, and $t' = t+O(q_s(n_u+n_m)\rho+(q_k+q_s)\tau)$, where q_s is the number of queries made to the **Sign** oracle, q_k the number of queries made to the oracles **Secret-Value-Extract** and **Create-User** altogether, and ρ and τ the time for a multiplication and an exponentiation in $\mathbb{G}_1$, respectively.*

The proof of this theorem is similar to that of Theorem 4.1 and thus is omitted. Interested readers can refer to [60,107] for the details.

4.4.2 Yuan–Wang CLS

In [135], Yuan and Wang proposed a concrete CLE scheme and showed that it is proven secure against the malicious-but-passive KGC attacks in the standard model. The basic reason their scheme can resist the malicious-but-passive KGC attacks depends on the wise construction of the user public key. It consists of the following algorithms:

Setup: The KGC chooses two cyclic groups $\mathbb{G}$ and $\mathbb{G}_T$ of prime order p, a random generator g of $\mathbb{G}$, and a bilinear map $\hat{e} : \mathbb{G} \times \mathbb{G} \to \mathbb{G}_T$. It also randomly chooses $s \in \mathbb{Z}_p^*$ and sets $g_1 = g^s$. Furthermore, it chooses four random elements $u', m_0, m_1, v \in \mathbb{G}$, and a random vector $\mathbf{U} = (u_i) \in \mathbb{G}^n$. $H_0 : \{0,1\}^* \to \{0,1\}^n$ and $H : \{0,1\}^* \times \mathbb{G}^6 \to \mathbb{Z}_p^*$ are two collision-resistant hash functions. Define a function $f(Q)$ for a point Q in $\mathbb{G}$ as follows. If the x-coordinate of Q is odd, then $f(Q) = 1$; else, $f(Q) = 0$. The public parameters are params $= \{\mathbb{G}, \mathbb{G}_T, \hat{e}, g, g_1, u', m_0, m_1, v, \mathbf{U}, H_0, H, f\}$ and the master secret key master-key is g^{s^2}.

Extract-Partial-Private-Key: Given an identity ID, the KGC first computes $H_0(\mathsf{ID})$. Let $u[i]$ denote the i-th bit of $u = H_0(\mathsf{ID})$ and $\mathcal{U} \subset \{1, \ldots, n\}$ be the set of indices i such that $u[i] = 1$. The KGC randomly selects $r \in \mathbb{Z}_p$, and computes $\mathsf{psk}_{\mathsf{ID}} = (\mathsf{psk}_{\mathsf{ID},1}, \mathsf{psk}_{\mathsf{ID},2}) = (g_1^s \cdot (u' \prod_{i \in \mathcal{U}_{\mathsf{ID}}} u_i)^r, g^r)$ as the partial secret key associated with the user ID.

Set-Public-Key: By randomly choosing a secret value $x_{\mathsf{ID}} \in \mathbb{Z}_p^*$, the user ID computes his/her public key $\mathsf{upk}_{\mathsf{ID}} = (g_1^{x_{\mathsf{ID}}}, v^{1/x_{\mathsf{ID}}}) = (\mathsf{upk}_{\mathsf{ID},1}, \mathsf{upk}_{\mathsf{ID},2})$.

Set-Private-Key: Featured with a random chosen $r_u \in \mathbb{Z}_p^*$ and partial private key $\mathsf{psk}_{\mathsf{ID}}$, the user ID computes his/her full private key $\mathsf{usk}_{\mathsf{ID}} = (\mathsf{usk}_{\mathsf{ID},1}, \mathsf{usk}_{\mathsf{ID},2}) = (\mathsf{psk}_{\mathsf{ID},1}^{x_{\mathsf{ID}}^2} \cdot (u' \prod_{i \in \mathcal{U}_{\mathsf{ID}}} u_i)^{r_u}, \mathsf{psk}_{\mathsf{ID},2}^{x_{\mathsf{ID}}^2} \cdot g^{r_u})$.

Sign: Given a message m to be signed, the signer associated with identity ID randomly chooses $r_m \in \mathbb{Z}_p^*$ and computes $b = f(\mathsf{usk}_{\mathsf{ID},2})$ and $h = H(m, \mathsf{ID}, \mathsf{upk}_{\mathsf{ID}}, \mathsf{usk}_{\mathsf{ID},2}, g^{r_m}, m_b, v)$. Then, the signer computes signature $\sigma = (\sigma_1, \sigma_2, \sigma_3)$ with the support of full private key $\mathsf{usk}_{\mathsf{ID}}$ as follows:

$$\sigma_1 = \mathsf{usk}_{\mathsf{ID},1}(\mathsf{upk}_{\mathsf{ID},2}^h m_b)^{r_m}, \sigma_2 = \mathsf{usk}_{\mathsf{ID},2}, \sigma_3 = g^{r_m}$$

Verify: After receiving a signature $\sigma = (\sigma_1, \sigma_2, \sigma_3)$ on message m under the identity ID and user public key $\mathsf{upk}_{\mathsf{ID}}$, the verifier performs the following steps:

1. Verifies whether

$$\hat{e}(\mathsf{upk}_{\mathsf{ID},1}, \mathsf{upk}_{\mathsf{ID},2}) = \hat{e}(g_1, v)$$

If not, it then provides the output and aborts.

2. Computes $b = f(\sigma_2)$ and $h = H(m, \mathsf{ID}, \mathsf{upk}_{\mathsf{ID}}, \sigma_2, \sigma_3, m_b, v)$.

3. Verifies whether

$$\hat{e}(\sigma_1, g) =$$

$$\hat{e}\left(\mathsf{upk}_{ID,1}, \mathsf{upk}_{\mathsf{ID},1}\right) \hat{e}\left(u' \prod_{i \in \mathcal{U}_{\mathsf{ID}}} u_i, \sigma_2\right) \cdot \hat{e}(\mathsf{upk}_{\mathsf{ID},2}^{h} m_b, \sigma_3)$$

If the equation holds, 1 is returned. Otherwise, 0 is returned.

The proof of this scheme is similar to the security proof in [107] and thus is omitted. Interested readers can refer to [135] for details.

III

CL-PKC in Random Oracle Models

CHAPTER 5

Random Oracle Models

5.1 RANDOM ORACLE METHODOLOGY

In the previous two chapters, constructions of secure certificateless encryption (CLE) and certificateless signature (CLS) schemes in the standard model are discussed and analyzed. However, these schemes suffer from the following clear disadvantages:

- The security of these schemes rests on a relatively small set of strong complexity assumptions (e.g., 3-Decisional Diffie–Hellman (DDH) [54], Squ-Computational Diffie–Hellman (CDH) [135], nonpairing-based generalized bilinear Diffie–Hellman (NGBDH) [60,107], and Many-DH [60,107]). In particular, none of these schemes is constructed based on the hardness of well-studied assumptions such as factoring, discrete logarithm assumptions, or even the computational Diffie–Hellman assumption.

- The existing secure schemes in the standard model are currently regarded as not being efficient *enough* for most practical cases. Notably, the computational complexity and the size of the public parameters depend linearly on the number of bits of identity and messages to be involved. This is especially true compared to various "heuristically secure" schemes (i.e., schemes whose security has not been broken thus far) that are much more efficient than these provably secure schemes in the standard model.

One approach to eliminating these disadvantages is to introduce new number-theoretic assumptions and in turn design more efficient schemes or maybe reduce the security of the existing efficient schemes on those assumptions. Despite this approach being certainly fascinating, we are still left in practice with the issue that a new assumption turns out to be not as reasonable as it appeared on first sight. Furthermore, it is also unclear how to determine when the new assumption should be introduced to prove the security of the existing schemes. Thus, it is desirable to prove the security of the schemes on older and widely accepted problems rather than newer ones.

Another approach to addressing these issues has been hugely successful in spite of the fact that the soundness of this approach has yet to be rigorously validated. This mechanism incorporates a idealized model, named the random oracle model [75,149–151], to prove the security of cryptographic schemes. In the random oracle model, a public random function H is assumed to be accessed by all parties to obtain $H(x)$ with the input of any desired value x, and parties needs to interact with an oracle computing H instead of computing H by themselves for any input. The oracle to compute H can be implemented by maintaining an initially empty table with tuples $\{(x_i, y_i)\}$. On input of a query x, this oracle first checks whether x has been queried already and returns the corresponding y_i if $x = x_i$ for some i. Otherwise, this oracle selects a random string y with appropriate length as the answer and stores the item (x, y) in its table to keep consistency. In this way, the same value can be outputted by the oracle once the same input is queried again. Furthermore, queries sent to the oracle from an honest party are assumed to be private and will not be disclosed to any adversary.

The methodology in which the random oracle model is adopted to design and validate cryptographic primitives is described as follows:

1. A cryptographic scheme is constructed and proven secure in the random oracle model under some relatively weak cryptographic assumptions. That is to say, this scheme is designed with the assumption that the idealized random oracle exists in the real world.

2. In view of the fact that no random oracle is available in practice, the random oracle is instantiated with a suitable (or sufficiently good) cryptographic hash function (such as Secure Hash Algorithm 1 [SHA-1] and Message-Digest Algorithm [MD5]) to implement this scheme.

A difficulty in the above methodology is that there is no theoretical benchmark to validate whether a hash function is "sufficiently good" at simulating a random oracle. Thus, proofs of security associated with a given scheme in the random oracle model cannot be regarded as proofs that apply to any "real-world" instantiation of this scheme. A detailed discussion about how the random oracle can be instantiated with an appropriate hash function is really beyond the scope of this book. Interested readers can refer to [75,149–151] for details.

5.2   SECURITY PROOFS IN THE RANDOM ORACLE MODEL

We describe chosen-plaintext attack (CPA)-secure RSA encryption in the random oracle model as an example to show why the random oracle model is so useful in offering security of cryptographic schemes.

Intuitively speaking, the random oracle model is applied in the following way: Given an adversary $\mathcal{A}$ breaking some scheme/violating some cryptographic assumption in the random oracle model, an algorithm $\mathcal{C}$ is constructed with the support of adversary $\mathcal{A}$ to violate some cryptographic assumption by means of simulating the random oracle for $\mathcal{A}$. The algorithm $\mathcal{C}$ obtains three advantages compared to $\mathcal{A}$: (1) $\mathcal{C}$ observes the queries that $\mathcal{A}$ makes to the random oracle; (2) $\mathcal{C}$ in turn answers these queries in any manner it likes as long as these queries have been answered in a "random-looking" way; and (3) the value of $H(x)$ for any input x not explicitly queried by $\mathcal{A}$ is completely random from the perspective of $\mathcal{A}$.

One quick example of proofs is shown to provide the reader with enough intuition so that the later proofs in the random oracle model can be easily understood.

For example, we consider the CPA-secure RSA encryption to be secure in the random oracle model (see Table 5.1): $\mathcal{C}$ carries out the GenRSA(1^n) algorithm to generate an RSA key (N, e), chooses random $m \in \{0,1\}^\ell$ and $r \in \mathbb{Z}_N^*$, and sends $(N, e, r^e \bmod N, H(r) \oplus m)$ to the adversary $\mathcal{A}$, where $H : \mathbb{Z}_N^* \to \{0,1\}^\ell$ is considered a random oracle. It is noted that no probabilistic polynomial time (PPT) adversary $\mathcal{A}$ can obtain any information about m under the RSA assumption except with negligible probability. The only way $\mathcal{A}$ can obtain anything about m is by explicitly querying the random oracle on the input r due to the fact that $H(r)$ is completely random from the perspective of $\mathcal{A}$ unless $\mathcal{A}$ has already queried H at this point. In other words, $\mathcal{A}$ learns no

TABLE 5.1 Chosen-Plaintext Attack (CPA)-Secure RSA Encryption in the Random Oracle Model

---

Let GenRSA be a PPT algorithm that, on input 1^n, outputs a modulus N as the product of two n-bit primes e and d satisfying $ed = 1 \bmod \phi(N)$, and let $H : \mathbb{Z}_N^* \to \{0,1\}^\ell$ be a function for ℓ, an arbitrary polynomial.

Key generation. The GenRSA(1^n) algorithm is performed to compute (N, e, d) such that N is of length $2n$ and elements of $\mathbb{Z}_N^*$ are represented by $2n$-bit strings. After that, $\langle N, e \rangle$ is published as the public key and (N, d) is kept as a secret key.

Encryption. On input of a message $m \in \{0,1\}^\ell$ to be encrypted under the public key $\langle N, e \rangle$, this algorithm chooses random $r \leftarrow \mathbb{Z}_N^*$ and outputs the ciphertext as follows:

$$\langle [r^e \bmod N], H(r) \oplus m \rangle$$

Decryption. On input of the ciphertext $\langle c_1, c_2 \rangle$ and the private key $\langle N, d \rangle$, this algorithm computes $r = [c_1^d \bmod N]$ and then outputs the message $H(r) \oplus c_2$.

---

information about m except with probability ε, where ε represents the probability that $\mathcal{A}$ does indeed query $H(r)$.

Also, $\mathcal{A}$ can query the random oracle $H : \mathbb{Z}_N^* \to \mathbb{Z}_N^*$ at any sequence of points $x_1, \ldots, x_\ell \in \mathbb{Z}_N^*$ (we assume without loss of generality that these are distinct), receiving in return the output values $k_1 = H(x_1), \ldots, k_\ell = H(x_\ell)$; the challenger then gives to $\mathcal{A}$ the values $k_i^{1/e} \bmod N$ for all i (assume the challenger knows the factorization of N and so can compute these values). We claim that $\mathcal{A}$ still cannot compute $k^{1/e} \bmod N$ except with negligible probability. To see this, construct the following adversary $\mathcal{C}$, which computes $k^{1/e} \bmod N$ with the same probability at $\mathcal{A}$, but without any additional "help" from the challenger:

Algorithm $\mathcal{C}$: The algorithm is given (N, e, c_1) as input, and its goal is to compute $c_1^{1/e} \bmod N$:

1. Choose random $k^* \leftarrow \{0,1\}^\ell$. ($H(r)$ is implicitly set as k^* such that $r^e \bmod N \overset{\text{def}}{=} c_1$. Meanwhile, r has not been disclosed to $\mathcal{C}$.)

2. Run the algorithm $\mathcal{A}$ on input of the public key $pk = \langle N, e \rangle$. Maintain an initially empty table with pairs of strings $(\cdot, \cdot)$. On input of the query $H(x_i)$ from $\mathcal{A}$, $\mathcal{C}$ responds as follows:

   - If there is an entry (x_i, k_i) in the table, return k_i as the answer.

   - If $x_i^e = c_1 \bmod N$, return k^* as the answer and insert the item (x_i, k^*) in the table.

   - Otherwise, choose a random $k_i \leftarrow \{0,1\}^\ell$, return k_i to $\mathcal{A}$ as the answer, and insert the item (x_i, k_i) in the table.

3. After deciding that all queries are resolved, $\mathcal{A}$ outputs message $m_0, m_1 \in \{0,1\}^\ell$.

4. Choose random $b \leftarrow \{0,1\}$ and set $c_2 := k^* \oplus m_b$. Give $\mathcal{A}$ the ciphertext $\langle c_1, c_2 \rangle$.

5. After $\mathcal{A}$ outputs its guess b', let $x_1, \ldots, x_p$ be the list of all oracle queries made by $\mathcal{A}$. If there exists an i for which $x_i^e = c_1 \bmod N$, output x_i.

The trick behind the random oracle model is that $\mathcal{C}$ perfectly simulates the random oracle queries in the example of $\mathcal{A}$ in such a way that $\mathcal{C}$ chooses the corresponding inverses $x_i = k_i^{1/e} \bmod N$ on the input k_i. Thus, the view of $\mathcal{A}$ in the example is identically distributed to its perspective in the real experiment, and so $\mathcal{C}$ outputs the correct inverse of k_i with exactly the same probability with which $\mathcal{A}$ breaks the security of the CPA-secure RSA encryption scheme.

5.3 CONTROVERSY ABOUT THE RANDOM ORACLE MODEL

Despite the proofs shown in the previous example being rather straightforward, they rely heavily on the existence of the random oracle model, and thus cannot be converted to the "real world" when the random oracle H is instantiated with any concrete hash function. In the previous two examples, the proof relies on the assumption that the output value $H(x_i)$ is completely random provided x_i has not been explicitly queried to the oracle, and on the assumption of $\mathcal{C}$'s ability to observe the queries sent from $\mathcal{A}$. These assumptions are not reasonable for any concrete function H in the real world since $\mathcal{A}$ may be able to evaluate

$H(x_i)$ by itself using the hash function other than by explicitly making a query to $\mathcal{C}$, who in turn computes H. When $\mathcal{A}$ is given a function to compute H, the output value $H(x_i)$ is no longer random from the view of $\mathcal{A}$. To make matters worse, there is no way for $\mathcal{C}$ to falsify the items corresponding to these queries and obtain an inverse of k_i once $\mathcal{A}$ no longer needs to make explicit queries to compute $H(x_i)$.

In the two-step methodology to designing schemes in the random oracle model, a scheme is first designed and proven secure in the random oracle model and then this scheme is in turn instantiated in the real world with the random oracle simulated by a sufficiently good hash function. Unfortunately, a more general problem with the random oracle model is identified in this methodology such that it is nontrivial to validate whether a given concrete hash function is good enough to simulate a random oracle. Therefore, a proof of security in the random oracle model cannot be translated into a proof of security in the real world. In fact, a number of negative results concerning the use of the random oracle model are known [76,77]. The major criticism on the soundness of the random oracle model was initially suggested by Canetti et al. [77], who constructed a secure scheme in the random oracle model and showed the insecurity of this scheme for any concrete instantiation of the random oracle. Thus, a proof of security in the random oracle model is generally regarded as less desirable than a proof of security in the so-called standard model that does not depend on random oracles.

Despite the theoretical problems and the negative results discussed with the random oracle model, our confidence in the random oracle assumption is unshaken [3,42,151] due to the following reasons:

- A potential weakness can arise in the secure scheme in a random oracle model only from the weaknesses of the hash function used to instantiate the random oracle. Correspondingly, the only way to break the converted scheme is to break the hash function involved. In this way, the security of the scheme can be trusted if the hash function is good enough.

- On the other hand, the existing attack associated with the scheme proven secure in the random oracle model is contrived and bizarre from the perspective of real-world cryptography. This factor gives us confidence to trust the usefulness of the random oracle model in designing schemes in practice.

CHAPTER 6

CLE, CLS, and CL-AKE Secure in Random Oracle Models

6.1 INTRODUCTION

With the support of the random oracle model, numerous efficient and natural constructions have been proposed with provable security in the field of certificateless public-key encryption (CL-PKC). We begin by describing the first certificateless encryption (CLE) scheme invented by Al-Riyami and Paterson [17] in their seminar work based on bilinear pairing. We then introduce Zhang and Zhang's [138] pairing-based certificateless signature (CLS) scheme, which is more efficient than the other existing CLS schemes secure against a super type I/II adversary. Finally, we focus on the construction of certificateless authenticated key agreement (CL-AKA) by formalizing the security model of two-party CL-AKA and describing an efficient and practical pairing-based CL-AKA protocol [21], where each party only needs to perform one pairing operation and five multiplications to share a session key.

6.2 AL-RIYAMI–PATERSON CLE

Similar to [9], a pair of CLE schemes are proposed in [17] such that the first scheme is constructed by extending the basic Boneh–Franklin identity-based encryption (IBE) scheme and the second scheme is in turn an analogue of the full Boneh–Franklin IBE scheme. Furthermore, the second CLE scheme is proved to achieve indistinguishability under chosen-ciphertext attack (IND-CCA) security assuming the hardness of the generalized bilinear Diffie–Hellman problem (GBDHP) defined as follows.

Definition 6.1 Let $\hat{e}$: $\mathbb{G}_1 \times \mathbb{G}_1 \rightarrow \mathbb{G}_2$ be a symmetric bilinear pairing defined in Section 2.2.4 and P be a generator of group $\mathbb{G}_1$. The generalized bilinear Diffie–Hellman problem (GBDHP) defined in $< \mathbb{G}_1, \mathbb{G}_2, e >$ is described as follows: Given $< P, aP, bP, cP >$ with uniformly random choices of $a, b, c \in \mathbb{Z}_q^*$, the goal of a GBDHP breaker is to output a pair $< Q \in \mathbb{G}_1^*, e(P, Q)^{abc} \in \mathbb{G}_2 >$. We define the advantage of $\mathcal{A}$ as $Adv(\mathcal{A})$, which is assumed to be negligible.

6.2.1 Concrete Construction

6.2.1.1 Basic CLE Scheme

The first basic CLE scheme consists of the following seven algorithms:

Setup: This algorithm runs as follows:

1. Let $\hat{e} : \mathbb{G}_1 \times \mathbb{G}_1 \rightarrow \mathbb{G}_2$ be a symmetric bilinear pairing defined in Section 2.2.4.

2. Choose an arbitrary generator $P \in \mathbb{G}_1$.

3. Select s uniformly at random from $\mathbb{Z}_q^*$ as **master-key** and set $P_{\text{pub}} = sP$.

4. Choose cryptographic hash functions $H_1 : \{0,1\}^* \rightarrow \mathbb{G}_1^*$ and $H_2 : \mathbb{G}_2 \rightarrow \{0,1\}^n$. Here n will be the bit-length of plaintexts.

The system parameters **params** $= \langle \mathbb{G}_1, \mathbb{G}_2, e, n, P, P_{\text{pub}}, H_1, H_2 \rangle$ are published and the **master-key** $s \in \mathbb{Z}_q^*$ is kept secret. The message space is $\mathcal{M} = \{0,1\}^n$ and the ciphertext space is $\mathcal{C} = \mathbb{G}_1 \times \{0,1\}^n$.

Extract-Partial-Private-Key: On input of an identifier $\text{ID} \in \{0,1\}^*$, this algorithm carries out the following steps to construct the partial private key for the user-associated identifier ID:

1. Compute $Q_{\text{ID}} = H_1(\text{ID}) \in \mathbb{G}_1^*$.

2. Output the partial private key $\text{psk}_{\text{ID}} = sQ_{\text{ID}} \in \mathbb{G}_1^*$.

Set-Secret-Value: On input of params and a user's identifier ID, this algorithm selects $x_{\mathsf{ID}} \in \mathbb{Z}_q^*$ at random and outputs x_{ID} as the user ID's secret value.

Set-Private-Key: On input of params, a user ID's partial private key $\mathsf{psk}_{\mathsf{ID}}$, and ID's secret value $x_{\mathsf{ID}} \in \mathbb{Z}_q^*$, this algorithm transforms partial private key $\mathsf{psk}_{\mathsf{ID}}$ to private key $\mathsf{usk}_{\mathsf{ID}}$ by computing $\mathsf{usk}_{\mathsf{ID}} = x_{\mathsf{ID}}\mathsf{psk}_{\mathsf{ID}} = x_{\mathsf{ID}}sQ_{\mathsf{ID}}$.

Set-Public-Key: On input of params and user ID's secret value $\mathsf{usk}_{\mathsf{ID}}$ as input, this algorithm outputs ID's public key $\mathsf{upk}_{\mathsf{ID}} = \langle x_{\mathsf{ID}}P, x_{\mathsf{ID}}P_{PUB} \rangle$.

Encrypt: To encrypt $m \in \mathcal{M}$ under the identity $\mathsf{ID} \in \{0,1\}^*$ and user public key $\mathsf{upk}_{\mathsf{ID}}$, this algorithm performs the following steps:

1. Check the correctness of the user public key $\mathsf{upk}_{\mathsf{ID}}$ by checking if the equality $\hat{e}(x_{\mathsf{ID}}P, P_{\mathrm{pub}}) = \hat{e}(x_{\mathsf{ID}}P_{\mathrm{pub}}, P)$ holds or not. If not, output $\perp$ and abort encryption.

2. Compute $Q_{\mathsf{ID}} = H_1(\mathsf{ID})$.

3. Choose a random value $r \in \mathbb{Z}_q^*$.

4. Compute and output the ciphertext: $c = \langle rP, m \oplus H_2(\hat{e}(Q_{\mathsf{ID}}, x_{\mathsf{ID}}P_{\mathrm{pub}})^r) \rangle$.

Decrypt: On the input of the ciphertext $c = \langle U, V \rangle \in \mathcal{C}$, this algorithm performs the decryption using the private key $\mathsf{usk}_{\mathsf{ID}}$ by computing $V \oplus H_2(\hat{e}(\mathsf{usk}_{\mathsf{ID}}, U))$.

6.2.1.2   Full CLE Scheme

Based on the basic CLE scheme, an improved CLE scheme achieving CCA security has been proposed by adapting the Fujisaki–Okamoto padding technique [152]. The full CLE scheme consists of the following algorithms:

Setup: This algorithm is identical to the Setup algorithm for the basic CLE scheme with the exception that two additional cryptographic hash functions are selected: $H_3 : \{0,1\}^n \times \{0,1\}^n \rightarrow \mathbb{Z}_q^*$ and $H_4 : \{0,1\}^n \rightarrow \{0,1\}^n$.

The system parameters $\mathsf{params} = \langle \mathbb{G}_1, \mathbb{G}_2, \hat{e}, n, P, P_{\mathrm{pub}}, H_1, H_2,$ $H_3, H_4 \rangle$ are published and the master-key as well as the message space $\mathcal{M}$ are the same as in the basic CLE scheme. The ciphertext space is now $\mathcal{C} = \mathbb{G}_1 \times \{0,1\}^{2n}$.

Extract-Partial-Private-Key, Set-Secret-Value, Set-Private-Key, and Set-Public-Key: These algorithms are identical to those in the basic CLE scheme.

Encrypt: To encrypt $m \in \mathcal{M}$ under the identity $\mathsf{ID} \in \{0,1\}^*$ and user public key $\mathsf{upk}_{\mathsf{ID}}$, this algorithm performs the following steps:

1. Check the correctness of the user public key $\mathsf{upk}_{\mathsf{ID}}$ by checking if the equality $\hat{e}(x_{\mathsf{ID}}P, P_{\mathrm{pub}}) = \hat{e}(x_{\mathsf{ID}}P_{\mathrm{pub}}, P)$ holds or not. If not, output $\bot$ and abort encryption.

2. Compute $Q_{\mathsf{ID}} = H_1(\mathsf{ID})$.

3. Choose a random $\sigma \in \{0,1\}^n$.

4. Set $r = H_3(\sigma, m)$.

5. Compute and output: $c = \langle rP, \sigma \oplus H_2(\hat{e}(Q_{\mathsf{ID}}, x_{\mathsf{ID}}P_{\mathrm{pub}})^r), m \oplus H_4(\sigma) \rangle$.

Decrypt: On the input of the ciphertext $c = \langle U, V, W \rangle \in \mathcal{C}$, this algorithm performs the decryption using the private key $\mathsf{usk}_{\mathsf{ID}}$ as follows:

1. Compute $V \oplus H_2(\hat{e}(\mathsf{usk}_{\mathsf{ID}}, U))) = \sigma'$.

2. Compute $W \oplus H_4(\sigma') = m'$.

3. Set $r' = H_3(\sigma', m')$ and test if $U = r'P$. If not, output $\bot$ and reject c.

4. Output m' as the decryption of c.

Theorem 6.1 *Let hash functions $H_1, H_2, H_3,$ and H_4 be random oracles. The GBDH assumption will fail with a nonnegligible advantage in the case that the IND-CCA security of the full CLE scheme has been broken by a type I/II adversary.*

Proof 6.1 *The details of the proof for this theorem can be found in [17] and so has been omitted here.*

6.3   ZHANG–ZHANG CLS

Zhang and Zhang [138] proposed a pairing-based CLS scheme secure against a super type I/II adversary. This scheme is more efficient than the other CLS schemes featured with the same security level.

6.3.1   Concrete Construction

The construction of Zhang and Zhang's CLS scheme consists of the following algorithms:

Setup: Let $\hat{e} : \mathbb{G}_1 \times \mathbb{G}_1 \to \mathbb{G}_2$ be a symmetric bilinear pairing defined in Section 2.2.4. Also let P be a generator for the group $\mathbb{G}_1$. This algorithm is carried out by the key-generation center (KGC) to choose a random $\lambda \in \mathbb{Z}_q^*$ as the **master-key** and set $P_{\text{pub}} = \lambda P$. After that, the KGC chooses three cryptographic hash functions $H_1 : \{0,1\}^* \to \mathbb{G}_1$, $H_2 : \{0,1\}^* \to \mathbb{Z}_q^*$, and $H_3 : \{0,1\}^* \to \mathbb{Z}_q^*$. The system parameters $\text{params} = (\mathbb{G}_1, \mathbb{G}_2, \hat{e}, P, P_{\text{pub}}, H_1, H_2, H_3)$ are published. The message space is $\mathcal{M} = \{0,1\}^*$.

Extract-Partial-Private-Key: On input of params, master-key λ, and a user's identity $\text{ID}_i \in \{0,1\}^*$, this algorithm generates the partial private key for the user as follows:

1. Compute $Q_{\text{ID}_i} = H_1(\text{ID}_i \| P)$.
2. Output the partial private key $\text{psk}_{\text{ID}_i} = \lambda Q_{\text{ID}_i}$.

Set-Secret-Value: On input of params and a user's identity ID_i, this algorithm selects a random $x_{\text{ID}_i} \in \mathbb{Z}_q^*$ and outputs x_{ID_i} as the user's secret value.

Set-Public-Key: On input of params, a user's identity ID_i, and this user's secret value $x_{\text{ID}_i} \in \mathbb{Z}_q^*$, this algorithm produces the user's public key $\text{upk}_{\text{ID}_i} = x_{\text{ID}_i} P$.

Sign: To sign a message $m \in \mathcal{M}$ using the partial private key psk_{ID_i} and the secret value x_{ID_i}, the signer associated with the identity ID_i and the corresponding public key upk_{ID_i} performs the following steps:

1. Choose a random $r \in \mathbb{Z}_q^*$; compute $R = rP$.
2. Compute $u = H_2(R \| \text{upk}_{\text{ID}_i} \| m)$ and $v = H_3(R \| \text{upk}_{\text{ID}_i} \| m)$.

3. Compute $V = (u \cdot x_{\mathsf{ID}_i} + r)Q_{\mathsf{ID}_i} + v \cdot \mathsf{psk}_{\mathsf{ID}_i}$.

4. Output $\sigma = (R, V)$ as the signature on m.

Verify: To verify a signature σ on a message m under an identity ID_i and public key $\mathsf{upk}_{\mathsf{ID}_i}$, the verifier performs the following steps:

1. Compute $Q_{\mathsf{ID}_i} = H_1(\mathsf{ID}_i \| P)$, $u = H_2(R \| \mathsf{upk}_{\mathsf{ID}_i} \| m)$, and $v = H_3(R \| \mathsf{upk}_{\mathsf{ID}_i} \| m)$.

2. Check whether $\hat{e}(V, P) \stackrel{?}{=} \hat{e}(u \cdot \mathsf{upk}_{\mathsf{ID}_i} + v P_{\mathrm{pub}} + R, Q_{\mathsf{ID}_i})$ holds or not. If the equation holds, output 1. Otherwise, output 0.

6.3.2 Security Analysis

Theorem 6.2 *This CLS scheme is unforgeable against a super type I adversary in the random oracle model under the CDH assumption.*

Proof 6.2 *The intuition behind Theorem 6.2 can be found in Figure 6.1. Let $\mathcal{C}$ be a CDH attacker who receives a random instance*

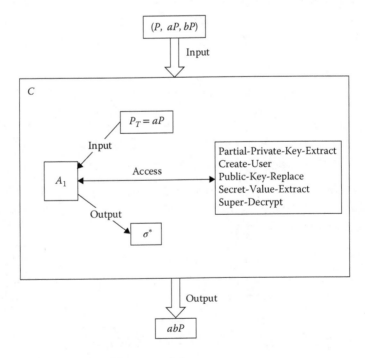

Figure 6.1 Intuition for Theorem 6.2.

(P, aP, bP) of the CDH problem in $\mathbb{G}_1$ and has to compute the value of abP. $\mathcal{A}_1$ is a super type I adversary who interacts with $\mathcal{C}$ as modeled in the CMA-CIDA-Super-I security game. We show how $\mathcal{C}$ can use $\mathcal{A}_1$ to solve the CDH problem, that is, to compute abP.

Initial: $\mathcal{C}$ sets $P_{\text{pub}} = aP$, selects params $= (\mathbb{G}_1, \mathbb{G}_2, e, P, P_{\text{pub}}, H_1, H_2, H_3)$, and sends params to $\mathcal{A}_1$. We consider hash functions H_1, H_2, and H_3 random oracles.

Attack: H_1 Queries: Suppose $\mathcal{A}_1$ can make at most q_{H_1} times H_1 queries, $\mathcal{C}$ chooses $J \in [1, q_{H_1}]$. $\mathcal{C}$ maintains an initially empty list $\mathbf{H_1}$ of tuples $(\text{ID}_j, \alpha_j, Q_{\text{ID}_j})$. The same answer from the list $\mathbf{H_1}$ will be given if the request has been asked before. On receiving a new query $H_1(\text{ID}_i \| P)$, $\mathcal{C}$ simulates the random oracle H_1 as follows:

1. If $i = J$, set $Q_{\text{ID}_j} = bP$, add $(\text{ID}_i, \perp, Q_{\text{ID}_j})$ to $\mathbf{H_1}$, and return Q_i as answer.

2. Otherwise, pick $\alpha_i \in \mathbb{Z}_q^*$ at random, set $Q_{\text{ID}_j} = \alpha_i P$, add $(\text{ID}_i, \alpha_i, Q_{\text{ID}_j})$ to $\mathbf{H_1}$, and return Q_{ID_j} as the answer.

H_2 Queries: $\mathcal{C}$ keeps an initially empty list $\mathbf{H_2}$ of tuples $(R_j, \text{upk}_{\text{ID}_j}, m_j, u_j)$. Whenever $\mathcal{A}_1$ issues a query $(R_i \| \text{upk}_{\text{ID}_i} \| m_i)$ to H_2, the same answer from the list $\mathbf{H_2}$ will be given if the request has been asked before. If the query $(R_i \| \text{upk}_{\text{ID}_i} \| m_i)$ is new, $\mathcal{C}$ selects a random $u_i \in \mathbb{Z}_q^*$, adds $(R_i, \text{upk}_{\text{ID}_i}, m_i, u_i)$ to $\mathbf{H_2}$, and returns u_i as answer.

H_3 Queries: $\mathcal{C}$ keeps an initially empty list $\mathbf{H_3}$ of tuples $(R_j, \text{upk}_{\text{ID}_j}, m_j, v_j)$. Whenever $\mathcal{A}_1$ issues a query $(R_i \| \text{upk}_{\text{ID}_i} \| m_i)$ to H_3, the same answer from the list $\mathbf{H_3}$ will be given if the request has been asked before. For a new query $(R_i \| \text{upk}_{\text{ID}_i} \| m_i)$, $\mathcal{C}$ selects a random $v_i \in \mathbb{Z}_q^*$, adds $(R_i, \text{upk}_{\text{ID}_i}, m_i, v_i)$ to $\mathbf{H_3}$, and returns v_i as answer.

Partial-Private-Key-Extract Queries: $\mathcal{C}$ keeps an initially empty list $\mathbf{K}$ of tuples $(\text{ID}_j, x_{\text{ID}_j}, \text{psk}_{\text{ID}_j}, \text{upk}_{\text{ID}_j})$. When $\mathcal{A}_1$ issues a query **Partial-Private-Key-Extract**(ID_i), the same answer from the list $\mathbf{K}$ will be given if the request has been asked before. If the query is new, $\mathcal{C}$ does the following:

1. If $\text{ID}_i = \text{ID}_J$, aborts.

2. Else if there's a tuple $(\mathsf{ID}_i, x_{\mathsf{ID}_i}, \mathsf{psk}_{\mathsf{ID}_i}, \mathsf{upk}_{\mathsf{ID}_i})$ on $\mathbf{K}$:

   (a) If there is a tuple $(\mathsf{ID}_i, \alpha_i, Q_{\mathsf{ID}_i})$ on $\mathbf{H}_1$, set $\mathsf{psk}_{\mathsf{ID}_i} = \alpha_i P_{\mathrm{pub}}$ and return $\mathsf{psk}_{\mathsf{ID}_i}$ as answer.

   (b) Otherwise, first make an H_1 query on $(\mathsf{ID}_i \| P)$ to generate $(\mathsf{ID}_i, \alpha_i, Q_{\mathsf{ID}_i})$, and then set $\mathsf{psk}_{\mathsf{ID}_i} = \alpha_i P_{\mathrm{pub}}$ and return $\mathsf{psk}_{\mathsf{ID}_i}$ as the answer.

3. Otherwise, do the following:

   (a) If there's a tuple $(\mathsf{ID}_i, \alpha_i, Q_{\mathsf{ID}_i})$ on $\mathbf{H}_1$, compute $\mathsf{psk}_{\mathsf{ID}_i} = \alpha_i P_{\mathrm{pub}}$, set $x_{\mathsf{ID}_i} = \mathsf{upk}_{\mathsf{ID}_i} = \perp$, return $\mathsf{psk}_{\mathsf{ID}_i}$ as the answer, and add $(\mathsf{ID}_i, x_{\mathsf{ID}_i}, \mathsf{psk}_{\mathsf{ID}_i}, \mathsf{upk}_{\mathsf{ID}_i})$ to $\mathbf{K}$.

   (b) Else, generate the tuple $(\mathsf{ID}_i, \alpha_i, Q_{\mathsf{ID}_i})$ the same way as he/she simulates the random oracle H_1. Compute $\mathsf{psk}_{\mathsf{ID}_i} = \alpha_i P_{\mathrm{pub}}$, set $x_{\mathsf{ID}_i} = \mathsf{upk}_{\mathsf{ID}_i} = \perp$, and then return $\mathsf{psk}_{\mathsf{ID}_i}$ as the answer and add $(\mathsf{ID}_i, x_{\mathsf{ID}_i}, \mathsf{psk}_{\mathsf{ID}_i}, \mathsf{upk}_{\mathsf{ID}_i})$ to $\mathbf{K}$.

Create-User Queries: On receiving a query **Create-User**(ID_i), the current public key from the list $\mathbf{K}$ will be given if the request has been asked before. Otherwise, $\mathcal{C}$ does as follows:

1. If there's a tuple $(\mathsf{ID}_i, x_{\mathsf{ID}_i}, \mathsf{psk}_{\mathsf{ID}_i}, \mathsf{upk}_{\mathsf{ID}_i})$ on $\mathbf{K}$ (in this case, the public key $\mathsf{upk}_{\mathsf{ID}_i}$ of ID_i has not been set), choose $x'_{\mathsf{ID}_i} \in \mathbb{Z}_q^*$, compute $\mathsf{upk}'_{\mathsf{ID}_i} = x'_{\mathsf{ID}_i} P$, return $\mathsf{upk}'_{\mathsf{ID}_i}$ as the answer, and update $(\mathsf{ID}_i, x_{\mathsf{ID}_i}, \mathsf{psk}_{\mathsf{ID}_i}, \mathsf{upk}_{\mathsf{ID}_i})$ to $(\mathsf{ID}_i, x'_{\mathsf{ID}_i}, \mathsf{psk}_{\mathsf{ID}_i}, \mathsf{upk}'_{\mathsf{ID}_i})$.

2. Otherwise, choose $x_{\mathsf{ID}_i} \in \mathbb{Z}_q^*$, set $\mathsf{upk}_{\mathsf{ID}_i} = x_{\mathsf{ID}_i} P$, return $\mathsf{upk}_{\mathsf{ID}_i}$ as the answer, set $\mathsf{psk}_{\mathsf{ID}_i} = \perp$, and add $(\mathsf{ID}_i, x_{\mathsf{ID}_i}, \mathsf{psk}_{\mathsf{ID}_i}, \mathsf{upk}_{\mathsf{ID}_i})$ to $\mathbf{K}$.

Secret-Value-Extract Queries: On receiving a query **Secret-Value-Extract** (ID_i), if the public key of ID_i has been replaced, $\mathcal{C}$ returns $\perp$. Otherwise, if there is a tuple $(\mathsf{ID}_i, x_{\mathsf{ID}_i}, \mathsf{psk}_{\mathsf{ID}_i}, \mathsf{upk}_{\mathsf{ID}_i})$ on $\mathbf{K}$, $\mathcal{C}$ returns x_{ID_i} as the answer; else, $\mathcal{C}$ first makes **Create-User** (ID_i) and then returns x_{ID_i} as the answer.

Public-Key-Replace Queries: $\mathcal{A}_1$ can choose a new public key for the user whose identity is ID_i. On receiving a query **Public-Key-Replace**$(\mathsf{ID}_i, \mathsf{upk}'_{\mathsf{ID}_i})$, $\mathcal{C}$ first finds the tuple $(\mathsf{ID}_i, x_{\mathsf{ID}_i}, \mathsf{psk}_{\mathsf{ID}_i}, \mathsf{upk}_{\mathsf{ID}_i})$ on $\mathbf{K}$ (if such a tuple does not exist on $\mathbf{K}$ or $\mathsf{upk}_{\mathsf{ID}_i} = \perp$, $\mathcal{C}$ first makes $PK(\mathsf{ID}_i)$), and then $\mathcal{C}$ updates $\mathsf{upk}_{\mathsf{ID}_i}$ to $\mathsf{upk}'_{\mathsf{ID}_i}$.

Super-Sign Queries: On receiving a **Super-Sign** query on the input $(m_i, \mathsf{ID}_i, \mathsf{upk}_{\mathsf{ID}_i})$, where $\mathsf{upk}_{\mathsf{ID}_i}$ denotes the public key chosen by $\mathcal{A}_1$, $\mathcal{C}$ generates the signature as follows (note $\mathcal{A}_1$ need not supply the secret value that is used to generate $\mathsf{upk}_{\mathsf{ID}_i}$):

1. Choose $u_i, v_i, r_i \in \mathbb{Z}_q^*$ at random; set $R_i = r_i P - (u_i \mathsf{upk}_{\mathsf{ID}_i} + v_i P_{\mathrm{pub}})$.

2. Set $H_2(R_i \| \mathsf{upk}_{\mathsf{ID}_i} \| m_i) = u_i$ and $H_3(R_i \| \mathsf{upk}_{\mathsf{ID}_i} \| m_i) = v_i$.

3. Compute $V_i = r_i H_1(\mathsf{ID}_i \| P)$ and output $\sigma_i = (R_i, V_i)$.

Forgery: Finally, $\mathcal{A}_1$ returns a successful forgery $(m^*, \sigma^* = (R^*, V^*), \mathsf{ID}^*, \mathsf{upk}_{\mathsf{ID}^*})$, which means (R^*, V^*) is a valid signature on message m^* under identity ID^* and public key $\mathsf{upk}_{\mathsf{ID}^*}$. If $\mathsf{ID}^* \neq \mathsf{ID}_J$, $\mathcal{C}$ aborts. According to the forking lemma [153], $\mathcal{C}$ replays $\mathcal{A}_1$ with the same random tape but different choice of the hash function H_3' to get another forged signature $(m^*, \sigma^{*'} = (R^*, V^{*'}), \mathsf{ID}^*, P_{\mathsf{ID}^*})$.

Since σ^* and $\sigma^{*'}$ must satisfy $\hat{e}(V^*, P) = \hat{e}(u^* \mathsf{upk}_{\mathsf{ID}}^* + v^* P_{\mathrm{pub}} + R^*, Q^*)$ and $\hat{e}(V^{*'}, P) = \hat{e}(u^* \mathsf{upk}_{\mathsf{ID}}^* + v^{*'} P_{\mathrm{pub}} + R^*, Q^*)$, respectively (where $u^* = H_2(R^* \| \mathsf{upk}_{\mathsf{ID}^*} \| m^*)$, $v^* = H_3(R^* \| \mathsf{upk}_{\mathsf{ID}^*} \| m^*)$, $v^{*'} = H_3'(R^* \| \mathsf{upk}_{\mathsf{ID}^*} \| m^*)$, $Q^* = H_1(\mathsf{ID}^* \| P)$, and $v^* \neq v^{*'}$), we have $\hat{e}(V^* - V^{*'}, P) = \hat{e}((v^* - v^{*'}) P_{\mathrm{pub}}, Q^*)$. By setting $P_{\mathrm{pub}} = aP$, $Q^* = bP$, $\mathcal{C}$ can compute $abP = (v^* - v^{*'})^{-1}(V^* - V^{*'})$. So $\mathcal{C}$ has successfully obtained the solution of the CDH problem.

Theorem 6.3 *This CLS scheme is unforgeable against a super type II adversary in the random oracle model under the CDH assumption.*

Proof 6.3 *The intuition behind Theorem 6.3 can be found in Figure 6.2. Let $\mathcal{C}$ be a CDH attacker who receives a random instance (P, aP, bP) of the CDH problem in $\mathbb{G}_1$ and has to compute the value of abP. $\mathcal{A}_2$ is a type II adversary who interacts with $\mathcal{C}$ as defined in game 2. We show how $\mathcal{C}$ can use $\mathcal{A}_2$ to solve the CDH problem, that is, to compute abP.*

Initial: $\mathcal{C}$ selects $\lambda \in \mathbb{Z}_q^*$ as the **master-key**, computes $P_{PUB} = \lambda P$, and selects the system parameters $\mathsf{params} = (\mathbb{G}_1, \mathbb{G}_2, \hat{e}, P, P_{\mathrm{pub}}, H_1, H_2, H_3)$. When the simulation is started, $\mathcal{A}_2$ is provided with params and the **master-key** λ.

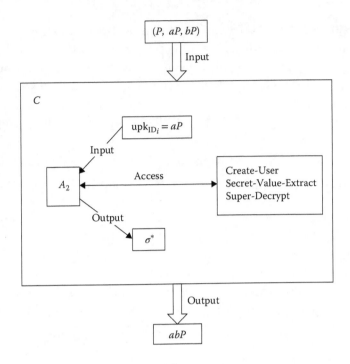

Figure 6.2 Intuition for Theorem 6.3.

Attack: H_1 Queries: Suppose $\mathcal{A}_2$ can make at most q_{H_1} times H_1 queries, $\mathcal{C}$ chooses $J \in [1, q_{H_1}]$. $\mathcal{C}$ maintains an initially empty list $\mathbf{H_1}$ of tuples $(\mathsf{ID}_j, \alpha_j, Q_{\mathsf{ID}_j})$. Whenever receiving an H_1 query on $(\mathsf{ID}_i \| P)$, the same answer from the list $\mathbf{H_1}$ will be given if the request has been asked before. For a new query, if $\mathsf{ID}_i = \mathsf{ID}_J$, $\mathcal{C}$ sets $Q_{\mathsf{ID}_i} = bP$, adds $(\mathsf{ID}_i, \perp, Q_{\mathsf{ID}_i})$ to $\mathbf{H_1}$, and returns Q_i as the answer; else, $\mathcal{C}$ picks $\alpha_i \in Z_q^*$ at random, sets $Q_{\mathsf{ID}_i} = \alpha_i P$, adds $(\mathsf{ID}_i, \alpha_i, Q_{\mathsf{ID}_i})$ to $\mathbf{H_1}$, and returns Q_{ID_i} as the answer.

H_2 Queries: $\mathcal{C}$ keeps a list $\mathbf{H_2}$ of tuples $(R_j, \mathsf{upk}_{\mathsf{ID}_j}, m_j, u_j)$. This list is initially empty. Whenever $\mathcal{A}_2$ issues a query $(R_i \| \mathsf{upk}_{\mathsf{ID}_i} \| m_i)$ to H_2, the same answer from the list $\mathbf{H_2}$ will be given if the request has been asked before. If the query is new, $\mathcal{C}$ selects a random $u_i \in Z_q^*$, adds $(R_i, \mathsf{upk}_{\mathsf{ID}_i}, m_i, u_i)$ to $\mathbf{H_2}$, and returns u_i as the answer.

H_3 Queries: $\mathcal{C}$ keeps a list $\mathbf{H_3}$ of tuples $(R_j, \mathsf{upk}_{\mathsf{ID}_j}, m_j, v_j)$. This list is initially empty. Whenever $\mathcal{A}_2$ issues a query $(R_i \| \mathsf{upk}_{\mathsf{ID}_i} \| m_i)$ to H_3, the same answer from the list $\mathbf{H_3}$ will be given if the request has been asked before. For a new query,

$\mathcal{C}$ selects a random $v_i \in Z_q^*$, adds $(R_i, \mathsf{upk}_{\mathsf{ID}_i}, m_i, v_i)$ to $\mathbf{H_3}$, and returns v_i as the answer.

Create-User Queries: $\mathcal{C}$ keeps an initially empty list $\mathbf{K}$ of tuples $(\mathsf{ID}_j, x_{\mathsf{ID}_j}, \mathsf{upk}_{\mathsf{ID}_j})$. On receiving a query **Create-User**(ID_i), the current public key from the list $\mathbf{K}$ of the user whose identity is ID_i will be given if the request has been asked before. For a new query, if $\mathsf{ID}_i = \mathsf{ID}_J$, $\mathcal{C}$ returns $\mathsf{upk}_{\mathsf{ID}_i} = aP$ as the answer and adds $(\mathsf{ID}_i, \bot, \mathsf{upk}_{\mathsf{ID}_i})$ to $\mathbf{K}$; else, $\mathcal{C}$ picks $x_{\mathsf{ID}_i} \in Z_q^*$, computes $\mathsf{upk}_{\mathsf{ID}_i} = x_{\mathsf{ID}_i} P$, adds $(\mathsf{ID}_i, x_{\mathsf{ID}_i}, \mathsf{upk}_{\mathsf{ID}_i})$ to $\mathbf{K}$, and returns $\mathsf{upk}_{\mathsf{ID}_i}$ as the answer.

Secret-Value-Extract Queries: On receiving a query $SV(\mathsf{ID}_i)$, if the public key of ID_i has been replaced, $\mathcal{C}$ returns $\bot$; otherwise, if $\mathsf{ID}_i = \mathsf{ID}_J$, $\mathcal{C}$ aborts; else if there is a tuple $(\mathsf{ID}_i, x_{\mathsf{ID}_i}, \mathsf{upk}_{\mathsf{ID}_i})$ on $\mathbf{K}$, $\mathcal{C}$ returns x_{ID_i} as the answer; else, $\mathcal{C}$ first makes **Create-User**(ID_i), then recovers the tuple $(\mathsf{ID}_i, x_{\mathsf{ID}_i}, \mathsf{upk}_{\mathsf{ID}_i})$ from $\mathbf{K}$, and returns x_{ID_i} as answer.

Public-Key-Replace Queries: $\mathcal{A}_2$ can choose a new public key for the user whose identity is ID_i. On receiving a query **Public-Key-Replace**$(\mathsf{ID}_i, \mathsf{upk}'_{\mathsf{ID}_i})$, if $\mathsf{ID}_i = \mathsf{ID}_J$, $\mathcal{C}$ aborts; otherwise, $\mathcal{C}$ finds the tuple $(\mathsf{ID}_i, x_{\mathsf{ID}_i}, \mathsf{upk}_{\mathsf{ID}_i})$ on $\mathbf{K}$ (if such a tuple does not exist on $\mathbf{K}$, $\mathcal{C}$ makes **Create-User**(ID_i) first and updates $\mathsf{upk}_{\mathsf{ID}_i}$ to $\mathsf{upk}'_{\mathsf{ID}_i}$).

Super-Sign Queries: On receiving a **Super-Sign** query on the input $(m_i, \mathsf{ID}_i, \mathsf{upk}_{\mathsf{ID}_i})$, $\mathcal{C}$ generates the signature as follows:

1. Choose $u_i, v_i, r_i \in Z_q^*$ at random; set $R_i = r_i P - (u_i \cdot \mathsf{upk}_{\mathsf{ID}_i} + v_i P_{\mathrm{pub}})$.
2. Set $H_2(R_i \| \mathsf{upk}_{\mathsf{ID}_i} \| m_i) = u_i$ and $H_3(R_i \| \mathsf{upk}_{\mathsf{ID}_i} \| m_i) = v_i$.
3. Compute $V_i = r_i H_1(\mathsf{ID}_i \| P)$ and output $\sigma_i = (R_i, V_i)$.

Forgery: Eventually, $\mathcal{A}_2$ returns a tuple $(m^*, \sigma^* = (R^*, V^*), \mathsf{ID}^*, \mathsf{upk}_{\mathsf{ID}^*})$ meaning that (R^*, V^*) is a valid signature on message m^* under identity ID^* and public key $\mathsf{upk}_{\mathsf{ID}^*}$. If $\mathsf{ID}^* \neq \mathsf{ID}_J$, $\mathcal{C}$ aborts. According to the forking lemma [153], $\mathcal{C}$ replays $\mathcal{A}_2$ with the same random tape but different choice of the hash function H_2' to get another forged signature $\sigma^{*'} = (R^*, V^{*'})$.

Since σ^* and $\sigma^{*'}$ must satisfy $\hat{e}(V^*, P) = \hat{e}(u^* \cdot \mathsf{upk}_{\mathsf{ID}^*} + v^* P_{\mathrm{pub}} + R^*, Q^*)$ and $\hat{e}(V^{*'}, P) = \hat{e}(u^{*'} \cdot \mathsf{upk}_{\mathsf{ID}^*} + v^* P_{\mathrm{pub}} +$

R^*, Q_i^*), respectively (where $u^* = H_2(R^*\|\mathsf{upk}_{\mathsf{ID}^*}\|m^*)$, $u^{*'} = H_2'(R^*\|\mathsf{upk}_{\mathsf{ID}^*}\|m^*)$, $v^* = H_3(R^*\|\mathsf{upk}_{\mathsf{ID}^*}\|m^*)$, $Q^* = H_1(\mathsf{ID}^*\|P)$, and $u^* \neq u^{*'}$), we have $\hat{e}(V^* - V^{*'}, P) = \hat{e}((u^* - u^{*'})\mathsf{upk}_{\mathsf{ID}^*}, Q^*)$. By setting $\mathsf{upk}_{\mathsf{ID}^*} = aP$, $Q^* = bP$, C can compute $abP = (u^* - u^{*'})^{-1}(V^* - V^{*'})$. So C has successfully obtained the solution of the computational Diffie–Hellman (CDH) problem.

6.4   ZHANG ET AL.'S CL-AKA

AKA is one of the fundamental cryptographic primitives. Such a protocol allows two or more parties to exchange information among themselves over an adversatively controlled insecure network and agree upon a common session key, which may be used for later secure communication among these parties. Thus, secure AKA protocols serve as basic building blocks for constructing secure, complex, higher-level protocols. In 1976, Diffie and Hellman [4] proposed the first key agreement protocol that enables two parties to establish a session key. Over the years, different approaches have been developed to solve the problem in order to improve the security and efficiency of the protocols [1,154]. AKA protocols can be realized under the traditional public-key infrastructure (PKI) or identity-based (ID-based) cryptosystem. However, PKI-based protocols suffer from a heavy certificate management overhead and ID-based systems are subject to the so-called key escrow problem. Thus, the AKA protocol has been investigated in the CL-PKC setting to eliminate such limitations. Pioneered by the work of Al-Riyami and Paterson (the first CL-AKA from pairings [17]), many CL-AKA protocols have been proposed making use of bilinear pairings [17,21,155–159]. All of these protocols realize secure session key establishment and continuously reduce the employment of pairings: of note is Zhang et al.'s protocol [21], which requires only one pairing operation. Recently, Zhang [160,161] formalized a security model for certificateless one-pass AKA protocols for two parties and then proposed a concrete construction, where only one entity is required to transmit information to its communicating peer during their authentication protocol.

6.4.1   Framework of CL-AKA Protocol

In general [21,160,161], a CL-AKA protocol consists of four polynomial-time algorithms: Setup, Extract-Parital-Private-Key, Set-User-Keys, and Key-Agreement. These algorithms are defined as follows:

Setup: On input of a security parameter k, this algorithm is performed to return a **master-key** and a list of system parameters **params**.

Extract-Partial-Private-Key: On input of the public parameters **params**, **master-key**, and an entity's identity ID_i, this algorithm is also performed by the KGC to produce the entity's partial private key psk_{ID_i}.

Set-User-Keys: On input of the public parameters **params**, and an entity's identity ID_i, this algorithm is carried out by the user himself/herself to produce a secret value usk_{ID_i} and public key upk_{ID_i} for this entity.

Key-Agreement: This is a probabilistic polynomial-time interactive algorithm that involves two entities A and B. The inputs are the system parameters **params** for both A and B, plus $\{psk_{ID_A}, usk_{ID_A}, upk_{ID_A}, ID_A\}$ for A and $\{psk_{ID_B}, usk_{ID_B}, upk_{ID_B}, ID_B\}$ for B. Here, psk_{ID_A}, psk_{ID_B} are the respective partial private keys of A and B and $\{usk_{ID_A}, upk_{ID_A}\}, \{usk_{ID_B}, upk_{ID_B}\}$ are the user secret value and public key of A and B, respectively; ID_A is the identity of A and ID_B is the identity of B. Eventually, if the protocol does not fail, A and B obtain a secret session key $K_{AB} = K_{BA} = K$.

6.4.2 Security Definitions

Motivated by the model of Zhang et al. [21] and modified Bellare–Rogaway model (mBR model) [75], a security model for CL-AKA protocols has been defined here. The security of CL-AKA protocol Π is defined by the following game between a challenger $\mathcal{C}$ and an adversary $\mathcal{A} \in \{\mathcal{A}_1, \mathcal{A}_2\}$. Here, type I adversary $\mathcal{A}_1$ models an adversary who does not know the master key of the KGC, but who has the ability to replace the public key of any entity with a value of his/her choice. Type II adversary $\mathcal{A}_2$ models a malicious KGC who knows the master key, but who cannot replace the target user's public key. We use the oracle $\Pi_{i,j}^s$ to represent the s-th instance between participant i and partner participant j in a session. At the beginning of the game, $\mathcal{C}$ runs the Setup algorithm and takes as input a security parameter k to obtain the master key and the system parameters **params**. If $\mathcal{A}$ is a type I adversary $\mathcal{A}_1$, $\mathcal{C}$ sends **params** to $\mathcal{A}$ and keeps the master key secret;

otherwise, $\mathcal{A}$ is a type II adversary $\mathcal{A}_2$, and $\mathcal{C}$ sends **params** with the master key to $\mathcal{A}$.

$\mathcal{A}$ is modeled by a probabilistic polynomial-time Turing machine. All communications go through the adversary $\mathcal{A}$. Participants only respond to the queries by $\mathcal{A}$ and do not communicate directly among themselves. $\mathcal{A}$ can relay, delete, modify, interleave, or delete all the message flows in the system. Note that $\mathcal{A}$ is allowed to make a polynomial number of queries, including one **Test** query defined as follows:

- **Create-User**(ID_i): This allows $\mathcal{A}$ to ask $\mathcal{C}$ to set up a new participant i with identity ID_i. On receiving such a query, $\mathcal{C}$ generates the public/private key pair for i.

- **Public-Key-Request**(ID_i): $\mathcal{A}$ can request the public key of a participant i whose identity is ID_i. To respond, $\mathcal{C}$ outputs the public key $\mathsf{upk}_{\mathsf{ID}_i}$ of participant i.

- **Partial-Private-Key-Extract**(ID_i): On input of an identity ID_i, $\mathcal{C}$ outputs the corresponding partial private key $\mathsf{psk}_{\mathsf{ID}_i}$ of participant i.

- **Corrupt**(ID_i): On input of an identity ID_i, $\mathcal{C}$ outputs the partial private key psk_{ID_i} and secret value $\mathsf{usk}_{\mathsf{ID}_i}$ of participant i.

- **Public-Key-Replace**($\mathsf{ID}_i, \mathsf{upk}'_{\mathsf{ID}_i}$): For a participant i whose identity is ID_i, $\mathcal{A}$ can choose a new public key $\mathsf{upk}'_{\mathsf{ID}_i}$ and then set $\mathsf{upk}'_{\mathsf{ID}_i}$ as the new public key of this participant. $\mathcal{C}$ will record these replacements, which will be used later.

- **Send**($\Pi^t_{j,i}, m$): $\mathcal{A}$ can send a message m of his/her choice to an oracle, say $\Pi^t_{j,i}$, in which case participant i assumes that the message has been sent by participant j. $\mathcal{A}$ may also make a special Send query with $m = \lambda$ to the oracle $\Pi^t_{j,i}$, which demonstrates i to initiate a protocol run with j. An oracle is an initiator if the first message it has received is λ. If an oracle does not receive a message λ as its first message, then it is a responder oracle.

- **Reveal**($\Pi^t_{j,i}$): $\mathcal{A}$ can ask a particular oracle to reveal the session key (if any) it currently holds to $\mathcal{A}$.

- **Test**($\Pi^T_{I,J}$): At some point, $\mathcal{A}$ has to make a Test query to a *fresh* oracle $\Pi^T_{I,J}$ (see Definition 6.2). To answer the query, $\mathcal{C}$ flips a fair coin $b \in \{0, 1\}$ and returns the session key held by $\Pi_{I,J}^T$ if $b = 0$, or a random sample from the distribution of the session key if $b = 1$.

Definition 6.2 *(Fresh Oracle). Here, $\Pi_{i,j}^s$ is fresh if (1) $\Pi_{i,j}^s$ has accepted the request to establish a session key; (2) $\Pi_{i,j}^s$ has not been revealed; (3) there is no matching conversation[a] of oracle $\Pi_{i,j}^s$ has been revealed; (4) participant $j \neq i$ has not been corrupted; and (5) if A is a type I adversary, A has never requested the partial private key of participant j; and, if A is a type II adversary, A has never replaced the public key of participant j.*

Note that Definition 6.2 allows participant i to be corrupted, and thus can be used to address the key-compromise impersonation property as well as the partial forward secrecy property. After a Test query, A can continue to query the oracles except that it cannot make a Reveal query to the test oracle $\Pi_{I,J}^T$ or $\Pi_{J,I}^S$ who has a matching conversation with $\Pi_{I,J}^T$ (if it exists). In addition, if A is a type I adversary, A cannot request the partial private key of the participant, J, and if A is a type II adversary, A cannot replace the public key of the participant J. Finally, A outputs its guess b' for b. A's advantage $Adv^A(k)$ is defined as the probability $b = b'$.

The security of the CL-AKA protocol can be defined using the concept of A's advantage as follows:

Definition 6.3 *A certificateless two-party AKA protocol is said to be secure if the following conditions are met:*

1. *In the presence of a benign adversary, two oracles, $\Pi_{i,j}^s$ and $\Pi_{j,i}^t$, running the protocol both accept holding the same session key, and the session key is distributed uniformly at random on $\{0, 1\}^k$.*

2. *For any adversary A, $Adv^A(k)$ is negligible.*

Similar to [21], since A is formalized in a way that it can perform all kinds of known attacks in the real world, then the protocol provides desirable security attributes including *known session key security, forward secrecy, key compromise impersonation resilience,* and *unknown key-share resilience* when it satisfies Definition 6.3.

---

[a]Let the session ID be the concatenation of the messages in a session. Two oracles $\Pi_{i,j}^s$ and $\Pi_{j,i}^t$ are said to have a matching conversation with each other if they have the same session ID.

6.4.3   Concrete Construction

In [21], an efficient certificateless two-party AKA protocol has been introduced based on bilinear pairing. It consists of the following algorithms:

Setup: On input of a security parameter ℓ, this algorithm runs as follows:

1. Select a cyclic additive group $\mathbb{G}_1$ of prime order q, a cyclic multiplicative group $\mathbb{G}_2$ of the same order, a generator P of $\mathbb{G}_1$, and a bilinear map $e : \mathbb{G}_1 \times \mathbb{G}_1 \to \mathbb{G}_1$.

2. Choose $s \in \mathbb{Z}_q^*$ randomly as **master-key** and set $P_{\text{pub}} = sP$.

3. Choose cryptographic hash functions $H_1 : \{0,1\}^* \to \mathbb{G}_1$ and $H_2 : \{0,1\}^{*2} \times \mathbb{G}_1^2 \times \mathbb{G}_2 \times \mathbb{G}_1^4 \to \{0,1\}^l$. The system parameters $\text{params} = (\mathbb{G}_1, \mathbb{G}_2, \hat{e}, P, P_{\text{pub}}, H_1, H_2, l)$ are published and the **master-key** $s \in \mathbb{Z}_q^*$ is kept secret.

Extract-Partial-Private-Key: On input of params, master-key, and an entity's identity $\text{ID}_i \in \{0,1\}^*$, this algorithm is performed by the KGC to generate the partial private key for the entity as follows:

1. Compute $Q_{\text{ID}_i} = H(\text{ID}_i)$.

2. Output the partial private key $\text{psk}_{\text{ID}_i} = sQ_{\text{ID}_i}$.

Set-User-Keys: On input of params and an entity's identity $\text{ID}_i \in \{0,1\}^*$, this algorithm is run by the user himself/herself to generate the user secret/public key pair $(\text{usk}_{\text{ID}_i}, \text{upk}_{\text{ID}_i})$ by randomly choosing $x_i \in \mathbb{Z}_q^*$ as the user secret key usk_{ID_i} and computing $\text{upk}_{\text{ID}_i} = x_i P$.

Key-Agreement: Assume that an entity A with identity ID_A has user secret/public key pair $(\text{usk}_{\text{ID}_A}, \text{upk}_{\text{ID}_A})$ and partial private key psk_{ID_A} and an entity B with identity ID_B has user secret/public key pair $(\text{usk}_{\text{ID}_B}, \text{upk}_{\text{ID}_B})$ and partial private key psk_{ID_B}. A and B run the protocol interactively as follows:

1. A randomly chooses $r_A \in \mathbb{Z}_q^*$, computes $R_A = r_A P$, and sends $(\text{ID}_A, \text{upk}_{\text{ID}_A}, R_A)$ to B.

2. After receiving $(\text{ID}_A, \text{upk}_{\text{ID}_A}, R_A)$ from A, B selects $r_B \in \mathbb{Z}_q^*$ at random, computes $R_B = r_B P$, and sends

$(\mathsf{ID}_B, \mathsf{upk}_{\mathsf{ID}_B}, R_B)$ to A. Finally, B computes the session key $K_{BA} = H_2(\mathsf{ID}_A, \mathsf{ID}_B, R_A, R_B, r_B R_A, \hat{e}(R_A + Q_{\mathsf{ID}_A}, r_B P_{\mathrm{pub}} + \mathsf{psk}_{\mathsf{ID}_B}), \mathsf{upk}_{\mathsf{ID}_A}, \mathsf{upk}_{\mathsf{ID}_B}, x_{\mathsf{ID}_B} R_A, r_B \mathsf{upk}_{\mathsf{ID}_A})$, where $Q_{\mathsf{ID}_A} = H_{\mathsf{ID}_A}$.

3. After receiving $(\mathsf{ID}_B, \mathsf{upk}_{\mathsf{ID}_B}, R_B)$ from B, A computes the session key $K_{AB} = H_2(\mathsf{ID}_A, \mathsf{ID}_B, R_A, R_B, r_A R_B, \hat{e}(R_B + Q_{\mathsf{ID}_B}, r_A P_{\mathrm{pub}} + \mathsf{psk}_{\mathsf{ID}_A}), \mathsf{upk}_{\mathsf{ID}_A}, \mathsf{upk}_{\mathsf{ID}_B}, r_A \mathsf{upk}_{\mathsf{ID}_B}, x_A R_B)$, where $Q_{\mathsf{ID}_B} = H_{\mathsf{ID}_B}$.

In such a protocol run, the session ID of the protocol instance is $\mathsf{ID}_A \| \mathsf{ID}_B \| \mathsf{upk}_{\mathsf{ID}_A} \| \mathsf{upk}_{\mathsf{ID}_B} \| R_A \| R_B$.

We briefly check the correctness of the protocol. Since $\hat{e}(R_A + Q_{\mathsf{ID}_A}, r_B P_{\mathrm{pub}} + \mathsf{psk}_{\mathsf{ID}_B}) = \hat{e}(R_A + Q_{\mathsf{ID}_A}, r_B P + Q_{\mathsf{ID}_B})^s = \hat{e}(s R_A + s Q_{\mathsf{ID}_A}, r_B P + Q_{\mathsf{ID}_B}) = \hat{e}(r_A P_{\mathrm{pub}} + \mathsf{psk}_{\mathsf{ID}_A}, R_B + Q_{\mathsf{ID}_B}) = \hat{e}(R_B + Q_{\mathsf{ID}_B}, r_A P_{\mathrm{pub}} + \mathsf{psk}_{\mathsf{ID}_A})$, it is easy to see that $K_{AB} = K_{BA}$ holds. Hence, the correctness of the protocol holds.

Theorem 6.4 *Under the bilinear Diffie–Hellman (BDH) assumption, the advantage of a type I/II adversary against this certificateless two-party AKA protocol is negligible in the random oracle model.*

Proof 6.4 *The security proof is omitted and the interested reader can refer to [21] for more detail.*

CHAPTER 7

CL-PKC without Pairings

7.1 INTRODUCTION

Bilinear pairing, a mathematical tool that maps two elements in an elliptic-curve group to an element in the related finite field, was originally brought to the cryptographic community to attack elliptic-curve systems [162,163]. These attacks originate from the fact that pairings can be used to transform the discrete logarithm problem on a certain class of elliptic curves or hyperelliptic curves to the discrete logarithm problem on a smaller finite field. Furthermore, a subexponential index calculus attack can be mounted to solve the latter problem. Since the seminar work in [9,144,164], bilinear pairing has found various applications in the field of cryptography. More precisely, this powerful tool can be used to construct identity (ID)-based and certificateless cryptographic schemes. Many ID-based and certificateless cryptographic schemes have been proposed using bilinear pairings. Examples include Boneh–Franklin's identity-based encryption (IBE) scheme [9], the Cha–Cheon identity-based signature (IBS) scheme [40], Smart's ID-based authentication key agreement protocol [165], certificateless encryption (CLE) schemes [17,60,69], and certificateless signature (CLS) schemes [17,19,107,138]. However, due to the large element size of the super singular elliptic-curve group that the bilinear pairing is always defined over, the operation time for pairings is significantly longer than that of RSA private key operations [166,167]. In addition, the state-of-the-art implementation result for a pairing operation is at least two (at most 10) times slower than that of a scalar multiplication operation in the elliptic curve depending on the selection of security parameters [168]. Thus, bilinear pairing is regarded as one of the most expensive cryptographic operations and it is desirable to devise pairing-free certificateless cryptographic primitives.

7.2 LAI–KOU CLE

7.2.1 Concrete Construction

In [63,67], a pairing-free CLE scheme has been proposed and proved secure in the random oracle model under the standard computational Diffie–Hellman (CDH) assumption. It consists of the following algorithms:

Setup: The key-generation center (KGC) generates two large primes p and q such that $q|p - 1$ and selects a generator g from the group $\mathbb{Z}_p^*$. After that, the KGC picks $x \in \mathbb{Z}_p^*$ uniformly at random and computes $y = g^x$. Then, the KGC chooses hash functions $H_1 : \{0,1\}^* \times \mathbb{Z}_p^* \times \mathbb{Z}_p^* \to \mathbb{Z}_p^*$, $H_2 : \{0,1\}^{l_0} \times \{0,1\}^{l_1} \to \mathbb{Z}_p^*$, and $H_3 : \mathbb{Z}_p^* \to \{0,1\}^l$, where $l = l_0 + l_1 \in \mathbb{N}$. Finally, the KGC publishes the public parameters params $=(p, q, g, y, H_1, H_2, H_3)$ and keeps master-key $= x$ secret.

Set-User-Keys: The user associated with the identity ID picks $z \in \mathbb{Z}_p^*$ at random and computes $\mu = g^z$. After that, (z, μ) are returned as the user secret key and the first user public key $(\text{usk}_{\text{ID}}, \text{upk}_{\text{ID},1})$, respectively.

Extract-Partial-Private-Key: After receiving the identity ID and the user public key upk_{ID}, the KGC selects $s \in \mathbb{Z}_p^*$ at random and computes $\omega = g^s$ as well as $t = s + xH_1(\text{ID}, \omega, \text{upk}_{\text{ID},1}) = s + xH_1(\text{ID}, \omega, \mu)$. Finally, ω and t are returned as partial private key psk_{ID} and the second part of the user public key $\text{upk}_{\text{ID},2}$, respectively.

Encrypt: To encrypt a message m with message length l_0 under the identity ID and the user public key $(\text{upk}_{\text{ID},1}, \text{upk}_{\text{ID},2})$, the sender picks $\sigma \in \{0,1\}^{l_1}$ at random and computes $r = H_2(m, \sigma)$. Finally, the ciphertext (c_1, c_2) is output such that $c_1 = g^r$ and $c_2 = H_3((\mu\omega y^{H_1(\text{ID},\omega,\mu)})^r) \oplus (m \parallel \sigma)$.

Decrypt: After receiving the ciphertext (c_1, c_2), the user can perform the decryption operation with his/her partial private key $\mathsf{psk}_{\mathsf{ID}}$ and user secret key $\mathsf{usk}_{\mathsf{ID}}$ by computing $m \parallel \sigma = H_3((c_1)^{z+t}) \oplus c_2$. If $g^{H_1(m,\sigma)} = c_1$, this returns the message m; else it returns $\perp$.

7.2.2 Security Analysis

The main idea of the security proofs given in this section is to have the challenger $\mathcal{C}$ compute g^{ab} from the given g^a and g^b for unknown a and b by invoking adversary $\mathcal{A}_1$ or $\mathcal{A}_2$ as a subroutine. The following two theorems show that this CLE scheme is indistinguishability under chosen-ciphertext attack (IND-CCA) secure in the random oracle under the CDH assumption.

Theorem 7.1 *Let hash functions H_1, H_2, and H_3 be random oracles. The CDH assumption will fail with nonnegligible advantage when the IND-CCA security of this CLE scheme has been broken by a type I adversary $\mathcal{A}_1$.*

Proof 7.1 *The detail of Theorem 7.1 is omitted due to the similarity with Theorem 7.2.*

Theorem 7.2 *Let hash functions H_1, H_2, and H_3 be random oracles. The CDH assumption will fail with nonnegligible advantage when the IND-CCA security of this CLE scheme has been broken by a type II adversary $\mathcal{A}_2$.*

Proof 7.2 *The intuition behind Theorem 7.2 can be found in Figure 7.1. Let $\mathcal{C}$ be a challenger who receives a random instance (p, q, g, g^a, g^b) of the CDH problem and has to compute the value of g^{ab} for unknown a and b. $\mathcal{A}_2$ is a type II adversary who interacts with $\mathcal{C}$ as modeled in the IND-CCA2 security game. We show how $\mathcal{C}$ can use $\mathcal{A}_2$ to solve the CDH problem, that is, to compute g^{ab}.*

Initial: $\mathcal{C}$ picks $x \in \mathbb{Z}_q^*$ uniformly at random and computes $y = g^x$, then sets $\mathsf{params} = (p, q, g, y, H_1, H_2, H_3)$ and $\mathsf{master\text{-}key} = x$. After that, both params and $\mathsf{master\text{-}key}$ are given to $\mathcal{A}_2$.

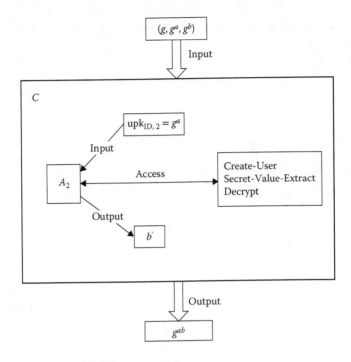

Figure 7.1 Intuition for Theorem 7.2.

Phase 1: $\mathcal{A}_2$ can issue the following oracle queries in an adaptive manner:

H_1 Queries: After receiving a query (ID, ω, μ) to oracle H_1, $\mathcal{C}$ responds as follows:

1. If there is an item $\langle (\text{ID}, \omega, \mu), e \rangle$ in list $\mathbf{H}_1$, e is returned as the answer.
2. Otherwise, $\mathcal{C}$ picks $e \in \mathbb{Z}_p^*$ at random, inserts the item $\langle (\text{ID}, \omega, \mu), e \rangle$ into list $\mathbf{H}_1$, and returns e as the answer.

H_2 Queries: After receiving a query (m, σ) to oracle H_2, $\mathcal{C}$ responds as follows:

1. If there is an item $\langle (m, \sigma), r \rangle$ in list $\mathbf{H}_2$, r is returned as the answer.
2. Otherwise, $\mathcal{C}$ picks $r \in \mathbb{Z}_p^*$ at random, inserts the item $\langle (M, \sigma), r \rangle$ into list $\mathbf{H}_2$, and returns r as the answer.

H_3 Queries: After receiving a query k to oracle H_3, $\mathcal{C}$ responds as follows:

1. If there is an item $\langle k, R \rangle$ in list $\mathbf{H}_3$, R is returned as the answer.

2. Otherwise, $\mathcal{C}$ picks $R \in \{0,1\}^l$ at random, inserts the item $\langle k, R \rangle$ into list $\mathbf{H}_3$, and returns R as the answer.

Create-User Queries: After receiving a query ID to the **Create-User** oracle, $\mathcal{C}$ responds as follows:

1. If there is an item $\langle \text{ID}, (\mu, \omega), coin \rangle$ in the list $\mathcal{PK}$, $\text{upk}_{\text{ID}} = (\mu, \omega)$ is returned as the answer.

2. Otherwise, $\mathcal{C}$ it picks a random coin $c_i \in \{0,1\}$ at random such that $Pr[c_i = 0] = \delta$. (δ will be determined later.)

   - When $c_i = 0$, picks $z, s \in \mathbb{Z}_p^*$ at random and computes $\mu = g^z$, $\omega = g^s$, and $t = s + x H_1(\text{ID}, \omega, \mu)$; inserts items $\langle \text{ID}, (z, t) \rangle$ and $\langle \text{ID}, (\mu, \omega), c_i \rangle$ into lists $\mathcal{SK}$ and $\mathcal{PK}$, respectively; and returns $\text{upk}_{\text{ID}} = (\mu, \omega)$ as an answer.

   - When $c_i = 1$, it picks $z, s \in \mathbb{Z}_p^*$ at random and computes $\mu = g^z$, $\omega = (g^b)^s$; inserts items $\langle \text{ID}, (z, \perp) \rangle$ and $\langle \text{ID}, (\mu, \omega), c_i \rangle$ into lists $\mathcal{SK}$ and $\mathcal{PK}$, respectively; and returns $\text{upk}_{\text{ID}} = (\mu, \omega)$ as an answer.

Secret-Value-Extract Queries: After receiving a query ID to the **Secret-Value-Extract** oracle, $\mathcal{C}$ responds as follows:

1. Runs **Create-User** on the identity ID to obtain a tuple $\langle \text{ID}, (\mu, \omega), c_i \rangle \in \mathcal{PK}$.

2. When $c_i = 0$, searches $\mathcal{SK}$ for a tuple $\langle \text{ID}, (z, t) \rangle$ and returns $(\text{usk}_{\text{ID}}, \text{psk}_{\text{ID}}) = (z, t)$ as an answer.

3. Otherwise, terminates the simulation.

Decrypt Queries: After receiving a query $(\text{ID}, \text{upk}_{\text{ID}}, (c_1, c_2))$ to the **Decrypt** oracle such that $\text{upk}_{\text{ID}} = (\mu, \omega)$, $\mathcal{C}$ responds as follows:

1. Searches $\mathcal{PK}$ for tuple $\langle \text{ID}, (\mu, \omega), c_i \rangle$. If $c_i = 0$, searches $\mathcal{SK}$ for a tuple $\langle \text{ID}, (z, t) \rangle$. (Note that $\langle \text{ID}, (\mu, \omega), c_i \rangle$ must exist in $\mathcal{PK}$ and when $c_i = 0$, $\langle \text{ID}, (z, t) \rangle$ exist in $\mathcal{SK}$.) Then it sets $(\text{usk}_{\text{ID}}, \text{psk}_{\text{ID}}) = (z, t)$ and performs Decrypt(param, $(\text{usk}_{\text{ID}}, \text{psk}_{\text{ID}}), (c_1, c_2))$. Finally, it returns the result of Decrypt algorithm.

2. When $c_i = 1$, runs H_1 queries to get a tuple $\langle (m, \sigma), r \rangle \in \mathbf{H}_2$ and $\langle k, R \rangle \in \mathbf{H}_3$ such that $c_1 = g^r$, $c_2 = R \oplus (m || \sigma)$, and $k = (\mu \omega y^e)^r$; returns m or $\perp$ otherwise.

Challenge: A_2 outputs two messages (m_0, m_1) and a challenge identity ID^*. C runs **Create-User** taking ID^* as input to get a tuple $\langle \text{ID}^*, (\mu^*, \omega^*), c_i \rangle \in \mathcal{PK}$.

1. If $c_i = 0$ returns, it terminates the simulation.
2. Otherwise, it does the following:
   a. Searches $\mathcal{SK}$ for a tuple $\langle \text{ID}^*, (z^*, \perp), s^* \rangle$.
   b. Picks $\sigma^* \in \{0, 1\}^{l_1}$, $c_2^* \in \{0, 1\}^l$, and $\beta \in \{0, 1\}$ at random.
   c. Sets $c_1^* = g^a$ and $e^* = H_1(\text{ID}^*, \omega^*, \mu^*)$.
   d. Defines $a = H_2(m_b, \sigma^*)$ and $H_3((\mu^*\omega^*y^{e^*})^a)$. (Note that C can compute $(\mu^*\omega^*y^{e^*})^a = (\mu^*\omega^*y^{e^*})^a = (g^a)^{z^*} \cdot (g^{ab})^{s^*} \cdot (g^a)^{xe^*}$ without knowledge of a.)
3. Returns (c_1^*, c_2^*) as a target ciphertext.

Phase 2: C repeats the same method it used in **phase 1**.

Guess: Finally, A_2 outputs a guess b'. Now C chooses a tuple $\langle k, R \rangle$ from $\mathbf{H_3}$ and outputs $(k/(g^a)^{z^*} \cdot (g^a)^{xe^*})^{1/s^*}$ as the solution to the CDH problem.

7.3 XIONG–WU–CHEN CERTIFICATELESS AUTHENTICATED KEY AGREEMENT (CL-AKA)

In 2009, Catalano et al. [22] proposed a certificateless *anonymous* key agreement protocol based on Fiore–Gennaro's [88] ID-based key agreement. After that, two certificateless authenticated key agreement (CL-AKA) protocols without bilinear pairing have been proposed in [169,170]. However, Yang and Tan [73] showed that both protocols are insecure and proposed a strongly secure pairing-free CL-AKA protocol along with a new security model for CL-AKA. Nevertheless, the protocol in [73] cannot be considered a *pure* CL-AKA protocol. The merits of certificateless cryptography have been sacrificed to some degree due to the signature embedded in the public key in Yang–Tan's protocol. In fact, the signature included in the public key in [73] is similar to the certificate in traditional public-key infrastructure (PKI). Independent of Yang and Tan's work, He et al. [171] and Xiong et al. [172] proposed two CL-AKA protocols without pairing recently. Unfortunately, Han [173] later showed that He et al.'s protocol cannot resist a type I adversary in certificateless public-key encryption (CL-PKC).

Recently, Tu et al. [174] presented a new CL-AKA protocol without pairing suitable for smart media and mobile environments.

7.3.1 Concrete Construction

Based on the idea in [21,166], Xiong et al. [172] proposed a novel pairing-free CL-AKA protocol. Similarly to other CL-AKA protocols, this protocol requires a KGC and consists of four phases: system setup, partial key extraction, user key generation, and a key agreement phase.

Setup: Given a security parameter $k \in \mathbb{Z}$, the algorithm works as follows:

1. Runs the parameter generator on input k to generate a prime p and determines the tuple $\{\mathbb{F}_p, E/\mathbb{F}_p, \mathbb{G}, P\}$ as defined in Section 2.2.3.
2. Chooses a **master-key** $x \in_R \mathbb{Z}_p^*$, and computes $P_{\text{pub}} = xP$.
3. Chooses cryptographic hash functions $H_1 : \{0,1\}^* \times G \to \mathbb{Z}_p^*$ and $H_2 : \{0,1\}^{*2} \times G^9 \to \{0,1\}^k$. Finally the PKG's **master-key** x is kept secret and the system parameters $\{\mathbb{F}_p, E/\mathbb{F}_p, G, P, P_{\text{pub}}, H_1, H_2\}$ are published.

Extract-Partial-Private-Key: Given a user's identity $\text{ID}_U \in \{0,1\}^*$, the KGC first chooses at random $r_{\text{ID}_U} \in_R \mathbb{Z}_p^*$ and computes $R_{\text{ID}_U} = r_{\text{ID}_U} P$, $h = H_1(\text{ID}_U \| R_{\text{ID}_U})$, and $s_{\text{ID}_U} = (r_{\text{ID}_U} + hx)^{-1}$. It then sets this user's partial private key $(s_{\text{ID}_U}, R_{\text{ID}_U})$ and transmits it to user ID_i secretly.

It is easy to see that user ID_U can validate his/her partial private key by checking whether the equation $s_{\text{ID}_U}(R_{\text{ID}_U} + H_1(\text{ID}_U \| R_{\text{ID}_U}) P_{\text{pub}}) = P$ holds. The partial key is valid if the equation holds and vice versa.

Set-User-Keys: The user ID_U selects a secret value $x_{\text{ID}_U} \in_R \mathbb{Z}_p^*$ as his/her user secret key usk_{ID_U} and computes his/her public key as $\text{upk}_{\text{ID}_U} = x_{\text{ID}_U} P$.

Key Agreement: Assume that an entity A with identity ID_A has full private key $(s_{\text{ID}_A}, R_{\text{ID}_A}, x_{\text{ID}_A})$ and public key upk_{ID_A}, and an entity B with identity ID_B has full private key $(s_{\text{ID}_B}, R_{\text{ID}_B}, x_{\text{ID}_B})$ and public key upk_{ID_B}. The message flows and computations of a protocol run are described below:

1. To start an authenticated key agreement (AKA) session with the intended responder B, the initiator A will

send $\{\mathsf{ID}_A, \mathsf{upk}_{\mathsf{ID}_A}, R_{\mathsf{ID}_A}\}$ to B. On receiving the initiation message from A, B does the following:

    a. Chooses at random the ephemeral key $b \in_R \mathbb{Z}_p^*$ and computes the key token $T_B = b(R_{\mathsf{ID}_A} + H_1(\mathsf{ID}_A\|R_{\mathsf{ID}_A})P_{\text{pub}})$.

    b. Sends $\{\mathsf{ID}_B, \mathsf{upk}_{\mathsf{ID}_B}, R_{\mathsf{ID}_B}\}$ and the key token T_B to A.

2. On receiving $\{\mathsf{ID}_B, \mathsf{upk}_{\mathsf{ID}_B}, R_{\mathsf{ID}_B}, T_B\}$, A does the following:

    a. Chooses at random the ephemeral key $a \in_R \mathbb{Z}_p^*$ and computes the key token $T_A = a(R_{\mathsf{ID}_B} + H_1(\mathsf{ID}_B\|R_{\mathsf{ID}_B})P_{\text{pub}})$.

    b. Sends the key token T_A to B.

3. Then both A and B can compute the shared secrets as follows:

A computes $s_{\mathsf{ID}_A}T_B = bP$ and

$K_{AB}^1 = bP + aP$, $K_{AB}^2 = a \cdot bP$ and $K_{AB}^3 = a \cdot \mathsf{upk}_{\mathsf{ID}_B} + \mathsf{usk}_{\mathsf{ID}_A} \cdot bP$.

B computes $s_{\mathsf{ID}_B}T_A = aP$ and

$K_{BA}^1 = aP + bP$, $K_{BA}^2 = b \cdot aP$ and $K_{BA}^3 = b \cdot \mathsf{upk}_{\mathsf{ID}_A} + \mathsf{usk}_{\mathsf{ID}_B} \cdot aP$.

The shared secrets agree because of the following:

$K_{AB}^1 = bP + aP = K_{BA}^1$,

$K_{AB}^2 = abP = K_{BA}^2$,

$K_{AB}^3 = a \cdot \mathsf{upk}_{\mathsf{ID}_B} + \mathsf{usk}_{\mathsf{ID}_A} \cdot bP = \mathsf{usk}_{\mathsf{ID}_B} \cdot aP + b \cdot \mathsf{upk}_{\mathsf{ID}_A} = K_{BA}^3$.

Thus the agreed session key for A and B can be computed as follows:

$$K = H_2(\mathsf{ID}_A, \mathsf{ID}_B, \mathsf{upk}_{\mathsf{ID}_A}, \mathsf{upk}_{\mathsf{ID}_B}, R_{\mathsf{ID}_A}, R_{\mathsf{ID}_B}, T_A, T_B, K_{AB}^1, K_{AB}^2, K_{AB}^3).$$

7.3.2 Modular Approach for Security Proof in Modified Bellare–Rogaway (mBR) Model

The mBR model [75] is a well-defined model that describes the security of AKA protocols. However, proofs in the mBR model are always error-prone. In order to simplify security proofs in the mBR model, Kudla and Paterson [175] proposed a reduced game called the computational no reveal (cNR)-mBR game. In this section, we introduce the approach.

7.3.2.1 mBR Model

In the mBR model [75], which provides a formal definition for the security of AKA protocols, a protocol is modeled as a pair $P = (\pi, \mathcal{G})$. Here, π specifies how honest players behave, and $\mathcal{G}$ generates key pairs for each entity. π takes as input the security parameter 1^k, identity of initiator i, identity of the responder j, i's public/private key pair together with j's public key $K_{i,j}$, and a transcript $tran$ of the protocol run so far. $\pi(1^k, i, j, K_{i,j}, \mathsf{tran})$ outputs a triple (m, δ, κ), where m is the next message being sent from i to j, $\delta \in \{\mathsf{Accept, Reject}\}$ is i's current decision, and κ is the agreed session key.

The security of π is defined between an adversary $\mathcal{A}$ and a challenger $\mathcal{C}$ by the mBR game. In the game, $\mathcal{A}$ has access to a collection of oracles $\pi_{i,j}^s$, which means the s-th instance between participant i and partner participant j in a session, and is allowed to make a polynomial number of queries including Send, Reveal, and Corrupt to any oracle in any order. Then at some point, $\mathcal{A}$ has to make a Test query to a *fresh* oracle $\pi_{i,j}^s$. Here, $\pi_{i,j}^s$ is called *unfresh* if it is revealed, or has a revealed partner, or its partner $\pi_{j,i}^t$ was corrupted. If an oracle is not *unfresh*, then the oracle is *fresh*. Then $\mathcal{C}$ chooses $b \in_R \{0,1\}$ and responds to $\mathcal{A}$ with the session key of $\pi_{i,j}^s$ if $b = 0$, and otherwise a random value in the key space. After a Test query, $\mathcal{A}$ can continue to query the oracles except that it cannot make a Reveal query to the test oracle $\pi_{i,j}^s$ or to $\pi_{j,i}^t$ who has a matching conversation with $\pi_{i,j}^s$ (if it exists), and it cannot corrupt participant j. Finally, $\mathcal{A}$ outputs its guess b' for b. $\mathcal{A}$'s advantage $Adv^{\mathcal{A}}(k)$ is defined as the probability $b = b'$.

The security of the AKA protocol can be defined using the concept of $\mathcal{A}$'s advantage as follows:

Definition 7.1 *A protocol is said to be an mBR-secure AKA protocol if the following conditions are met:*

1. *In the presence of a benign adversary, two oracles running the protocol both accept holding the same session key, and the session key is distributed uniformly at random on $\{0,1\}^k$.*

2. *For any adversary $\mathcal{A}$, $Adv^{\mathcal{A}}(k)$ is negligible.*

Since $\mathcal{A}$ is formalized in a way that it can perform all kinds of known attacks in the real world, a protocol provides desirable security attributes including known session key security, forward secrecy, key compromise impersonation resilience, and unknown key-share resilience when it satisfies Definition 7.1.

7.3.2.2 Kudla and Paterson's Modular Approach

To provide a concise but precise security proof for AKA protocols in the mBR model, Kulda and Paterson [175] proposed a modular approach (cNR-mBR game), which is regarded as one of the best solutions to prove AKA protocols [167,176]. A cNR-mBR game is identical to an mBR game except that A is not allowed to ask **Reveal** queries and A no longer makes a **Test** query. Instead, an adversary must choose an accepted and fresh oracle $\pi_{i,j}^s$ at the end of the game, and it must compute the session key instead of deciding between a session key and a random value to win the game. In such a game, $Adv^A(k)$ is defined as follows:

Definition 7.2 *A protocol is said to be an cNR-mBR-secure AKA protocol if the following conditions are met:*

1. *In the presence of a benign adversary, two oracles running the protocol both accept holding the same session key, and the session key is distributed uniformly at random on $\{0,1\}^k$.*

2. *For any adversary A, $Adv^A(k)$ in the cNR-mBR game is negligible.*

To employ the modular approach, one should first transform the target protocol π into a corresponding protocol $\overline{\pi}$, which is identical to π except that π produces a hashed session key while $\overline{\pi}$ utilizes the input string of the hash function as the session key. Then prove the security of $\overline{\pi}$ in the cNR-mBR game using Definition 9.5. Finally, the security of π in the cNR-mBR game can be related to that of π in the mBR game according to the following theorem.

Theorem 7.3 *Suppose that a key agreement protocol π produces a hashed session key on completion of the protocol (via hash function) and that π has strong partnering. If the cNR-mBR security of the corresponding $\overline{\pi}$ is probabilistic polynomial time reducible to the hardness of the computational problem of some relation f, and the session string decisional problem for $\overline{\pi}$ is polynomial time reducible to the decisional problem of f, then the mBR security of π is probabilistic polynomial time reducible to the hardness of the Gap problem of f, assuming the hash function is a random oracle.*

The definition for strong partnering in Theorem 7.3 is denoted as follows:

Definition 7.3 *If there exists an adversary $\mathcal{A}$, which when attacking π in an mBR game with nonnegligible probability in the security parameter k can make any two oracles $\pi_{a,b}^u$ and $\pi_{b,a}^v$ accept holding the same session key when they are not partners, then we say that π has weak partnering. If π does not have weak partnering, then we say that π has strong partnering.*

For a comprehensive study of Kudla and Paterson's modular proof, we refer readers to [175].

7.3.2.3 Hard Problems

The following problems defined over G are assumed to be intractable within polynomial time:

Definition 7.4 *Divisible CDH (DCDH) problem: Given a tuple $\{P, aP, bP\} \in G$ for some random values $a, b \in \mathbb{Z}_p$, compute the element $ab^{-1}P$.*

As for the relationship between the CDH problem and DCDH problem, we have the following theorem [177]:

Theorem 7.4 *The DCDH problem is equivalent to the CDH problem; that is, by solving two instances of the DCDH problem, one can solve an instance of the CDH problem.*

7.3.3 Security Analysis

In this section, we prove the security of Xiong et al.'s protocol using Kudla and Paterson's model.

Lemma 7.1 *Suppose that if there is a type I adversary $\mathcal{A}_1$ that breaks the security of our protocol with advantage at least ε, then the CDH problem can be solved with nonnegligible advantage by an algorithm $\mathcal{C}$.*

Proof 7.3 *Suppose $\mathcal{C}$ is given an instance $(aP, bP) \in G$ of the CDH problem and is tasked to compute $cP \in G$ with $c = ab \bmod p$. To do this, $\mathcal{C}$ simulates a challenger with $\mathcal{A}_1$. $\mathcal{C}$ stipulates the hash function H_1 and maintains an H_1-list which is initialized empty. The number* *of participants in the game is denoted by $n_p(k)$ and the number of sessions each participant may be involved in is denoted by $n_s(k)$. The full private key for the i-th participant ID_i is $(s_{\text{ID}_i}, R_{\text{ID}_i}, x_{\text{ID}_i})$ and ID_i is the corresponding identifier. $\mathcal{C}$ generates ID_i's partial private key as follows:*

$\mathcal{C}$ first chooses at random $I \in \{1, \ldots, n_p(k)\}$, then chooses $R_{\text{ID}_I} \in_R G$, and sets $\{\perp, R_{\text{ID}_I}\}$ as ID_I's partial private key. The system public key can be denoted as $P_{pub} = H_1(\text{ID}_I, R_{\text{ID}_I})^{-1}(bP - R_{\text{ID}_I})$, which implicitly means that $s_{\text{ID}_I}^{-1}P = bP$. For ID_i with $i \in \{1, \ldots, n_p(k)\}$ and $i \neq I$, $\mathcal{C}$ sets the partial private key by first choosing at random $(s_{\text{ID}_i}, h_i) \in_R \mathbb{Z}_p^*$. Then $\mathcal{C}$ computes $R_{\text{ID}_i} = s_{\text{ID}_i}^{-1}P - h_i P_{pub}$ and sets $(s_{\text{ID}_i}, R_{\text{ID}_i})$ as ID_i's partial private key. After that, $\mathcal{C}$ passes R_{ID_i} and ID_i to $\mathcal{A}_1$ and adds $\{\text{ID}_i, R_{\text{ID}_i}, s_{\text{ID}_i}, h_i\}$ to the H_1-list for $i \in \{1, \ldots, n_p(k)\}$.

Then $\mathcal{C}$ picks at random $J \in \{1, \ldots, n_p(k)\} \neq I$, $v \in \{1, \ldots, n_s(k)\}$, and $\mathcal{C}$ starts $\mathcal{A}_1$ by answering $\mathcal{A}_1$'s queries as follows:

$H_1(\text{ID}_i, R_{\text{ID}_i})$ query: If the tuple $\{\text{ID}_i, R_{\text{ID}_i}, s_{\text{ID}_i}, h_i\}$ is already in the H_1-list, $\mathcal{C}$ responds with h_i; otherwise, $\mathcal{C}$ chooses $l_i \in_R \mathbb{Z}_p^*$, adds $\{\text{ID}_i, R_{\text{ID}_i}, s_{\text{ID}_i}, l_i\}$ to the H_1-list, and returns l_i to $\mathcal{A}_1$.

__Create-User__(ID_i): $\mathcal{C}$ maintains an initially empty list $\mathbf{C}$ consisting of tuples of the form $(\text{ID}_i, R_{\text{ID}_i}, s_{\text{ID}_i}, x_{\text{ID}_i}, \text{upk}_{\text{ID}_i})$. For simplicity, we assume that all the __Create__ queries are distinct. On receiving a __Create__ query on ID_i, $\mathcal{C}$ first makes an H_1 query to obtain a tuple $\{\text{ID}_i, R_{\text{ID}_i}, s_{\text{ID}_i}, h_i\}$, then chooses a random $x_{\text{ID}_i} \in_R \mathbb{Z}_p^*$, and computes the public key $\text{upk}_{\text{ID}_i} = x_{\text{ID}_i}P$ for ID_i with $i \in \{1, \ldots, n_p(k)\}$. Finally the tuple $(\text{ID}_i, R_{\text{ID}_i}, s_{\text{ID}_i}, x_{\text{ID}_i}, \text{upk}_{\text{ID}_i})$ is added to $\mathbf{C}$. Without loss of generality, we assume that, before asking the following queries, $\mathcal{A}_1$ has already asked some __Create__ queries on the related queries.

__Public-Key-Request__(ID_i): On receiving this query, $\mathcal{C}$ first searches for a tuple $(\text{ID}_i, R_{\text{ID}_i}, s_{\text{ID}_i}, x_{\text{ID}_i}, \text{upk}_{\text{ID}_i})$ in $\mathbf{C}$, which is indexed by ID_i, and then returns upk_{ID_i} as the answer.

__Partial-Private-Key-Extract__(ID_i): Whenever $\mathcal{C}$ receives this query, if $\text{ID}_i = \text{ID}_I$, $\mathcal{C}$ aborts; else, $\mathcal{C}$ searches for a tuple $(\text{ID}_i, R_{\text{ID}_i}, s_{\text{ID}_i}, x_{\text{ID}_i}, \text{upk}_{\text{ID}_i})$ in $\mathbf{C}$, which is indexed by ID_i, and returns $(R_{\text{ID}_i}, s_{\text{ID}_i})$ as the answer.

__Corrupt__(ID_i): Whenever $\mathcal{C}$ receives this query, if $\text{ID}_i = \text{ID}_I$, $\mathcal{C}$ aborts; else, $\mathcal{C}$ searches for a tuple $(\text{ID}_i, R_{\text{ID}_i}, s_{\text{ID}_i}, x_{\text{ID}_i}, \text{upk}_{\text{ID}_i})$ in $\mathbf{C}$, which is indexed by ID_i, and if $x_{\text{ID}_i} = \text{null}$, $\mathcal{C}$ returns null; otherwise, $\mathcal{C}$ returns $(R_{\text{ID}_i}, s_{\text{ID}_i}, x_{\text{ID}_i})$ as the answer.

Public-Key-Replace($\text{ID}_i, upk'_{\text{ID}_i}$): *On receiving this query, $\mathcal{C}$ searches for a tuple* ($\text{ID}_i, R_{\text{ID}_i}, s_{\text{ID}_i}, x_{\text{ID}_i}, upk_{\text{ID}_i}$) *in $\mathbf{C}$, which is indexed by ID_i, and then updates upk_{ID_i} to upk'_{ID_i} and sets x_{ID_i} = null.*

Send($\pi_{i,j}^s, m$): *If $\pi_{i,j}^s \neq \pi_{J,j}^v$, then $\mathcal{C}$ acts according to the protocol specification. Otherwise, $\mathcal{C}$ responds with the tuple* ($\text{ID}_j, upk_{\text{ID}_j}, R_{\text{ID}_j}, aP$).

The probability that $\mathcal{A}_1$ chooses $\pi_{J,j}^v$ as the Test *oracle and that $\text{ID}_j = \text{ID}_I$ is $1/n_p^2(k)n_s(k)$. In this case, $\mathcal{A}_1$ would not have corrupted ID_I, and so $\mathcal{C}$ would not have aborted. If $\mathcal{A}_1$ can win such a game, then at the end of this game, $\mathcal{A}_1$ will output its guess of the session key of the form $\{0,1\}^* \times \{0,1\}^* \times A \times B \times C \times D \times E \times F \times G \times H \times I$, and $\mathcal{C}$ can output $G - s_J m$, where m is the input message of the* Send($\pi_{J,j}^v, m$) *query. Thus, $\mathcal{C}$ can solve the DCDH problem with nonnegligible probability $c1/n_p^2(k)n_s(k)$ within $t(k)$, where c is a constant. Then according to Theorem 7.4, the CDH problem can be solved with an advantage of at least $(c1/n_p^2(k)n_s(k))^2$.*

Lemma 7.2 *Suppose that if there is a type II adversary $\mathcal{A}_2$ that breaks the security of our protocol with an advantage of at least ε, then the CDH problem can be solved with nonnegligible advantage by an algorithm $\mathcal{C}$.*

Proof 7.4 *Suppose that there exists a type II adversary $\mathcal{A}_2$ that can win the game with a nonnegligible advantage in polynomial time. Then we show that there is an algorithm $\mathcal{C}$ that solves the CDH problem with nonnegligible probability. Suppose $\mathcal{C}$ is given an arbitrary input $(P, aP, bP) \in G$ of the CDH problem. We show how $\mathcal{C}$ can use $\mathcal{A}_2$ to solve the CDH problem, that is, to compute abP. $\mathcal{C}$ first chooses $x \in_R \mathbb{Z}_p^*$ at random and sets $P_{pub} = xP$ as the system public key. After that, x is sent to $\mathcal{A}_2$ by $\mathcal{C}$. $\mathcal{C}$ stipulates the hash function H_1 and maintains an H_1-list, which is initialized empty. The number of participants in the game is denoted by $n_p(k)$ and the number of sessions each participant may be involved in is denoted by $n_s(k)$. The full private key for the i-th participant ID_i is $(s_{\text{ID}_i}, R_{\text{ID}_i}, x_{\text{ID}_i})$ and ID_i is the corresponding identifier. $\mathcal{C}$ chooses at random $r_{\text{ID}_i} \in_R \mathbb{Z}_p^*$, computes $R_{\text{ID}_i} = r_{\text{ID}_i} P$ and $s_{\text{ID}_i} = r_{\text{ID}_i} + H_1(\text{ID}_i \| R_{\text{ID}_i})x$, and sets $(s_{\text{ID}_i}, R_{\text{ID}_i})$ as ID_i's partial private key.*

Then $\mathcal{C}$ picks at random $I, J \in \{1, \ldots, n_p(k)\}$, $v \in \{1, \ldots, n_s(k)\}$, and $\mathcal{C}$ starts $\mathcal{A}_2$ by answering $\mathcal{A}_2$'s queries as follows:

$H_1(\mathsf{ID}_i, R_{\mathsf{ID}_i})$ *query: If the tuple* $\{\mathsf{ID}_i, R_{\mathsf{ID}_i}, s_{\mathsf{ID}_i}, h_i\}$ *is already in the* H_1*-list,* $\mathcal{C}$ *responds with* h_i*; otherwise,* $\mathcal{C}$ *chooses* $l_i \in_R \mathbb{Z}_p^*$*, adds* $\{\mathsf{ID}_i, R_{\mathsf{ID}_i}, s_{\mathsf{ID}_i}, l_i\}$ *to the* H_1*-list, and returns* l_i *to* $\mathcal{A}_2$*.*

Create-User(ID_i)*:* $\mathcal{C}$ *maintains an initially empty list* $\boldsymbol{C}$ *consisting of tuples of the form* $(\mathsf{ID}_i, R_{\mathsf{ID}_i}, s_{\mathsf{ID}_i}, x_{\mathsf{ID}_i}, \mathsf{upk}_{\mathsf{ID}_i})$*. For simplicity, we assume that all the* **Create** *queries are distinct. On receiving a* **Create** *query on* ID_i*,* $\mathcal{C}$ *sets the public key as* bP *and the user secret key as* $\perp$ *for* ID_i *with* $i = I$*; otherwise,* $\mathcal{C}$ *chooses a random* $x_{\mathsf{ID}_i} \in_R \mathbb{Z}_p^*$ *and computes the public key as* $x_{\mathsf{ID}_i}P$ *and user secret key as* x_{ID_i} *for* ID_i *with* $i \in \{1, \ldots, n_p(k)\}$ *and* $i \neq I$*. After that,* $\mathcal{C}$ *makes an* H_1 *query to obtain a tuple* $\{\mathsf{ID}_i, R_{\mathsf{ID}_i}, s_{\mathsf{ID}_i}, h_i\}$*. Finally the tuple* $(\mathsf{ID}_i, R_{\mathsf{ID}_i}, s_{\mathsf{ID}_i}, x_{\mathsf{ID}_i}, \mathsf{upk}_{\mathsf{ID}_i})$ *is added to* $\boldsymbol{C}$*. Without loss of generality, we assume that, before asking the following queries,* $\mathcal{A}_2$ *has already asked some* **Create** *queries on the related queries.*

Public-Key-Request(ID_i)*:* *On receiving this query,* $\mathcal{C}$ *first searches for a tuple* $(\mathsf{ID}_i, R_{\mathsf{ID}_i}, s_{\mathsf{ID}_i}, x_{\mathsf{ID}_i}, \mathsf{upk}_{\mathsf{ID}_i})$ *in* $\boldsymbol{C}$*, which is indexed by* ID_i*, and then returns* $\mathsf{upk}_{\mathsf{ID}_i}$ *as the answer.*

Corrupt(ID_i)*: Whenever* $\mathcal{C}$ *receives this query, if* $\mathsf{ID}_i = \mathsf{ID}_I$*,* $\mathcal{C}$ *aborts; else,* $\mathcal{C}$ *searches for a tuple* $(\mathsf{ID}_i, R_{\mathsf{ID}_i}, s_{\mathsf{ID}_i}, x_{\mathsf{ID}_i}, \mathsf{upk}_{\mathsf{ID}_i})$ *in* $\boldsymbol{C}$*, which is indexed by* ID_i*, and returns* $(R_{\mathsf{ID}_i}, s_{\mathsf{ID}_i}, x_{\mathsf{ID}_i})$ *as the answer.*

Public-Key-Replace$(ID_i, \mathsf{upk}'_{\mathsf{ID}_i})$*: On receiving this query, if* $\mathsf{ID}_i = \mathsf{ID}_I$*,* $\mathcal{C}$ *aborts; otherwise,* $\mathcal{C}$ *searches for a tuple* $(\mathsf{ID}_i, R_{\mathsf{ID}_i}, s_{\mathsf{ID}_i}, x_{\mathsf{ID}_i}, \mathsf{upk}_{\mathsf{ID}_i})$ *in* $\boldsymbol{C}$*, which is indexed by* ID_i*, and then updates* $\mathsf{upk}_{\mathsf{ID}_i}$ *to* $\mathsf{upk}'_{\mathsf{ID}_i}$ *and sets* $x_{\mathsf{ID}_i} = null$*.*

Send$(\pi_{i,j}^s, m)$*: If* $\pi_{i,j}^s \neq \pi_{J,j}^v$*, then* $\mathcal{C}$ *acts according to the protocol specification. Otherwise,* $\mathcal{C}$ *responds with the tuple* $(\mathsf{ID}_j, \mathsf{upk}_{\mathsf{ID}_j}, R_{\mathsf{ID}_j}, aP)$*.*

The probability that $\mathcal{A}_2$ *chooses* $\pi_{J,j}^v$ *as the* **Test** *oracle and that* $\mathsf{ID}_j = \mathsf{ID}_I$ *is* $1/n_p^2(k)n_s(k)$*. In this case,* $\mathcal{A}_2$ *would not have corrupted* ID_I*, and so* $\mathcal{C}$ *would not have aborted. If* $\mathcal{A}_2$ *can win such a game, then at the end of this game,* $\mathcal{A}_2$ *will output its guess of the session key of the form* $\{0,1\}^* \times \{0,1\}^* \times A \times B \times C \times D \times E \times F \times G \times H \times I$*, and* $\mathcal{C}$ *can output* $I - x_J m$*, where* m *is the input message of the* **Send**$(\pi_{J,j}^v, m)$ *query. Thus,* $\mathcal{C}$ *can solve the divisible CDH (DCDH) problem with nonnegligible probability* $c1/n_p^2(k)n_s(k)$ *within* $t(k)$*, where* c *is a constant. Then according to Theorem 7.4, the CDH problem can be solved with an advantage of at least* $(c1/n_p^2(k)n_s(k))^2$*.*

Lemma 7.3 *Our protocol has strong partnering in the random oracle model.*

Proof 7.5 *Let pa denote the partner of user a. Suppose an adversary $\mathcal{A}$ can have two oracles $\pi_{i,pi}^s$ and $\pi_{j,pj}^t$ accept holding the same session key when $pi \neq j$ and $pj \neq i$.*

If $\pi_{i,pi}^s$ is an initiator for the session key, it has to make a query of the form $\{ID_i, ID_{pi}, A, B, C, D, E, F, G, H, I\}$ to the random oracle H_2 and to receive h_2^i as the session key. For $\pi_{j,pj}^t$ to have the same session key, it must have made the H_2 query of the form $\{ID_{pj}, ID_j, A, B, C, D, E, F, G, H, I\}$ since $\mathsf{ID}_j \neq \mathsf{ID}_i$. Then it must have $\mathsf{ID}_{pj} = \mathsf{ID}_i$ and vice versa. Thus, $\pi_{i,pi}^s$ and $\pi_{j,pj}^t$ are partners, which contradicts the assumption.

Theorem 7.5 *Our protocol is secure in the random oracle model assuming the hardness of the Gap Diffie–Hellman problem.*

Proof 7.6 *The theorem follows directly from Lemmas 7.1 to 7.3. Thus, the protocol provides known session key security, key compromise impersonation resilience, and unknown key share resilience, which is satisfied even in face of Kaliski's unknown key-share attack, as shown in [178].*

Theorem 7.6 *Our protocol has the perfect forward secrecy property if the CDH problem in G is hard.*

Proof 7.7 *Suppose that A and B established a session key K using this CL-AKA protocol, and later, their full private keys $(s_{\mathsf{ID}_A}, R_{\mathsf{ID}_A}, x_{\mathsf{ID}_A})$ and $(s_{\mathsf{ID}_B}, R_{\mathsf{ID}_B}, x_{\mathsf{ID}_B})$ were compromised. Let a and b be the secret random numbers chosen by A and B, respectively, during the establishment of their session key. It is easy to see that, to compute the established session key K, the adversary who owns $(s_{\mathsf{ID}_A}, R_{\mathsf{ID}_A}, x_{\mathsf{ID}_A})$, $(s_{\mathsf{ID}_B}, R_{\mathsf{ID}_B}, x_{\mathsf{ID}_B})$, $s_{\mathsf{ID}_B} T_a = aP$, and $s_{\mathsf{ID}_A} T_b = bP$ for unknown a, b must know the value of abP. However, to compute the value of abP without the knowledge of either a or b, the adversary must have the ability to solve the CDH problem in $\mathbb{G}$. Under the CDH assumption, this probability is negligible. Hence, this protocol has the perfect forward secrecy property.*

7.3.4 Performance

In this section, we compare the efficiency of the proposed protocols and Zhang et al.'s [21] protocol (the known most-efficient certificateless authenticated two-party key agreement protocol from pairings). In the computation efficiency comparison, we obtain the running time for cryptographic operations using MIRACAL [179], a standard cryptographic library.

The hardware platform is a PIV 3 GHz processor with 512 MB memory and the Windows XP operating system. For the pairing-based protocols, to achieve 1024-bit RSA-level security, we used the Tate pairing defined over the supersingular elliptic curve $E/\mathbb{F}_p : y^2 = x^3 + x$ with embedding degree 2. q is a 160-bit Solinas prime $q = 2^{159} + 2^{17} + 1$ and p a 512-bit prime satisfying $p + 1 = 12qr$. For the elliptic curve cryptography (ECC)-based protocols, to achieve the same security level, we employed the ECC group on the Koblitz elliptic curve $y^2 = x^3 + ax^2 + b$ defined on $\mathbb{F}_{2^{163}}$ with $a = 1$ and b a 163-bit random prime. The running times are listed in Table 7.1, where sca.mul. stands for scalar multiplication.

To evaluate the computation efficiency of different protocols, we use the simple method from [167]. For example, in Zhang et al.'s protocol [21], to establish a session key, one pairing operation and five pairing-based scalar multiplications are needed, and the resulting computation time is $20.01 + 6.38 \times 5 = 54.16$ ms. Bandwidth is measured by the maximal length of a single message in transmission (auxiliary messages such as entity identifier and public key are not counted). In Zhang et al.'s protocol, the longest message contains one point in the pairing-based group; thus the bandwidth for Zhang et al.'s protocol is $512/8 = 64$ bytes.

According to Table 7.2, the computation cost and bandwidth load of Xiong et al.'s protocol is 10.7% and 68.3% of Zhang et al.'s protocol, respectively.

TABLE 7.1   Cryptographic Operation Time (in ms)

Pairing	Pairing-Based sca.mul.	Exponential in $\mathbb{F}_{p^2}$	ECC-Based sca.mul.
20.01	6.83	11.20	0.83

TABLE 7.2   Performance Comparison of Different Protocols

Protocol	Computation (in ms)	Bandwidth (in bytes)
Zhang et al. [21]	54.16	64
Xiong et al.	5.81	41

IV

Applications, Extensions, and Related Paradigms

CHAPTER 8

Applications of CL-PKC

8.1 INTRODUCTION

Due to its unique characteristics, certificateless public-key encryption (CL-PKC) has been found applicable in numerous scenarios including anonymous communication [22], cloud computing [25,28,99], vehicle ad hoc networks (VANETs) [26], vehicle to grid networks [180], ad hoc networks [181], and wireless body area networks (WBANs) [24,101,182, 183]. In general, the main objective of the CL-PKC applications is to reduce trust in the private key generator (PKG) and retain the good aspects of identity-based public-key cryptography (ID-PKC) simultaneously. The purpose of this chapter is to provide a brief discussion of these applications. This discussion is not meant to be comprehensive, but rather to provide the reader with an intuition of the technical flexibility that the notion of CL-PKC offers. We primarily discuss certificateless onion routing [22] and the anonymous certificateless remote authentication protocol for extrabody communication in WBANs [183].

8.2 ONION ROUTING

8.2.1 Motivation

To decouple the user's identity from her/his network activities in a public network like the Internet, the notion of mix-net has been introduced by Chaum [184] to achieve an anonymous channel. Informally speaking, the basic idea of mix-net is that the messages are wrapped in several layers of encryption before sending to the first node in the mixnet. After receiving a number of ciphertexts, the node in the mix-net peels off a layer of encryption from each of the ciphertexts and sends the resulting values in permuted order to the next node sequentially until the messages are delivered to the recipients by the last node. The link between the sender and the receiver will not be disclosed provided that each node in the mix-net permutes the messages in a randomized order before forwarding.

Based on the idea of mix-nets, Reed et al. [185] and Syverson et al. [186] introduced the *onion routing* approach to achieve anonymous communication as follows. An onion routing protocol involves a service provider, a set of users, and a set of nodes (called onion routers). To establish an anonymous channel with the service provider over the public network, the user first selects a random set of nodes (called a circuit), then wraps the message with several layers of encryption, one for each node, and sends it to the service provider through these intermediate nodes. The layered composition where transmitted messages are wrapped is called the onion, and thus the nodes in the circuit are called onion routers. On receiving a message from another node, the onion router decrypts it and immediately sends the resulting value to the next node. This way, anonymity can be achieved since each onion router obtains only the identities of the two nodes adjacent to him/her in the circuit. Neither the first node nor the last node can recognize if the message is receiving from/sending to a user or another onion router. Different from the mix-net in [184], an onion router does not batch and permute a number of received messages before forwarding, but rather immediately forwards what it receives. Since its introduction, onion routing has received a lot of attention and led to several constructions and implementations (e.g., [187–191]). Notably, the famous onion routing project, known as Tor [192], now offers privacy and anonymity service to huge number of users over the Internet.

As the most important component of an onion routing protocol, circuit construction allows a user to build a circuit by establishing a secure channel through each onion router. According to [22,187,188,190–192], the circuit construction is expected to feature a forward secrecy property where a router's corruption does not disclose the session keys of this router before the corruption. A straightforward and naive way to offer forward secrecy is to frequently update the keys shared between the user and the onion router. However, such a naive solution can be very complicated in practice since the users are required to repeatedly share new keys with the routers. As a solution for Tor [192], the circuit is built by using the routers' public keys to establish a temporary session key between the user and the corresponding router via an interactive key exchange protocol [4]. Despite this solution being analyzed [193] and improved [194], the main issue of this approach is the bandwidth cost such that $O(n^2)$ symmetrically encrypted messages are required in case n routers are involved in a circuit. After that, Kate et al. [190,191] incorporated ID-PKC [9] to propose a new approach to this problem such that messages are encrypted under the identity of the routers and validity period. Two major drawbacks are identified in [190,191]: (1) the key escrow problem inherent in ID-PKC and (2) the frequent interaction between the routers and the PKG to allow routers to derive new secret keys in each validity period. To solve these issues, Catalano et al. [22] suggested using certificateless encryption (rather than identity-based) to construct the onions to enjoy the merits of ID-PKC without suffering the key escrow problem.

8.2.2 Catalano–Fiore–Gennaro Scheme

8.2.2.1 Framework of Onion Routing

In general, an onion routing protocol involves a service provider, a set of onion routers, and users. The goal of users is to establish an anonymous channel with the service provider over the hostile networks by sending their traffic through a circuit of randomly chosen onion routers. In particular, a protocol is typically defined by the following two phases:

Setup and Key Generation: In this phase, the service provider initializes the system by setting up the public parameters. After that, each user generates a pair of public/private keys.

Circuit Construction: In this phase, the user firstly obtains a list $\mathcal{L}$ containing the identities of all the onion routers available in the system from the service provider. Then, the user selects an ordered set of n onion routers $\{OR_1, \ldots, OR_n\}$ (which is called a circuit) randomly from the list $\mathcal{L}$. To route the traffic through such a circuit, the user builds a specific ciphertext such that each onion router OR_i in the circuit can partially decrypt the ciphertext by peeling off a layer of encryption and obtain (1) the address of the next router OR_{i+1} in the circuit and (2) another onion ciphertext that is then forwarded to the next router OR_{i+1}. Finally, the user sends this ciphertext to the first router and each router in the circuit will decrypt and forward it to the next router until the last router sends the message to the service provider.

8.2.2.2 Security of Onion Routing

In [195], Camenisch and Lysyanskaya formalized the security of the onion routing protocol in the universally composable framework and proposed a generic construction based on the chosen-ciphertext attack (CCA) encryption with tags and pseudorandom permutations. However, satisfying the security requirement defined in [195] results in inefficient constructions of onion routing since all potential attacks are captured in the Camenisch–Lysyanskaya model. Therefore, the security of onion routing protocols are revisited in [22,187,188,190,191].

Cryptographic Unlinkability: This property means that it is infeasible for an adversary to identify a link between the sender and the receiver. Note that the attacks in the network level are not considered by this property [190,191]. A formal definition of this property is given by the following game between an adversary $\mathcal{A}$ and a simulator/challenger $\mathcal{C}$ [22,190,191]:

Setup: $\mathcal{C}$ initializes the system by generating the public system parameters and distributes the parameters to $\mathcal{A}$.

Phase 1: The following oracles are allowed to be queried by $\mathcal{A}$ in an adaptive manner:

- **Corruption**: After receiving an onion router OR, the secret keys are returned to $\mathcal{A}$ by this oracle.
- **Decrypt**: After receiving an onion router OR and a ciphertext c, this oracle decrypts the ciphertext c with OR's secret key.

Challenge: After deciding the query phase is over, $\mathcal{A}$ is enabled to select a message m and routers $OR_1, OR_1', OR_2, OR_2', OR_H$ such that OR_H has not been corrupted in the previous phase. $\mathcal{C}$ flips a binary coin $b \in \{0,1\}$ and performs the following steps. When $b = 0$:

- An onion ciphertext c_1 is created for the circuit (OR_1, OR_H, OR_2).
- Another onion ciphertext c_1' is created for the circuit (OR_1', OR_H, OR_2').

When $b = 1$:

- An onion ciphertext c_1 is created for the circuit (OR_1, OR_H, OR_2').

- Another onion ciphertext c_1' is created for the circuit (OR_1', OR_H, OR_2).

Finally, $\mathcal{C}$ sends (c_1, c_1') to $\mathcal{A}$.

Phase 2: $\mathcal{A}$ can proceed as in phase 1 with the following restrictions:

1. OR_H cannot be corrupted in this phase.
2. $\mathcal{A}$ cannot submit (OR_H, c_1) and (OR_H, c_1') to the decryption oracle.

Guess: At the end of this game, $\mathcal{A}$ outputs a guess b' for b and it wins if $b' = b$.

The advantage of $\mathcal{A}$ in this game is defined as $\mathrm{Adv}_{OR}^{anon}(\mathcal{A}) = 2 \cdot Pr[b' = b] - 1$.

Definition 8.1 *An onion routing protocol is regarded as offering cryptographic unlinkability if for any PPT adversary $\mathcal{A}$, the probability $Adv_{OR}^{anon}(\mathcal{A})$ is negligible.*

Integrity and Correctness: Correctness ensures that if all parties execute the protocol honestly, then the recipient should derive the message encrypted by the sender and forwarded by the circuit. On the other hand, integrity states that the onion routers can be recognized even if the number of encryption layers of an onion ciphertext is longer than a prespecified upper-bound.

Onion-Security: Onion security guarantees that the adversary controlling all but one honest router in a circuit is not able to disclose the session key shared between the user and the honest node. Following the Canetti–Krawczyk model for key-agreement protocols [196,197], a formal definition of onion security is presented in [22,190,191].

Circuit Position Secrecy: Circuit position secrecy means that the position of a given onion router in the circuit should not be disclosed to this router. In fact, it is nontrivial to offer this property since the ciphertext size depends proportionally on the number of times it is encrypted in randomized encryption schemes as shown by Camenisch and Lysyanskaya in [195]. Some solutions for this issue can be found in [190,191,195].

8.2.2.3 Building Blocks

A certificateless anonymous key agreement protocol has been proposed in this section, which is used as a building block to construct a certificateless onion routing protocol.

Setup: The key-generation center (KGC) chooses a group $\mathbb{G}$ with the prime order q and a random generator $g \in \mathbb{G}$. After that, two hash functions $H_1 : \{0,1\}^* \to \mathbb{Z}_q$ and $H_2 : \mathbb{Z}_q \times \mathbb{Z}_q \to \{0,1\}^l$ are also selected by the KGC. Then the KGC picks a random $x \in \mathbb{Z}_q$ and computes $y = g^x$. Finally, the KGC distributes the public parameters $\mathsf{params} = (q, \mathbb{G}, g, y, H_1, H_2)$ and keeps the master-secret x secret.

Extract-Partial-Private-Key: After receiving a valid identity ID, the KGC generates the corresponding partial private key as follows. First, the KGC selects a random $k \in \mathbb{Z}_q$ and computes $r = g^k$ and $s = k + H_1(\mathsf{ID}, r)x$. After that, the partial private key $\mathsf{psk}_{\mathsf{ID}} = (r, s)$ is returned to the user.

Set-User-Keys: After receiving a partial private key $\mathsf{psk}_{\mathsf{ID}} = (r, s)$ from the KGC, the user picks a random $t \in \mathbb{Z}_q$ and computes $u = g^t$. Then the user public key $\mathsf{upk}_{\mathsf{ID}}$ and user secret key $\mathsf{usk}_{\mathsf{ID}}$ are defined as (r, u) and (s, t), respectively.

Key-Agreement: If a user U intends to anonymously authenticate to Bob, U chooses $\omega \in \mathbb{Z}_q$ at random and computes its pseudonym identity $P_U = g^\omega$. After obtaining Bob's identity ID_B and user public key $\mathsf{upk}_{\mathsf{ID}_B} = (r_{\mathsf{ID}_B}, u_{\mathsf{ID}_B})$, U computes the session key $K = H_2(z_1, z_2)$ such that $z_1 = (r_{\mathsf{ID}_B} y^{H_1(\mathsf{ID}_B, r_{\mathsf{ID}_B})})^\omega$ and $z_2 = u_{\mathsf{ID}_B}^\omega$ and sends P_U to Bob. Upon receiving the pseudonym identity P_U, Bob generates the session key $z_1 = P_U^{s_{\mathsf{ID}_B}}$ and $z_2 = P_U^{t_{\mathsf{ID}_B}}$. It is obvious to observe that $z_1 = g^{\omega s_{\mathsf{ID}_B}}$ and $z_2 = g^{\omega t_{\mathsf{ID}_B}}$.

Lemma 8.1 *Suppose that if there is a type I adversary $\mathcal{A}_1$ who breaks the security of this key agreement protocol, then the computational Diffie–Hellman (CDH) problem can be solved with nonnegligible advantage by an algorithm $\mathcal{C}$.*

Lemma 8.2 *Suppose that if there is a type II adversary $\mathcal{A}_2$ who breaks the security of this key agreement protocol, then the CDH problem can be solved with nonnegligible advantage by an algorithm $\mathcal{C}$.*

Proof. The proofs of both theorems are omitted due to space limitations and interested readers can refer to [22] for more details.

8.2.2.4 Concrete Construction

The certificateless onion routing protocol is described as follows [22]:

Setup and Key Generation: The KGC is acted by the service provider for the anonymous key agreement protocol. In this phase, the KGC generates the public parameters and a list $\mathcal{L}$ containing the identities of all the onion routers and issues partial private keys for the onion routers. After receiving the partial private key $\mathsf{psk}_{\mathsf{ID}_i}$ from the KGC, an onion router OR_i generates a pair of user public/secret keys $(\mathsf{upk}_i, \mathsf{usk}_{\mathsf{ID}_i})$ and distributes $\mathsf{upk}_{\mathsf{ID}_i}$ in the system.

Circuit Construction: To build a circuit, the user selects n onion routers $OR_1, \ldots, OR_n$ from $\mathcal{L}$ at random. After that, the anonymous certificateless key agreement protocol is performed by the user and each onion router in the circuit in Section 8.2.2.3 to establish a shared session key. Finally, an onion ciphertext is created as follows:

$$P_1, \{OR_2, P_2, \{\ldots \{OR_n, P_n, \{\emptyset\}_{K_n}\} \ldots\}_{K_2}\}_{K_1}$$

where $\{m\}_{K_i}$ denotes that the message m is encrypted using the session key K_i with symmetric encryption. It is obvious to see that an onion is defined by a pair (P, c), where P denotes a pseudonym and c is a ciphertext. On receiving an onion (P_i, c_i), the router OR_i recovers the session key K_i using its user secret key and the pseudonym P_i, and in turn decrypts c_i with the session key K_i. Finally, OR_i sends (P_{i+1}, c_{i+1}) to the next onion router OR_{i+1}. This way, the ciphertext can be forwarded to the real receiver. After the last onion router in the circuit obtains $\emptyset$ from the decrypting ciphertext, a confirmation message will be sent back along the circuit to the user such that this confirmation message is encrypted by each router using the session key K_i.

8.2.2.5 Security Analysis

The certificateless onion routing protocol described above satisfies all security requirements defined in Section 8.2.2.2.

Cryptographic Unlinkability: This property depends on the IND-CPA security of the symmetric encryption scheme adopted in the onion routing protocol. Thus, Catalano et al.'s protocol automatically features cryptographic unlinkability provided that the indistinguishability under chosen-plaintext attack (IND-CPA) secure symmetric encryption scheme is adopted.

Integrity and Correctness: An onion ciphertext containing more than n layers of encryption can be trivially identified by the first router from the ciphertext length where n denotes the upper bound on the number of routers in the circuit. Correctness originates from the construction of a certificateless onion routing protocol and the correctness of the underlying certificateless anonymous key agreement protocol.

Onion Security: It is obvious that onion security directly originates from the security of the underlying certificateless anonymous key agreement protocol. The adversary, who is allowed to corrupt routers and ask for decryption of onions, can be simulated by the adversary defined in type I and type II security games for the underlying certificateless anonymous key agreement protocol.

Circuit Position Secrecy: Despite the position in the circuit of a router being identified from the length of a receiving ciphertext in Catalano et al.'s protocol, the trick in [190] can be used to offer circuit position security at the cost of efficiency.

8.3 ANONYMOUS REMOTE AUTHENTICATION FOR WBANs

8.3.1 Motivation

The increasing demand for providing expert-level medical diagnosis and treatment remotely has attracted wide interest on WBANs [198,199]. As a subgroup of wireless sensor networks (WSNs), WBANs have been implemented to continuous measure and monitor vital parameters of the aging population and patients with chronic diseases [200]. A WBAN mainly consists of wearable/implanted (bio-)medical sensors and portable personal devices (PPDs) [201], where the intelligent sensors of WBAN can monitor the health/motion information of people with different degrees of physical and mental disabilities, while the PPD is employed to ensure reliable message delivery between the sensors and the application providers (APs) such as the physician and hospital or medical staff [202–205]. Several key applications ranging from remote health monitoring to military/fitness training can be enabled by intra-body communication (between the WBAN sensors and the PPD) and extra-body communication (between the PPD and the APs) in WBANs. An example of intra-body and extra-body communication in a WBAN is shown in Figure 8.1. Due to the potential of minimizing the need of caregivers and improving the patient/elder's experience, WBANs have become increasingly attractive to industry and academia [206–211].

With the continuing development of WBANs, users' concerns about the privacy of their sensitive physiological information such that these data can only be accessed by the authorized parties become the main obstacles that impede WBANs from wide adoption [212,213]. However, security design for WBANs is nontrivial when the unique features of WBANs, such as the limited resources and mobility of body sensors, open medium of the communication channel, and the lack of infrastructure, are taken into account. To allow the neighboring nodes in WBANs to share a common key, Zhang and Mao [139] proposed a novel key agreement scheme by using electrocardiogram signals. Li et al. [214] suggested a group key agreement protocol that establishes shared secret keys between the WBAN sensors and the PPD *from scratch*.

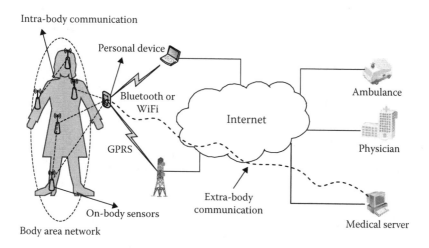

Figure 8.1 Wireless body area network (WBAN) example of intra-body and extra-body communication.

He et al. [215] developed a secure admission and transmission protocol for WBANs based on polynomial-based authentication to allow each sensor to establish an individual key shared with the PPD and a pairwise key shared with another sensor node. Most of the existing security protocols were proposed for securing intra-body communication in WBANs [214–216] or simply for privacy protection without an authentication mechanism [217,218].

Regarding the security issues in the extra-body communication field, Liu et al. [24,219] suggested two certificateless remote anonymous authentication protocols along with an efficient certificateless signature by incorporating the idea of certificateless cryptography [17,19] and an identity-based remote anonymous authentication protocol [166] recently. Using the remote authentication protocols reported in [24,219], a WBAN client and the requested AP can authenticate each other and share a session key to secure the subsequent communication. Furthermore, the privacy of the client can be realized without encryption operation. The certificateless anonymous remote authentication protocols in [24,219] combine the merits of the remote anonymous authentication in the traditional public-key infrastructure (PKI) [1] and ID-PKC [166], while preventing the inborn key escrow problem in ID-PKC [8] and the heavy certificate management overhead in conventional PKI.

Unfortunately, Xiong [183] observes that the certificateless signature in [24] cannot resist the attack mounted by the key replacement adversary [50,116]. Moreover, Liu et al.'s certificateless authentication protocols cannot offer the feature of forward security (FS) [220–222]. In particular, the session key in the previous round will be revealed if the long-term private key of the AP is corrupted. Finally, Liu et al.'s protocols did not address the scalability issue in the sense that the account information of the WBAN client must be distributed to the APs before the client can access the service offered by these APs.

8.3.2 Xiong's Protocol

In this section, Xiong's protocol is presented along with the basic mathematic background, the system model, and the objectives.

8.3.2.1 Notations

The notations used throughout Xiong's protocol are listed in Table 8.1 to improve readability.

TABLE 8.1 Notations and Descriptions

Notations	Descriptions
WBANs	**W**ireless **B**ody **A**rea **N**etworks
WSNs	**W**ireless **S**ensor **N**etworks
PPD	**P**ortable **P**ersonal **D**evice
APs	**A**pplication **P**roviders
NM	**N**etwork **M**anager
$\mathbb{F}_p$	A prime finite field
$E/\mathbb{F}_p$	The elliptic curve over $\mathbb{F}_p$
G	A cyclic additive group defined over the curve E
$H_1(\cdot), H_2(\cdot)$	Secure hash functions such as $H_1 : \{0,1\}^* \times G^2 \to \mathbb{Z}_p^*$
$H_3(\cdot), H_4(\cdot)$	$H_2 : \{0,1\}^* \times G^3 \times \{0,1\}^* \to \mathbb{Z}_p^*$
	$H_3 : G \to \{0,1\}^* \times G^3 \times \{0,1\}^*$
	$H_4 : \{0,1\}^* \times \{0,1\}^* \times G^8 \to \{0,1\}^*$
$\mathrm{MAC}_{(\cdot)}(\cdot)$	A message authentication code
$a \parallel b$	String concatenation of a and b

8.3.2.2 System Model

The considered system consists of three types of entities: the WBAN client, the AP, and the network manager (NM), and the system model for a WBAN can be found in Figure 8.2.

- WBAN Client: All WBAN clients, equipped with certain WBAN terminals, that is, wearable sensors, biosensors, and portable medical devices, need to be preloaded with public parameters and registered with the NM before they can access the medical services provided by the AP.

- AP: Medical institutions such as hospitals, clinics, or even weather forecast centers also need to be preloaded with public parameters and registered with the NM before they serve as APs to offer expert-level medical treatment remotely to WBAN clients. The services provided by APs include patient status monitoring and physician consultation.

- NM: The NM is in charge of the registration of WBAN clients and APs. In general, the NM is always assumed to be a commercial organization instead of a fully trusted third party. To derive commercial benefits, it is very likely the NM will illegally collect a client's personal health status by impersonating the AP or access the service

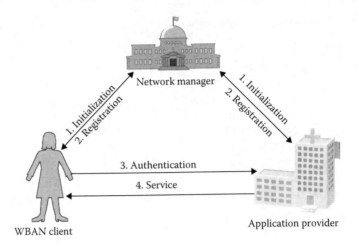

Figure 8.2 WBAN system model.

offered by APs free of charge by impersonating the legitimate WBAN client. Therefore, it is desirable to avoid the key escrow problem in the sense that the NM cannot impersonate the clients or APs without being detected.

8.3.2.3 Objectives

According to [24,183,219], the design objectives are straightforward. (1) Anonymity (ANO): The real identity of the requesting client cannot be revealed by anyone. (2) Unlinkability (UL): Any two sessions should not be linked to the same client. (3) Mutual authentication (MA): The WBAN client and AP should be allowed to authenticate each other to avoid potential malicious attacks. (4) Session key establishment (SKE): A session key to secure the later communication should be established between the WBAN client and AP after successful authentication. (5) FS: The exchanged data in the previous session will still be secure even if the long-term private key of the participant has been corrupted. (6) Key escrow resilience (KER): The NM cannot impersonate the registered client or AP without being detected. (7) Nonrepudiation (NR): The requesting client cannot deny its behavior in case of dispute. (8) Scalability (SC): The account information of the WBAN client does not need to be distributed to the APs before this client requests the services.

8.3.2.4 Concrete Construction

In this section, Xiong's scalable certificateless remote authentication protocol with anonymity is presented. Similar to [24,219], this protocol involves three entities, that is, NM, AP, and the WBAN clients, and consists of the *Initialization, Registration,* and *Authentication* phases.

Initialization. Given the security parameter l, NM performs the following steps:

- NM generates a prime p and determines the tuple $\{\mathbb{F}_p, E/\mathbb{F}_p, G, P\}$ according to the definition in Section 2.2.3.
- It chooses $x \in_R \mathbb{Z}_p^*$ and computes $P_{\text{pub}} = xP$.
- It picks a message authentication code $\text{MAC}_{(.)}(\cdot)$ and four hash functions $H_1, H_2, H_3,$ and H_4 satisfying $H_1 : \{0,1\}^* \times G^2 \to \mathbb{Z}_p^*$, $H_2 : \{0,1\}^* \times G^3 \times \{0,1\}^* \to \mathbb{Z}_p^*$, $H_3 : G \to \{0,1\}^* \times G^3 \times \{0,1\}^*$, and $H_4 : \{0,1\}^* \times \{0,1\}^* \times G^8 \to \{0,1\}^*$.

The NM loads the public parameters $\{\mathbb{F}_p, E/\mathbb{F}_p, G, P, P_{\text{pub}}, H_1, H_2, H_3, H_4, \text{MAC}_{(.)}(\cdot)\}$ to the WBAN clients and APs. Also, the NM keeps secret the master secret key x.

Registration. An AP with identity $\text{ID}_{AP} \in \{0,1\}^{l_1}$ needs to perform the following operations with the NM once before it can provide services to the WBAN clients:

1. The AP associated with identity ID_{AP} selects a secret value $x_{\text{ID}_{AP}} \in_R \mathbb{Z}_p^*$ as its user secret key $usk_{\text{ID}_{AP}}$ and computes his/her public key as $upk_{\text{ID}_{AP}} = x_{\text{ID}_{AP}}P$. This AP sends its identity ID_{AP} and user public key $upk_{\text{ID}_{AP}}$ to the NM.

2. On receiving this AP's identity ID_{AP} and user public key $upk_{\text{ID}_{AP}}$, NM first chooses at random $r_{\text{ID}_{AP}} \in_R \mathbb{Z}_p^*$ and computes $R_{\text{ID}_{AP}} = r_{\text{ID}_{AP}}P$, $h_{\text{ID}_{AP}} = H_1(\text{ID}_{AP}\|R_{\text{ID}_{AP}}\| upk_{\text{ID}_{AP}})$, and $s_{\text{ID}_{AP}} = r_{\text{ID}_{AP}} + h_{\text{ID}_{AP}}x$. The NM then transmits the partial private key $(s_{\text{ID}_{AP}}, R_{\text{ID}_{AP}})$ to this AP secretly.

Likewise, a WBAN client with the real identity $\text{ID}_R \in \{0,1\}^{l_1}$ needs to perform the following operations with the NM once before this client uses any of the services provided by the APs:

1. The user associated with the real identity ID_R selects a secret value $x_{\text{ID}_C} \in_R \mathbb{Z}_p^*$ as his/her user secret key usk_{ID_C} and computes his/her public key as $upk_{\text{ID}_C} = x_{\text{ID}_C}P$. After that, this client picks a pseudo-identity $\text{ID}_C \in \{0,1\}^{l_1}$ and

sends the real identity ID_R, pseudo-identity ID_C, and user public key upk_{ID_C} to the NM.

2. On receiving this user's real identity ID_R, pseudo-identity ID_C, and user public key upk_{ID_C}, the NM first chooses at random $r_{ID_C} \in_R \mathbb{Z}_p^*$ and computes $R_{ID_C} = r_{ID_C} P$, $h_{ID_C} = H_1(ID_C \| R_{ID_C} \| upk_{ID_C})$, and $s_{ID_C} = r_{ID_C} + h_{ID_C} x$. The NM then transmits the partial private key (s_{ID_C}, R_{ID_C}) and a group of $\{ID_{AP}, upk_{ID_{AP}}, R_{ID_{AP}}\}$ for different APs to this user secretly.

Authentication. The WBAN client can authenticate anonymously itself to the AP of interest by performing the following steps:

- The WBAN client associated with the pseudo-identity ID_C performs the following steps:
    1. Chooses at random the ephemeral key $a \in_R \mathbb{Z}_p^*$ and computes the key token $T_A = aP$.
    2. Picks up the time $t_c \in \{0,1\}^{l_2}$ at the terminal,[a] and computes $r = H_2(ID_C, upk_{ID_C}, R_{ID_C}, T_A, t_c)$.
    3. Computes $C_1 = rP$ and $C_2 = H_3(r(upk_{ID_{AP}} + R_{ID_{AP}} + H_1(ID_{AP} \| R_{ID_{AP}} \| upk_{ID_{AP}}) P_{\text{pub}})) \oplus (ID_C \| upk_{ID_C} \| R_{ID_C} \| T_A \| t_c)$.
    4. Sends a service request message $\text{Req} = (C_1, C_2)$ to the target AP.
- On receiving the request message $\text{Req} = (C_1, C_2)$ from the client, the requested AP performs the following steps to authenticate the requesting client:
    1. Computes $ID_C \| upk_{ID_C} \| R_{ID_C} \| T_A \| t_c = H_3((x_{ID_{AP}} + s_{ID_{AP}}) C_1) \oplus C_2$.
    2. Checks the freshness of t_c and checks if $H_2(ID_C, upk_{ID_C}, R_{ID_C}, T_A, t_c) P \overset{?}{=} C_1$ holds or not.

---

[a] Similar to [24,166,219], the security provided by the proposed protocol relies on loose time synchronization between the WBAN client and the AP in the sense that the WBAN client knows an upper bound on the AP's local time. Since WBAN clients and APs are assumed to be registered with centralized NM and the clock synchronization does not need to be very accurate, it is not difficult to realize loose time synchronization by adopting the indirect time synchronization technique in [223–225]. Specifically, the synchronization can be achieved through a global positioning system or Galileo device or thanks to Network Time Protocol version 4 (NTPv4). The details of loose synchronization can be found in [223–225] and is really outside the scope of this chapter.

3. Chooses at random the ephemeral key $b \in_R \mathbb{Z}_p^*$ and computes the key token $T_B = bP$.

4. Computes $K_{AP-C}^1 = s_{ID_{AP}}T_A + b(R_{ID_C} + H_1(ID_C\| R_{ID_C}\|upk_{ID_C})P_{\text{pub}}) + x_{ID_{AP}}T_A + b \cdot upk_{ID_C}$ and $K_{AP-C}^2 = bT_A$.

5. Computes $key = H_4(ID_C, ID_{AP}, upk_{ID_C}, upk_{ID_{AP}}, R_{ID_C}, R_{ID_{AP}}, T_A, T_B, K_{AP-C}^1, K_{AP-C}^2)$.

6. Computes $\text{MAC}_{key}(T_B)$ and sends $(\text{MAC}_{key}(T_B), T_B)$ back to the requesting client.

- On receiving the reply $(\text{MAC}_{key}(T_B), T_B)$ from the AP, the client C performs the following steps:

    1. Computes $K_{C-AP}^1 = s_{ID_C}T_B + a(R_{ID_{AP}} + H_1(ID_{ID_{AP}}\| R_{ID_{AP}}\|upk_{ID_{AP}})P_{\text{pub}}) + a \cdot upk_{ID_{AP}} + x_{ID_C}T_B$ and $K_{C-AP}^2 = aT_B$.

    2. Computes $key = H_4(ID_C, ID_{AP}, upk_{ID_C}, upk_{ID_{AP}}, R_{ID_C}, R_{ID_{AP}}, T_A, T_B, K_{C-AP}^1, K_{C-AP}^2)$.

    3. Checks the validity of $\text{MAC}_{key}(T_B)$ using session key key. If this check fails, C will reject this session. Otherwise, C will authenticate AP and regard key as the session key in the later communications.

We first analyze the correctness of the decryption and key agreement procedure. Upon receiving the request message $\text{Req} = (C_1, C_2)$ from the client, the AP decrypts this ciphertext using its user secret key $x_{ID_{AP}}$ and partial private key $s_{ID_{AP}}$ as follows:

$$H_3((x_{ID_{AP}} + s_{ID_{AP}})C_1) \oplus C_2$$
$$= H_3((x_{ID_{AP}} + s_{ID_{AP}})rP) \oplus H_3(r(upk_{ID_{AP}} + R_{ID_{AP}}$$
$$+ h_{ID_{AP}}P_{\text{pub}})) \oplus (ID_C\|upk_{ID_C}\|R_{ID_C}\|T_A\|t_c)$$
$$= H_3(r(upk_{ID_{AP}} + R_{ID_{AP}} + h_{ID_{AP}}P_{\text{pub}})) \oplus H_3(r(upk_{ID_{AP}}$$
$$+ R_{ID_{AP}} + h_{ID_{AP}}P_{\text{pub}})) \oplus (ID_C\|upk_{ID_C}\|R_{ID_C}\|T_A\|t_c)$$
$$= ID_C\|upk_{ID_C}\|R_{ID_C}\|T_A\|t_c.$$

Here, $h_{ID_{AP}} = H_1(ID_{AP}\|R_{ID_{AP}}\|upk_{ID_{AP}})$. Furthermore, the shared secrets agree due to the following facts:

$$K_{AP-C}^1 = s_{ID_{AP}}T_A + bs_{ID_C}P + x_{ID_{AP}}T_A + b \cdot upk_{ID_C} = bs_{ID_C}P$$
$$+ s_{ID_{AP}}T_A + x_{ID_{AP}}T_A + b \cdot upk_{ID_C} = s_{ID_C}T_B + a(s_{ID_{AP}}P)$$
$$+ a \cdot upk_{ID_{AP}} + x_{ID_C}T_B = K_{C-AP}^1, K_{AP-C}^2 = abP = baP$$
$$= K_{C-AP}^2.$$

Thus, the agreed session key for the authentication provider AP and the client C can be computed as:

$$key = H_4(ID_C, ID_{AP}, upk_{ID_C}, upk_{ID_{AP}}, R_{ID_C}, R_{ID_{AP}}, T_A, T_B,$$
$$K_{AP-C}^1, K_{AP-C}^2)$$
$$H_4(ID_C, ID_{AP}, upk_{ID_C}, upk_{ID_{AP}}, R_{ID_C}, R_{ID_{AP}}, T_A, T_B,$$
$$K_{C-AP}^1, K_{C-AP}^2)$$

8.3.2.5 Security Analysis

In this section, we analyze the security of the proposed protocol in terms of correctness and the security requirements mentioned in Section 8.3.2.3.

Theorem 8.1 (Anonymity) *Anonymity in this protocol means that except for the requesting WBAN client and the requested AP, any outsider (including the NM) is unable to link a particular protocol session to a particular identity.*

Proof 8.1 *In this protocol, the anonymity of the requesting WBAN client is achieved by adopting the certificateless encryption in [63]. On the one hand, the AP can decrypt the Req = (C_1, C_2) using its full private key $(x_{ID_{AP}}, s_{ID_{AP}}, R_{ID_{AP}})$ and then obtain the pseudo-identity ID_C and the public key (upk_{ID_C}, R_{ID_C}) of the client. However, the real identity pertaining to this pseudo-identity cannot be revealed by the AP.*

On the other hand, the pseudo-identity of the requesting client is only involved in Req = (C_1, C_2) in this protocol. Any third party who eavesdrops on the communication channel and wants to reveal the real identity of the WBAN client faces the decryption operation. According to [63], the certificateless encryption adopted in this protocol can resist the adaptive CCA provided that the standard CDH problem is hard to solve. Thus, the adversary (including the NM) cannot obtain the real identity of the WBAN client without the knowledge of the full private key of the AP.

Theorem 8.2 (Unlinkability) *Unlinkability is a stronger property than anonymity and requires that except for the requesting WBAN client and the requested AP, any outsider (including the NM) is unable to link two different protocol sessions to the same WBAN client. In other words, the adversary cannot distinguish whether she/he has seen the same WBAN client twice.*

Proof 8.2 *Suppose that* $\text{Req}_i = (C_{1i}, C_{2i})$ *and* $\text{Req}_j = (C_{1j}, C_{2j})$ *are two requesting messages produced by one client in two different authentication sessions, where*

$$C_{1i} = r_i P, C_{2i} = H_3(r_i(upk_{ID_{AP}} + R_{ID_{AP}} + H_1(ID_{AP}\|R_{ID_{AP}}\|$$
$$upk_{ID_{AP}})P_{\text{pub}})) \oplus (ID_C\|upk_{ID_C}\|R_{ID_C}\|T_{A_i}\|t_{ci}),$$
$$C_{1j} = r_j P, C_{2j} = H_3(r_j(upk_{ID_{AP}} + R_{ID_{AP}} + H_1(ID_{AP}\|R_{ID_{AP}}\|$$
$$upk_{ID_{AP}})P_{\text{pub}})) \oplus (ID_C\|upk_{ID_C}\|R_{ID_C}\|T_{A_j}\|t_{cj}).$$

One may wonder at first glance whether these ciphertexts (C_{1i}, C_{2i}) *and* (C_{1j}, C_{2j}) *would leak some relation since they are generated by the same client with the same identity and user public key. However, due to the usage of the random factors* r_i *and* r_j, C_{1i} *is independent of* C_{1j}. *As* H_3 *is a secure cryptographic hash function, the same is true for* C_{2i} *and* C_{2j}.

To sum up, (C_{1i}, C_{2i}) *gains independence from* (C_{1j}, C_{2j}), *and thus, any adversary over the communication channel has no ability to distinguish whether the clients in two authentication sessions are identical.*

Theorem 8.3 (Mutual authentication) *This protocol can achieve MA in the sense that a requesting WBAN client authenticates itself to a requested AP and that AP authenticates itself to the client at the same time and both parties are assured of the others' identity.*

Proof 8.3 *The security of this protocol is defined by two security games between the challenger* $\mathcal{C}$ *and an adversary* $\mathcal{A}_1$ *or* $\mathcal{A}_2$, *respectively. To capture the attack launched by the outside adversary,* $\mathcal{A}_1$ *is simulated as the attacker who can replace the public key of any entity in the system but cannot access the NM's master secret key. To catch the attack mounted by the malicious NM,* $\mathcal{A}_2$ *is assumed to be an attacker who has the ability to access the master key with the restriction that any user's public key cannot be replaced by* $\mathcal{A}_2$. *Interested readers can refer to [17,19] for more details. This theorem follows directly from Lemmas 8.3 and 8.4 corresponding to* $\mathcal{A}_1$ *and* $\mathcal{A}_2$, *respectively.*

Lemma 8.3 *The widely accepted CDH assumption will fail with nonnegligible advantage when the security of this authentication protocol is broken by a type I adversary* $\mathcal{A}_1$.

Proof 8.4 *Given an instance* $(aP, bP) \in G$ *of the CDH problem, the task of the challenger* $\mathcal{C}$ *with type I adversary* $\mathcal{A}_1$ *is to compute* $cP \in G$

with $c = ab \bmod p$. The hash function H_1 will be simulated as the random oracle and an initially empty H_1 list associated with this oracle will also be maintained by $\mathcal{C}$. The number of participants in the game and the number of sessions each participant may be involved in is denoted as $n_p(k)$ and $n_s(k)$, respectively. $(s_{ID_i}, R_{ID_i}, x_{ID_i})$ represents the full private key for the i-th participant associated with the identifier ID_i. The partial private key (s_{ID_i}, R_{ID_i}) with ID_i can be generated by $\mathcal{C}$ as follows:

At first, $\mathcal{C}$ chooses a random point $P_0 \in_R G$, sets $P_{\text{pub}} = P_0$, and chooses a random index $I \in_R \{1, \ldots, n_p(k)\}$. To generate a partial private key for the identifier ID_I, $\mathcal{C}$ chooses a random $x_{ID_I} \in_R \mathbb{Z}_p^*$ and computes the public key $upk_{ID_I} = x_{ID_I}P$. $\mathcal{C}$ then chooses $h_{ID_I} \in_R \mathbb{Z}_p^*$ and computes $R_{ID_I} = bP - h_{ID_I}P_0$, which implies that $s_{ID_I} = b$. Then $(\perp, R_{ID_I})$ is set as ID_I's partial private key and $\{ID_I, R_{ID_I}, upk_{ID_I}, \perp, h_{ID_I}, x_{ID_I}\}$ is inserted into the H_1 list. Regarding ID_i with $i \in \{1, \ldots, n_p(k)\}$ and $i \neq I$, $\mathcal{C}$ chooses a random $x_{ID_i} \in_R \mathbb{Z}_p^*$ and computes the public key $upk_{ID_i} = x_{ID_i}P$. Then, $\mathcal{C}$ generates the partial private key by first choosing $(s_{ID_i}, h_{ID_i}) \in_R \mathbb{Z}_p^*$. Next $\mathcal{C}$ computes $R_{ID_i} = s_{ID_i}P - h_{ID_i}P_0$ and sets (s_{ID_i}, R_{ID_i}) as ID_i's partial private key. Then, $\mathcal{C}$ adds $\{ID_i, R_{ID_i}, upk_{ID_i}, s_{ID_i}, h_{ID_i}, x_{ID_i}\}$ to the H_1 list for $i \in \{1, \ldots, n_p(k)\}$ and $i \neq I$. Without loss of generality, we assume that, before asking the following queries, $\mathcal{A}_1$ has already created the partial private key on the related identifiers.

Then $\mathcal{C}$ picks another random index $J \neq I \in_R \{1, \ldots, n_p(k)\}$, $v \in \{1, \ldots, n_s(k)\}$, and C starts the simulation by answering $\mathcal{A}_1$'s adaptive queries as follows:

$H_1(ID_i, R_{ID_i}, upk_{ID_i})$ Queries: Suppose the item $\{ID_i, R_{ID_i}, upk_{ID_i}, s_{ID_i}, h_{ID_i}, x_{ID_i}\}$ has already been inserted in the H_1 list, $\mathcal{C}$ responds with h_{ID_i} as the answer; otherwise, $\mathcal{C}$ chooses $h_{ID_i} \in_R \mathbb{Z}_p^*$, adds the item $\{ID_i, R_{ID_i}, upk_{ID_i}, s_{ID_i}, h_{ID_i}, x_{ID_i}\}$ to the H_1 list, and returns h_{ID_i} to $\mathcal{A}_1$ as the answer.

Public-Key-Request(ID_i): On receiving this query, $\mathcal{C}$ first searches for the item $\{ID_i, R_{ID_i}, upk_{ID_i}, s_{ID_i}, h_{ID_i}, x_{ID_i}\}$ in the H_1 list, which is indexed by ID_i, and then returns upk_{ID_i} as the answer.

Partial-Private-Key-Extract(ID_i): On receiving this query, $\mathcal{C}$ aborts the simulation when $ID_i = ID_I$; otherwise, $\mathcal{C}$ searches for the item $\{ID_i, R_{ID_i}, upk_{ID_i}, s_{ID_i}, h_{ID_i}, x_{ID_i}\}$ in the H_1 list, which is indexed by ID_i, and returns (R_{ID_i}, s_{ID_i}) as the answer.

Corrupt(ID_i): On receiving this query, $\mathcal{C}$ aborts the simulation when $ID_i = ID_I$; else, $\mathcal{C}$ searches for the item $\{ID_i, R_{ID_i}, upk_{ID_i}, s_{ID_i}, h_{ID_i}, x_{ID_i}\}$ in the H_1 list, which is indexed by ID_i, and if

s_{ID_i} = null, $\mathcal{C}$ returns null; otherwise, $\mathcal{C}$ returns $(R_{ID_i}, s_{ID_i}, x_{ID_i})$ as the answer.

Public-Key-Replace(ID_i, upk'_{ID_i}): On receiving this query, $\mathcal{C}$ searches for the item $\{ID_i, R_{ID_i}, upk_{ID_i}, s_{ID_i}, h_{ID_i}, x_{ID_i}\}$ in the H_1 list, which is indexed by ID_i, and then updates upk_{ID_i} to upk'_{ID_i} and sets x_{ID_i} = null.

Send$(\Pi^s_{i,j}, M)$: If $\Pi^s_{i,j} \neq \Pi^v_{J,j}$, then $\mathcal{C}$ carries out the protocol normally according to the protocol specification. Otherwise, $\mathcal{C}$ responds with the tuple $(ID_j, upk_{ID_j}, R_{ID_j}, aP)$ as the answer.

The probability that $\Pi^v_{J,j}$ is chosen by $\mathcal{A}_1$ as the Test oracle and $ID_j = ID_I$ is $1/n_p^2(k)n_s(k)$. In this case, $\mathcal{C}$ would not have aborted the simulation in the sense that ID_I has not been corrupted by $\mathcal{A}_1$. Therefore, at the end of the security game, $\mathcal{A}_1$ will output its guess of the session key of the form $\{0,1\}^{l_1} \times \{0,1\}^{l_1} \times G^6 \times A \times B$. On receiving this guess, $\mathcal{C}$ can output $A - s_{ID_J}M - x_{ID_J}M - x_{ID_I}aP$ as the solution of the CDH problem, where M is the input message of Send$(\Pi^v_{J,j}, M)$ query. In this way, the CDH problem can be solved by $\mathcal{C}$ with nonnegligible probability $c/n_p^2(k)n_s(k)$ within $t(k)$, where c is a constant.

Lemma 8.4 *The widely accepted CDH assumption will fail with nonnegligible advantage when the security of this authentication protocol is broken by a type II adversary $\mathcal{A}_2$.*

Proof 8.5 *Given an input $(P, aP, bP) \in G$ of the CDH problem, the challenger $\mathcal{C}$ can use type II adversary $\mathcal{A}_2$ as a subroutine to compute $cP \in G$ with $c = ab \bmod p$. At first, $\mathcal{C}$ chooses $x \in_R \mathbb{Z}_p^*$ randomly and assigns $P_{\text{pub}} = xP$. x is then sent to $\mathcal{A}_2$ by $\mathcal{C}$. The hash function H_1 will be simulated as the random oracle and an initially empty H_1 list associated with this oracle will also be maintained by $\mathcal{C}$. The number of participants in the game and the number of sessions each participant may be involved in is denoted as $n_p(k)$ and $n_s(k)$, respectively. $(s_{ID_i}, R_{ID_i}, x_{ID_i})$ represents the full private key for the i-th participant associated with the identifier ID_i. $\mathcal{C}$ picks two random indexes $I, J \in \{1, \ldots, n_p(k)\}$ at random, along with a random protocol session $v \in \{1, \ldots, n_s(k)\}$. The user secret key x_{ID_i} with ID_i can be generated by $\mathcal{C}$ as follows:*

To generate a user secret key for the identifier ID_I, $\mathcal{C}$ sets the user public key as bP and the user secret key as $\perp$. $\mathcal{C}$ then chooses $r_{ID_I} \in_R \mathbb{Z}_p^*$ at random and computes $R_{ID_I} = r_{ID_I}P$ and $s_{ID_I} = r_{ID_I}+$

$H_1(ID_I \| R_{ID_I} \| upk_{ID_I}) x$. Then, $\{ID_I, R_{ID_I}, upk_{ID_I}, \perp, h_{ID_I}, x_{ID_I}\}$ is inserted into the H_1 list by C. With regard to ID_i with $i \in \{1, \ldots, n_p(k)\}$ and $i \neq I$, C chooses a random $x_{ID_i} \in_R \mathbb{Z}_p^*$ and computes the public key $upk_{ID_i} = x_{ID_i} P$. Then, C chooses $(s_{ID_i}, h_{ID_i}) \in_R \mathbb{Z}_p^*$ and computes $R_{ID_i} = s_{ID_i} P - h_{ID_i} P_0$. C sets the user public key as upk_{ID_i} and the user secret key as x_{ID_i}. Then, C adds $\{ID_i, R_{ID_i}, upk_{ID_i}, s_{ID_i}, h_{ID_i}, x_{ID_i}\}$ to the H_1 list for $i \in \{1, \ldots, n_p(k)\}$ and $i \neq I$. Without loss of generality, we assume that, before asking the following queries, A_2 has already created the user secret key on the related identifiers.

$H_1(ID_i, R_{ID_i}, upk_{ID_i})$ Queries: Suppose the item $\{ID_i, R_{ID_i}, upk_{ID_i}, s_{ID_i}, h_{ID_i}, x_{ID_i}\}$ has already been inserted in the H_1 list. C responds with h_{ID_i} as the answer; otherwise, C chooses $h_{ID_i} \in_R \mathbb{Z}_p^*$, adds the item $\{ID_i, R_{ID_i}, upk_{ID_i}, s_{ID_i}, h_{ID_i}, x_{ID_i}\}$ to the H_1 list, and returns h_{ID_i} to A_1 as the answer.

Public-Key-Request(ID_i): On receiving this query, C aborts the simulation in case $ID_i = ID_I$; otherwise, C searches for the item $\{ID_i, R_{ID_i}, upk_{ID_i}, s_{ID_i}, h_{ID_i}, x_{ID_i}\}$ in the H_1 list, which is indexed by ID_i, and then returns upk_{ID_i} as the answer.

Partial-Private-Key-Extract(ID_i): On receiving this query, C first searches for the item $\{ID_i, R_{ID_i}, upk_{ID_i}, s_{ID_i}, h_{ID_i}, x_{ID_i}\}$ in the H_1 list, which is indexed by ID_i and returns (R_{ID_i}, s_{ID_i}) as the answer.

Corrupt(ID_i): On receiving this query, C aborts the simulation when $ID_i = ID_I$; else, C searches for the item $\{ID_i, R_{ID_i}, upk_{ID_i}, s_{ID_i}, h_{ID_i}, x_{ID_i}\}$ in the H_1 list, which is indexed by ID_i, and if $x_i = \text{null}$, C returns null; otherwise, C returns $(R_{ID_i}, s_{ID_i}, x_{ID_i})$ as the answer.

Public-Key-Replace(ID_i, upk'_{ID_i}): On receiving this query, C searches for the item $\{ID_i, R_{ID_i}, upk_{ID_i}, s_{ID_i}, h_{ID_i}, x_{ID_i}\}$ in the H_1 list, which is indexed by ID_i, and then updates upk_{ID_i} to upk'_{ID_i} and sets $x_{ID_i} = \text{null}$.

Send$(\Pi^s_{i,j}, M)$: If $\Pi^s_{i,j} \neq \Pi^v_{J,j}$, then C carries out the protocol normally according to the protocol specification. Otherwise, C responds with the tuple $(ID_j, upk_{ID_j}, R_{ID_j}, aP)$ as the answer.

The probability that $\Pi^v_{J,j}$ is chosen by A_2 as the Test oracle and $ID_j = ID_I$ is $1/n_p^2(k) n_s(k)$. In this case, C would not have aborted the simulation in the sense that ID_I has not been corrupted by A_2. Therefore, at the end of the security game, A_2 will output its guess of the session key of the form $\{0,1\}^{l_1} \times \{0,1\}^{l_1} \times G^6 \times A \times B$. On receiving this guess, C can output $A - s_{ID_J} M - x_{ID_J} M - s_{ID_I} aP$ as the solution of the CDH problem, where M is the input message of the Send$(\Pi^v_{J,j}, M)$ query. In this way, the CDH problem can be solved by C with nonnegligible probability $c/n_p^2(k)n_s(k)$ within $t(k)$, where c is a constant.

Theorem 8.4 (Session key establishment) *The requested AP and the requesting client can share the secure session key after successful authentication.*

Proof 8.6 *Observe that* $K^1_{AP-C} = K^1_{C-AP}$ *and* $K^2_{AP-C} = K^2_{C-AP}$ *are secrets shared between the AP and the client. Namely, the session key can only be shared by the AP and the client. More specifically,* $K^1_{AP-C} = s_{ID_{AP}}T_A + b(R_{ID_C} + H_1(ID_C \| R_{ID_C} \| upk_{ID_C})P_{pub}) + x_{ID_{AP}}T_A + b \cdot upk_{ID_C}$, $K^2_{AP-C} = bT_A$ *can only be generated by the AP with the full private key* $(s_{ID_{AP}}, x_{ID_{AP}})$ *and the ephemeral key* b*. Similarly,* $K^1_{C-AP} = s_{ID_C}T_B + a(R_{ID_{AP}} + H_1(ID_{ID_{AP}} \| R_{ID_{AP}} \| upk_{ID_{AP}})P_{pub}) + a \cdot upk_{ID_{AP}} + x_{ID_C}T_B$, $K^2_{C-AP} = aT_B$ *can only be computed by the client with the full private key* (s_{ID_C}, x_{ID_C}) *and the ephemeral key* a*. Hence, based on the exchanged messages in the authentication phase, this proposed protocol can afford the* explicit *key confirmation in the sense that the AP and client can confirm the peer generates the session key correctly.*

Theorem 8.5 (Forward security) *This protocol can offer the forward secrecy property, which guarantees that the session key established in the previous round will not be disclosed even if the full private key of the client or the AP has been corrupted.*

Proof 8.7 *Suppose that the full private key* $(s_{ID_{AP}}, R_{ID_{AP}}, x_{ID_{AP}})$ *of the AP and* $(s_{ID_C}, R_{ID_C}, x_{ID_C})$ *of the C were corrupted after the establishment of a shared session key between the AP and C. Let* a *and* b *be the ephemeral key chosen by AP and C, respectively, during the establishment of the session key. It is obvious to observe that, to compute the established session key, the adversary who owns* $(s_{ID_{AP}}, R_{ID_{AP}}, x_{ID_{AP}})$, $(s_{ID_C}, R_{ID_C}, x_{ID_C})$, $T_a = aP$, *and* $T_b = bP$ *must know the value of* abP*. However, in order to compute* abP *without the knowledge of either* a *or* b*, the adversary must solve the CDH problem in* G*. Thus, this protocol features the forward secrecy property.*

Theorem 8.6 (Key escrow resilience) *The NM cannot impersonate the client or the AP without being detected.*

Proof 8.8 *According to Lemma 8.4, the type II adversary (namely, NM) cannot mount the impersonation attack successfully provided that the CDH problem is hard. The basic reason is that the client (resp. the AP) generates the user secret key x_{ID_C} (resp. $x_{ID_{AP}}$) itself in this protocol, and thus the client's (resp. the AP's) full private key is not available to the NM. We emphasize that the NM never mounts a public key replacement attack with a false public key against a target client since two legitimate public keys associated with one identity in the system will badly destroy the NM's reputation.*

Theorem 8.7 (Nonrepudiation) *Client ID_C cannot deny that she/he has accessed the service provided by the AP after a successful access.*

Proof 8.9 *Client ID_C is the unique client who can authenticate with AP under the identity ID_C and public key (R_{ID_C}, upk_{ID_C}). Even the NM cannot impersonate the client ID_C according to Theorem 8.3.*

8.3.2.6 Comparison with Previous Protocols

In this section, we compare the security properties and efficiency of the proposed protocols, Cao et al.'s [166] protocol, which is the most efficient existing ID-based remote anonymous authentication protocol, and Liu et al.'s [24] protocol, which is the only certificateless remote authentication protocol with anonymity for WBANs. The comparison results are shown in Table 8.2, which includes ANO, UL, MA, SKE, FS, KER, NR, and SC. Here, the entry ✓ means that the protocol satisfied the requirement and × indicates that the protocol did not meet the goal. The above comparison shows that this protocol conforms to all of the security requirements, whereas the competitive protocols satisfy only partial security properties.

As for the computation efficiency comparison, the benchmark (the running time of the cryptographic operations) is obtained by using the Multiprecision Integer and Rational Arithmetic Cryptographic Library

TABLE 8.2   Security Properties Comparison of Different Protocols

Schemes	ANO	UL	MA	SKE	FS	KER	NR	SC
Cao et al.-I [166]	✓	✓	✓	✓	×	×	✓	×
Liu et al.-I [24]	✓	×	✓	✓	×	✓	✓	✓
Liu et al.-II [24]	✓	✓	✓	✓	×	✓	✓	×
Xiong [183]	✓	✓	✓	✓	✓	✓	✓	✓

(MIRACAL) [179]. The hardware environment for the AP is adopted by a Windows XP OS equipped with a PIV 3-GHz processor and 512 MB memory, whereas the simulation platform of the WBAN client is set as a Linux personal digital assistant over an Intel® PXA270 624-MHz processor. With regard to the pairing-based protocol [24,166], to achieve a comparable level of security to 1024-bit RSA, we employed a supersingular elliptic curve $E/\mathbb{F}_p : y^2 = x^3 + x$ providing groups in which a Tate pairing $e : G_1 \times G_1 \to G_2$ is defined. Here, the embedding degree of this curve is 2, q is a 160-bit Solinas prime equal to $2^{159} + 2^{17} + 1$, and p is a 512-bit prime such that $p = 12qr - 1$. With regard to elliptic curve cryptography (ECC)-based protocol, to offer the security with the equivalent level, we used the Koblitz elliptic curve $y^2 = x^3 + ax^2 + b$ defined on $\mathbb{F}_{2^{163}}$ to provide ECC group. Here, a is equal to 1 and b is a 163-bit random prime. The running time of the cryptographic operations on AP is derived by a repeated simulation experiment, and the running time on the client terminal can be easily estimated according to [226]. The running time of the involved cryptographic operations on the AP and client are listed in Table 8.3. To be compatible with Liu et al.'s **Setup** and **Extract-Partial-Private-Key** algorithms, the signature in Liu et al.'s first authentication protocol has been instantiated by the efficient identity-based signature in [227]. Figure 8.3 shows the time consumption on computation of the AP in Cao et al.'s protocol, Liu et al.'s protocols, and Xiong's protocol as the number of requesting clients increases. Obviously, we observe that Xiong's protocol offers a much lower time consumption compared with the other protocols. Figure 8.4 illustrates the time consumption on computation of client in Cao et al.'s protocol, Liu et al.'s protocols, and Xiong's protocol when the number of requested APs increases. The facts drawn from Figure 8.3 and Figure 8.4 indicate that compared with the most efficient ID-based remote anonymous authentication protocol, Xiong's protocol reduces at least 52.6% of the overall running time; the reduction in the computation cost reaches at least

TABLE 8.3   Cryptographic Operation Time on AP and Client (in ms)

Operations	Client	AP
ECC-based scalar multiplication	3.99	0.83
Exponential in $\mathbb{F}_{p^2}$	53.85	11.20
Pairing-based scalar multiplication	30.67	6.38
Pairing	96.20	20.01

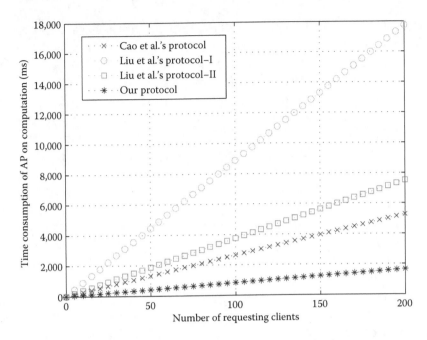

Figure 8.3 Time consumption on computation of the application provider (AP) with regard to the number of requesting clients.

73.8% compared with the up-to-date certificateless remote authentication protocol with anonymity.

We compare the communication overhead by evaluating the overall size of the request and response messages during one round of a protocol. For example, in Cao et al.'s protocol [166], a client's request message consists of two points of G_1 and the response message from AP contains a hash value.[a] The resulting bandwidth for Cao et al.'s protocol is $64 * 2 + 20 = 148B$ when a 160-bit hash is employed. As shown in Figure 8.5, the communication overhead of Xiong's protocol is 82.43% of Cao et al.'s protocol, 30.20% of Liu et al.'s first protocol, and 44.20% of Liu et al.'s second protocol.

The performance comparison between this protocol and the related work in terms of energy consumption at the client side has also been evaluated. The MICA2 sensor mote equipped with the eight-bit processor ATmega128L is set as the simulation platform of the WBAN client. Per the Crossbow data sheet [228], the power level of MICA2 is 3.0 V and the current draw in active mode is 8 mA. According

---

[a]Note that an auxiliary message such as a time stamp or entity identifier is not counted in this protocol and the related work.

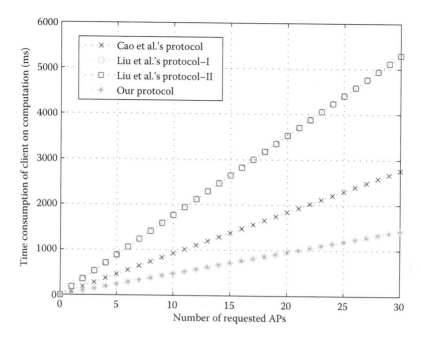

Figure 8.4 Time consumption on computation of WBAN client with regard to the number of requested APs it will roam to and from.

to the implementation results in [85,86], the time required for a ECC-based scalar multiplication to achieve an 80-bit security level on the binary Koblitz curve is 0.33 s. Also, Oliveira et al. [86] showed that the pairing computation and a pairing-based scalar multiplication to reach the same security level take 1.90 s and 0.95 s on ATmega128L, respectively. The time for a modular exponentiation in the same curve is very similar to that of a scalar multiplication. In this protocol, 10 ECC-based scalar multiplications are required at the client side, and the resulting computational energy consumption is $3.0 \times 8.0 \times (10 \times 0.33) = 79.2$ mJ. Now we analyze the communication energy cost. In MICA2, the receiving current draw and the transmitting current draw are assumed to be 10 mA and 27 mA, respectively [229]. Hence, the energy consumption due to transmitting and receiving messages is $3.0 \times 27 \times 82 \times 8/12,400 = 4.285$ mJ and $3.0 \times 10 \times 41 \times 8/12,400 = 0.794$ mJ, respectively. The total energy consumptions of the four protocols are summarized in Figure 8.6. Though the energy consumption in Cao et al.'s protocol is the most efficient, their scheme does not offer the property of key escrow, which, nonetheless, is not the case in the other protocols.

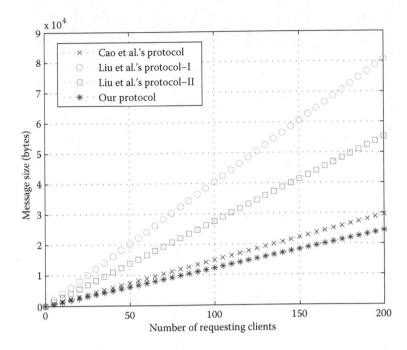

Figure 8.5 Message size with regard to the number of requesting clients.

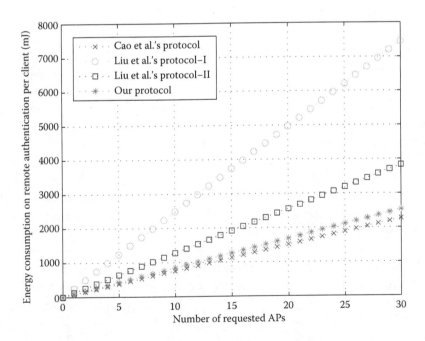

Figure 8.6 Comparison of energy consumption per client.

8.4 SECURE DATA SHARING IN CLOUD COMPUTING

8.4.1 Motivation

With the rapid development of cloud computing, the security of outsourced data in the cloud has attracted a lot of concern from industry and academia recently. When data is outsourced to a semitrust cloud service provider (CSP), the data owner cannot take control of his/her own data directly. To avoid disclosing the outsourced data to CSP or other unauthorized users, it is essential for data owners to preserve the privacy of the outsourced data in the cloud [230–233]. Intuitively, a traditional asymmetric encryption scheme can be adopted to enforce the access control of data outsourced in the cloud. It seems to be feasible for data owners to outsource encrypted data to the semitrusted cloud if only the data owner himself/herself can access the encrypted data. However, it becomes cumbersome to share encrypted data between different users based on traditional encryption mechanisms. To share the encrypted data with other users, a data owner needs to download and decrypt the requested data, and further re-encrypt it using a target user's public key to accomplish data sharing. Another naive approach for the data owner is to share his/her private key with the target user who is authorized to decrypt the outsourced data directly. Obviously, the former method renders heavy communication overhead and computation cost, and thus mismatches the purpose of cloud computing. The idea of disclosing private keys to authorized users in the latter method violates the least privilege principle. Thus, it is challenging to share encrypted data in the cloud computing environment.

Proxy re-encryption (PRE) [234], which enables a semitrusted proxy to transform a ciphertext that has been encrypted under one public key into a ciphertext under another public key of the same message without leaking any information to the proxy, is considered a promising candidate to achieve secure data sharing in cloud computing. Consider the following scenario: the data owner, say Alice, wants to share sensitive data outsourced in the cloud with a third party, Bob. It is natural for Alice to desire that the requested data only be accessed by Bob. Inspired by the primitive of PRE, Alice can encrypt the sensitive data before outsourcing these data to the semitrusted cloud. After receiving the request of decryption delegation from Bob, Alice generates a PRE key using her own private key and Bob's public key and sends this PRE key to the semitrusted cloud. Equipped with this PRE key, CSP can transform the ciphertext encrypted under the public key of Alice into the ciphertext under the public key of Bob. Meanwhile, the outsourced data can only be accessed by Bob since the CSP cannot decrypt the encrypted data with the PRE key. Finally, Bob can download and decrypt the outsourced data with his own private key.

Before PRE can be widely deployed in the cloud environment, several issues should be addressed. Observing the heavy management of public key certificates in traditional public-key encryption (PKE) [234–236] and the key escrow problem in ID-based public key encryption (ID-PKE) [59,237], it is natural to investigate PRE in the certificateless public-key encryption (CL-PKE) setting [17]. To enjoy the merits of traditional PKE and ID-PKE without suffering the corresponding criticisms, Sur et al. [96] introduced the primitive of PRE into CL-PKE [59] and proposed the first concrete certificateless proxy re-encryption (CL-PRE) scheme. Concretely, CL-PRE leverages the identity of a user as an ingredient of its public key, which eliminates the key escrow problem in ID-PKE, and does not require the use of certificates to guarantee the authenticity of public keys in traditional PKE.

Since Sur et al. [96] introduced CL-PRE, this cryptosystem has attracted more attention. In 2012, Xu et al. [97] constructed a CL-PRE scheme, which is claimed to be chosen-plaintext attack (CPA) secure and is introduced to a cloud-based data sharing scenario. In 2013, Yang et al. [98] constructed the first CCA secure pairing-free CL-PRE scheme based on Baek et al.'s [51] CL-PKE scheme. In 2014, Wang et al. [238] also proposed a CCA secure CL-PRE scheme without bilinear pairings under Yang et al.'s security models [98]. Compared to the previous CL-PRE schemes, an attractive feature in Yang et al.'s scheme is the efficiency gained from removing computationally heavy pairing operations. However, the untransformed ciphertexts in their scheme may greatly consume computation and storage resources for data owners. In addition, Qin et al. [99] point out that the security models for CL-PRE in [98] are slightly weak in a sense that the type I adversary is not allowed to replace the public key associated with the challenge identity. After that, Qin et al. defined an architecture of cloud-based data sharing using the primitive of CL-PRE. To this end, Qin et al. further proposed a strongly secure and pairing-free CL-PRE scheme based on Yang et al.'s [98] scheme. That is, Qin et al.'s CL-PRE scheme is cost-effective and provably secure against the type I and II adversaries in a strong sense where the type I adversary is able to replace the public key associated with the challenge identity (before the challenge phase). Moreover, Qin et al. evaluated communication overhead and computation cost in terms of a data owner, the CSP, and the data recipient. Qin et al.'s results demonstrate that their CL-PRE scheme outperforms other existing works at the requirements of large-scale data sharing.

8.4.2 Qin–Wu–Xiong Scheme

8.4.2.1 Formal Definition

In this section, a system architecture is described and definition of CL-PRE for cloud-based data sharing is given. Then, the security assumptions and security model for secure data sharing with a public cloud are also given.

We consider an architecture of cloud-based data sharing by introducing the primitive of CL-PRE as shown in Figure 8.7, which involves a data owner, the CSP, and the data recipients. A data owner creates the encrypted data and hosts his/her data to the semitrusted CSP. The CSP stores the data owner's data and provides the data access to the data owner and the authorized data recipients. The data owner is able

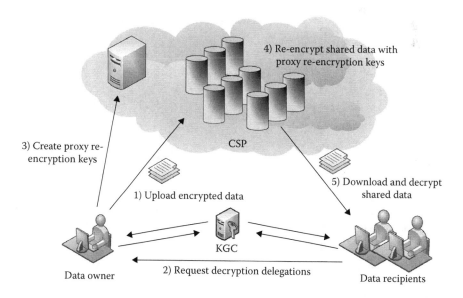

Figure 8.7 Architecture of certificateless proxy re-encryption (CL-PRE) for secure data sharing in cloud computing.

to share his/her encrypted data to data recipients, who should first request decryption delegations. After receiving the requests, the data owner produces a PRE key for each data recipient and sends it to the CSP through a secure channel. Utilizing these PRE keys, the CSP can transform the data owner's encrypted data into each data recipient's encrypted data without disclosing any information. Then, data recipients can download and decrypt the data owner's outsourced data by themselves. As mentioned above, we assume that the CSP itself is semitrusted, which means it follows protocols and does not pollute data confidentiality actively as a malicious adversary, but it may be curious about the received data and may collude with data recipients to launch attacks on the data owner.

Furthermore, a PRE key is produced by inputting a data owner's private key and a data recipient's public key. Since the number of cloud users participating in data sharing may be large, the traditional PKE-based approach has the public key management issue, and the ID-PKE–based approach has the private key escrow problem. Uniquely, we adopt CL-PRE for data sharing in the cloud.

A cloud-based data sharing mechanism designed by the primitive of CL-PRE consists of the following nine algorithms:

Setup: Taking a security parameter k as input, this algorithm is run by the KGC to produce a master secret key master-secret and a list of public parameters params.

Extract-Partial-Private-Key: Taking a list of public parameters params, a master key master-secret, and a cloud user's identifier ID_i as input, this algorithm is performed by the KGC to return a partial public/private key pair psk_{ID_i} to the user with an identifier ID_i.

Set-Secret-Value: Taking a list of public parameters params and an identifier ID_i as input, this algorithm is executed by the user ID_i to set a secret value z_i.

Set-Private-Key: Taking a list of public parameters params, a partial private key psk_{ID_i}, and a secret value z_i as input, this algorithm is carried out by user ID_i to set a private key usk_{ID_i}.

Set-Public-Key: Taking a list of public parameters params and a secret value z_i as input, this algorithm is carried out by user ID_i to set a public key upk_{ID_i}.

Encrypt: Taking a list of public parameters params, plaintext data m, an identity ID_A, and a public key $\mathsf{upk}_{\mathsf{ID}_A}$ as input, this algorithm is performed by data owner Alice to produce a ciphertext c_A. Then Alice uploads her ciphertext to CSP.

Re-Encrypt-Key: Taking a list of public parameters params, Alice's user public/private key pair $(\mathsf{upk}_{\mathsf{ID}_A}, \mathsf{usk}_{\mathsf{ID}_A})$ associated with an identifier ID_A and data recipient Bob's public key $\mathsf{upk}_{\mathsf{ID}_B}$ associated with an identifier ID_B as input, this algorithm is implemented by Alice to generate a PRE key $\mathsf{rk}_{A \to B}$, which is further sent to CSP through a secure channel.

Re-Encrypt: Taking a list of public parameters params, a ciphertext c_A for Alice, and a PRE key $\mathsf{rk}_{A \to B}$ as input, this algorithm is executed by the CSP to produce a transformed ciphertext c_B for Bob.

Decrypt: Taking a list of public parameters params, a private key $\mathsf{upk}_{\mathsf{ID}_i}$, and a ciphertext c_i, this algorithm is run by the data owner/recipient associated with an identifier ID_i to obtain the underlying encrypted data m or return a distinguished symbol $\bot$.

The above CL-PRE scheme allows the CSP using a PRE key $\mathsf{rk}_{A \to B}$ to transform a ciphertext encrypted under data owner Alice's public key $\mathsf{upk}_{\mathsf{ID}_A}$ into another ciphertext encrypted under data recipient Bob's public key $\mathsf{upk}_{\mathsf{ID}_B}$ on the same message m without leaking m or $\mathsf{usk}_{\mathsf{ID}_A}/\mathsf{usk}_{\mathsf{ID}_B}$ of the data owner/data recipient to the CSP.

Correctness: For all data $m \in \mathcal{M}$, key pair $(\mathsf{upk}_{\mathsf{ID}_A}, \mathsf{usk}_{\mathsf{ID}_A})$ for Alice and $(\mathsf{upk}_{\mathsf{ID}_B}, \mathsf{usk}_{\mathsf{ID}_B})$ for Bob, Alice is able to correctly share her underlying encrypted data m with Bob in the cloud if and only if the following conditions are satisfied:

- $\mathsf{Decrypt}_1(\mathsf{params}, \mathsf{usk}_{\mathsf{ID}_A}, \mathsf{Encrypt}(\mathsf{params}, \mathsf{ID}_A, \mathsf{upk}_{\mathsf{ID}_A}, m)) = m$

- $\mathsf{Decrypt}_2(\mathsf{params}, \mathsf{usk}_{\mathsf{ID}_B}, \mathsf{ReEncrypt}(\mathsf{params}, \mathsf{rk}_{A \to B}, c_A)) = m$

8.4.2.2 Security Model

First, we recall the security models of CL-PRE, given by Yang et al. [98] based on Baek et al.'s [51] security models of CL-PKE. Their definition considers two types of adversaries, types I and II. The difference between them is that a type I adversary $\mathcal{A}_1$ does not have access to the master key but may replace public keys of arbitrary identities with values of its own choice, whereas a type II adversary $\mathcal{A}_2$ does have access to the master key but may not replace public keys of entities. It must be pointed that Yang et al.'s security model for a type I adversary is slightly weak in a sense that $\mathcal{A}_1$ is not allowed to replace the public key of the challenge identity ID^* in any phase in order to prove the second-level ciphertext security of their CL-PRE scheme. However, Sun et al. [70] eliminated Baek et al.'s limitation and presented an improved CL-PKE scheme with a strong type I adversary. As a result, the security models of CL-PRE that we formalize by taking account of strong CL-PKE security notions [17] [70] and PRE security notions [98,234,235] are the strong type I and II adversaries, where $\mathcal{A}_1$ is able to replace the public key associated with the challenge identity. Furthermore, our CL-PRE scheme does not depend on bilinear pairings. Our strong security model is enough for many practical applications such as secure data sharing with a public cloud [97].

We formalize the security model of CL-PRE schemes by taking account of the CL-PKE security notion [17,70] and PRE security notion [98,234,235]. As usual, we consider $\mathcal{A}_1$ and $\mathcal{A}_2$ as two types of adversaries of types I and II, respectively. In our security model, different from Yang et al.'s definition, a type I adversary $\mathcal{A}_1$ does not have access to the master key but is allowed to replace the public key associated with the challenge identity, whereas a type II adversary $\mathcal{A}_2$ does have access to the master key but may not replace public keys of entities.

Let games I and II denote two games played between a challenger $\mathcal{C}$ and type I adversary $\mathcal{A}_1$ and type II adversary $\mathcal{A}_2$ for the CL-PRE scheme, respectively. Note that the challenger $\mathcal{C}$ maintains a list of queries-answers while interacting with the adversaries.

Game I (for adversary $\mathcal{A}_1$):

Initial: Taking a security parameter k as input, the challenger $\mathcal{C}$ runs the Setup algorithm to produce a master key master-secret kept secret and a list of public parameters params for $\mathcal{A}_1$.

Phase 1: In this phase, $\mathcal{A}_1$ issues a series of queries and acquires answers from the challenger $\mathcal{C}$ as follows:

  Partial-Private-Key-Extract Queries: On input of ID by $\mathcal{A}_1$, $\mathcal{C}$ produces the partial private key $\mathsf{psk_{ID}}$ for ID by running the Extract-Partial-Private-Key algorithm, and then answers $\mathsf{psk_{ID}}$ to $\mathcal{A}_1$.

Create-User Queries: On input of ID by $\mathcal{A}_1$, $\mathcal{C}$ produces the public key $\mathsf{upk_{ID}}$ for ID by running the Set-Secret-Value and Set-Public-Key algorithms, and then answers $\mathsf{upk_{ID}}$ to $\mathcal{A}_1$.

Secret-Value-Extract Queries: On input of ID by $\mathcal{A}_1$, $\mathcal{C}$ produces the private key $\mathsf{usk_{ID}}$ for ID by running Set-Secret-Value and Set-Private-Key, and then answers $\mathsf{usk_{ID}}$ to $\mathcal{A}_1$.

Public-Key-Replace Queries: The adversary $\mathcal{A}_1$ can repeatedly replace the public key $\mathsf{upk_{ID}}$ for any ID with any valid public key $\mathsf{upk'_{ID}}$ of its choice. The current value of an entity's public key is used by the challenger in any computation or response to the adversary's requests.

Re-Encrypt-Key Extract Queries: On input of $(\mathsf{ID}_1, \mathsf{ID}_2)$ by $\mathcal{A}_1$, $\mathcal{C}$ produces the re-encryption key $\mathsf{rk}_{1\to2}$ by running Re-Encrypt-Key, and then answers $\mathsf{rk}_{1\to2}$ to $\mathcal{A}_1$.

Re-Encrypt Queries: On input $(\mathsf{ID}_1, \mathsf{ID}_2, c_{\mathsf{ID}_1})$ by $\mathcal{A}_1$, $\mathcal{C}$ produces re-encrypted ciphertext c_{ID_2} for ID_2 by running the Re-Encrypt algorithm to transform c_{ID_1} into c_{ID_2} with the re-encryption key $\mathsf{rk}_{1\to2}$, which should be answered to $\mathcal{A}_1$.

Decrypt Queries: On input of $(\mathsf{ID}, c_{\mathsf{ID}})$ by $\mathcal{A}_1$,

1. If c_{ID} is a non-re-encrypted ciphertext, $\mathcal{C}$ answers the decryption of c_{ID} to $\mathcal{A}_1$ by running Decrypt$_1$, utilizing the private key that is associated with the current public key.

2. If c_{ID} is a re-encrypted ciphertext, $\mathcal{C}$ answers the decryption of c_{ID} to $\mathcal{A}_1$ by running Decrypt$_2$, utilizing the private key that is associated with the current public key.

Challenge: Once the adversary $\mathcal{A}_1$ decides to finish *phase 1*, it outputs a challenging identity ID^* and two plaintexts $m_0, m_1 \in \mathcal{M}$ with equal length. Note that ID^* has not been issued to extract a partial private key, a private key, or a re-encryption key at any time. The challenger $\mathcal{C}$ picks $b \in \{0,1\}$ and answers the challenge ciphertext $c^*=\mathsf{Encrypt}(\mathsf{params}, \mathsf{ID}^*, \mathsf{upk_{ID^*}}, m_b)$ to $\mathcal{A}_1$.

Phase 2: In this phase, the adversary $\mathcal{A}_1$ issues more queries adaptively, and the challenger $\mathcal{C}$ answers as in *phase 1*. Note that $\mathcal{A}_1$ cannot be issued to extract a partial private key, a private key, or a re-encryption key on ID^* at any time, and **Decrypt** queries on both (ID^*, c^*) and any derivative ciphertexts [234,236] of (ID^*, c^*) should not be made.

Guess: In the end, $\mathcal{A}_1$ outputs a guess $b' \in \{0, 1\}$. If $b = b'$, $\mathcal{A}_1$ wins this game.

Game II (for adversary $\mathcal{A}_2$): We do not describe the full details of game II and only present the differences from **game I** as follows:

- In **game II**, due to the fact that $\mathcal{A}_2$ has access to master key master-secret but may not be allowed to replace public key for any ID, the **Partial-Private-Key-Extract** and **Public-Key-Replace** queries cannot be queried by $\mathcal{A}_2$.

- In the **challenge** phase, ID^* has not been issued to extract a private key or a re-encryption key at any time.

We define $\mathcal{A}_i$'s advantage in **game** i above by $\text{Adv}(\mathcal{A}_i) = 2(\Pr[b' = b] - 1/2), i \in \{1, 2\}$. A CL-PRE scheme is considered to be IND-CCA secure if no probabilistic polynomial-time adversary has a nonnegligible advantage in the above games.

8.4.2.3 Concrete Construction

In this section, Qin et al.'s [99] CL-PRE scheme is presented. The detailed description of their CL-PRE scheme is as follows:

Setup: Taking a security parameter k as input, this algorithm produces a prime q and a group $\mathbb{G}$ of order q. Then it performs as follows:

1. Chooses a random generator $g \in \mathbb{G}$.
2. Picks $s \in \mathbb{Z}_q^*$ at random and computes $h = g^s$.
3. Selects hash functions $H_1 : \{0, 1\}^* \times \mathbb{G} \to \mathbb{Z}_q^*$, $H_2 : \{0, 1\}^* \times \mathbb{G} \times \mathbb{G} \to \mathbb{Z}_q^*$, $H_3 : \{0, 1\}^* \to \mathbb{Z}_q^*$, $H_4 : \mathbb{G} \to \{0, 1\}^{n+k_0}$, and $H_5 : \mathbb{G} \to \mathbb{Z}_q^*$.

The system public parameters are $\text{params} = \{q, n, k_0, g, h, H_1, H_2, H_3, H_4, H_5\}$, where n, k_0 mean the bit-length of a plaintext and a random bit string, respectively. The system master key master-secret $= s$. Note that plaintext space is $\mathcal{M} = \{0, 1\}^n$ and the ciphertext space is $\mathcal{C} = \{0, 1\}^{n+k_0}$.

Extract-Partial-Private-Key: Taking params, master-secret, and an identifier ID_A for Alice as input, this algorithm picks $\alpha_1, \alpha_2 \in \mathbb{Z}_q^*$ at random and computes $a_1 = g^{\alpha_1}$, $a_2 = g^{\alpha_2}$, $x_1 = \alpha_1 + sH_1(ID_A, a_1)$, and $x_2 = \alpha_2 + sH_1(ID_A, a_1, a_2)$. Then it returns a partial private key $\text{psk}_{ID_A} = (a_1, a_2, x_1, x_2)$ for Alice.

Set-Secret-Value: Taking params and ID_A as input, this algorithm randomly picks $z_A \in \mathbb{Z}_q^*$ as a secret value for Alice.

Set-Private-Key: Taking params, Alice's partial private key $\mathsf{psk}_{\mathsf{ID}_A}$, and secret value z_A as input, this algorithm returns a user secret key $\mathsf{usk}_{\mathsf{ID}_A} = (x_1, z_A)$ for Alice.

Set-Public-Key: Taking params, Alice's partial private key $\mathsf{psk}_{\mathsf{ID}_A}$, and secret value z_A as input, this algorithm computes $u_A = g^{z_A}$ and returns a public key $\mathsf{upk}_{\mathsf{ID}_A} = (u_A, a_1, a_2, x_2)$ for that user.

Re-Encrypt-Key: Taking params, an identifier ID_A and a public/private key pair $(\mathsf{upk}_{\mathsf{ID}_A}, \mathsf{usk}_{\mathsf{ID}_A})$ for Alice, and an identifier ID_B and a public key $\mathsf{upk}_{\mathsf{ID}_B}$ for Bob as input, this algorithm computes $t_B = b_1 h^{H_1(\mathsf{ID}_B, b_1)}$ and $t_{AB} = H_3(t_B^{z_A} \| u_B^{x_1} \| \mathsf{ID}_A \| \mathsf{upk}_{\mathsf{ID}_A} \| \mathsf{ID}_B \| \mathsf{upk}_{\mathsf{ID}_B})$. Then it returns a re-encryption key $\mathsf{rk}_{A \to B} = (x_1 H_5(u_A) + z_A) t_{AB}$.

Encrypt: Taking params, a plaintext message $m \in \mathcal{M}$, and Alice's public key $\mathsf{upk}_{\mathsf{ID}_A}$ as input, this algorithm performs as follows:

1. Checks $g^{x_2} \stackrel{?}{=} a_2 h^{H_2(\mathsf{ID}_A, a_1, a_2)}$.

2. Selects $\sigma \in \{0,1\}^{k_0}$ at random and computes $t_A = a_1 h^{H_1(\mathsf{ID}_A, a_1)}$ and $r = H_3(m \| \sigma \| \mathsf{ID}_A \| u_A)$.

3. Computes $c_1 = g^r$ and $c_2 = (m \| \sigma) \oplus H_4((t_A^{H_5(u_A)} \cdot u_A)^r)$.

Then it returns a ciphertext $c_A = (c_1, c_2)$ for Alice.

Re-Encrypt: Taking params, Alice's ciphertext c_A, and a re-encryption key $\mathsf{rk}_{A \to B}$ as input, this algorithm computes $c_1' = c_1^{\mathsf{rk}_{A \to B}}$ and $c_2' = c_2$. Then it outputs re-encrypted ciphertext $c_B = (c_1', c_2')$ for Bob or a distinguished symbol $\perp$.

Decrypt: Taking params, a user secret key $\mathsf{usk}_{\mathsf{ID}}$, and a ciphertext c_{ID} for user ID, this algorithm performs as follows:

- Decrypt$_1$: To decrypt non-re-encrypted ciphertext $c_A = (c_1, c_2)$ with $\mathsf{usk}_{\mathsf{ID}_A} = (x_1, z_A)$, this algorithm computes $(m \| \sigma) = c_2 \oplus H_4(c_1^{(x_1 H_5(u_A) + z_A)})$. Then it returns plaintext m, if $r' = H_3(m \| \sigma \| \mathsf{ID}_A \| u_A)$ and $g^{r'} = c_1$ holds. Otherwise, it outputs $\perp$.

- **Decrypt$_2$**: To decrypt re-encrypted ciphertext $c_B = (c'_1, c'_2)$ with $\mathsf{usk}_{\mathsf{ID}_B} = (y_1, z_B)$, this algorithm computes as follows:

  1. Computes $t_A = a_1 h^{H_1(\mathsf{ID}_A, a_1)}$ and $t_{BA} = H_3(u_A^{y_1} \| t_A^{z_B} \| \mathsf{ID}_A \| \mathsf{upk}_{\mathsf{ID}_A} \| \mathsf{ID}_B \| \mathsf{upk}_{\mathsf{ID}_B})$.

  2. Computes $(m \| \sigma) = c'_2 \oplus H_4((c'_1)^{1/t_{BA}})$.

  3. If $r' = H_3(m \| \sigma \| \mathsf{ID}_A \| u_A)$ and $(t_A^{H_5(u_A) \cdot u_A})^{r' t_{BA}} = c'_1$ holds, it returns m. Otherwise, it outputs $\perp$.

It is easy to check the correctness of the pairing-free CL-PRE scheme above; we omit it here.

Remark 8.1 *In our CL-PRE scheme, existentially unforgeable under an adaptive chosen-message attack (EUF-CMA), a secure Schnorr signature is used to protect the partial public key from being replaced by attackers with the values of their choices. $H_5(u_A)$ is necessary for resisting public key replacement attacks, where H_5 is a collision-free hash function.*

Remark 8.2 *The proposed scheme possesses properties such as unidirectionality, single hop, noninteractivity, nontransitivity, and collusion resistance, all of which are suitable for security requirements in cloud-based data sharing scenarios.*

8.4.2.4 Security Analysis

We have the following theorems about the security of the CL-PRE scheme. Due to space limitations, the proofs of these theorems are omitted.

Theorem 8.8 *Qin et al.'s CL-PRE scheme is an adaptive chosen ciphertext (IND-CCA) secure against the type I adversary in the random oracle model, if for any polynomial time adversary $\mathcal{A}_1$ the CDH problem is intractable in $\mathbb{G}$.*

Theorem 8.9 *Qin et al.'s CL-PRE scheme is an adaptive chosen ciphertext (IND-CCA) secure against the type II adversary in the random oracle model, if for any polynomial time adversary $\mathcal{A}_2$ the CDH problem is intractable in $\mathbb{G}$.*

8.4.2.5 Performance Evaluation

Data sharing is a very resource-demanding service with the public cloud in terms of computation cost, communication overhead, and storage space. In this section, we compare the performance of a data owner, CSP, and data recipient of our CL-PRE scheme with Xu et al.'s [97] scheme, Sur et al.'s [96] scheme, and Yang et al.'s [98] scheme. For both Xu et al.'s [97] and Sur et al.'s pairing-based schemes, to satisfy 1024-bit RSA-level security, we adopt the Tate pairing implemented over an elliptic curve defined on a 512-bit prime field with a generator of the order of 160 bits. For Yang et al.'s [98] and our pairing-free schemes, to achieve the same security level, we implement them over a 1024-bit prime finite field with a generator of the order of 160 bits. Additionally, we assume that the bit length of $|m|$ and $|\sigma|$ is 1024 bits and 160 bits, respectively. Note that we obtain the running time for cryptographic operations using the MIRACAL Library [179], a standard cryptographic library, on a PIV 3 GHz processor with 512 MB memory and a Windows XP operation system. The running times of one pairing operation, one exponentiation operation, and one map-to-point hash are 20.04 ms, 5.83 ms and 3.04 ms, respectively. According to the description of the multiple exponentiation algorithm in [98], we evaluate the concrete running time and communication cost in Table 8.4 to make the comparison more clear between our scheme and three existing works [96–98].

From Table 8.4, Qin et al.'s scheme is more efficient than Xu et al.'s scheme and Sur et al.'s scheme in terms of running time and ciphertext length. Compared with Yang et al.'s scheme, the overall performance of our scheme is superior.

In cloud-based data sharing of CL-PRE, we assume that a data owner only has to do one encryption and decryption. From observation of Table 8.4, the sum of running times on Encrypt and Decrypt$_1$ in our scheme is the shortest. We believe this cost is not significant. However, the data owner should perform the Re-Encrypt-Key algorithm to generate a decryption delegation for each data recipient. As shown in Figure 8.8, the computation cost of the data owner does increase linearly with the number of recipients. Our scheme and Yang et al.'s [98] scheme have the same overhead in Re-Encrypt-Key, so the curves coincide. For a data owner, both our scheme and Yang et al.'s scheme do not require high computational cost.

TABLE 8.4 Performance Comparison of CL-PRE Schemes

Schemes	Xu et al. [97]	Sur et al. [96]	Yang et al. [98]	Qin et al. [99]
Encrypt (ms)	37.53	32.66	18.95	23.32
ReEncryptKey (ms)	40.57	23.79	12.65	12.65
ReEncrypt (ms)	20.04	123.28	12.65	5.83
$\text{Decrypt}_1(C_A)$ (ms)	20.04	58.04	18.48	11.66
$\text{Decrypt}_2(C_B)$ (ms)	43.12	43.36	24.78	24.78
$|C_A|$ (bits)	3072	4256	3392	2208
$|rk_{A \rightarrow B}|$ (bits)	3072	3072	160	160
$|C_B|$ (bits)	4096	4256	2208	2208
Pairing-free	×	×	√	√
Security model	Weak	Weak	Weak	Strong
Assumption	DBDH	p-BDHI	CDH	CDH
Security	CPA	CCA	CCA	CCA

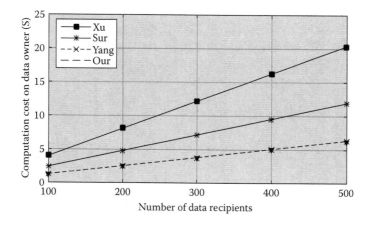

Figure 8.8 Computation cost of the data owner.

Next we analyze the computation cost of the CSP in different CL-PRE schemes. As a proxy, the CSP only has to carry out ciphertext transformations for a number of data recipients. Thus, the **Re-Encrypt** algorithm determines the computation cost of the CSP. Table 8.4 shows that the running time on **Re-Encrypt** in our scheme is superior to other schemes. The computation cost of the CSP increases accompanied by the number of data recipients. Clearly, Figure 8.9 reflects the advantage.

For a data recipient, there is no difference as it obtains re-encrypted messages from the CSP and decrypts in the same way. The data recipient has to do one decryption only. The running time on $Decrypt_2$ in our scheme is equal to Yang et al.'s [98] scheme. As a result, the computation cost of our CL-PRE is inexpensive for cloud-based data sharing.

For a data owner, the communication overhead is not constant and is relevant to the number of data recipients, since the data owner has to transport one encrypted message and one PRE key for each recipient to the CSP. Figure 8.10 shows the comparison of communication overhead for a data owner. Compared with Xu et al.'s [97] scheme and Sur et al.'s [96] scheme, our scheme has a great advantage. In addition, the data owner not only has to keep its own public/private key pair but also has to store all the generated PRE keys. Therefore, Figure 8.10 also reflects the storage overhead of the data owner.

For one data sharing operation, the CSP transports one re-encrypted message for one recipient, that is, the communication

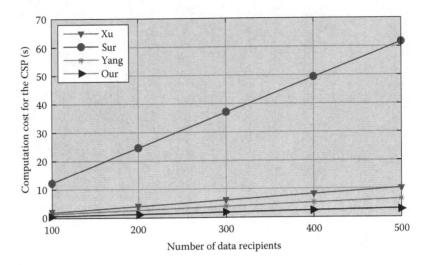

Figure 8.9 Computation cost of the cloud service provider (CSP).

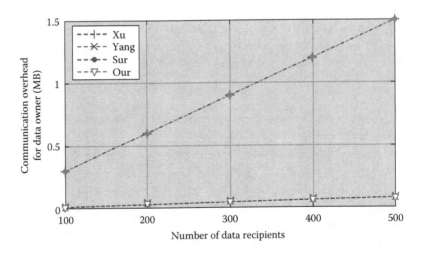

Figure 8.10 Communication overhead of the data owner.

overhead is proportional to the number of recipients. In addition, the CSP should store the data owner's encrypted message, PRE keys, and re-encrypted messages for a number of data recipients. Therefore, the storage overhead of the CSP is linear. We evaluate the storage overhead of the CSP with different CL-PRE schemes in Figure 8.11.

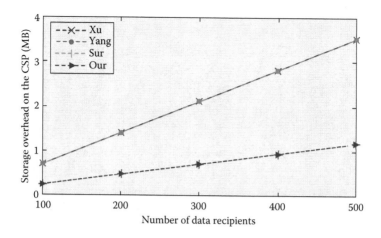

Figure 8.11 Storage overhead of the CSP.

In cloud-based data sharing of CL-PRE, a data recipient has to obtain only one re-encrypted message from the CSP, so the communication overhead and storage overhead of the data recipient are not significant.

CHAPTER 9

Extensions of CL-PKC

9.1 INTRODUCTION

To enjoy the good aspects of certificateless public-key cryptography (CL-PKC), numerous cryptographic primitives other than public-key encryption, signature, and key agreement have been introduced in the certificateless environment. Some of these primitives can be regarded as more general notions of CL-PKC. The purpose of this chapter is to provide a brief discussion of these issues. In this chapter, we briefly mention the connection of CL-PKC-based techniques to the construction of a few other primitives. We primarily discuss extensions of CL-PKC including certifcateless signcryption, certifcateless threshold signature, certifcateless ring signature, and certifcateless aggregate signature. We mostly describe these primitives along with their own formal definitions and security models to explain the connection to the techniques employed for CL-PKC.

9.2 CERTIFICATELESS SIGNCRYPTION

9.2.1 Related Work

Featured with confidentiality and nonrepudiation, the concept of signcryption originated by Zheng [102] in 1997 has found wide applications where both confidentiality and authentication are required. Compared with the traditional signature-then-encryption approach, signcryption enjoys a lower computational cost and communication overhead. The formal definition and security proof of signcryption was given in 2002 by Baek et al. [239]. Furthermore, this primitive has been extensively studied in traditional public-key cryptography (PKC) [240–246] and identity-based public-key cryptography (ID-PKC) [247–252] settings, respectively. As an extension of signcryption in the CL-PKC setting, Barbosa and Farshim [103] initialized the notion of certificateless signcryption (CL-SC) to gain the merits of CL-PKC and signcryption simultaneously. After that, several CL-SC schemes have also been proposed [104,105,253]. The security of all these CL-SC schemes has been proved in the random oracle model [75]. In view of the criticism on the random oracle model [77], the signcryption scheme secure in the standard model receives a lot of attention. To remove the random oracles in the security proof of CL-SC, Liu et al. [106] proposed the first efficient and provably secure CL-SC scheme in the standard model by integrating the idea of certificateless signature [60,107] and certificateless encryption [18,69]. However, Liu et al.'s scheme has been shown to be insecure against the outsider attack [108] and the malicious-but-passive key-generation center (KGC) attack [109], respectively. After that, Jin et al. [110] proposed an improvement to remedy the weakness in [106]. Unfortunately, Xiong [111] showed that Jin et al.'s CL-SC scheme still does not offer semantical security against chosen ciphertext attacks or existential unforgeability against chosen message attacks once the malicious-but-passive KGC is considered. The basic reason for Xiong's attack has also been analyzed. By exploiting Bellare and Shoup's one-time signature [112], Hwang et al.'s certificateless encryption [69] and Li et al.'s identity-based signcryption [254], Xiong proposed a new CL-SC scheme in the standard model. It is proven that this CL-SC scheme satisfies semantic security and unforgeability against outside adversary and malicious-but-passive KGC assuming the hardness of bilinear decision Diffie–Hellman (BDDH) and computational Diffie–Hellman (CDH) problems. The proofs do not rely on random oracles.

9.2.2   Formal Definition

Definitions of CL-SC Schemes. Generally speaking, a CL-SC scheme consists of a tuple (Setup, Extract-Partial-Private-Key, Set-User-Keys, Set-Private-Key, Signcrypt, Unsigncrypt) described as follows [106,110]:

Setup: Given a security parameter $k \in \mathbb{N}$ as input, this algorithm is executed by the KGC to generate the public system parameter params and a master secret key master-secret.

Extract-Partial-Private-Key: Given the master secret key master-secret along with the user identity ID $\in \{0,1\}^*$, this algorithm is executed by the KGC to generate a user partial key psk_{ID}, which will be sent to the corresponding user securely.

Set-User-Keys: Given the public system parameters and user identity ID, this algorithm is executed by the user itself to generate a user public/secret key pair (upk_{ID}, usk_{ID}). We stress that the user secret key that will be used in the Signcrypt and Unsigncrypt algorithm cannot be accessed by the KGC to avoid the key escrow problem in ID-PKC.

Set-Private-Key: On input of params and the entity's partial private key psk_{ID} and secret value usk_{ID}, this algorithm generates the entity's full private key sk_{ID}. Note that this algorithm can be omitted since the full private key sk_{ID} used in the Signcrypt or Unsigncrypt algorithms can be generated by integrating the partial private key psk_{ID} and user secret key usk_{ID} together in the process of performing the Signcrypt or Unsigncrypt algorithms.

Signcrypt: Given the system parameters params, a message m, a sender's user private key sk_{ID_S}, identity ID_S and user public key upk_{ID_S}, and a receiver's identity ID_R and public key upk_{ID_R}, this algorithm outputs a ciphertext σ or an error symbol $\perp$.

Unsigncrypt: Given a ciphertext σ, the receiver's user private key sk_{ID_S}, and the sender's identity ID_S and public key upk_{ID_S}, this algorithm outputs the plaintext m or an error symbol $\perp$.

Security models. According to [106], the outside attacker who can only compromise the user private key or replace the user public key and the malicious-but-passive KGC who is responsible for the generation of the public system parameters and master public/secret key pair should be considered in the security model of CL-SC. In this way, two types of security along with two types of adversaries $\mathcal{A}_1$ and $\mathcal{A}_2$ have been defined for the CL-SC scheme with the restriction that $\mathcal{A}_1$ cannot compromise the master secret key nor get access to the user partial key and $\mathcal{A}_2$ cannot mount the key replacement attack. The oracles that can be accessed by the adversaries are described as follows:

1. **Create-User** Oracle: Given a query on identity ID $\in \{0,1\}^*$, this oracle returns the matching user public key upk_{ID}.

2. **Partial-Private-Key-Extract** Oracle: Given a query on identity ID, this oracle outputs the partial secret key psk_{ID} associated with this identity.

3. **Secret-Value-Extract** Oracle: Given a query on identity ID, this oracle outputs a user secret key usk_{ID} associated with this identity.

4. **Public-Key-Replace** Oracle: Given an identity ID and a new user public key upk_{ID}, this oracle replaces the associated user's public key with the new public key upk'_{ID}.

5. **Signcrypt** Oracle: Upon receiving a sender with identity ID_S, a receiver with identity ID_R, and a message m, challenger $\mathcal{C}$ first runs **Signcrypt**$(params, m, sk_{ID_S}, ID_S, upk_{ID_S}, ID_R, upk_{ID_R})$, and then returns the resulting ciphertext to the adversary. Here, sk_{ID_S} denotes the sender's full private key. Note that it is possible for the challenger to be unaware of the sender's user secret value when the associated public key has been replaced by the adversary. In this case, we require the adversary to provide the sender's user secret value.

6. **Unsigncrypt** Oracle: Upon receiving a ciphertext σ, a sender with identity ID_S, and a receiver with identity ID_R, challenger $\mathcal{C}$ returns the result of **Unsigncrypt**$(\sigma, sk_{ID_R}, ID_S, upk_{ID_S})$. Note that it is possible for the challenger to be unaware of the receiver's user secret value when the associated public key has been replaced by the adversary. In this case, we require the adversary to provide the receiver's user secret value.

With regard to confidentiality, two games, one for $\mathcal{A}_1$ and the other for $\mathcal{A}_2$, have been defined as follows to capture the attacks launched by $\mathcal{A}_1$ and $\mathcal{A}_2$, respectively.

Game I: In this game, the outside attacker is modeled as type I adversary $\mathcal{A}_1$ and the game simulator/challenger is modeled as $\mathcal{C}$.

Initial: $\mathcal{C}$ first executes Setup to generate the master-secret and public system parameters params, and then publishes the public system params and keeps the master-secret secret.

Phase 1: In this phase, $\mathcal{C}$ runs $\mathcal{A}_1$ on 1^k and public system parameters. During the simulation, $\mathcal{A}_1$ can make queries to oracles

Create-User, **Partial-Private-Key-Extract**, **Secret-Value-Extract**, **Public-Key-Replace**, **Signcrypt**, and **Unsigncrypt**.

Challenge: Once $\mathcal{A}_1$ decides that *phase 1* is over, $\mathcal{A}_1$ generates two equal length messages m_0, m_1 and two identities ID_{S^*} and ID_{R^*} on which he/she wants to be challenged. Challenger $\mathcal{C}$ first chooses a bit b randomly, and then computes σ^*=**Signcrypt**$(\text{params}, m_b, \text{sk}_{\mathsf{ID}_S^*}, \mathsf{ID}_{S^*}, \text{upk}_{\mathsf{ID}_S^*}, \mathsf{ID}_{R^*}, \text{upk}_{\mathsf{ID}_R^*})$. Finally, $\mathcal{C}$ gives σ^* to $\mathcal{A}_1$.

Phase 2: Adversary $\mathcal{A}_1$ continues to issue queries as in *phase 1*, and $\mathcal{C}$ responds in the same way as in *phase 1*.

Guess: $\mathcal{A}_1$ produces a bit b' and wins the game if $b' = b$ and the following conditions are satisfied simultaneously:

1. $\mathcal{A}_1$ cannot extract the private key for any identity if the corresponding public key has been replaced.

2. $\mathcal{A}_1$ cannot extract the partial private key for ID_{R^*} if $\mathcal{A}_1$ has replaced the public key $\text{upk}_{\mathsf{ID}_R^*}$ before the challenge phase.

3. In *phase 2*, $\mathcal{A}_1$ cannot make an unsigncryption query on the challenge ciphertext σ^* under ID_{S^*} and ID_{R^*} unless the sender's public key $\text{upk}_{\mathsf{ID}_S^*}$ or the receiver's public key $\text{upk}_{\mathsf{ID}_R^*}$, which were used to signcrypt m_γ, has been replaced after the challenge phase.

The advantage of $\mathcal{A}_1$ is defined as $\text{Adv}_{\mathcal{A}_1}^{\text{IND}-\text{CL}-\text{SC}-\text{CCA2}} = |2Pr[b' = b] - 1|$, where $Pr[b' = b]$ denotes the probability that $b' = b$.

Game II: In this game, the insider attacker (malicious-but-passive KGC) is modeled as type II adversary $\mathcal{A}_2$ and the game simulator/challenger is modeled as $\mathcal{C}$.

Initial: $\mathcal{A}_2$ executes Setup to generate the master secret key master-secret and public system parameters params and sends the public system params and keeps the master secret master-secret to challenger $\mathcal{C}$. We should keep in mind that $\mathcal{A}_2$ generates params and master-secret by itself.

Phase 1: During the simulation, $\mathcal{A}_2$ can make queries to oracles **Create-User**, **Secret-Value-Extract**, **Signcrypt**, and

Unsigncrypt. Note that $\mathcal{A}_2$ can compute the partial private key of any identity by itself with the master secret key.

Challenge: Once $\mathcal{A}_2$ decides that *phase 1* is over, $\mathcal{A}_2$ generates two equal length messages m_0, m_1 and two identities ID_{S^*} and ID_{R^*} on which he wants to be challenged. Challenger $\mathcal{C}$ first chooses a bit b randomly, and then computes $\sigma^*=$**Signcrypt** (params, m_b, $\mathsf{sk}_{\mathsf{ID}_S^*}$, ID_{S^*}, $\mathsf{upk}_{\mathsf{ID}_S^*}$, ID_{R^*}, $\mathsf{upk}_{\mathsf{ID}_R^*}$). Finally, $\mathcal{C}$ gives σ^* to $\mathcal{A}_2$.

Phase 2: Adversary $\mathcal{A}_2$ continues to issue queries as in *phase 1*, and $\mathcal{C}$ responds in the same way as in *phase 1*.

Guess: $\mathcal{A}_2$ produces a bit b' and wins the game if $b' = b$ and the following conditions are satisfied. In *phase 2*, $\mathcal{A}_2$ cannot make an unsigncryption query on the challenge ciphertext σ^* under ID_{S^*} and ID_{R^*} unless the sender's public key $\mathsf{upk}_{\mathsf{ID}_S^*}$ or the receiver's public key $\mathsf{upk}_{\mathsf{ID}_R^*}$, which were used to signcrypt m_b, has been replaced after the challenge phase.

The advantage of $\mathcal{A}_2$ is defined as $Adv_{\mathcal{A}_2}^{IND-CL-SC-CCA2} = |2Pr[b' = b] - 1|$, where $Pr[b' = b]$ denotes the probability that $b' = b$.

A CL-SC scheme is said to be semantically secure against adaptively chosen ciphertext attacks, if there exists neither a polynomial-time type I adversary nor polynomial-time type II adversary who has a nonnegligible advantage in games I and II, respectively.

With regard to existential unforgeability, two games, one for $\mathcal{A}_1$ and the other for $\mathcal{A}_2$, have also been defined as follows to capture the attacks launched by $\mathcal{A}_1$ and $\mathcal{A}_2$, respectively.

Game III: Let $\mathcal{C}$ be the game simulator/challenger with the input of security parameter $k \in \mathbb{N}$.

Initial: $\mathcal{C}$ first executes **Setup** to generate the master secret key master-secret and public system parameters params, and then publishes the public system params and keeps the master secret key master-secret secret.

Attack: In this phase, $\mathcal{A}_1$ adaptively issues a polynomial bounded number of queries as in game I.

Forgery: Finally, $\mathcal{A}_1$ outputs a new triple $(\sigma^*, \mathsf{ID}_{S^*}, \mathsf{ID}_{R^*})$, which is not produced by the **Signcrypt** query. Adversary $\mathcal{A}_1$ wins this game if the result of $\mathsf{Unsigncrypt}(\sigma^*, \mathsf{ID}_{S^*}, \mathsf{upk}_{\mathsf{ID}_S^*}, \mathsf{sk}_{\mathsf{ID}_R^*})$ is not the symbol $\bot$ and the queries are subject to the following constraints:

1. $\mathcal{A}_1$ cannot extract the private key for any identity if the corresponding public key has been replaced.

2. $\mathcal{A}_1$ cannot extract the partial private key for ID_{S^*} if $\mathcal{A}_1$ has replaced the public key $\mathsf{upk}_{\mathsf{ID}_R^*}$ before the challenge phase.

The advantage of $\mathcal{A}_1$ is defined as $\mathrm{Adv}_{\mathcal{A}_1}^{\mathrm{EUF-CL-SC-CMA}} = Pr[\mathcal{A}_1$ wins].

Game IV: Let $\mathcal{C}$ be the game challenger with the input of security parameter $k \in \mathbb{N}$.

Initial: $\mathcal{A}_2$ executes Setup to generate the master secret key master-secret and public system parameters params and sends the public system params and keeps the master secret key master-secret to challenger $\mathcal{C}$. We should keep in mind that $\mathcal{A}_2$ generates params and master-secret by itself.

Attack: In this phase, $\mathcal{A}_2$ adaptively issues a polynomial bounded number of queries as in game II.

Forgery: Finally, $\mathcal{A}_2$ outputs a new triple $(\sigma^*, \mathsf{ID}_{S^*}, \mathsf{ID}_{R^*})$, which is not produced by the Signcrypt query. Adversary $\mathcal{A}_1$ wins this game if the result of $\mathsf{Unsigncrypt}(\sigma^*, \mathsf{ID}_{S^*}, \mathsf{upk}_{\mathsf{ID}_S^*}, \mathsf{sk}_{\mathsf{ID}_R^*})$ is not the symbol $\bot$.

The advantage of $\mathcal{A}_1$ is defined as $Adv_{\mathcal{A}_2}^{EUF-CL-SC-CMA} = Pr[\mathcal{A}_2$ wins].

A CL-SC scheme is said to be existentially unforgeable under adaptively chosen message attacks if there exists neither a polynomial-time type I adversary nor a polynomial-time type II adversary who has a nonnegligible success probability in games III and IV, respectively.

9.2.3 Xiong's Scheme

A new CL-SC scheme against type I and II adversaries has been proposed by Xiong [111] in the standard model by incorporating the idea of Bellare and Shoup's one-time signature [112], Hwang et al.'s certificateless encryption [69], and Li et al.'s identity-based signcryption [214]. To fight against the malicious KGC attack, our scheme uses a different user public/secret key generation algorithm and embeds the sender's public key in the ciphertext. In this way, the unforgeability of our scheme will be guaranteed since the secret key of the sender cannot be extracted by the malicious KGC.

Setup: Select a pairing $\hat{e} : \mathbb{G}_1 \times \mathbb{G}_1 \rightarrow \mathbb{G}_2$ where the order of $\mathbb{G}_1$ is p. Let g be a generator of $\mathbb{G}_1$. Randomly select $\alpha \leftarrow_R \mathbb{Z}_p$, and $g_2 \leftarrow_R \mathbb{G}_1$, and $K \in_R \{0,1\}^k$, and then compute $g_1 = g^\alpha$, $h = \hat{e}(g_1, g_2)$. Also select randomly the following elements: $u', m' \leftarrow_R \mathbb{G}_1$, $u_i \leftarrow_R \mathbb{G}_1$ for $i = 1, \ldots, n_u$, $m_i \leftarrow_R \mathbb{G}_1$ for $i = 1, \ldots, n_m$. Let $\mathbf{U} = (u_i)$, $\mathbf{M} = (m_i)$. Let $H_1 : \{0,1\}^* \rightarrow \mathbb{Z}_p$, $H_2 : \{0,1\}^* \rightarrow \mathbb{Z}_p$, and $H_m : \{0,1\}^* \rightarrow \{0,1\}^{n_m}$ be three collision-resistant cryptographic hash functions for some $n_m \in \mathbb{Z}$. The public parameters are params $= \{\mathbb{G}_1, \mathbb{G}_2, \hat{e}, g, g_1, g_2, h, u', \mathbf{U}, m', \mathbf{M}, K, H_1, H_2, H_m\}$ and master-secret is g_2^α.

Partial-Private-Key-Gen: Let ID be a bit string of length n_{ID} representing an identity and let $\text{ID}[i]$ be the i-th bit of ID. Define $\mathcal{U} \subset \{1, \ldots, n_{\text{ID}}\}$ to be the set of indices i such that $\text{ID}[i] = 1$. To construct the partial secret key of identity ID, the KGC randomly picks $r_{\text{ID}} \leftarrow_R \mathbb{Z}_p$ and computes the following:

$$\left(g_2^\alpha \left(u' \prod_{i \in \mathcal{U}} u_i \right)^{r_{\text{ID}}}, g^{r_{\text{ID}}} \right) = (psk_{\text{ID},1}, psk_{\text{ID},2})$$

Therefore, the sender and the receiver's partial private keys are

$$\left(g_2^\alpha \left(u' \prod_{i \in \mathcal{U}_S} u_i \right)^{r_S}, g^{r_S} \right) = (\mathsf{psk}_{\text{ID}_S,1}, \mathsf{psk}_{\text{ID}_S,2})$$

and

$$\left(g_2^\alpha \left(u' \prod_{i \in \mathcal{U}_R} u_i \right)^{r_R}, g^{r_R} \right) = (\mathsf{psk}_{\text{ID}_R,1}, \mathsf{psk}_{\text{ID}_R,2})$$

User-Key-Gen: An entity selects two secret values $x_{\text{ID}}, y_{\text{ID}} \leftarrow_R \mathbb{Z}_p$ as his/her user secret key usk_{ID} such that $\mathsf{usk}_{\text{ID}} = (x_{\text{ID}}, y_{\text{ID}})$ and computes the corresponding user public key as $\mathsf{upk}_{\text{ID}} = (\mathsf{upk}_{\text{ID},1}, \mathsf{upk}_{\text{ID},2}, \mathsf{upk}_{\text{ID},3}) = (h^{x_{\text{ID}}}, g_2^{y_{\text{ID}}}, g^{y_{\text{ID}}})$. After that, the corresponding signature associated with the public key is computed as $z_{\mathsf{ID}} = y_{\mathsf{ID}} + c_{1,\mathsf{ID}} x_{\mathsf{ID}}$, where $c_{1,\mathsf{ID}} = H_1(K, \mathsf{upk}_{\mathsf{ID}} \parallel \mathsf{params})$. According to [69], this one-time signature can be generated by applying the technique of the Fiat-Shamir transform without random oracles as described in [112].

Signcrypt: To send a message $m \in \mathbb{G}_2$ to the receiver associated with identity ID_R and user public key $\mathsf{upk}_{\mathsf{ID}_R}$, the sender associated with identity ID_S, user public key $\mathsf{upk}_{\mathsf{ID}_S}$, partial private key $(\mathsf{psk}_{\mathsf{ID}_S,1}, \mathsf{psk}_{\mathsf{ID}_S,2})$, and user secret key $\mathsf{usk}_{\mathsf{ID}_S}$ first checks if the receiver's user public key has the right form such that $\hat{e}(g_1, g_2)^{z_{\mathsf{ID}_R}} = \mathsf{upk}_{\mathsf{ID}_R,1}^{c_{1,\mathsf{ID}_R}} \cdot \hat{e}(g_1, \mathsf{upk}_{\mathsf{ID}_R,2})$ and $\hat{e}(\mathsf{upk}_{\mathsf{ID}_R,2}, g) = \hat{e}(\mathsf{upk}_{\mathsf{ID}_R,3}, g_2)$, where $c_{1,\mathsf{ID}_R} = H_1(K, \mathsf{upk}_{\mathsf{ID}_R} \parallel \mathsf{params})$. After that, the sender picks $k \leftarrow_R \mathbb{Z}_p$ and performs the following steps:

1. Computes $\sigma_1 = m \cdot \mathsf{upk}_{\mathsf{ID}_R,1}^{k}$, $\sigma_2 = g^k$, $\sigma_3 = (u' \prod_{i \in \mathcal{U}_R} u_i)^k$, and $\sigma_4 = \mathsf{psk}_{\mathsf{ID}_S,2}^{x_{\mathsf{ID}_S}}$.

2. Computes $\mathsf{m} = H_{\mathsf{m}}(\sigma_1, \sigma_2, \sigma_3, \sigma_4, u_S, u_R, upk_S, upk_R) \in \{0,1\}^{n_m}$ and assumes $\mathsf{m}[i]$ to be the i-th bit of m and $\mathcal{M} \subset \{1, \ldots, n_m\}$ to be the set of indices i such that $\mathsf{m}[i] = 1$,

3. Computes $\sigma_5 = \mathsf{psk}_{\mathsf{ID}_S,1}^{x_{\mathsf{ID}_S}} \cdot \mathsf{upk}_{\mathsf{ID}_S,3}^{kc_2} \cdot (m' \prod_{j \in \mathcal{M}} m_j)^k$, where $c_2 = H_2(\sigma_1, \sigma_2, \sigma_3, \sigma_4, \mathsf{ID}_S, \mathsf{ID}_R, \mathsf{upk}_{\mathsf{ID}_S}, \mathsf{upk}_{\mathsf{ID}_R})$.

4. Outputs the ciphertext $\sigma = (\sigma_1, \sigma_2, \sigma_3, \sigma_4, \sigma_5)$.

Unsigncrypt: Given a ciphertext $\sigma = (\sigma_1, \sigma_2, \sigma_3, \sigma_4, \sigma_5)$ from the user associated with an identity ID_S and public key $\mathsf{upk}_{\mathsf{ID}_S}$, a verifier associated with partial private key $(\mathsf{psk}_{\mathsf{ID}_R,1}, \mathsf{psk}_{\mathsf{ID}_R,2})$ and user secret key $\mathsf{usk}_{\mathsf{ID}_R}$ performs the following steps to decrypt the ciphertext:

1. Checks if the sender's user public key has the right form such that $\hat{e}(g_1, g_2)^{z_{\mathsf{ID}_S}} = \mathsf{upk}_{\mathsf{ID}_S,1}^{c_{1,\mathsf{ID}_S}} \cdot \hat{e}(g_1, \mathsf{upk}_{\mathsf{ID}_S,2})$ and $\hat{e}(\mathsf{upk}_{\mathsf{ID}_S,2}, g) = \hat{e}(\mathsf{upk}_{\mathsf{ID}_S,3}, g_2)$, where $c_{1,\mathsf{ID}_S} = H_1(K, \mathsf{upk}_{\mathsf{ID}_S} \parallel \mathsf{params})$.

2. Computes $\mathsf{m} = H_{\mathsf{m}}(\sigma_1, \sigma_2, \sigma_3, \sigma_4, \mathsf{ID}_S, \mathsf{ID}_R, \mathsf{upk}_{\mathsf{ID}_S}, \mathsf{upk}_{\mathsf{ID}_R}) \in \{0,1\}^{n_m}$, assumes $\mathsf{m}[i]$ to be the i-th bit of m and $\mathcal{M} \subset \{1, \ldots, n_m\}$ to be the set of indices i such that $\mathsf{m}[i] = 1$,

and checks whether the following equation holds:

$$\hat{e}(\sigma_5, g) \;=\; \mathsf{upk}_{\mathsf{ID}_S,1} \cdot \hat{e}\left(\sigma_4, u' \prod_{i \in \mathcal{U}_S} u_i\right)$$

$$\cdot \hat{e}\left(\sigma_2, \mathsf{upk}_{\mathsf{ID}_S,3}^{c_2} \cdot \left(m' \prod_{j \in \mathcal{M}} m_j\right)\right)$$

where $c_2 = H_2(\sigma_1, \sigma_2, \sigma_3, \sigma_4, \mathsf{ID}_S, \mathsf{ID}_R, \mathsf{upk}_{\mathsf{ID}_S}, \mathsf{upk}_{\mathsf{ID}_R})$. If the above equation holds, output $m = \sigma_1 \cdot \hat{e}(\sigma_3, \mathsf{psk}_{\mathsf{ID}_R,2}^{x_{\mathsf{ID}_R}}) / \hat{e}(\sigma_2, \mathsf{psk}_{\mathsf{ID}_R,1}^{x_{\mathsf{ID}_R}})$; otherwise, output $\perp$.

9.2.4 Analysis

Theorem 9.1 *Our CL-SC scheme is existentially unforgeable against chosen-message attacks (EUF-CL-SC-CMA) in the standard model assuming the CDH problem is hard.*

This theorem follows Lemma 9.1.

Lemma 9.1 *(Type I Existential Unforgeability). Our CL-SC scheme is (ϵ, t)-existential unforgeable against a type I adversary with advantage at most ϵ and runs in time at most t, assuming that the (ϵ', t')-CDH assumption holds in $\mathbb{G}_1$, where $\epsilon' \geq \epsilon/16(q_{pp}+q_s+q_u)q_u(n_u+1)(n_m+1)$ and $t' = t + O((q_{pp}n_u + q_s(n_u + n_m))\rho + (q_k + q_{pp} + q_s)\tau)$, where q_{pp} is the number of queries made to the Reveal-Partial-Private-Key oracle, q_s the number of queries made to the Signcrypt oracle, q_u the number of queries made to the Unsigncrypt oracle, q_k the number of queries made to the Reveal-Secret-Key and Request-Public-Key oracles altogether, and ρ and τ the time for a multiplication and an exponentiation in $\mathbb{G}_1$, respectively.*

Theorem 9.2 *Our CL-SC scheme is indistinguishable against chosen-ciphertext attacks (IND-CL-SC-CCA) in the standard model assuming the decisional BDDH problem is hard.*

This theorem follows Lemmas 9.2 and 9.3.

Lemma 9.2 *(Type I Confidentiality). Our CL-SC scheme is (ϵ, t)-indistinguishable against a type I chosen-ciphertext adversary with* advantage at most ϵ and runs in time at most t, assuming that the (ϵ', t')-BDDH assumption holds in $\mathbb{G}_1$, where $\epsilon' \geq \epsilon/32(q_e + q_s)q_s(n_u + 1)(n_m + 1)$ and $t' = t + O((q_e n_u + q_s(n_u + n_m))\rho + (q_k + q_e + q_s)\tau)$.

Lemma 9.3 *(Type II Confidentiality). Our CL-SC scheme is (ϵ, t)-indistinguishable against a type II chosen-ciphertext adversary with advantage at most ϵ and runs in time at most t, assuming that the (ϵ', t')-BDDH assumption holds in $\mathbb{G}_1$, where $\epsilon' \geq \epsilon/32(q_s + q_u)q_u(n_u + 1)(n_m + 1)$ and $t' = t + O((q_{pp}n_u + q_s(n_u + n_m))\rho + (q_k + q_s)\tau)$.*

The proof of Theorems 9.6 and 9.7 is omitted due to the similarity to the security proof in [69,107].

9.3 CERTIFICATELESS AGGREGATE SIGNATURE

9.3.1 Related Work

In the notion of aggregate signatures introduced by Boneh et al. [255], given n signatures (as well as the associated public keys) on n messages from n users, anyone can combine all of these signatures into a single one. The resulting signature can convince a verifier that the n users indeed signed the n corresponding messages. This feature greatly reduces the computational overhead to verify signatures and the communication/storage cost to relay/store signatures.

Since Boneh el al.'s scheme, a number of aggregate signature schemes have been proposed in traditional PKC [256–261] and ID-PKC [262–266], respectively. To obtain the merits of aggregate signature and CL-PKC simultaneously, the concept of CL-AS has been introduced and several CL-AS schemes have been proposed [21,141,267,268]. Unfortunately, most CL-AS schemes are only provably secure against the strong type I/II adversary [21,141,267]. Only one scheme in [268] is provably secure against the super type I/II adversary. Furthermore, Zhang et al.'s schemes [21,268] require certain synchronization, that is, all signers must share the same string based on synchronized clocks to generate the aggregate signature. One may observe that it is not easy to achieve synchronization in many mobile computing scenarios. Also, many schemes [141,267,268] require a large number of pairing operations and a long signature size, which deviates from the main goals of aggregate signatures. To solve these problems, Xiong et al. [269,270] proposed an efficient CL-AS scheme and showed its security in the random oracle model against the super type I/II adversary under the standard CDH assumption. However, Shen and Sun [271] demonstrated two kinds of concrete attacks against Xiong et al.'s CL-AS scheme in their security model. After that, Xiong et al. [272] proposed another CL-AS scheme suitable for ad hoc networks. The security of such a scheme is theoretically proven. Unfortunately, He et al. [273] and Cheng et al. [274] pointed out that an adversary could forge a legal signature for any message against Xiong et al.'s CL-AS scheme, respectively. Recently, Horng et al. [275] proposed a novel CL-AS scheme that featured conditional anonymity for secure vehicle-to-infrastructure communications in vehicular ad hoc networks (VANETs). Furthermore, their scheme has been proven to be existentially unforgeable under adaptive chosen-message attacks under the standard CDH assumption.

9.3.2 Formal Definition

Components of CL-AS schemes. A CL-AS scheme CL-AS= (Setup, Extract-Partial-Private-Key, Set-User-Keys, Sign, Aggregate and Aggregate Verify) is specified by six polynomial time algorithms with the following functionality:

The randomized parameters generation algorithm Setup takes as input 1^k, where k is the security parameter params, and outputs a master secret key master-secret. The algorithm is assumed to be run by a KGC for the initial setup of a CL-AS scheme.

The randomized private key generation algorithm Extract-Partial-Private-Key takes as input master-secret and user's identity $\mathsf{ID}_i \in \{0,1\}^*$ and generates a key $\mathsf{psk}_{\mathsf{ID}_i}$ called the partial private key. This algorithm is run by the KGC once for each user, and the partial private key is assumed to be distributed securely to the corresponding user.

The randomized user key generation algorithm Set-User-Keys takes as input params and user's identity ID_i and generates a user public/secret key pair $(\mathsf{upk}_{\mathsf{ID}_i}, \mathsf{usk}_{\mathsf{ID}_i})$. This algorithm is supposed to be run by each user in the system.

The randomized signing algorithm Sign is run by a signer ID_i that takes as input a signing key $(\mathsf{psk}_{\mathsf{ID}_i}, \mathsf{usk}_{\mathsf{ID}_i})$ and a message $m_i \in \{0,1\}^*$ and outputs a signature $\sigma_i \leftarrow \mathsf{Sign}(\mathsf{psk}_{\mathsf{ID}_i}, \mathsf{usk}_{\mathsf{ID}_i}, m_i)$.

The randomized aggregating algorithm **Aggregate** takes as input an aggregating set U of n users $\{\mathfrak{U}_1, \ldots, \mathfrak{U}_n\}$ with the identity ID_i and the corresponding public key $\mathsf{upk}_{\mathsf{ID}_i}$ of each user $\mathfrak{U}_i$, a signature σ_i on a message m_i under identity ID_i, and the public key $\mathsf{upk}_{\mathsf{ID}_i}$ for each user $\mathfrak{U}_i \in U$. The output of this algorithm is an aggregate signature σ on messages $\{m_1, \ldots, m_n\}$.

The randomized verification algorithm **Aggregate Verify** takes as input **params**, an aggregating set U of n users $\{\mathfrak{U}_1, \ldots, \mathfrak{U}_n\}$ with the identity ID_i and the corresponding public key $\mathsf{upk}_{\mathsf{ID}_i}$ of each user $\mathfrak{U}_i$, and an aggregate signature σ on messages $\{m_1, \ldots, m_n\}$. It outputs **True** if the signature is correct, or $\perp$ otherwise.

Adversaries model of CL-AS scheme. Combining the security notions of CL-PKC and security models of aggregate signature schemes in traditional PKC and ID-PKC, two types of security, type-I and type-II security, for the CL-AS scheme along with two types of adversaries, $\mathcal{A}_1$ and $\mathcal{A}_2$, have been defined [21,118,268,272]. Adversary $\mathcal{A}_1$ models a malicious adversary that compromises the user secret key $\mathsf{usk}_{\mathsf{ID}}$ or replaces the user public key $\mathsf{upk}_{\mathsf{ID}}$ but cannot compromise the master secret key **master-secret** nor get access to the partial private key $\mathsf{psk}_{\mathsf{ID}}$. Adversary $\mathcal{A}_2$ models the malicious-but-passive KGC that controls the generation of the master public/secret key pair, and that of any partial private key $\mathsf{psk}_{\mathsf{ID}}$. The following are five oracles that can be accessed by the adversaries:

1. **Create-User**: On input of an identity $\mathsf{ID}_i \in \{0,1\}^*$, if ID_i has already been created, nothing is to be carried out. Otherwise, the oracle generates $\mathsf{psk}_{\mathsf{ID}_i} \leftarrow$ Extract-Partial-Private-Key(master-secret, ID_i) and $(\mathsf{upk}_{\mathsf{ID}_i}, \mathsf{usk}_{\mathsf{ID}_i}) \leftarrow$ Set-User-Keys(params, ID_i). It then stores $(\mathsf{ID}_i, \mathsf{psk}_{\mathsf{ID}_i}, \mathsf{upk}_{\mathsf{ID}_i}, \mathsf{usk}_{\mathsf{ID}_i})$ into a list L. In both cases, $\mathsf{upk}_{\mathsf{ID}_i}$ is returned.

2. **Partial-Private-Key-Extract**: On input of an identity ID_i, the oracle searches L for a corresponding entry to ID_i. If it is not found, $\perp$ is returned; otherwise, the corresponding $\mathsf{psk}_{\mathsf{ID}_i}$ is returned.

3. **Secret-Value-Extract**: On input of an identity ID_i, the oracle searches L for a corresponding entry to ID_i. If it is not found, $\perp$ is returned; otherwise, the corresponding $\mathsf{usk}_{\mathsf{ID}_i}$ is returned.

4. **Public-Key-Replace**: On input of an identity ID_i and a user public/secret key pair $(\mathsf{upk}^*_{\mathsf{ID}_i}, \mathsf{usk}^*_{\mathsf{ID}_i})$, the oracle searches L for the entry of ID_i. If it is not found, nothing will be carried. Otherwise, the oracle updates $(\mathsf{ID}, \mathsf{psk}_{\mathsf{ID}_i}, \mathsf{upk}_{\mathsf{ID}_i}, \mathsf{usk}_{\mathsf{ID}_i})$ to $(\mathsf{ID}, \mathsf{psk}_{\mathsf{ID}_i}, \mathsf{upk}^*_{\mathsf{ID}_i}, \mathsf{usk}^*_{\mathsf{ID}_i})$.

5. **Super-Sign**: On input of a message $m_i \in \{0,1\}^*$ for ID_i, the signing oracle returns a valid signature σ_i such that $\mathsf{True}\leftarrow$ $\mathsf{Verify}(\mathsf{params}, \mathsf{ID}_i, \mathsf{upk}_{\mathsf{ID}_i}, m_i, \sigma_i)$, where $\mathsf{upk}_{\mathsf{ID}_i}$ is the current public key corresponding to ID_i and it may be replaced by the **Public-Key-Replace** query.

Note that when the oracle **Public-Key-Replace** is queried, $\mathsf{usk}^*_{\mathsf{ID}_i}$ can be an empty string. In this case, it means that the user secret key is not provided. If $\mathsf{usk}^*_{\mathsf{ID}_i}$ is an empty string and the original user secret key of an identity ID_i is replaced with $\mathsf{usk}^*_{\mathsf{ID}_i}$, then the empty string will be returned if the **Secret-Value-Extract** oracle is queried on ID_i. Also note that even if $\mathsf{usk}^*_{\mathsf{ID}_i}$ is not an empty string, it does not mean that $\mathsf{usk}^*_{\mathsf{ID}_i}$ is the corresponding secret key of $\mathsf{upk}^*_{\mathsf{ID}_i}$. Hence as mentioned, the signature generated by the signing oracle **Super-Sign** will be a valid signature under the replaced user public key $\mathsf{upk}^*_{\mathsf{ID}_i}$.

We define two games, one for $\mathcal{A}_1$ and the other for $\mathcal{A}_2$.

Game I: Let $\mathcal{S}_1$ be the game simulator/challenger and $k \in \mathbb{N}$ be a security parameter.

1. $\mathcal{S}_1$ executes $\mathsf{Setup}(1^k)$ to get (mpk, msk).

2. $\mathcal{S}_1$ runs $\mathcal{A}_1$ on 1^k and mpk. During the simulation, $\mathcal{A}_1$ can make queries to oracles **Create-User**, **Partial-Private-Key-Extract**, **Secret-Value-Extract**, **Public-Key-Replace**, and **Super-Sign**.

3. $\mathcal{A}_1$ outputs a set of n users whose identities form the set $L^*_{\mathsf{ID}} = \{\mathsf{ID}^*_1, \ldots, \mathsf{ID}^*_n\}$ and corresponding public keys that from the set $L^*_{\mathsf{upk}} = \{\mathsf{upk}^*_1, \ldots, \mathsf{upk}^*_n\}$, n messages $L^*_m = \{m^*_1, \ldots, m^*_n\}$, and an aggregate signature σ^*.

We say that $\mathcal{A}_1$ wins **game I**, iff

- σ^* is a valid aggregate signature on messages $\{m^*_1, \cdots, m^*_n\}$ under identities $\{\mathsf{ID}^*_1, \ldots, \mathsf{ID}^*_n\}$ and the corresponding public keys $\{\mathsf{upk}^*_1, \ldots, \mathsf{upk}^*_n\}$.

- At least one of the identities, without loss of generality, say $\mathsf{ID}_1^* \in L_{\mathsf{ID}}^*$, has not submitted during the **Partial-Private-Key-Extract**(ID_1^*) queries to get the user partial key $\mathsf{psk}_{\mathsf{ID}_1}^*$. And the oracle **Super-Sign** has never been queried with (ID_1^*, m_1^*).

Definition 9.1 *A CL-AS scheme is said to be type-I secure if there is no probabilistic polynomial-time adversary $\mathcal{A}_1$ that wins **game I** with a nonnegligible advantage.*

Game II: Let $\mathcal{S}_2$ be the game challenger and $k \in \mathbb{N}$ be a security parameter. There are two phases of interactions between $\mathcal{S}_2$ and $\mathcal{A}_2$.

1. $\mathcal{S}_2$ executes $\mathcal{A}_2$ on input 1^k, which returns a master secret key master-secret and public parameters params to $\mathcal{A}_2$. Note that $\mathcal{A}_2$ cannot make any query at this stage.

2. During this stage of the simulation, $\mathcal{A}_2$ can make queries to oracles **Secret-Value-Extract** and **Super-Sign**. $\mathcal{A}_2$ can also make queries to **Create-User**. Note that oracle **Partial-Private-Key-Extract** is not accessible and no longer needed as $\mathcal{A}_2$ has the master secret key, and when $\mathcal{A}_2$ issues a query to the **Create-User** oracle, it has to additionally provide the user partial key $\mathsf{psk}_{\mathsf{ID}}$.

3. At the end of this phase, $\mathcal{A}_2$ is to output a set of n users whose identities form the set $L_{\mathsf{ID}}^* = \{\mathsf{ID}_1^*, \ldots, \mathsf{ID}_n^*\}$ and corresponding public keys that form the set $L_{\mathsf{upk}}^* = \{\mathsf{upk}_1^*, \ldots, \mathsf{upk}_n^*\}$, n messages $L_m^* = \{m_1^*, \ldots, m_n^*\}$, and an aggregate signature σ^*.

We say that $\mathcal{A}_2$ wins **game II**, iff

- σ^* is a valid aggregate signature on messages $\{m_1^*, \ldots, m_n^*\}$ under identities $\{\mathsf{ID}_1^*, \ldots, \mathsf{ID}_n^*\}$ and the corresponding public keys $\{\mathsf{upk}_1^*, \ldots, \mathsf{upk}_n^*\}$.

- At least one of the identities, without loss of generality, say $\mathsf{ID}_1^* \in L_{\mathsf{ID}}^*$, has not submitted during the **Secret-Value-Extract**(ID_1^*) queries to get the user secret key $\mathsf{usk}_{\mathsf{ID}_1}^*$. And the oracle **Super-Sign** has never been queried with (ID_1^*, m_1^*).

Definition 9.2 *A CL-AS scheme is said to be type-II secure if there is no probabilistic polynomial-time adversary $\mathcal{A}_2$ that wins **Game II** with a nonnegligible advantage.*

9.3.3 Xiong–Wu–Chen's Scheme

In this section, Xiong et al.'s [269,270] CL-AS scheme is presented. Although this scheme was shown to be vulnerable to the forgery attack [271], the intention of including this scheme is merely to offer a gentle introduction to the CL-AS scheme.

Setup: Given a security parameter $k \in \mathbb{Z}$, the algorithm works as follows:

1. Run the parameter generator on input k to generate a prime q, two groups $\mathbb{G}_1$, $\mathbb{G}_2$ of prime order q, two different generators P and Q in $\mathbb{G}_1$, and an admissible pairing $\hat{e} : \mathbb{G}_1 \times \mathbb{G}_1 \to \mathbb{G}_2$.

2. Select a master-key $s \in_R \mathbb{Z}_q^*$ and set $P_{\text{pub}} = sP$.

3. Choose cryptographic hash functions $H_0, H_0' : \{0,1\}^* \to \mathbb{G}_1$ and $H_1, H_2, H_2' : \{0,1\}^* \to \mathbb{Z}_q^*$. The security analysis will review H_1 and H_2 as random oracles. The system parameters params are $\{q, \mathbb{G}_1, \mathbb{G}_2, \hat{e}, P, Q, P_{\text{pub}}, H_0, H_0', H_1, H_2, H_2'\}$. The master-key is s.

Extract-Partial-Private-Key: Given a user's identity $\mathsf{ID}_i \in \{0,1\}^*$, the KGC first computes $Q_{\mathsf{ID}_i} = H_0(\mathsf{ID}_i)$ and $Q'_{\mathsf{ID}_i} = H_0'(\mathsf{ID}_i)$. It then sets this user's partial key $\mathsf{psk}_{\mathsf{ID}_i} = (sQ_{\mathsf{ID}_i}, sQ'_{\mathsf{ID}_i})$ and transmits it to user ID_i secretly.

Set-User-Keys: The user ID_i selects a secret value $x_{\mathsf{ID}_i} \in_R \mathbb{Z}_q^*$ as his secret key $\mathsf{usk}_{\mathsf{ID}_i}$, and computes his public key as $\mathsf{upk}_{\mathsf{ID}_i} = x_{\mathsf{ID}_i} P$.

Sign: Given its signing key $(\mathsf{usk}_{\mathsf{ID}_i}, \mathsf{psk}_{\mathsf{ID}_i})$, and a message $m_i \in \{0,1\}^*$, the signer, whose identity is ID_i with a corresponding public key $\mathsf{upk}_{\mathsf{ID}_i}$, performs the following steps:

1. Computes $h_{i1} = H_1(m_i, \mathsf{ID}_i, \mathsf{upk}_{\mathsf{ID}_i})$, $h_{i2} = H_2(m_i, \mathsf{ID}_i, \mathsf{upk}_{\mathsf{ID}_i})$ and $h'_{i2} = H_2'(m_i, \mathsf{ID}_i, \mathsf{upk}_{\mathsf{ID}_i})$.

2. Computes $\sigma_i = h_{i1} \cdot x_{\mathsf{ID}_i} \cdot Q + h_{i2} \cdot sQ_{\mathsf{ID}_i} + h'_{i2} \cdot sQ'_{\mathsf{ID}_i}$.

3. Outputs σ_i as the signature on m_i.

Aggregate: Anyone can act as an aggregate signature generator who can aggregate a collection of individual signatures. For an aggregating set of n users$\{\mathfrak{U}_1, \ldots, \mathfrak{U}_n\}$ with identities $\{\mathsf{ID}_1, \ldots, \mathsf{ID}_n\}$

and the corresponding public keys $\{\mathsf{upk}_1, \ldots, \mathsf{upk}_n\}$, and message-signature pairs $(m_1, \sigma_1), \ldots, (m_n, \sigma_n)$ from $\{\mathfrak{U}_1, \ldots, \mathfrak{U}_n\}$ respectively, the aggregate signature generator computes $\sigma = \sum_{i=1}^{n} \sigma_i$ and outputs σ as an aggregate signature.

Aggregate Verify: To verify an aggregate signature σ signed by n users $\{\mathfrak{U}_1, \ldots, \mathfrak{U}_n\}$ with identities $\{\mathsf{ID}_1, \ldots, \mathsf{ID}_n\}$ and the corresponding public keys $\{\mathsf{upk}_1, \ldots, \mathsf{upk}_n\}$ on messages $\{m_1, \ldots, m_n\}$, the verifier performs the following steps:

1. Computes $Q_{\mathsf{ID}_i} = H_0(\mathsf{ID}_i)$, $Q'_{\mathsf{ID}_i} = H'_0(\mathsf{ID}_i)$, $h_{i1} = H_1(m_i, \mathsf{ID}_i, \mathsf{upk}_{\mathsf{ID}_i})$, $h_{i2} = H_2(m_i, \mathsf{ID}_i, \mathsf{upk}_{ID_i})$ and $h'_{i2} = H'_2(m_i, \mathsf{ID}_i, \mathsf{upk}_{\mathsf{ID}_i})$ for $i = 1, \ldots, n$.

2. Verifies the equation

$$\hat{e}(\sigma, P) = \hat{e}(\sum_{i=1}^{n} h_{i1}\mathsf{upk}_{\mathsf{ID}_i}, Q)\hat{e}(\sum_{i=1}^{n}(h_{i2}Q_{\mathsf{ID}_i} + h'_{i2}Q'_{\mathsf{ID}_i}), P_{\mathrm{pub}})$$

If it holds, the verifies accepts the signature; else it rejects it.

9.3.4 Security Proof

Assuming that the CDH problem is hard, we now show the security of our CL-AS scheme.

Theorem 9.3 *In the random oracle model, our CL-AS scheme is existentially unforgeable against adaptive chosen-message attacks under the assumption that the CDH problem in $\mathbb{G}_1$ in intractable.*

The theorem follows at once from Lemmas 9.6 and 9.7, according to Definitions 9.1 and 9.2.

Lemma 9.4 *If a probabilistic polynomial-time forger $\mathcal{A}_1$ has an advantage ε in forging a signature in an attack modeled by **game I** of Definition 9.1 after running in time t and making q_{H_0} queries to random oracles H_0 and H'_0, q_{H_1} queries to random oracle H_1, q_{H_2} queries to random oracles H_2 and H'_2, q_{CreU} queries to the **Create-User** request oracle, q_{RPar} queries to the **Partial-Private-Key-Extract** extraction oracle, q_{RSec} queries to the **Secret-Value-Extract** extraction oracle, and q_{SupSig} queries to the **Super-Sign** oracle, then the CDH problem can be solved with probability $\varepsilon' > (1 - 1/q_{H_0})^{q_{RPar}+n-1}q_{H_0}\varepsilon$.*

Proof 9.1 *Let* $(X = aP, Y = bP)$ *be a random instance of the CDH problem in* $\mathbb{G}_1$. *Here* P *is a generator of* $\mathbb{G}_1$, *with prime order* q, *and the elements* a, b *are taken uniformly at random in* $\mathbb{Z}_q^*$. *By using the forgery algorithm* $\mathcal{A}_1$, *we will construct an algorithm* $\mathcal{S}_1$ *that outputs the CDH solution* abP *in* $\mathbb{G}_1$.

Initial: Algorithm $\mathcal{S}_1$ chooses a random $t \in \mathbb{Z}_q^*$, and sets $P_{\text{pub}} = X$ and $Q = tP$, and then starts performing oracle simulation. Without loss of generality, we assume that, for any key extraction or signature query involving an identity, a $H_0(\cdot)$ and $H_0'(\cdot)$ oracle query has previously been made on that identity. And $\mathcal{S}_1$ maintains a list $L = \{(\text{ID}_i, \text{psk}_{\text{ID}_i}, \text{upk}_{\text{ID}_i}, \text{usk}_{\text{ID}_i})\}$ while $\mathcal{A}_1$ is making queries throughout the game. $\mathcal{S}_1$ responds to $\mathcal{A}_1$'s oracle as follows.

Attack: **Queries on Oracle** H_0, H_0'**:** Suppose $\mathcal{A}_1$ makes at most q_{H_0} queries to the H_0, H_0' oracle. First, $\mathcal{S}_1$ chooses $j \in [1, q_{H_0}]$ randomly. When $\mathcal{A}_1$ makes an H_0, H_0' query on ID_i, where $1 \leq i \leq q_{H_0}$, if $i = j$ (we let $\text{ID}_i = \text{ID}^*$ at this point), $\mathcal{S}_1$ picks two random $\alpha, \beta \in \mathbb{Z}_q^*$ and returns $(Q_{\text{ID}_i} = Y, Q_{\text{ID}_i}' = \alpha(\beta P - Y))$. Then $\mathcal{S}_1$ inserts a tuple $(\text{ID}_i, Q_{\text{ID}_i}, Q_{\text{ID}_i}', \alpha, \beta)$ in a list L_0. Otherwise, $\mathcal{S}_1$ picks two random $r_i, r_i' \in \mathbb{Z}_q^*$ and returns $(Q_{\text{ID}_i} = r_i P, Q_{\text{ID}_i}' = r_i' P)$ and also adds $(\text{ID}_i, Q_{\text{ID}_i}, Q_{\text{ID}_i}', r_i, r_i')$ to L_0.

Queries on Oracle H_1**:** Suppose $(m_i, \text{ID}_i, \text{upk}_{\text{ID}_i})$ is submitted to oracle $H_1(\cdot)$. $\mathcal{S}_1$ first scans $L_1 = \{(m_i, \text{ID}_i, \text{upk}_{\text{ID}_i}, h_{1i})\}$ to check whether H_1 has already been defined for that input. If so, the previously defined value is returned. Otherwise, $\mathcal{S}_1$ picks at random $h_{1i} \in \mathbb{Z}_q^*$ and returns h_{1i} as a hash value of $H_1(m_i, \text{ID}_i, \text{upk}_{\text{ID}_i})$ to $\mathcal{A}_1$ and also stores the values in the list L_1.

Queries on Oracle H_2, H_2'**:** Suppose $(m_i, \text{ID}_i, \text{upk}_{\text{ID}_i})$ is submitted to oracle $H_2(\cdot)$ and $H_2'(\cdot)$. $\mathcal{S}_1$ first scans $L_2 = \{(m_i, \text{ID}_i, \text{upk}_{\text{ID}_i}, h_{2i}, h_{2i}')\}$ to check whether H_2 and H_2' have already been defined for that input. If so, the previously defined value is returned. Otherwise, $\mathcal{S}_1$ picks at random $h_{2i}, h_{2i}' \in \mathbb{Z}_q^*$ and returns h_{2i} and h_{2i}' as the hash value of $H_2(m_i, \text{ID}_i, \text{upk}_{\text{ID}_i})$ and $H_2'(m_i, \text{ID}_i, \text{upk}_{\text{ID}_i})$ to $\mathcal{A}_1$ and also stores the values in the list L_2.

Partial-Private-Key-Extract Oracle: Suppose the request is on an identity ID_i. If $\text{ID}_i \neq \text{ID}^*$, $\mathcal{S}_1$ recovers the corresponding

$(\mathsf{ID}_i, Q_{\mathsf{ID}_i}, Q'_{\mathsf{ID}_i}, r_i, r'_i)$ from the list L_0 and returns $\mathsf{psk}_{\mathsf{ID}_i} = (r_i X, r'_i X)$. Otherwise $\mathcal{S}_1$ outputs "failure" and halts because it is unable to coherently answer the query.

Create-User Oracle: Suppose the request is on an identity ID_i.

- If the list L contains $(\mathsf{ID}_i, \mathsf{psk}_{\mathsf{ID}_i}, \mathsf{upk}_{\mathsf{ID}_i}, \mathsf{usk}_{\mathsf{ID}_i})$, $\mathcal{S}_1$ checks whether $\mathsf{upk}_{\mathsf{ID}_i} = \perp$. If $\mathsf{upk}_{\mathsf{ID}_i} \neq \perp$, $\mathcal{S}_1$ returns $\mathsf{upk}_{\mathsf{ID}_i}$ to $\mathcal{A}_1$. Otherwise, $\mathcal{S}_1$ randomly chooses $\nu_i \in \mathbb{Z}_q^*$ and $\mathsf{upk}_{\mathsf{ID}_i} = \nu_i P$ and $\mathsf{usk}_{\mathsf{ID}_i} = \nu_i$. $\mathcal{S}_1$ returns $\mathsf{upk}_{\mathsf{ID}_i}$ to $\mathcal{A}_1$ and saves $(\mathsf{upk}_{\mathsf{ID}_i}, \mathsf{usk}_{\mathsf{ID}_i})$ to the list L.
- If the list L does not contain $(\mathsf{ID}_i, \mathsf{psk}_{\mathsf{ID}_i}, \mathsf{upk}_{\mathsf{ID}_i}, \mathsf{usk}_{\mathsf{ID}_i})$, $\mathcal{S}_1$ sets $\mathsf{psk}_{\mathsf{ID}_i} = \perp$, and then randomly chooses $\nu_i \in \mathbb{Z}_q^*$ and sets $\mathsf{upk}_{\mathsf{ID}_i} = \nu_i P$ and $\mathsf{usk}_{\mathsf{ID}_i} = \nu_i$. $\mathcal{S}_1$ returns $\mathsf{upk}_{\mathsf{ID}_i}$ to $\mathcal{A}_1$ and adds $(\mathsf{ID}_i, \mathsf{psk}_{\mathsf{ID}_i}, \mathsf{upk}_{\mathsf{ID}_i}, \mathsf{usk}_{\mathsf{ID}_i})$ to the list L.

Secret-Value-Extract Oracle: Suppose the request is on an identity ID_i.

- If the list L contains $(\mathsf{ID}_i, \mathsf{psk}_{\mathsf{ID}_i}, \mathsf{upk}_{\mathsf{ID}_i}, \mathsf{usk}_{\mathsf{ID}_i})$, $\mathcal{S}_1$ checks whether $\mathsf{usk}_{\mathsf{ID}_i} = \perp$. If $\mathsf{usk}_{\mathsf{ID}_i} \neq \perp$, $\mathcal{S}_1$ returns $\mathsf{usk}_{\mathsf{ID}_i}$ to $\mathcal{A}_1$. Otherwise, $\mathcal{S}_1$ makes a **Create-User** query itself to generate $(\mathsf{upk}_{\mathsf{ID}_i} = \nu_i P, \mathsf{usk}_{\mathsf{ID}_i} = \nu_i)$. Then $\mathcal{S}_1$ saves these values in the list L and returns $\mathsf{usk}_{\mathsf{ID}_i} = \nu_i$ to $\mathcal{A}_1$.
- If the list L does not contain $(\mathsf{ID}_i, \mathsf{psk}_{\mathsf{ID}_i}, \mathsf{upk}_{\mathsf{ID}_i}, \mathsf{usk}_{\mathsf{ID}_i})$, $\mathcal{S}_1$ makes a **Create-User** query itself, and then adds $(\mathsf{ID}_i, \mathsf{psk}_{\mathsf{ID}_i}, \mathsf{upk}_{\mathsf{ID}_i}, \mathsf{usk}_{\mathsf{ID}_i})$ to the list L and returns $\mathsf{usk}_{\mathsf{ID}_i}$.

Public-Key-Replace Oracle: Suppose $\mathcal{A}_1$ makes the query with $(\mathsf{ID}_i, \mathsf{upk}'_{\mathsf{ID}_i})$.

- If the list L contains an element $(\mathsf{ID}_i, \mathsf{psk}_{\mathsf{ID}_i}, \mathsf{upk}_{\mathsf{ID}_i}, \mathsf{usk}_{\mathsf{ID}_i})$, $\mathcal{S}_1$ sets $\mathsf{upk}_{\mathsf{ID}_i} = \mathsf{upk}'_{\mathsf{ID}_i}$ and $\mathsf{usk}_{\mathsf{ID}_i} = \perp$.
- If the list L does not contain an item $(\mathsf{ID}_i, \mathsf{psk}_{\mathsf{ID}_i}, \mathsf{upk}_{\mathsf{ID}_i}, \mathsf{usk}_{\mathsf{ID}_i})$, $\mathcal{S}_1$ sets $\mathsf{psk}_{\mathsf{ID}_i} = \perp$, $\mathsf{upk}_{\mathsf{ID}_i} = \mathsf{upk}'_{\mathsf{ID}_i}$ and $\mathsf{usk}_{\mathsf{ID}_i} = \perp$, and adds an element $(\mathsf{ID}_i, \mathsf{psk}_{\mathsf{ID}_i}, \mathsf{upk}_{\mathsf{ID}_i}, \mathsf{usk}_{\mathsf{ID}_i})$ to L.

Super-Sign Oracle: When $\mathcal{A}_1$ makes a **Super-Sign** query on m_i with ID_i, $\mathcal{S}_1$ first finds the corresponding $(\mathsf{ID}_i, Q_{\mathsf{ID}_i}, Q'_{\mathsf{ID}_i}, r_i, r'_i)$ and $(\mathsf{ID}_i, \mathsf{upk}_{\mathsf{ID}_i}, \mathsf{usk}_{\mathsf{ID}_i})$ from the list L_0 and L, respectively. Then, $\mathcal{S}_1$ performs as follows:

- If $\mathsf{ID}_i = \mathsf{ID}^*$, $\mathcal{S}_1$ picks two random $h_{i1}, h_{i2} \in \mathbb{Z}_q^*$ and computes $h'_{i2} = h_{i2}\alpha^{-1}$, $\sigma_i = h_{i1} \cdot t \cdot \mathsf{upk}_{\mathsf{ID}_i} + h_{i2}\beta X$. $\mathcal{S}_1$ then returns σ_i and adds $(m_i, \mathsf{ID}_i, \mathsf{upk}_{\mathsf{ID}_i}, h_{1i})$ and $(m_i, \mathsf{ID}_i, \mathsf{upk}_{\mathsf{ID}_i}, h_{2i}, h'_{2i})$ to L_1 and L_2, respectively.

- Otherwise, $\mathcal{S}_1$ picks three random $h_{i1}, h_{i2}, h'_{i2} \in \mathbb{Z}_q^*$ and computes $\sigma_i = h_{i1} \cdot t \cdot \mathsf{upk}_{\mathsf{ID}_i} + h_{i2}r_i X + h'_{i2}r'_i X$. $\mathcal{S}_1$ then returns σ_i and adds $(m_i, \mathsf{ID}_i, \mathsf{upk}_{\mathsf{ID}_i}, h_{1i})$ and $(m_i, \mathsf{ID}_i, \mathsf{upk}_{\mathsf{ID}_i}, h_{2i}, h'_{2i})$ to L_1 and L_2, respectively.

Forgery: Eventually, $\mathcal{A}_1$ outputs a set of n users whose identities form the set $L_{\mathsf{ID}}^* = \{\mathsf{ID}_1^*, \ldots, \mathsf{ID}_n^*\}$ with corresponding public keys that form the set $L_{\mathsf{upk}}^* = \{\mathsf{upk}_1^*, \ldots, \mathsf{upk}_n^*\}$, n messages $L_m^* = \{m_1^*, \ldots, m_n^*\}$, and an aggregate signature σ^*. It is required that there exists $\mathsf{ID}^* \in \{\mathsf{ID}_1^*, \ldots, \mathsf{ID}_n^*\}$ for which $\mathcal{A}_1$ has not asked for the partial private key. Without loss of generality, we assume that $\mathsf{ID}^* = \mathsf{ID}_1^*$. And $\mathcal{A}_1$ has not made a (m_1^*, ID_1^*) query to the **Super-Sign** oracle. Furthermore, the aggregate signature σ^* should satisfy the aggregate verification as follows:

$$\hat{e}(\sigma^*, P) = \hat{e}\left(\sum_{i=1}^{n} h_{i1}^* \mathsf{upk}_{\mathsf{ID}_i^*}, Q\right) \hat{e}\left(\sum_{i=1}^{n} \left(h_{i2}^* Q_{\mathsf{ID}_i^*} + h_{i2}'^* Q'_{\mathsf{ID}_i^*}\right), P_{\mathrm{pub}}\right)$$

Then, $\mathcal{S}_1$ finds the corresponding tuples $(\mathsf{ID}_i^*, Q_{\mathsf{ID}_i^*}, Q'_{\mathsf{ID}_i^*}, r_i, r'_i)$ for $2 \le i \le n$ and $(\mathsf{ID}_1^*, Q_{\mathsf{ID}_1^*}, Q'_{\mathsf{ID}_1^*}, \alpha, \beta)$ from the list L_0, respectively. The public keys $\mathsf{upk}_{\mathsf{ID}_i^*}$ may be replaced by $\mathcal{A}_1$. The following equation holds because the aggregate signature is valid:

$$\hat{e}(\sigma^*, P) = \hat{e}\left(\sum_{i=1}^{n} h_{i1}^* \mathsf{upk}_{\mathsf{ID}_i^*}, Q\right) \hat{e}\left(\sum_{i=1}^{n} (h_{i2}^* Q_{\mathsf{ID}_i^*} + h_{i2}'^* Q'_{\mathsf{ID}_i^*}), P_{\mathrm{pub}}\right)$$

$$= \hat{e}\left(\sum_{i=1}^{n} h_{i1}^* \mathsf{upk}_{\mathsf{ID}_i^*}, tP\right) \hat{e}\left(\sum_{i=2}^{n} (h_{i2}^* r_i P + h_{i2}'^* r'_i P), X\right)$$

$$\times \hat{e}\left(h_{12}^* Y + h_{12}'^* \alpha(\beta P - Y), X\right)$$

$$= \hat{e}\left(\sum_{i=1}^{n} t h_{i1}^* \mathsf{upk}_{\mathsf{ID}_i^*}, P\right) \hat{e}\left(\sum_{i=2}^{n} (h_{i2}^* r_i + h_{i2}'^* r'_i) X, P\right)$$

$$\times \hat{e}((h_{12}^* - h_{12}'^* \alpha)Y, X)\hat{e}(h_{12}'^* \alpha\beta X, P)$$

Finally, $\mathcal{S}_1$ outputs abP as a solution to the CDH instance by computing

$$abP = (h_{12}^* - h_{12}'^*\alpha)^{-1}(\sigma^* - \sum_{i=1}^{n} th_{i1}^* \mathsf{upk}_{\mathsf{ID}_i^*}$$

$$- \sum_{i=2}^{n} (h_{i2}^* r_i + h_{i2}'^* r_i')X - h_{12}'^*\alpha\beta X)$$

This completes the description of $\mathcal{S}_1$. It remains to show that $\mathcal{S}_1$ solves the given instance of the CDH problem with probability at least ε'. To do so, we analyze three events needed for $\mathcal{S}_1$ to succeed:

- E_1 : $\mathcal{S}_1$ does not abort as a result of any of $\mathcal{A}_1$'s **Partial-Private-Key-Extract** queries.

- E_2 : $\mathcal{A}_1$ generates a valid and nontrivial aggregate signature forgery.

- E_3 : Event E_2 occurs, $\mathsf{ID}_1^* = \mathsf{ID}^*$ and $\mathsf{ID}_i^* \neq \mathsf{ID}^*$ for all $i, 2 \leq i \leq n$.

$\mathcal{S}_1$ succeeds if all of these events happen. The probability $Pr[E_1 \wedge E_2 \wedge E_3]$ is decomposed as $Pr[E_1 \wedge E_2 \wedge E_3] = Pr[E_1] \cdot Pr[E_2 \mid E_1] \cdot Pr[E_3 \mid E_1 \wedge E_2]$.

The following claims give a lower bound for each of these terms.

Claim 9.1 *The probability that algorithm $\mathcal{S}_1$ does not abort as a result of any of $\mathcal{A}_1$'s **Partial-Private-Key-Extract** queries is at least $(1 - 1/q_{H_0})^{q_{RPar}}$.*

Proof 9.2 *As $Pr[E_1] = 1 - 1/q_{H_0}$, for a partial private key extraction query, the probability $\mathcal{S}_1$ does not abort is $1 - 1/q_{H_0}$. Since $\mathcal{A}_1$ makes at most q_{RPar} queries to the partial private key extraction oracle, the probability that $\mathcal{S}_1$ does not abort as a result of $\mathcal{A}_1$'s partial private key extraction queries is at least $(1 - 1/q_{H_0})^{q_{RPar}}$.*

Claim 9.2 *If $\mathcal{S}_1$ does not abort as a result of $\mathcal{A}_1$'s **Super-Sign** queries and **Partial-Private-Key-Extract** queries, then $\mathcal{A}_1$'s view is identical to its view in the attack. Hence, $Pr[E_2 \mid E_1] \geq \varepsilon$.*

Claim 9.3 *The probability that algorithm S_1 does not abort after A_1 outputs a valid and nontrivial forgery is at least $q_{H_0}(1 - 1/q_{H_0})^{n-1}$. Hence, $Pr[E_3 \mid E_1 \wedge E_2] \geqslant q_{H_0}(1 - 1/q_{H_0})^{n-1}$.*

Proof 9.3 *Algorithm S_1 succeeds only if A_1 generates a forgery such that $\mathsf{ID}_1^* = \mathsf{ID}^*$ and $\mathsf{ID}_i^* \neq \mathsf{ID}^*$ for all $i, 2 \leq i \leq n$. Hence, $Pr[E_3 \mid E_1 \wedge E_2] \geqslant q_{H_0}(1 - 1/q_{H_0})^{n-1}$.*

Therefore, the result is that S_1's advantage in solving the CDH problem in $\mathbb{G}_1$ is at least $(1 - 1/q_{H_0})^{q_{\text{RPar}}+n-1}q_{H_0}\varepsilon$.

Lemma 9.5 *If a probabilistic polynomial-time forger A_2 has an advantage ε in forging a signature in an attack modeled by **game II** of Definition 9.3 after running in time t and making q_{H_2} queries to random oracles H_2, q_{CreU} queries to the **Create-User** request oracle, q_{RSec} queries to the **Secret-Value-Extract** extraction oracle, and q_{SupSig} queries to the **Super-Sign** oracle, then the CDH problem can be solved with probability $(1 - 1/q_{\text{CreU}})^{q_{\text{SupSig}}+q_{\text{RSec}}+n-1}q_{\text{CreU}}\varepsilon$.*

Proof 9.4 *Suppose A_2 is a **type II** adversary that (t, ε)-breaks our CL-AS scheme. We show how to construct a t'-time algorithm S_2 that solves the CDH problem on $\mathbb{G}_1$ with probability at least ε'. Let $(X = aP, Y = bP) \in \mathbb{G}_1 \times \mathbb{G}_1$ be a random instance of the CDH problem taken as input by S_2.*

Initial: S_2 randomly chooses $s \in \mathbb{Z}_q^*$ as the master key, and then initializes A_2 with $P_{\text{pub}} = sP$ and also the master key s. After that, S_2 sets $Q = X$. The adversary A_2 then starts making oracle queries as described in Definition 9.3. Note that the user's partial key $\mathsf{psk}_{\mathsf{ID}_i} = (sH_0(\mathsf{ID}_i), sH_0'(\mathsf{ID}_i))$ can be computed by both S_2 and A_2; thus, the hash functions $H_0(\cdot)$ and $H_0'(\cdot)$ are not modeled as a random oracle in this case.

Attack: Create-User Oracle: Suppose A_2 makes at most q_{CreU} queries to the **Create-User** oracle. First, S_2 chooses $j \in [1, q_{\text{CreU}}]$ randomly. When A_2 makes a **Create-User** query on ID_i where $1 \leq i \leq q_{\text{CreU}}$, if $i = j$ (we let $\mathsf{ID}_i = \mathsf{ID}^*$ at this point), S_2 returns $\mathsf{upk}_{\mathsf{ID}_i} = Y$. Then S_1 inserts a tuple $(\mathsf{ID}_i, \mathsf{upk}_{\mathsf{ID}_i}, \perp)$ in a list L. Otherwise, S_2 chooses $\nu_i \in \mathbb{Z}_q^*$, sets $\mathsf{upk}_{\mathsf{ID}_i} = \nu_i P$ and $\mathsf{usk}_{\mathsf{ID}_i} = \nu_i$, and adds $(\mathsf{ID}_i, \mathsf{upk}_{\mathsf{ID}_i}, \mathsf{usk}_{\mathsf{ID}_i})$ to L.

Secret-Value-Extract Oracle: Suppose the request is on an identity ID_i. If $\mathsf{ID}_i \neq \mathsf{ID}^*$, $\mathcal{S}_2$ finds $(\mathsf{ID}_i, \mathsf{upk}_{\mathsf{ID}_i}, \mathsf{usk}_{\mathsf{ID}_i})$ in L and returns $\mathsf{usk}_{\mathsf{ID}_i}$. Otherwise, $\mathcal{S}_2$ halts the simulation.

Queries on Oracle H_0, H_0': Suppose ID_i is submitted to oracles $H_2(\cdot)$ and $H_2'(\cdot)$. $\mathcal{S}_2$ first scans $L_0 = \{(\mathsf{ID}_i, Q_{\mathsf{ID}_i}, Q_{\mathsf{ID}_i}')\}$ to check whether H_0 and H_0' have already been defined for that input. If so, the previously defined value is returned. Otherwise, $\mathcal{S}_2$ picks at random $Q_{\mathsf{ID}_i}, Q_{\mathsf{ID}_i}' \in \mathbb{G}_1$ and returns Q_{ID_i} and Q_{ID_i}' as the hash values of $H_0(\mathsf{ID}_i)$ and $H_0'(\mathsf{ID}_i)$ to $\mathcal{A}_2$ and also stores the values in the list L_0.

Queries on Oracle H_1: Suppose $(m_i, \mathsf{ID}_i, \mathsf{upk}_{\mathsf{ID}_i})$ is submitted to oracle $H_1(\cdot)$. $\mathcal{S}_2$ first scans $L_1 = \{(m_i, \mathsf{ID}_i, \mathsf{upk}_{\mathsf{ID}_i}, h_{1i})\}$ to check whether H_1 has already been defined for that input. If so, the previously defined value is returned. Otherwise, $\mathcal{S}_2$ picks at random $h_{1i} \in \mathbb{Z}_q^*$ and returns h_{1i} as a hash value of $H_1(m_i, \mathsf{ID}_i, \mathsf{upk}_{\mathsf{ID}_i})$ to $\mathcal{A}_2$ and also stores the values in the list L_1.

Queries on Oracle H_2, H_2': Suppose $(m_i, \mathsf{ID}_i, \mathsf{upk}_{\mathsf{ID}_i})$ is submitted to oracles $H_2(\cdot)$ and $H_2'(\cdot)$. $\mathcal{S}_2$ first scans $L_2 = \{(m_i, \mathsf{ID}_i, \mathsf{upk}_{\mathsf{ID}_i}, h_{2i}, h_{2i}')\}$ to check whether H_2 and H_2' have already been defined for that input. If so, the previously defined value is returned. Otherwise, $\mathcal{S}_2$ picks at random $h_{2i}, h_{2i}' \in \mathbb{Z}_q^*$ and returns h_{2i} and h_{2i}' as the hash values of $H_2(m_i, \mathsf{ID}_i, \mathsf{upk}_{\mathsf{ID}_i})$ and $H_2'(m_i, \mathsf{ID}_i, \mathsf{upk}_{\mathsf{ID}_i})$ to $\mathcal{A}_2$ and also stores the values in the list L_2.

Super Sign Oracle: When $\mathcal{A}_2$ makes a **Super-Sign** query on m_i with ID_i, $\mathcal{S}_2$ first finds the corresponding $(\mathsf{ID}_i, Q_{\mathsf{ID}_i}, Q_{\mathsf{ID}_i}')$ and $(\mathsf{ID}_i, \mathsf{upk}_{\mathsf{ID}_i}, \mathsf{usk}_{\mathsf{ID}_i})$ from the lists L_0 and L, respectively. Then, $\mathcal{S}_2$ performs as follows:

- If $\mathsf{ID}_i = \mathsf{ID}^*$, $\mathcal{S}_2$ aborts the simulation.
- Otherwise, $\mathcal{S}_2$ picks three random $h_{i1}, h_{i2}, h_{i2}' \in \mathbb{Z}_q^*$ and computes $\sigma_i = h_{i1} \cdot \mathsf{usk}_{\mathsf{ID}_i} \cdot X + h_{i2}sQ_{\mathsf{ID}_i} + h_{i2}'sQ_{\mathsf{ID}_i}'$. $\mathcal{S}_2$ then returns σ_i and adds $(m_i, \mathsf{ID}_i, \mathsf{upk}_{\mathsf{ID}_i}, h_{1i})$ and $(m_i, \mathsf{ID}_i, \mathsf{upk}_{\mathsf{ID}_i}, h_{2i}, h_{2i}')$ to L_1 and L_2, respectively.

Forgery: Eventually, $\mathcal{A}_2$ outputs a set of n users whose identities form the set $L_{\mathsf{ID}}^* = \{\mathsf{ID}_1^*, \ldots, \mathsf{ID}_n^*\}$ with corresponding public keys that form the set $L^*_{\text{upk}} = \{\text{upk}^*_1, \ldots, \text{upk}^*_n\}$, n messages $L^*_m = \{m^*_1, \ldots, m^*_n\}$, and an aggregate signature σ^*. It is required that there exists $\text{ID}^* \in \{\text{ID}^*_1, \ldots, \text{ID}^*_n\}$ for which $\mathcal{A}_2$ has not asked for the secret key. Without loss of generality, we assume that $\text{ID}^* = \text{ID}^*_1$. And $\mathcal{A}_2$ has not made a (m^*_1, ID^*_1) query to **Super Sign oracle**. Furthermore, the aggregate signature σ^* should satisfy the aggregate verification as follows:

$$\hat{e}(\sigma^*, P) = \hat{e}(\textstyle\sum_{i=1}^{n} h^*_{i1}\text{upk}_{\text{ID}^*_i}, Q)\hat{e}(\textstyle\sum_{i=1}^{n}(h^*_{i2}Q_{\text{ID}^*_i} + h'^*_{i2}Q'_{\text{ID}^*_i}), P_{\text{pub}})$$

Then, $\mathcal{S}_2$ finds the corresponding tuples $(\text{ID}_i, \text{upk}_{\text{ID}_i}, \text{usk}_{\text{ID}_i})$ for $2 \le i \le n$ from the list L. The following equation holds because the aggregate signature is valid:

$$\hat{e}(\sigma^*, P) = \hat{e}(\sum_{i=1}^{n} h^*_{i1}\text{upk}_{\text{ID}^*_i}, X)\hat{e}\left(\sum_{i=1}^{n}(h^*_{i2}Q_{\text{ID}^*_i} + h'^*_{i2}Q'_{\text{ID}^*_i}), P_{\text{pub}}\right)$$

$$= \hat{e}(h^*_{11}Y, X)\hat{e}\left(\sum_{i=2}^{n} h^*_{i1}\text{usk}_{\text{ID}^*_i}P, X\right)$$

$$\hat{e}\left(\sum_{i=1}^{n}(h^*_{i2}Q_{\text{ID}^*_i} + h'^*_{i2}Q'_{\text{ID}^*_i}), sP\right)$$

$$= \hat{e}(h^*_{11}Y, X)\hat{e}\left(\sum_{i=2}^{n} h^*_{i1}\text{usk}_{\text{ID}^*_i}X, P\right)$$

$$\hat{e}\left(\sum_{i=1}^{n} s(h^*_{i2}Q_{\text{ID}^*_i} + h'^*_{i2}Q'_{\text{ID}^*_i}), P\right)$$

Finally, $\mathcal{S}_2$ outputs abP as a solution to the CDH instance by computing

$$abP = (h^*_{11})^{-1}\left(\sigma^* - \sum_{i=2}^{n} h^*_{i1}\text{usk}_{\text{ID}^*_i}X - \sum_{i=1}^{n} s\left(h^*_{i2}Q_{\text{ID}^*_i} + h'^*_{i2}Q'_{\text{ID}^*_i}\right)\right)$$

This completes the description of $\mathcal{S}_2$. It remains to show that $\mathcal{S}_2$ solves the given instance of the CDH problem with probability at least ε'. To do so, we analyze three events needed for $\mathcal{S}_2$ to succeed:

- E_1 : $\mathcal{S}_2$ does not abort as a result of any of $\mathcal{A}_2$'s **Secret-Value-Extract** and **Super Sign** queries.

- E_2 : $\mathcal{A}_2$ generates a valid and nontrivial aggregate signature forgery.

- E_3 : Event E_2 occurs, $\mathsf{ID}_1^* = \mathsf{ID}^*$ and $\mathsf{ID}_i^* \neq \mathsf{ID}^*$ for all $i, 2 \leq i \leq n$.

$\mathcal{S}_2$ succeeds if all of these events happen. The probability $Pr[E_1 \wedge E_2 \wedge E_3]$ is decomposed as $Pr[E_1 \wedge E_2 \wedge E_3] = Pr[E_1] \cdot Pr[E_2 \mid E_1] \cdot Pr[E_3 \mid E_1 \wedge E_2]$.

Similar to Lemma 9.1, the result is that $\mathcal{S}_2$'s advantage in solving the CDH problem in $\mathbb{G}_1$ is at least $(1 - \frac{1}{q_{\mathrm{CreU}}})^{q_{\mathrm{SupSig}}+q_{\mathrm{RSec}}+n-1} q_{\mathrm{CreU}} \varepsilon$.

9.4   CERTIFICATELESS RING SIGNATURE

9.4.1   Related Work

The ring signature, initially formalized by Rivest et al. [276], features anonymity and spontaneity. The anonymity means that a signer can represent a group of potential signers (called a ring) including himself/herself in signing a message while preserving unconditionally the anonymity for the signer; the spontaneity states that the signature generation procedure requires neither group managers to initialize the system nor the cooperation from the other ring members; that is, the real signer can decide for other ring members in an *ad hoc* way. Therefore, ring signatures can be applied in the above scenarios.

Since its introduction [276,277], the ring signature has been well studied along several research lines. Many ring signature schemes have been proposed in various mathematical settings such as pairing-based [255], discrete-log-based [278], mixture-based (trapdoor-permutation-type and discrete-log-type) [279], code-based [280,281], lattice-based [282], and multivariate-based [283]. According to the adversary's attack power, security models for ring signature schemes fall into three categories. The security model where the adversary is only allowed to mount a chosen-message attack was introduced in [276]. Later Abe et al. [279] proposed an improved model achieving unforgeability against chosen-subring attacks. Finally, the insider attack resilient model where the adversary can adaptively corrupt honest participants and obtain their secret keys has been introduced in [284]. The former two models were defined in the random oracle model [75], and the latter was defined in the standard model [79]. Furthermore, the forking lemma for the ring signature has also been given in [278]. To respond to the different scenarios, researchers have extended basic ring signatures with more versatile properties and proposed variations such as the proxy ring signature [285], threshold ring signature [286], concurrent signature [287], and linkable ring signature [288].

Observe that the management of certificates is usually considered to be expensive and unaffordable for ring signatures, and involves validating a large number of public keys; Zhang and Kim [289] proposed the first ID-based ring signature based on bilinear pairings. Subsequently, a more efficient construction has been given by Lin and Wu [290]. Another ID-based ring signature scheme along with the extension for anonymous subsets was presented by Herranz and Sáez [291]. After that, Chow et al. [292] and Nguyen's [293] constructions achieved a constant number of pairing computations and a constant size signature, respectively. In addition, an ID-based ring signature secure in the standard model has been given by Au et al. [294]. To avoid the expensive pairing operation, Herranz [295] and Tsang et al. [296] suggested two pairing-free ID-based ring signatures from RSA independently. The motivation and design philosophy of an ID-based ring signature have been insightfully surveyed in [297].

To gain the merits of traditional public-key infrastructure (PKI) and ID-PKC simultaneously, Zhang et al. [298] introduced the ring signature into the CL-PKC environment and proposed two concrete certificateless ring signature (CL-RS) schemes. After that, Chang et al. [299] suggested a more efficient construction along with the t-out-of-n threshold extension. Similar to CL-RS, ring signature schemes in a certificate-based and self-certified setting have also been proposed to solve the certificate management problem in PKI and key escrow problem in ID-PKC in [300,301], respectively. Unfortunately, all of these CL-RS schemes are derived from bilinear pairings, a powerful but computationally expensive primitive. Compared with other problems from number theory such as discrete logarithms, factoring, and RSA, bilinear pairings were only investigated recently and did not enjoy the same exposure to cryptanalysis attacks [139]. In addition, many companies or official organizations may have already invested in the development and deployment of traditional cryptosystems and thus a new pairing technique may not be worth the reinvestment in terms of industry implementation. Thus, Qin et al. [302] presented a certificateless pairing-free ring signature scheme. Under the standard RSA and discrete-logarithm assumptions, the proposed scheme can be formally proved to be existentially unforgeable against adaptive chosen-message attacks in the random oracle model. The scheme allows a user to sign any documents anonymously on behalf of a ring of users including himself/herself. The signer can form the user ring in an *ad hoc* way. That is, the other members in the ring can be chosen on demand, even without letting the chosen users know that they appear in the ring. Our scheme is also very efficient in computation due to the removal of time-consuming bilinear pairing operations in the signing and verifying procedures. This implies that our scheme is very applicable to *ad hoc* anonymous authentication.

9.4.2 Formal Definition

Modeling CL-RS schemes. A CL-RS scheme consists of the following five algorithms: Setup, Extract-Partial-Private-Key, Set-User-Keys, Ring-Sign, Verify. The first four algorithms may be randomized but the last one is usually not:

Setup: On input of 1^k where $k \in \mathbb{N}$ is a security parameter, this algorithm generates the public parameters params and master secret master-secret.

Extract-Partial-Private-Key: On input of master-secret and user identity $\text{ID} \in \{0,1\}^*$, this algorithm generates a key psk_{ID} called the partial private key.

Set-User-Keys: On input of params and user identity $\text{ID} \in \{0,1\}^*$, this algorithm generates the corresponding user public/secret key pair $(\text{upk}_{\text{ID}}, \text{usk}_{\text{ID}})$

Ring-Sign: On input of a set of n group members whose identities form the set $L_{\text{ID}} = \{\text{ID}_1, \ldots, \text{ID}_n\}$ and their corresponding public keys $L_{\text{upk}} = \{\text{upk}_{\text{ID}_1}, \ldots, \text{upk}_{\text{ID}_n}\}$, a signer's secret key usk_{ID_s}, partial key psk_{ID_s} and message $m \in \{0,1\}^*$, this algorithm generates a ring signature σ. Here, usk_{ID_s} and psk_{ID_s} are the s-th ring member's user secret key and partial private key, respectively.

Verify: On input of params, the set L_{ID} of the group members' identities and the set L_{upk} of the corresponding public keys of the ring members, message m, and ring signature σ, this returns 1 for accept or 0 for reject.

Generally, the KGC could be the entity that performs the algorithms Setup and Extract-Partial-Private-Key. We assume that everyone in the system has gotten a legitimate copy of public parameters params and the partial private key is also assumed to be issued securely to the intended user. This is usually done in the setup stage of the system. Each user in the system is supposed to be able to carry out the Set-User-Keys, Ring-Sign, and Verify algorithms.

Adversaries model of CL-RS scheme. By integrating the security notion for the CL-PKC and security models for ring signature in the traditional PKI and ID-PKC, two types of security for a CL-RS scheme along with two types of adversaries, $\mathcal{A}_1$ and $\mathcal{A}_2$, have been defined in [298]. In terms of the outsider who can replace the user's public key of his/her choice, $\mathcal{A}_1$ models the adversary that replaces the user public key and cannot extract the user's partial private key $\mathsf{psk}_{\mathsf{ID}}$. On the other hand, adversary $\mathcal{A}_2$ models the malicious-but-passive KGC that generates the master public and secret key pair, and thus controls the generation of any user partial key $\mathsf{psk}_{\mathsf{ID}}$.

We define two games, one for $\mathcal{A}_1$ and the other for $\mathcal{A}_2$.

Game I: Unforgeability of CL-RS against type I adversary $\mathcal{A}_1$

Setup: The game simulator $\mathcal{S}_1$ obtains the master secret key master-secret and public parameters params by executing the Setup(1^k) algorithm, where $k \in \mathbb{N}$ is the security parameter. Then $\mathcal{S}_1$ sends params to $\mathcal{A}_1$ while keeping the master-secret secret. After that, three lists L_1, L_2, and L_3 will be initiated and maintained by $\mathcal{S}_1$ as follows:

1. List L_1 will be initiated empty and used to record the identities that have been chosen by $\mathcal{A}_1$ in the **Extract-Partial-Private-Key** queries.

2. List L_2 will be initiated empty and used to record the identities whose public keys have been replaced by $\mathcal{A}_1$.

3. List L_3 will be initiated empty and used to record the identities that have been chosen by $\mathcal{A}_1$ in the **Corruption** queries.

Query: During the simulation, $\mathcal{A}_1$ can adaptively make a polynomially bounded number of queries as defined below:

1. **Create-User:** On input of an identity $\mathsf{ID} \in \{0,1\}^*$, if ID has already been created, nothing is to be carried out. Otherwise, $\mathcal{S}_1$ generates $(\mathsf{upk}_{\mathsf{ID}}, \mathsf{usk}_{\mathsf{ID}}) \leftarrow$ Set-User-Keys(ID, params). In both cases, $\mathsf{upk}_{\mathsf{ID}}$ is returned.

2. **Extract-Partial-Private-Key:** $\mathcal{A}_1$ can request the partial private key of any user whose identity is ID. In response, $\mathcal{S}_1$ first resets $L_1 = L_1 \cup \{\text{ID}\}$, then runs the algorithm Partial-Private-Key-Extract, and outputs the partial private key psk_{ID} as an answer.

3. **Public-Key-Replace:** On input of an identity ID and a user public key upk^*, $\mathcal{S}_1$ searches L_2 for the entry of ID. If it is not found, nothing will be performed. Otherwise, $\mathcal{S}_1$ updates $(\text{ID}, \text{upk}_{\text{ID}})$ to $(\text{ID}, \text{upk}_{\text{ID}}^*)$ and resets $L_2 = L_2 \cup \{\text{ID}\}$.

4. **Corruption:** $\mathcal{A}_1$ can request the secret key of any user whose identity is ID. In response,

   a. $\mathcal{S}_1$ first checks the set L_2. If $\text{ID} \in L_2$ (i.e., the public key of the user ID has been replaced), $\mathcal{S}_1$ will return the symbol $\perp$, which means $\mathcal{S}_1$ cannot output the user secret key and partial private key of an identity whose public key has been replaced.

   b. Otherwise, $\text{ID} \notin L_2$ and $\mathcal{S}_1$ resets $L_3 = L_3 \cup \{\text{ID}\}$. $\mathcal{S}_1$ then runs the algorithms Set-User-Keys and Extract-Partial-Private-Key to output the user secret key usk_{ID} and the partial private key psk_{ID}, respectively, as an answer.

5. **Ring-Sign:** On input of a message $m \in \{0,1\}^*$ on behalf of a group whose identities are listed in the set $L_{\text{ID}} = \{\text{ID}_1, \ldots, \text{ID}_n\}$ with the corresponding public keys in the set $L_{\text{upk}} = \{\text{upk}_{\text{ID}_1}, \ldots, \text{upk}_{\text{ID}_n}\}$, $\mathcal{S}_1$ outputs a ring signature σ for the message m. It is required that the algorithm Verify will output 1 for the input $(\text{params}, L_{\text{ID}}, L_{\text{upk}}, m, \sigma)$.

Forgery: Finally, $\mathcal{A}_1$ outputs $(L_{\text{ID}}^*, L_{\text{upk}}^*, m^*, \sigma^*)$ as the forgery. We say that $\mathcal{A}_1$ wins if $\text{Verify}(\text{params}, L_{\text{ID}}^*, L_{\text{upk}}^*, m^*, \sigma^*) = 1$ for the oracle **Ring-Sign** has never been queried with $(L_{\text{ID}}^*, L_{\text{upk}}^*, m^*)$. One additional restriction is that $L_{\text{ID}}^* \cap L_1 \cap L_2 = \emptyset$ and $L_{\text{ID}}^* \cap L_3 = \emptyset$.

Game II: Unforgeability of CL-RS against type II adversary $\mathcal{A}_2$

Setup: The game challenger $\mathcal{S}_2$ executes $\mathcal{A}_2$ on input 1^k, where $k \in \mathbb{N}$ is a security parameter. Then $\mathcal{S}_2$ returns the master secret key master-secret and public parameters params to $\mathcal{A}_2$, who cannot make any query at this stage. Two lists L_1 and L_2 will be initiated and maintained by S_2 as follows:

1. L_1 will be initiated empty and used to record the identities whose public keys have been replaced by A_2.

2. L_2 will be initiated empty and used to record the identities that have been chosen by A_2 in the **Corruption** queries.

Query: During this stage of the simulation, A_2 can make queries to oracles **Corruption**, **Public-Key-Replace**, **Ring-Sign**, and **Create-User**. Note that oracle **Partial-Private-Key-Extract** is no longer needed since A_2 has a master secret key of his/her own. Those queries will be answered by S_2 in the same way in **game I**.

Forgery: At the end of **game II**, A_2 outputs a triple $(L_{\mathsf{ID}}^*, L_{\mathsf{upk}}^*, m^*, \sigma^*)$. A_2 wins if $\mathsf{Verify}(\mathsf{params}, L_{\mathsf{ID}}^*, L_{\mathsf{upk}}^*, m^*, \sigma^*) = 1$ for the oracle **Ring-Sign** has never been queried with $(L_{\mathsf{ID}}^*, L_{\mathsf{upk}}^*, m^*)$. One additional restriction is that $L_{\mathsf{ID}}^* \cap L_1 = \emptyset$ and $L_{\mathsf{ID}}^* \cap L_2 = \emptyset$.

Definition 9.3 *A CL-RS scheme is existentially unforgeable under an adaptive chosen-message attack iff the success probability of any polynomially bounded adversary in **games I** and **II** is negligible.*

Definition 9.4 *A CL-RS scheme is said to achieve unconditional anonymity if for any ring of n signers whose identities form the set L_{ID} with corresponding public keys L_{upk}, any message m, and any ring signature from $\sigma = \mathsf{Ring\text{-}Sign}(L_{\mathsf{ID}}, L_{\mathsf{upk}}, \mathsf{psk}_{\mathsf{ID}_s}, \mathsf{usk}_{\mathsf{ID}_s}, m)$, any verifier cannot identify the actual signer with probability better than a random guess, even when the verifier knows the user secret keys and partial private keys of all the ring members. In other words, the verifier can only output the identity of the actual signer with probability no better than $1/n$ $(1/n - 1$ if this verifier is in the ring).*

9.4.3 Qin et al.'s Scheme

In this section, Qin et al.'s pairing-free CL-RS scheme is presented. The proposal is motivated by the ID-based ring signature scheme in [296] and the certificateless signature scheme in [139]. The notation used throughout this chapter is listed in Table 9.1 to improve readability and the proposed scheme is defined by the following algorithms:

Setup: On input of a security parameter 1^k, the KGC chooses two k-bit prime numbers p and q randomly and computes $N = pq$.

TABLE 9.1   Notations

Notations	Descriptions
ID_i	The identity of the user i
(upk_{ID_i}, usk_{ID_i})	The user public/secret key pair of the user i
psk_{ID_i}	The partial private key of the user i
$L_{ID} = \{ID_1, \ldots, ID_n\}$	The identity set of n ring members
$L_{upk} = \{upk_{ID_1}, \ldots, upk_{ID_n}\}$	The public key set of n ring members
N	A positive integer satisfying $N = pq$, where p and q are prime numbers.
$\phi(N)$	The Euler totient function that counts the number of positive integers less than or equal to N that are relatively prime to N [303]
(e, d)	The master public/secret key pair such that $ed = 1 \bmod \phi(N)$
H_1, H_2	Two hash functions such as $H_1 : \{0,1\}^* \to \mathbb{Z}_N^*$ and $H_2 : \{0,1\}^* \to \{0,1\}^l$
$a \parallel b$	String concatenation of a and b

For the fixed parameter l, the KGC picks a prime number e at random satisfying $2^l < e < 2^{l+1}$ and $gcd(e, \phi(N)) = 1$, where $\phi(N)$ is the Euler totient function. After that, the KGC computes $d = e^{-1} \bmod \phi(N)$. Finally, the KGC chooses two hash functions H_1 and H_2 satisfying $H_1 : \{0,1\}^* \to \mathbb{Z}_N^*$ and $H_2 : \{0,1\}^* \to \{0,1\}^l$. The KGC publishes the public parameters params=(k, l, N, e, H_1, H_2) and keeps secret the master private parameters (p, q, d).

Extract-Partial-Private-Key: To compute the partial private key of identity $ID \in \{0,1\}^*$, the KGC computes $psk_{ID} = H_1(ID)^d \bmod N$. After receiving the psk_{ID} from KGC, the user ID can verify the validity of the partial private key as follows: $psk_{ID}^e = H_1(ID) \bmod N$.

Set-User-Keys: On input of the public parameters and the identity ID, the user selects $x_{ID} \in \mathbb{Z}_{2^{|N|/2-1}}$ as his/her secret key usk_{ID} and computes his/her public key as $upk_{ID} = H_1(ID)^{usk_{ID}} \bmod N$. Here, $|N|$ denotes the binary length of N.

Ring-Sign: Let $L_{ID} = \{ID_1, \ldots, ID_n\}$ be the list of n identities to be included in the ring signature, with corresponding public keys that form the set $L_{upk} = \{upk_{ID_1}, \ldots, upk_{ID_n}\}$. To sign a message $m \in \{0,1\}^*$ on behalf of the group, the actual signer, indexed by π (where $\pi \in [1, n]$), with partial secret key psk_{ID_π} and user secret key usk_{ID_π}, performs the following steps:

1. Randomly chooses two numbers $r_{\pi 1}, r_{\pi 2} \in \mathbb{Z}_{2^{|N|/2-1}}$.

2. Computes $R_{\pi 1} = H_1(ID_\pi)^{r_{\pi 1}} \bmod N$ and $R_{\pi 2} = H_1(ID_\pi)^{r_{\pi 2}} \bmod N$.

3. For all $i \in \{1, \ldots, n\}$, $i \neq \pi$, chooses $u_{i1}, c_i \in \mathbb{Z}_N^*$, $u_{i2} \in \mathbb{Z}_{2^{|N|/2-1}}$ uniformly at random and pairwise different.

4. Computes $R_{i1} = u_{i1}^e H_1(ID_i)^{c_i} \bmod N$ and $R_{i2} = H_1(ID_i)^{u_{i2}} upk_{ID_i}^{c_i} \bmod N$ for all $i \in \{1, \ldots, n\}$, $i \neq \pi$.

5. Computes $c_0 = H_2(m \parallel L_{ID} \parallel L_{upk} \parallel (R_{i1}, R_{i2})_{i=1}^n)$.

6. Generates a polynomial f over $GF(2^k)$ of degree $n - 1$ such that $c_0 = f(0)$ and $c_i = f(i)$ for all $i \in \{1, \ldots, n\}$, $i \neq \pi$.

7. Computes $c_\pi = f(\pi)$ and $u_{\pi 1} = (psk_{ID_\pi})^{r_{\pi 1} - c_\pi} \bmod N$ and $u_{\pi 2} = r_{\pi 2} - x_{ID_\pi} c_\pi$. Note that $u_{\pi 2}$ is an integer of the real number field and does not require any modular operation.

8. Outputs the ring signature on m as $\{f, (u_{i1}, u_{i2})_{i=1}^n\}$.

Verify: To verify a signature $\{f, (u_{i1}, u_{i2})_{i=1}^n\}$ on a message m with identities in $L_{ID} = \{ID_1, \ldots, ID_n\}$ and corresponding public keys in $L_{upk} = \{upk_{ID_1}, \ldots, upk_{ID_n}\}$, the verifier performs the following steps:

1. Checks if f is a polynomial over $GF(2^k)$ of degree $n - 1$.

2. For all $i \in \{1, \ldots, n\}$, computes $c_i = f(i)$, $R_{i1} = u_{i1}^e H_1(ID_i)^{c_i} \bmod N$, and $R_{i2} = H_1(ID_i)^{u_{i2}} upk_{ID_i}^{c_i} \bmod N$.

3. Checks if $f(0) \stackrel{?}{=} H_2(m \parallel L_{ID} \parallel L_{upk} \parallel (R_{i1}, R_{i2})_{i=1}^n)$ holds or not.

The proof of correctness is straightforward and omitted.

9.4.4 Analysis

Unconditional anonymity. In terms of the anonymity of the scheme, we can argue as follows: let $\{f, (u_{i1}, u_{i2})_{i=1}^n\}$ be a valid CL-RS scheme of a message m on behalf of a ring specified by identities in L_{ID} and public keys in L_{upk}. We can find the probability that ID_π (a member of the ring) computes exactly the CL-RS of message m on behalf of the ring by following the proposed scheme.

The probability that ID_π computes all the values $R_{i1} = u_{i1}^e H_1(ID_i)^{c_i} \bmod N$ and $R_{i2} = H_1(ID_i)^{u_{i2}} upk_{ID_i}^{c_i} \bmod N$, pairwise different for $1 \leq i \leq n$, $i \neq \pi$, is $(1/N - 1 \cdot 1/N - 2 \cdots \cdots 1/N - n + 1)^2$. Then the probability that ID_π chooses the values $r_{\pi 1}, r_{\pi 2} \in \mathbb{Z}_{2^{|N|/2-1}}$ that lead to the value $R_{\pi 1} = H_1(ID_\pi)^{r_{\pi 1}} \bmod N$ and $R_{\pi 2} = H_1(ID_\pi)^{r_{\pi 2}} \bmod N$, among all possible values for $R_{\pi 1}, R_{\pi 2}$ different to 1 and different to all R_{i1}, R_{i2} with $i \neq \pi$, is $(1/N - n)^2$.

To sum up, the probability that the actual signer ID_π generates exactly the ring signature is $(1/N - 1 \cdot 1/N - 2 \cdots \cdots 1/N - n + 1 \cdot 1/N - n)^2$. In other words, this probability does not depend on the specific ring member ID_π, so it is the same for all the members of the signing ring and does not leak any information about the identity of the actual signer. And hence, the unconditional ambiguity of our proposed ring signature is proved.

Unforgeability. Assuming that the RSA problem and discrete logarithm problem are hard, we now show the unforgeability of our CL-RS scheme.

Theorem 9.4 (Unforgeability against Game I Adversary) *If a probabilistic polynomial-time forger $\mathcal{A}_1$ has an advantage ε in forging a CL-RS scheme in **game I** after running in time t and making q_h queries to hashing queries, q_u queries to the **Create-User** request oracle, q_p queries to the **Partial-Private-Key-Extract** extraction oracle, q_r queries to the **Public-Key-Replace** extraction oracle, q_c queries to the **Corruption** extraction oracle, and q_s queries to the **Ring-Sign** oracle, then the RSA problem can be solved with probability $((q_p + q_c/q_p + q_c + n)^{q_p+q_c} \cdot (n/q_p + q_c + n)^n \varepsilon)^2/66 P_n^{q_h}$ with time $t' < 2(t + q_h T_h + q_u T_u + q_p T_p + q_c T_c + q_s T_s)$, where n is the number of ring members and $P_n^{q_h}$ denotes the number of n-permutations of q_h elements, that is, $P_n^{q_h} = q_h \cdots \cdots (q_h - n + 1)$, T_h (resp. T_u, T_p, T_c, T_s, and T_r) is the time cost of a **Hash** query (resp. **Create-User, Partial-Private-Key-Extract, Corruption, Ring-Sign,** and **Public-Key-Replace** query).*

Proof 9.5 *Here we follow the idea from [139,296,298]. Assume there exists a forger $\mathcal{A}_1$. We construct an algorithm $\mathcal{S}_1$ that makes use of $\mathcal{A}_1$ to solve the RSA problem. Given (N, e, y), $\mathcal{S}_1$ is asked to find $z \in \mathbb{Z}_N^*$ such that $z^e = y$.*

Initial: Let (N, e) be the system parameters. $\mathcal{S}_1$ computes $d = e^{-1} \bmod \phi(N)$ as the master secret key and chooses two hash functions H_1 and H_2 as random oracles. Finally, $\mathcal{S}_1$ sends (N, e, H_1, H_2) to the adversary $\mathcal{A}_1$.

Attack: $\mathcal{A}_1$ can ask $\mathcal{S}_1$ H_1, H_2, **Create-User**, **Corruption**, **Partial-Private-Key-Extract**, **Public-Key-Replace**, and **Ring-Sign** queries a polynomial number of times. These oracles are all simulated by $\mathcal{S}_1$. To avoid conflict and maintain consistency, $\mathcal{S}_1$ maintains three lists $\mathbf{H_1}$, $\mathbf{H_2}$, and $\mathbf{K}$, which are initially empty. $\mathcal{S}_1$ also keeps three lists L_1, L_2, and L_3; the functions of these lists are the same as mentioned in **game I** in Section 9.4.2. In addition, modular N is omitted in the following expressions for simplicity:

H_1 *Queries:* On receiving a query $H_1(\mathsf{ID})$, $\mathcal{S}_1$ does as follows:

1. If there exists an item $(\mathsf{ID}, h_1^{\mathsf{ID}}, t_{\mathsf{ID}}, \mathrm{coin})$ in $\mathbf{H_1}$, then $\mathcal{S}_1$ returns h_1^{ID} as an answer.

2. Otherwise, $\mathcal{S}_1$ first picks $\mathrm{coin} \in \{0, 1\}$ at random such that $Pr[\mathrm{coin} = 0] = \rho$ (ρ will be determined later). Then it randomly selects $t_{\mathsf{ID}} \in \mathbb{Z}_N^*$ and defines $h_1^{\mathsf{ID}} = y^{\mathrm{coin}} t_{\mathsf{ID}}^e$ to return it to $\mathcal{A}_1$. Finally, $\mathcal{A}_1$ adds $(\mathsf{ID}, h_1^{\mathsf{ID}}, t_{\mathsf{ID}}, \mathrm{coin})$ to the $\mathbf{H_1}$ list and returns h_1 as an answer.

H_2 *Queries:* On receiving a query $H_2(m \parallel L_{\mathsf{ID}} \parallel L_{\mathsf{upk}} \parallel (R_{i1}, R_{i2})_{i=1}^n)$, $\mathcal{S}_1$ first checks if there exists an item $(m, L_{\mathsf{ID}}, L_{\mathsf{upk}}, (R_{i1}, R_{i2})_{i=1}^n, h_2)$ in $\mathbf{H_2}$; if so, it returns h_2 as answer. Otherwise, $\mathcal{S}_1$ picks a random $h_2 \in \mathbb{Z}_N^*$, which has not been used in the answers of the former H_2 queries, and then returns h_2 as an answer and adds $(m, L_{\mathsf{ID}}, L_{\mathsf{upk}}, R, h_2)$ to $\mathbf{H_2}$.

Create-User *Queries:* Whenever it receives a query ID, $\mathcal{S}_1$ randomly chooses $x_{\mathsf{ID}} \in \mathbb{Z}_{2^{|N|/2-1}}$ as his/her secret key $\mathsf{usk}_{\mathsf{ID}}$ and searches list $\mathbf{H_1}$ for a record $(\mathsf{ID}, h_1^{\mathsf{ID}}, t_{\mathsf{ID}}, \mathrm{coin})$. Then it sets $\mathsf{upk}_{\mathsf{ID}} = (h_1^{\mathsf{ID}})^{x_{\mathsf{ID}}}$, adds $(\mathsf{ID}, \mathsf{upk}_{\mathsf{ID}}, \mathsf{usk}_{\mathsf{ID}}, \mathsf{psk}_{\mathsf{ID}})$ to $\mathbf{K}$, and outputs $\mathsf{upk}_{\mathsf{ID}}$ as the answer.

Corruption *Queries:* Whenever it receives a **Corruption** query, if $\mathsf{ID} \in L_2$, $\mathcal{S}_1$ returns $\perp$; otherwise,

1. If there exists an item $(\mathsf{ID}, \mathsf{upk}_{\mathsf{ID}}, \mathsf{usk}_{\mathsf{ID}}, \mathsf{psk}_{\mathsf{ID}})$ in $\mathbf{K}$, $\mathcal{S}_1$ does the following:

a. If $usk_{ID} = \perp$, $\mathcal{S}_1$ first makes a **Create-User** query on ID, sets $L_3 = L_3 \cup \{ID\}$, and returns (usk_{ID}, psk_{ID}) as an answer.

b. Else if $psk_{ID} = \perp$, $\mathcal{S}_1$ first makes a **Partial-Private-Key-Extract** query on ID, sets $L_3 = L_3 \cup \{ID\}$, and returns (usk_{ID}, psk_{ID}) as an answer.

c. Otherwise, $\mathcal{S}_1$ sets $L_3 = L_3 \cup \{ID\}$ and returns (usk_{ID}, psk_{ID}) as an answer.

2. $\mathcal{S}_1$ first makes **Create-User** and **Partial-Private-Key-Extract** queries. Then $\mathcal{S}_1$ sets $L_3 = L_3 \cup \{ID\}$, returns (usk_{ID}, psk_{ID}) as an answer, and adds $(ID, upk_{ID}, usk_{ID}, psk_{ID})$ to **K**.

Partial-Private-Key-Extract *Queries*: $\mathcal{A}_1$ is allowed to make **Partial-Private-Key-Extract** queries for a public key upk_{ID} with identification string ID. $\mathcal{S}_1$ simulates the oracle as follows:

1. If there exists an item $(ID, upk_{ID}, usk_{ID}, psk_{ID})$ in **K**, $\mathcal{S}_1$ does the following:

a. If $psk_{ID} \neq \perp$, $\mathcal{S}_1$ returns psk_{ID} as an answer.

b. Else, if there exists an item $(ID, h_1^{ID}, t_{ID}, coin)$ in $\mathbf{H_1}$, $\mathcal{S}_1$ sets $L_1 = L_1 \cup \{ID\}$, $psk_{ID} = t_{ID}$, and returns psk_{ID} as the answer when $coin = 0$; when $coin = 1$, $\mathcal{S}_1$ aborts.

c. Otherwise, $\mathcal{S}_1$ first makes an H_1 query to obtain an item $(ID, h_1^{ID}, t_{ID}, coin)$. If $coin = 1$, $\mathcal{S}_1$ aborts; when $coin = 0$, $\mathcal{S}_1$ sets $L_1 = L_1 \cup \{ID\}$, $psk_{ID} = t_{ID}$, and returns psk_{ID} as the answer.

2. Otherwise $\mathcal{S}_1$ does the following:

a. If there exists an item $(ID, h_1^{ID}, t_{ID}, coin)$ in $\mathbf{H_1}$, $\mathcal{S}_1$ sets $L_1 = L_1 \cup \{ID\}$, computes $psk_{ID} = t_{ID}$, sets $usk_{ID} = \perp$, $upk_{ID} = \perp$, adds $(ID, upk_{ID}, usk_{ID}, psk_{ID})$ to **K**, and returns psk_{ID} as the answer when $coin = 0$; when $coin = 1$, $\mathcal{S}_1$ aborts.

b. Otherwise, $\mathcal{S}_1$ first makes an H_1 query to obtain an item $(ID, h_1^{ID}, t_{ID}, coin)$ in $\mathbf{H_1}$, then proceeds as in (2).

Public-Key-Replace *Queries*: Suppose $\mathcal{A}_1$ makes the query with an input (ID, upk'_{ID}). $\mathcal{S}_1$ first makes a **Partial-Private-Key-Extract** query to obtain an item $(ID, upk_{ID}, usk_{ID}, psk_{ID})$, then sets $L_2 = L_2 \cup \{\mathsf{ID}\}$, $\mathsf{upk}_{\mathsf{ID}} = \mathsf{upk}'_{\mathsf{ID}}$, updates the item as $(\mathsf{ID}, \mathsf{upk}'_{\mathsf{ID}}, \mathsf{usk}_{\mathsf{ID}}, \mathsf{psk}_{\mathsf{ID}})$, and inserts this item into **K** to record this replacement.

Ring-Sign *Queries*: $\mathcal{A}_1$ chooses a group of n users whose identities form the set $L_{\mathsf{ID}} = \{\mathsf{ID}_1, \ldots, \mathsf{ID}_n\}$ with the corresponding public keys forming the set $L_{\mathsf{upk}_{\mathsf{ID}}} = \{\mathsf{upk}_{\mathsf{ID}_1}, \ldots, \mathsf{upk}_{\mathsf{ID}_n}\}$ and may ask for a ring signature from a message m of this group. On receiving a **Ring-Sign** query on $(m, L_{\mathsf{ID}}, L_{\mathsf{upk}_{\mathsf{ID}}})$, $\mathcal{S}_1$ creates a ring signature as follows:

1. Chooses a random index $\pi \in \{1, \ldots, n\}$.

2. Randomly chooses two numbers $u_{\pi 1}, c_\pi \in \mathbb{Z}_N^*$, $u_{\pi 2} \in \mathbb{Z}_{2^{|N|/2-1}}$, and computes $R_{\pi 1} = u_{\pi 1}^e H_1(\mathsf{ID}_\pi)^{c_\pi} \bmod N$ and $R_{\pi 2} = H_1(\mathsf{ID}_\pi)^{u_{\pi 2}} \mathsf{upk}_{\mathsf{ID}_\pi}^{c_\pi} \bmod N$.

3. For all $i \in \{1, \ldots, n\} \setminus \{\pi\}$, chooses $r_{i1}, r_{i2}, u_{i1}, c_i \in \mathbb{Z}_N^*$, $u_{i2} \in \mathbb{Z}_{2^{|N|/2-1}}$ uniformly at random and pairwise different, and computes $R_{i1} = u_{i1}^e H_1(\mathsf{ID}_i)^{c_i} \bmod N$ and $R_{i2} = H_1(\mathsf{ID}_i)^{u_{i2}} \mathsf{upk}_{\mathsf{ID}_i}^{c_i} \bmod N$.

4. Generates a polynomial f over $GF(2^k)$ of degree $n-1$ such that $c_i = f(i)$ for all $i \in \{1, \ldots, n\}$.

5. At this point, $\mathcal{S}_1$ "falsifies" the random oracle H_2 by imposing the relation $H_2(m \parallel L_{\mathsf{ID}} \parallel L_{\mathsf{upk}} \parallel (R_{i1}, R_{i2})_{i=1}^n) = f(0)$. $\mathcal{S}_1$ will return $f(0)$ as the answer if $\mathcal{A}_1$ asks the random oracle H_2 for this input.

6. Returns the ring signature on m as $\{f, (u_{i1}, u_{i2})_{i=1}^n\}$ as the answer.

Forgery: Finally, $\mathcal{A}_1$ outputs a tuple $(m^*, L_{\mathsf{ID}}^*, L_{\mathsf{upk}_{\mathsf{ID}}}^*, f^*, (u_{i1}^*, u_{i2}^*)_{i=1}^n)$, which means $\{f^*, (u_{i1}^*, u_{i2}^*)_{i=1}^n\}$ is a ring signature on message m^* on behalf of the group specified by identities in L_{ID}^* and the corresponding public keys in L_{upk}^*. It is required that $\mathcal{S}_1$ does not know the secret key of any member in this group, $L_{\mathsf{ID}}^* \cap ((L_1 \cap L_2) \cup L_3) = \emptyset$, and the ring signature on message m^* on behalf of the group must be valid. According to the forking lemma [278,304], if $\mathcal{A}_1$ succeeds in forging a valid ring signature with probability $\epsilon \geq 7 P_n^{q_{H_1}} / 2^l$ in a time span time, then within 2 time and probability $\geq \epsilon^2 / 66 P_n^{q_{H_1}}$, $\mathcal{S}_1$ can get two valid ring signatures $(m^*, L^*_{\text{ID}}, L^*_{\text{upk}_{\text{ID}}}, f^*, (u^*_{i1}, u^*_{i2})^n_{i=1})$ and $(m^*, L^*_{\text{ID}}, L^*_{\text{upk}_{\text{ID}}}, f'^*, (u'^*_{i1}, u'^*_{i2})^n_{i=1})$. From these two valid ring signatures, $\mathcal{S}_1$ obtains

$$f^*(0) = H_2(m^* \parallel L^*_{\text{ID}} \parallel L^*_{\text{upk}} \parallel (u^{*e}_{i1} H_1(\text{ID}^*_i)^{c^*_i} \bmod N,$$

$$H_1(\text{ID}^*_i)^{u^*_{i2}} \text{upk}^{c^*_i}_{\text{ID}^*_i} \bmod N)^n_{i=1})$$

and

$$f'^*(0) = H_2(m^* \parallel L^*_{\text{ID}} \parallel L^*_{\text{upk}} \parallel (u'^{*e}_{i1} H_1(\text{ID}^*_i)^{c'^*_i} \bmod N,$$

$$H_1(\text{ID}^*_i)^{u'^*_{i2}} \text{upk}^{c'^*_i}_{\text{ID}^*_i} \bmod N)^n_{i=1})$$

where $c^*_i = f^*(i)$, $c'^*_i = f'^*(i)$, and for some $\pi \in \{1, \ldots, n\}$, $c^*_\pi \neq c'^*_\pi$, while for $i \in \{1, \ldots, n\}$ and $i \neq \pi$, $c^*_i = c'^*_i$. From the above two equations, we have $u^{*e}_{\pi 1} H_1(\text{ID}^*_\pi)^{c^*_\pi} = u'^{*e}_{\pi 1} H_1(\text{ID}^*_\pi)^{c'^*_\pi}$. At this stage, we look in the list $\mathbf{H_1}$ and look for the item $(\text{ID}^*_\pi, h^*_{\text{ID}_\pi}, t^*_{\text{ID}_\pi}, coin^*)$ corresponding to the identity ID^*_π. With probability $1 - \rho$, we have $coin^* = 1$ and $h^*_{\text{ID}_\pi} = yt^{*e}_{\text{ID}_\pi}$.

Then we have the following relation:

$$u^{*e}_{\pi 1}(yt^{*e}_{\text{ID}_\pi})^{c^*_\pi} = u'^{*e}_{\pi 1}(yt^{*e}_{\text{ID}_\pi})^{c'^*_\pi}$$

$$\Updownarrow$$

$$\left(\frac{u^*_{\pi 1}}{u'^*_{\pi 1}}\right)^e (t^{*e}_{\text{ID}_\pi})^{c^*_\pi - c'^*_\pi} = y^{c'^*_\pi - c^*_\pi}$$

$$\Updownarrow$$

$$\left(\frac{u^*_{\pi 1} t^{*(c^*_\pi - c'^*_\pi)}_{\text{ID}_\pi}}{u'^*_{\pi 1}}\right)^e = y^{c'^*_\pi - c^*_\pi}$$

Because e is a prime number, we have $gcd(e, c'^*_\pi - c^*_\pi) = 1$, and there exists two numbers a, b satisfying $ae + b(c'^*_\pi - c^*_\pi) = 1$. Thus, we can obtain

$$y = y^{ae + b(c'^*_\pi - c^*_\pi)} = y^{ae} y^{b(c'^*_\pi - c^*_\pi)} = y^{ae} \left(\frac{u^*_{\pi 1} t^{*(c^*_\pi - c'^*_\pi)}_{\text{ID}_\pi}}{u'^*_{\pi 1}}\right)^{eb}$$

$$\Rightarrow y = \left(y^a \left(\frac{u^*_{\pi 1} t^{*(c^*_\pi - c'^*_\pi)}_{\text{ID}_\pi}}{u'^*_{\pi 1}}\right)^b\right)^e$$

$$\Rightarrow z = y^a \left(\frac{u_{\pi 1}^* t_{ID_\pi}^{*(c_\pi^* - c_\pi'^*)}}{u_{\pi 1}'^*} \right)^b$$

This denotes that the RSA problem can be successfully solved by $\mathcal{S}_1$.

Probability analysis. Now we evaluate the value of ρ and determine the probability for $\mathcal{S}_1$ to successfully solve the given RSA problem. The probability that $\mathcal{S}_1$ does not abort in all the q_p **Partial-Private-Key-Extract** queries and q_c **Corruption** queries is at least $\rho^{q_p+q_c}$. The probability that the forged ring signature is effective for $\mathcal{S}_1$ in solving the RSA problem is $(1-\rho)^n$. Thus, the combined probability is computed as $\rho^{q_p+q_c}(1-\rho)^n$. We can find that the value of ρ that maximizes this probability is $q_p + q_c/q_p + q_c + n$ and the maximized probability is $(q_p + q_c/q_p + q_c + n)^{q_p+q_c} \cdot (n/q_p + q_c + n)^n$.

According to the ring forking lemma [278], if $\mathcal{S}_1$ succeeds in time t with probability $\epsilon \geq 7P_n^{q_{H_1}}/2^l$, then the RSA problem can be solved by $\mathcal{S}_1$ within time $2(t + q_h T_h + q_u T_u + q_p T_p + q_c T_c + q_s T_s)$ and with probability $((q_p + q_c/q_p + q_c + n)^{q_p+q_c} \cdot (n/q_p + q_c + n)^n \epsilon)^2/66P_n^{q_h}$.

Theorem 9.5 (Unforgeability against Game II adversary) *If a probabilistic polynomial-time forger $\mathcal{A}_2$ has an advantage ε in forging a certificate-based ring signature in an attack modeled by **game II** after running in time t and making q_h queries to hashing queries, q_u queries to the **Create-User** request oracle, q_c queries to the **Corruption** extraction oracle, and q_s queries to the **Ring-Sign** oracle, then the discrete logarithm problem can be solved with probability $((1 - \frac{1}{n})^{q_p+q_c}(\frac{1}{n})^n \epsilon)^2/66P_n^{q_h}$ with time $t' < 2(t + q_h T_h + q_u T_u + q_c T_c + q_s T_s)$, where T_h (resp. T_u, T_c, T_s) is the time cost of a **Hash** query (resp. **Create-User**, **Corruption**, and **Ring-Sign** query).*

Proof 9.6 *Assume there exists a forger $\mathcal{A}_2$. We construct an algorithm $\mathcal{S}_2$ that makes use of $\mathcal{A}_2$ to solve a discrete logarithm problem. $\mathcal{S}_2$ is given a number $g \in \mathbb{Z}_N^*$ and (N, p, q), a random number of $Y \in \mathbb{Z}_N$. $\mathcal{S}_2$ is asked to find x such that $g^x = Y \mod N$.*

Initial: *Let (N, e) be the system parameters. The master secret key is d satisfying $ed = 1 \mod \phi(N)$. $\mathcal{S}_2$ chooses two hash functions H_1 and H_2 as random oracles and sends $(N, e, H_1, H_2, H_3, d, p, q)$ to the adversary $\mathcal{A}_2$. Let $\text{upk}_{ID_\pi^*} = Y$ be the challenged user's public key and ID_π^* be the identity of the challenged user. $\mathcal{S}_2$ also keeps* two lists L_1 and L_2; the functions of these lists are the same as mentioned in **game II** in Section 9.4.2.

Attack: H_1 *Queries*: On receiving a query $H_1(\text{ID})$, $\mathcal{S}_2$ does as follows:

1. If there exists an item $(\text{ID}, h_1^{\text{ID}}, t_{\text{ID}})$ in $\mathbf{H_1}$, then $\mathcal{S}_2$ returns h_1^{ID} as an answer.

2. Otherwise, $\mathcal{S}_2$ first randomly selects $t_{\text{ID}} \in \phi(N)$ to set $h_1^{\text{ID}} = g^{t_{\text{ID}}}$ and returns it to $\mathcal{A}_2$, where $\phi(N)$ is the Euler totient function and can be computed by p, q. Finally, $\mathcal{A}_2$ adds $(\text{ID}, h_1^{\text{ID}}, t_{\text{ID}})$ to the $\mathbf{H_1}$ list and returns h_1^{ID} as the answer.

H_2 *Queries*: On receiving a query $H_2(m \parallel L_{\text{ID}} \parallel L_{\text{upk}} \parallel (R_{i1}, R_{i2})_{i=1}^{n})$, $\mathcal{S}_2$ first checks if there exists an item $(m, L_{\text{ID}}, L_{\text{upk}}, (R_{i1}, R_{i2})_{i=1}^{n}, h_2)$ in $\mathbf{H_2}$; if so, it returns h_2 as the answer. Otherwise, $\mathcal{S}_2$ picks a random $h_2 \in \mathbb{Z}_N^*$, which has not been used in the answers of the former H_2 queries, and then returns h_2 as the answer and adds $(m, L_{\text{ID}}, L_{\text{upk}}, (R_{i1}, R_{i2})_{i=1}^{n}, h_2)$ to $\mathbf{H_2}$.

Create-User *Queries*: On receiving a query ID, $\mathcal{S}_2$ randomly chooses $x_{\text{ID}} \in \mathbb{Z}_{2^{|N|/2-1}}$ as his/her secret key usk_{ID} and computes $\text{upk}_{\text{ID}} = h_1^{x_{\text{ID}}}$ if $\text{ID} \neq \text{ID}^*$. Otherwise, $\mathcal{S}_2$ searches list $\mathbf{H_1}$ for a record $(\text{ID}^*, h_1^{\text{ID}^*}, t_{\text{ID}^*})$ and computes $\text{upk}_{\text{ID}^*} = Y^{t_{\text{ID}^*}}$. In both cases, $\mathcal{S}_2$ adds $(\text{ID}, \text{upk}_{\text{ID}}, \text{usk}_{\text{ID}})$ to $\mathbf{K}$ and outputs upk_{ID} as the answer.

Corruption *Queries*: Whenever it receives a **Corruption** query, if $\text{ID} \in L_1$, $\mathcal{S}_2$ returns $\perp$, otherwise

1. If there exists an item $(\text{ID}, \text{upk}_{\text{ID}}, \text{usk}_{\text{ID}}, \text{psk}_{\text{ID}})$ in $\mathbf{K}$, $\mathcal{S}_2$ does the following:

   a. If $\text{usk}_{\text{ID}} = \perp$, $\mathcal{S}_2$ first makes a **Create-User** query on ID, sets $L_2 = L_2 \cup \{\text{ID}\}$, and returns usk_{ID} as the answer.

   b. Otherwise, $\mathcal{S}_2$ sets $L_2 = L_2 \cup \{\text{ID}\}$ and returns usk_{ID} as the answer.

2. $\mathcal{S}_2$ first makes **Create-User** queries. Then $\mathcal{S}_2$ sets $L_2 = L_2 \cup \{\text{ID}\}$, returns usk_{ID} as the answer, and adds $(\text{ID}, \text{upk}_{\text{ID}}, \text{usk}_{\text{ID}})$ to $\mathbf{K}$.

Replace-Key *Queries*: Suppose $\mathcal{A}_2$ makes the query with an input $(\text{ID}.\text{upk}_{\text{ID}}')$. $\mathcal{S}_2$ first makes a **Partial-Private-Key-Extract**

query to obtain an item $(\mathsf{ID}, \mathsf{upk}_{\mathsf{ID}}, \mathsf{usk}_{\mathsf{ID}})$, then sets $L_1 = L_1 \cup \{\mathsf{ID}\}$, $\mathsf{upk}_{\mathsf{ID}} = \mathsf{upk}'_{\mathsf{ID}}$, updates the item as $(\mathsf{ID}, \mathsf{upk}'_{\mathsf{ID}}, \mathsf{usk}_{\mathsf{ID}})$, and inserts this item into $\mathbf{K}$ to record this replacement.

Ring-Sign *Queries*: $\mathcal{A}_2$ chooses a group of n users whose identities form the set $L_{\mathsf{ID}} = \{\mathsf{ID}_1, \ldots, \mathsf{ID}_n\}$ with corresponding public keys forming the set $L_{\mathsf{upk}_{\mathsf{ID}}} = \{\mathsf{upk}_{\mathsf{ID}_1}, \ldots, \mathsf{upk}_{\mathsf{ID}_n}\}$ and may ask for a ring signature from a message m of this group. On receiving a **Ring-Sign** query on $(m, L_{\mathsf{ID}}, L_{\mathsf{upk}_{\mathsf{ID}}})$, $\mathcal{S}_2$ creates a ring signature as follows:

1. Chooses a random index $\pi \in \{1, \ldots, n\}$.

2. Randomly chooses two numbers $u_{\pi 1}, c_\pi \in \mathbb{Z}_N^*$, $u_{\pi 2} \in \mathbb{Z}_{2^{\lfloor N \rfloor / 2 - 1}}$, and computes $R_{\pi 1} = u_{\pi 1}^e H_1(\mathsf{ID}_\pi)^{c_\pi} \bmod N$ and $R_{\pi 2} = H_1(\mathsf{ID}_\pi)^{u_{\pi 2}} \mathsf{upk}_{\mathsf{ID}_\pi}^{c_\pi} \bmod N$.

3. For all $i \in \{1, \ldots, n\} \setminus \{\pi\}$, chooses $r_{i1}, r_{i2}, u_{i1}, c_i \in \mathbb{Z}_N^*$, $u_{i2} \in \mathbb{Z}_{2^{\lfloor N \rfloor / 2 - 1}}$ uniformly at random and pairwise different, and computes $R_{i1} = u_{i1}^e H_1(\mathsf{ID}_i)^{c_i} \bmod N$ and $R_{i2} = H_1(\mathsf{ID}_i)^{u_{i2}} \mathsf{upk}_{\mathsf{ID}_i}^{c_i} \bmod N$.

4. Generates a polynomial f over $GF(2^k)$ of degree $n - 1$ such that $c_i = f(i)$ for all $i \in \{1, \ldots, n\}$.

5. At this point, $\mathcal{S}_2$ "falsifies" the random oracle H_2 by imposing the relation $H_2(m \parallel L_{\mathsf{ID}} \parallel L_{\mathsf{upk}} \parallel (R_{i1}, R_{i2})_{i=1}^n) = f(0)$. $\mathcal{S}_2$ will return $f(0)$ as the answer if $\mathcal{A}_2$ asks the random oracle H_2 for this input.

6. Returns the ring signature on m as $\{f, (u_{i1}, u_{i2})_{i=1}^n\}$ as the answer.

***Forgery*:** Finally, $\mathcal{A}_2$ outputs a tuple $(m^*, L_{\mathsf{ID}}^*, L_{\mathsf{upk}_{\mathsf{ID}}}^*, f^*, (u_{i1}^*, u_{i2}^*)_{i=1}^n)$, which means $\{f^*, (u_{i1}^*, u_{i2}^*)_{i=1}^n\}$ is a ring signature on message m^* on behalf of the group specified by the identities in L_{ID}^* and the corresponding public keys in L_{upk}^*. It is required that the ring signature on message m^* on behalf of the group be valid, that $\mathcal{S}_2$ does not know the secret key of any member in this group, and that $L_{\mathsf{ID}}^* \cap ((L_1 \cap L_2) \cup L_3) = \emptyset$. Applying the forking lemma [278,304], $\mathcal{S}_2$ can get two valid ring signatures $(m^*, L_{\mathsf{ID}}^*, L_{\mathsf{upk}_{\mathsf{ID}}}^*, f^*, (u_{i1}^*, u_{i2}^*)_{i=1}^n)$ and $(m^*, L_{\mathsf{ID}}^*, L_{\mathsf{upk}_{\mathsf{ID}}}^*, f'^*, (u_{i1}'^*, u_{i2}'^*)_{i=1}^n)$. From these two valid ring signatures, $\mathcal{S}_2$ obtains

$$f^*(0) = H_2(m^* \parallel L_{\mathsf{ID}}^* \parallel L_{\mathsf{upk}}^* \parallel (u_{i1}^{*e} H_1(\mathsf{ID}_i^*)^{c_i^*} \bmod N,$$

$$H_1(\mathsf{ID}_i^*)^{u_{i2}^*} \mathsf{upk}_{\mathsf{ID}_i^*}^{c_i} \bmod N)_{i=1}^n)$$

and

$$f'^*(0) = H_2(m^* \parallel L_{\mathsf{ID}}^* \parallel L_{\mathsf{upk}}^* \parallel (u_{i1}'^{*e} H_1(\mathsf{ID}_i^*)^{c_i'^*} \bmod N,$$

$$H_1(\mathsf{ID}_i^*)^{u_{i2}'^*} \mathsf{upk}_{\mathsf{ID}_i^*}^{c_i'^*} \bmod N)_{i=1}^n)$$

where $c_i^* = f^*(i)$, $c_i'^* = f'^*(i)$, and for some $\pi \in \{1, \ldots, n\}$, $c_\pi^* \neq c_\pi'^*$, while for $i \in \{1, \ldots, n\}$ and $i \neq \pi$, $c_i^* = c_i'^*$. From the above two equations, we have $H_1(\mathsf{ID}_\pi^*)^{u_{\pi 2}^*} \mathsf{upk}_{\mathsf{ID}_\pi^*}^{c_\pi^*} = H_1(\mathsf{ID}_\pi^*)^{u_{\pi 2}'^*} \mathsf{upk}_{\mathsf{ID}_\pi^*}^{c_\pi'^*}$. At this stage, we look in the list $\mathbf{H_1}$, and look for the item $(\mathsf{ID}_\pi^*, h_{\mathsf{ID}_\pi}^*, t_{\mathsf{ID}_\pi}^*, coin^*)$ corresponding to the identity ID_π^*. Thus, we have the following relation:

$$H_1(\mathsf{ID}_\pi^*)^{u_{\pi 2}^*} \mathsf{upk}_{\mathsf{ID}_\pi^*}^{c_\pi^*} = H_1(\mathsf{ID}_\pi^*)^{u_{\pi 2}'^*} \mathsf{upk}_{\mathsf{ID}_\pi^*}^{c_\pi'^*}$$

$$\Updownarrow$$

$$(g^{t_{\mathsf{ID}_\pi}^*})^{u_{\pi 2}^* - u_{\pi 2}'^*} = Y^{c_\pi'^* - c_\pi^*}$$

$$\Updownarrow$$

$$g^{t_{\mathsf{ID}_\pi}^*(u_{\pi 2}^* - u_{\pi 2}'^*)/(c_\pi'^* - c_\pi^*)} = Y$$

It is obvious that the discrete logarithm of Y to the base g is $t_{\mathsf{ID}_\pi}^*(u_{\pi 2}^* - u_{\pi 2}'^*)/(c_\pi'^* - c_\pi^*)$. This denotes that the discrete logarithm problem can be successfully solved by $\mathcal{S}_2$.

Probability analysis. Now it is time to determine the probability for $\mathcal{S}_2$ to successfully solve the given discrete logarithm problem. The probability that $\mathcal{S}_2$ does not abort in all the q_u **Create-User** queries and q_c **Corruption** queries is at least $(1 - 1/n)^{q_p + q_c}$. The probability that the forged ring signature is effective for $\mathcal{S}_2$ in solving the discrete logarithm problem is $(\frac{1}{n})^n$. Thus, the combined probability is computed as $(1 - 1/n)^{q_p + q_c}(1/n)^n$.

According to the ring forking lemma [278], if $\mathcal{S}_2$ succeeds in time t with probability $\epsilon \geq 7 P_n^{q_{H_1}}/2^l$, then the discrete logarithm problem can be solved by $\mathcal{S}_2$ within time $2(t + q_h T_h + q_u T_u + q_c T_c + q_s T_s)$ and with probability $((1 - 1/n)^{q_p + q_c}(1/n)^n \epsilon)^2 / 66 P_n^{q_h}$.

Efficiency analysis. We now compare Qin et al.'s CL-RS [302] with the schemes proposed by Zhang et al. [298] and by Chang et al.

TABLE 9.2 Comparison of CL-RS Schemes

Schemes	Signing Computation	Verifying Computation	Signature Size
Zhang–Zhang–Wu [298]	$2P + (2n+3)S + nE$	$3P + 2nS$	$160 + 320n$
Chang–Wong–Mu [299]	$2P + (2n+2)S$	$2P + (2n+1)S$	$160(n+2)$
Qin–Xiong–Zhu–Chen [302]	$(4n-1)e + M$	$4ne$	$1536n + \lvert f \rvert$

Note: In terms of the chosen parameters provide unforgeability with $k = 80$ bits of security, RSA signatures are instantiated with a modulus of $\lvert N \rvert = 1024$ bits. With regard to bilinear pairings, elements in G_1 can be represented by $\lvert G_1 \rvert = 160$ bits, while an element G_2 can be represented $\lvert G_2 \rvert = 320$ bits.

[299] in terms of signing/verifying computation and signature size in Table 9.2. We denote by $\mathbb{G}_1$ and $\mathbb{G}_2$ two cyclic groups of prime order p, by P a pairing operation, by S a multiplication in $\mathbb{G}_1$, by E an exponentiation in $\mathbb{G}_1$, by e an exponentiation operator, and by M a multiplication operator in an RSA crypto-system.

The comparison shows that signing and verifying computation of Qin et al.'s scheme is considerably cheaper: Qin et al.'s scheme only needs multiple (linear to the ring size) exponentiation and multiplication operations in an RSA group, as opposed to multiple (linear to the ring size) pairing computations for the schemes of [298,299]. Signatures under Qin et al.'s scheme are $1536n + \lvert f \rvert$ bits[a] long for typical values of the security parameters, which is longer than the signatures in [298,299]. This is the major tradeoff of Qin et al.'s scheme. However, the security of Qin et al.'s scheme is based on relatively weak intractability assumptions such as the RSA and the discrete-logarithm assumptions, while the others are built on stronger assumptions such as the bilinear CDH assumption.

9.5 CERTIFICATELESS THRESHOLD SIGNATURE

9.5.1 Related Work

The idea of threshold cryptography is to distribute the secret information and computation (i.e., decryption or signature generation) among multiple parties in order to prevent a single point of failure or abuse. For example, let Alice be the president of a company. She shared her power of signing among a number of servers in such a way that only more than a certain number of secret shares can be used to sign a message or decrypt a ciphertext on behalf of her. There is plenty of research on threshold cryptographic schemes under traditional PKI [305–309].

---

[a]Here, $\lvert f \rvert$ represents the length of a polynomial with degree $n - 1$.

To avoid the necessity of certificates in PKI, Baek and Zheng [310] introduced a new approach for ID-based threshold decryption in which the private key associated with an identity rather than the master key of the PKG is shared. Moreover, they [311] first proposed an ID-based threshold signature without distributed PKGs. Chen et al. [312] proposed a new ID-based threshold signature scheme by combining the advantages of both certificate-based public-key cryptography and ID-based public-key cryptography. To solve the key escrow problem in ID-PKC, Wang et al. [313] and Yuan et al. [314] proposed the certificateless threshold signature in the random oracle model independently. After that, Xiong et al. [315] presented a certificateless threshold signature scheme secure in the standard mode. In addition, Long and Chen proposed a certificateless threshold decryption scheme [316] and certificateless threshold key encapsulation scheme [317], respectively, secure against a chosen-ciphertext attack

9.5.2 Formal Definition

A certificateless threshold signature is defined by five algorithms: Setup, Partial-Key-Gen-and-Share, User-Secret-Key-Gen-and-Share, Sign, and Verify. The first four algorithms may be randomized, but the last one is usually not. The description of each algorithm is as follows:

Setup: On input of a security parameter, this algorithm generates and publishes the public parameters **params** of the scheme.

Partial-Key-Gen-and-Share: Given an identity ID and **params**, n PKGs jointly generate the partial private key share d_{ID}^i and corresponding verification key share fvk_i to the player i such that the values $(d_{ID}^1, \ldots, d_{ID}^n)$ form a (t, n)-threshold secret sharing of d_{ID}, where d_{ID} is the private key of ID. PKGs will use this algorithm to generate partial private key shares for all entities participating in the scheme and send the partial private key shares to their respective owners through a secure channel.

User-Secret-Key-Gen-and-Share: On input of **params** and user identity ID, n players jointly generate the user public key upk_{ID}, the user secret key share usk_{ID}^j, and the corresponding verification key share svk_i such that the values $(usk_{ID}^1, \ldots, usk_{ID}^n)$ form a (t, n)-threshold secret sharing of usk_{ID}.

Sign: On input of message $m \in \{0, 1\}^*$, player i signs m using its partial private key share d_{ID}^i and user secret key share usk_{ID}^i. Then, a dealer (selected at random from the presented players) combines t valid signature shares together and outputs a whole valid signature σ.

Verify: On input of params, user identity ID, user public key upk_{ID}, message m, and σ, it returns 1 for accept or 0 for reject.

Existential unforgeability. There are two types of security for a certificateless threshold signature scheme, type-I and type-II security, along with two types of adversaries, $\mathcal{A}_1$ and $\mathcal{A}_2$, respectively. Adversary $\mathcal{A}_1$ models a malicious adversary that compromises the user secret key usk_{ID} or replaces the user public key upk_{ID}; however, it cannot compromise the master secret key or get access to the private key d_{ID}. Adversary $\mathcal{A}_2$ models the malicious-but-passive KGC who controls the generation of the private key d_{ID}. The following are seven oracles that can be accessed by the adversaries:

1. **Create-User**: On input of an identity $u \in \{0,1\}^*$, if u has already been created, nothing is to be carried out. Otherwise, the oracle generates $(d_{ID}^1, \dots, d_{ID}^n)$ ←Partial-Key-Gen-and-Share (params, ID) and $(upk_{ID}, usk_{ID}^1, \dots,$ $usk_{ID}^n)$ ← User-Secret-Key-Gen-and-Share(params, ID). It then stores $(ID, upk_{ID},$ $d_{ID}^1, \dots, d_{ID}^n, usk_{ID}^1, \dots, usk_{ID}^n)$ into a list List. In both cases, upk_{ID} is returned.

2. **Partial-Private-Key-Extract**: On input of an identity ID, the oracle searches List for an corresponding entry to ID. If it is not found, $\perp$ is returned; otherwise, the corresponding $(d_{ID}^1, \dots, d_{ID}^n)$ is returned.

3. **Secret-Value-Extract**: On input of an identity ID, the oracle searches List for an corresponding entry to ID. If it is not found, $\perp$ is returned; otherwise, the corresponding $(usk_{ID}^1, \dots, usk_{ID}^n)$ is returned.

4. **Reveal-Corrupted-Player-Key-Share**: Let $\phi(\leq t-1)$ be the set of corrupted players corresponding to entry ID. For $i \in \phi$, the oracle is allowed to search List for player i's user secret key share usk_{ID}^i. Additionally, the oracle can ask for all the players' verification keys.

5. **Reveal-Corrupted-PKG-Key-Share**: Let $\psi(\leq t-1)$ be the set of corrupted PKGs. For $j \in \psi$, the oracle is allowed to search List for PKG_j's secret share.

6. **Public-Key-Replace**: On input of an identity ID and the corresponding user public/secret key $(\mathsf{upk}_{\mathsf{ID}}^*, \mathsf{usk}_{\mathsf{ID}}^{1*}, \ldots, \mathsf{usk}_{\mathsf{ID}}^{n*})$, the oracle searches List for the entry of ID. If it is not found, nothing will be carried. Otherwise, the oracle updates $(\mathsf{ID}, \mathsf{upk}_{\mathsf{ID}}, d_{\mathsf{ID}}^1, \ldots, d_{\mathsf{ID}}^n, \mathsf{usk}_{\mathsf{ID}}^1, \ldots, \mathsf{usk}_{\mathsf{ID}}^n)$ to $(\mathsf{ID}, \mathsf{upk}_{\mathsf{ID}}^*, d_{\mathsf{ID}}^1, \ldots, d_{\mathsf{ID}}^n, \mathsf{usk}_{\mathsf{ID}}^{1*}, \ldots, \mathsf{usk}_{\mathsf{ID}}^{n*})$. Note that it is unreasonable for the oracle to issue a **Partial-Private-Key-Extract** query, **Secret-Value-Extract** query, and **Reveal-Corrupted-Player-Key-Share** query on an identity ID whose public key has been replaced.

7. **Sign**: On input of an identity ID and a message $m \in \{0,1\}^*$, the signing oracle proceeds in one of the three cases below:

   a. A valid signature σ returned if ID has been created but the user public/secret key $(\mathsf{upk}_{\mathsf{ID}}, \mathsf{usk}_{\mathsf{ID}}^1, \ldots, \mathsf{usk}_{\mathsf{ID}}^n)$ has not been replaced.

   b. If ID has not been created, the oracle **Create-User** will be queried to create it.

   c. If the user public/secret key pair of u has been replaced with, say $(\mathsf{ID}, \mathsf{upk}_{\mathsf{ID}}^*, d_{\mathsf{ID}}^1, \ldots, d_{\mathsf{ID}}^n, \mathsf{usk}_{\mathsf{ID}}^{1*}, \ldots, \mathsf{usk}_{\mathsf{ID}}^{n*})$, then the oracle returns the result of $\mathrm{Sign}(d_{\mathsf{ID}}^1, \ldots, d_{\mathsf{ID}}^n, \mathsf{usk}_{\mathsf{ID}}^{1*}, \ldots, \mathsf{usk}_{\mathsf{ID}}^{n*}, m)$.

Remark: When querying the oracle **Public-Key-Replace**, $(\mathsf{usk}_{\mathsf{ID}}^{1*}, \ldots, \mathsf{usk}_{\mathsf{ID}}^{n*})$ can be a set of empty strings. In this case, this means that the user secret key is not provided. If $(\mathsf{usk}_{\mathsf{ID}}^{1*}, \ldots, \mathsf{usk}_{\mathsf{ID}}^{n*})$ is a set of empty strings and the original user secret key of an identity u is replaced with $(\mathsf{usk}_{\mathsf{ID}}^{1*}, \ldots, \mathsf{usk}_{\mathsf{ID}}^{n*})$, then the empty strings will be returned if the **Secret-Value-Extract** oracle is queried on ID. Also note that even if $(\mathsf{usk}_{\mathsf{ID}}^{1*}, \ldots, \mathsf{usk}_{\mathsf{ID}}^{n*})$ is not a set of empty strings, it does not mean that $(\mathsf{usk}_{\mathsf{ID}}^{1*}, \ldots, \mathsf{usk}_{\mathsf{ID}}^{n*})$ is the corresponding user secret key of $\mathsf{upk}_{\mathsf{ID}}^*$. Hence as mentioned, the signature generated by the signing oracle **Sign** will be an execution of Sign using the replaced user secret key $(\mathsf{usk}_{\mathsf{ID}}^{1*}, \ldots, \mathsf{usk}_{\mathsf{ID}}^{n*})$ regardless of the value of $\mathsf{upk}_{\mathsf{ID}}^*$. In other words, the signature may not be valid.

We define two games, one for $\mathcal{A}_1$ and the other for $\mathcal{A}_2$.

Game I: Let $\mathcal{S}_1$ be the game simulator/challenger and $k \in \mathbb{N}$ be a security parameter.

1. $\mathcal{S}_1$ chooses to corrupt a fixed set $\phi(\le t-1)$ of players and a fixed set $\psi(\le t-1)$ of PKGs.

2. $\mathcal{S}_1$ executes **Setup**(1^k) to get params.

3. $\mathcal{S}_1$ runs $\mathcal{A}_1$ as a subroutine and gives 1^k and params to $\mathcal{A}_1$. During the simulation, $\mathcal{A}_1$ can make queries to oracles **Create-User, Partial-Private-Key-Extract, Secret-Value-Extract, Reveal-Corrupted-Player-Key-Share, Public-Key-Replace, Reveal-Corrupted-PKG-Key-Share,** and **Sign.**

4. $\mathcal{A}_1$ outputs $(\mathsf{ID}^*, m^*, \sigma^*)$.

$\mathcal{A}_1$ wins if $\mathsf{Verify}(\mathsf{params}, \mathsf{ID}^*, \mathsf{upk}_{\mathsf{ID}^*}, m^*, \sigma^*) = 1$ for some created ID^*. There are several natural restrictions on $\mathcal{A}_1$:

1. The oracle **Sign** has never been queried with (ID^*, m^*).

2. $\mathcal{A}_1$ has never queried **RevealPartialKey**(ID^*) to get the private key shares $(d_{\mathsf{ID}}^{1*}, \ldots, d_{\mathsf{ID}}^{n*})$.

3. $\mathcal{A}_1$ has never queried **RevealUserSecretKey**(ID^*) to get the user secret key $(\mathsf{usk}_{\mathsf{ID}}^{1*}, \ldots, \mathsf{usk}_{\mathsf{ID}}^{n*})$.

4. $\mathcal{A}_1$ cannot extract the partial private key shares of corrupted PKGs and the user secret key shares of corrupted players if the user's public key has been replaced.

Game II: Let $\mathcal{S}_2$ be the game challenger and $k \in \mathbb{N}$ be a security parameter. There are two phases of interactions between $\mathcal{S}_2$ and $\mathcal{A}_2$.

1. $\mathcal{S}_2$ chooses to corrupt a fixed set $\phi(\le t-1)$ of players.

2. $\mathcal{S}_2$ executes $\mathcal{A}_2$ on input 1^k, which returns partial private key shares $(d_{\mathsf{ID}}^1, \ldots, d_{\mathsf{ID}}^n)$ to $\mathcal{A}_2$. Note that $\mathcal{A}_2$ cannot make any query at this stage.

3. During this stage of simulation, $\mathcal{A}_2$ can make queries to oracles **Secret-Value-Extract, Reveal-Corrupted-Player-Key-Share,** and **Sign.** $\mathcal{A}_2$ can also make queries to **Create-User.** Note that oracle **Partial-Private-Key-Extract** is not accessible and no longer needed as $\mathcal{A}_2$ has the partial private key

shares, and when $\mathcal{A}_2$ issues a query to the **Create-User** oracle, it has to additionally provide the partial private key shares $(d_{\mathsf{ID}}^1, \ldots, d_{\mathsf{ID}}^n)$.

4. At the end of this phase, $\mathcal{A}_2$ outputs a triple $(\mathsf{ID}^*, m^*, \sigma^*)$.

$\mathcal{A}_2$ wins if Verify(params, ID^*, $\mathsf{upk}_{\mathsf{ID}^*}$, m^*, σ^*) $= 1$ for some created ID^* and the oracle **Sign** has never been queried with (ID^*, m^*). One additional restriction is that $\mathcal{A}_2$ has never queried **Secret-Value-Extract**(u^*) to get the user secret key $(\mathsf{usk}_{\mathsf{ID}}^{1*}, \ldots, \mathsf{usk}_{\mathsf{ID}}^{n*})$ nor queried **Public-Key-Replace**() to replace the user public key $\mathsf{upk}_{\mathsf{ID}^*}$.

Definition 9.5 *A certificateless threshold signature scheme is existentially unforgeable under an adaptive chosen-message attack iff the success probability of any polynomially bounded adversary in* **game I** *and* **game II** *is negligible.*

9.5.3   Xiong-Li-Qin Scheme

In this section, Xiong et al.'s [315] certificateless threshold signature scheme based on Paterson and Schuldt's ID-based signature scheme [148] is presented. The following shows the details of our scheme:

Setup: Let $\mathbb{G}_1$ and $\mathbb{G}_2$ be two cyclic groups of prime order p. Let g and h be generators of $\mathbb{G}_1$ where $\log_g h$ is unknown, and $\hat{e}$ be a bilinear map such that $\hat{e} : \mathbb{G}_1 \times \mathbb{G}_1 \to \mathbb{G}_2$. In the following, all identities and messages will be assumed to be bit strings of length n_{ID} and n_m, respectively. To construct a more flexible scheme that allows identities and messages of arbitrary lengths, collision-resistant hash functions, $H_{\mathsf{ID}} : \{0,1\}^* \to \{0,1\}^{n_{\mathsf{ID}}}$ and $H_m : \{0,1\}^* \to \{0,1\}^{n_m}$, can be defined and used to create identities and messages of the desired length. Choose $g_2 \leftarrow_R \mathbb{G}_1$. Furthermore, pick elements $u', m' \leftarrow_R \mathbb{G}_1$ and vectors $\mathbf{U} = (u_i), \mathbf{M} = (m_i)$ of length n_{ID} and n_m, respectively, whose entries are random elements from $\mathbb{G}_1$. The public parameters are params=$(\mathbb{G}_1, \mathbb{G}_2, \hat{e}, g, h, g_2, u', \mathbf{U}, m', \mathbf{M})$.

Partial-Key-Gen-and-Share: Let ID be a bit string of length n_{ID} representing an identity and let $\mathsf{ID}[i]$ be the i-th bit of ID. Define $\mathcal{U} \subset \{1, \ldots, n_{\mathsf{ID}}\}$ to be the set of indices i such that $\mathsf{ID}[i] = 1$.

1. In order to generate a partial private key $\mathsf{psk}_{\mathsf{ID}} = (\mathsf{psk}_{\mathsf{ID}1}, \mathsf{psk}_{\mathsf{ID}2}) = (g_2^\alpha (u' \prod_{i \in \mathcal{U}} u_i)^r, g^r)$, each partial private key generator PKG_i performs interactively as follows:

   a. PKG_i chooses two random polynomials $f_i(z)$ and $g_i(z)$ over Z_p of degree $t - 1$: $f_i(z) = a_{i0} + a_{i1}z + \cdots + a_{i,t-1}z^{t-1}$, $g_i(z) = b_{i0} + b_{i1}z + \cdots + b_{i,t-1}z^{t-1}$. Let $z_i = a_{i0} = f_i(0)$. PKG_i broadcasts $C_{il} = g^{a_{il}} h^{b_{il}} \bmod p$ for $l = 0, \ldots, t - 1$. PKG_i computes the shares $s_{ij} = f_i(j)$, $s'_{ij} = g_i(j) \bmod p$ for $j = 1, \ldots, n$ and sends s_{ij}, s'_{ij} to PKG_j.

   b. Each PKG_j verifies the shares he/she received from the other PKGs. For each $i = 1, \ldots, n$, PKG_j checks if $g^{s_{ij}} h^{s'_{ij}} = \prod_{l=0}^{t-1} (C_{il})^{j^l} \bmod p$. If the verification is not passed, then PKG_j broadcasts a complaint to PKG_i.

   c. Each PKG_i who received a complaint from PKG_j broadcasts the values s_{ij}, s'_{ij}. Otherwise, PKG_i is disqualified.

   d. Each PKG_i marks as disqualified any PKG_j that either received more than $t - 1$ complaints in Step 1 or answered a complaint in Step 1 with invalid values.

   e. Each PKG_i then builds the same set of nondisqualified PKGs $\mathrm{QUAL}_{\mathrm{PKG}}$ and sets his/her secret share as $\alpha_i = \sum_{j \in \mathrm{QUAL}_{\mathrm{PKG}}} s_{ji} \bmod p$ and the value r_i to $\sum_{j \in \mathrm{QUAL}_{\mathrm{PKG}}} s'_{ji} \bmod p$. The distributed master secret α is not explicitly computed by any party, but it equals $\sum_{i \in \mathrm{QUAL}_{\mathrm{PKG}}} z_i \bmod p$. Then PKG_i computes the partial private key share $\mathsf{psk}_{\mathsf{ID}}^i = (\mathsf{psk}_{\mathsf{ID}1}^i, \mathsf{psk}_{\mathsf{ID}2}^i) = (g_2^{\alpha_i} (u' \prod_{i \in \mathcal{U}} u_i)^{r_i}, g^{r_i})$ and transmits to the corresponding player i secretly.

2. PKGs generate the public key $Y (= \hat{e}(g_2, g_1))$, where $g_1 = g^\alpha$) and the first verification key share $fvk_i (= \hat{e}(g_2, g)^{\alpha_i})$ for $i \in \mathrm{QUAL}_{\mathrm{PKG}}$.

   a. Each PKG_i broadcasts $A_{il} = \hat{e}(g_2, g)^{a_{il}} \bmod p$ for $l = 0, \ldots, t - 1$.

   b. PKG_j verifies the values broadcast by the other PKGs; PKG_j checks if $\hat{e}(g_2, g)^{s_{ij}} = \prod_{l=0}^{t-1} (A_{il})^{j^l} \bmod p$ for $i \in \mathrm{QUAL}_{\mathrm{PKG}}$. If the check fails for an index i, PKG_j complains against PKG_i by broadcasting the values s_{ij}, s'_{ij}.

c. Each PKG_i in QUAL_{PKG} can compute and publish public parameter $Y = \prod_{j \in \text{QUAL}_{\text{PKG}}} A_{j0} \bmod p$ and $fvk_i = \hat{e}(g_2, g)^{\alpha_i} = \prod_{j \in \text{QUAL}_{\text{PKG}}} \prod_{l=0}^{t-1} (A_{jl})^{i^l} \bmod p$.

3. After receiving the partial private key shares $\mathsf{psk}_{\text{ID}}^i$ from the PKG_i, player i checks if the following equation holds:

$$\hat{e}(\mathsf{psk}_{\text{ID1}}^i, g) = \hat{e}\left(psk_{\text{ID2}}^i, u' \prod_{l \in \mathcal{U}} u_l\right) \cdot fvk_i$$

If the check fails, player i broadcasts a complaint against PKG_i.

User-Secret-Key-Gen-and-Share: 1. To generate the user secret key $\mathsf{usk}_{\text{ID}} = x$, each player i performs interactively as follows:

a. Player i chooses two random polynomials $f_i(z)$ and $g_i(z)$ over Z_p of degree $t - 1$: $f_i(z) = a_{i0} + a_{i1}z + \cdots + a_{i,t-1}z^{t-1}$, $g_i(z) = b_{i0} + b_{i1}z + \cdots + b_{i,t-1}z^{t-1}$. Let $z_i = a_{i0} = f_i(0)$. Player i broadcasts $C_{il} = g^{a_{il}} h^{b_{il}} \bmod p$ for $l = 0, \ldots, t-1$. Player i computes the shares $s_{ij} = f_i(j)$, $s'_{ij} = g_i(j) \bmod p$ for $j = 1, \ldots, n$ and sends s_{ij}, s'_{ij} to player j.

b. Each player j verifies the shares he/she received from the other players. For each $i = 1, \ldots, n$, player j checks if $g^{s_{ij}} h^{s'_{ij}} = \prod_{l=0}^{t-1} (C_{il})^{j^l} \bmod p$. If the verification is not passed, player j broadcasts a complaint to player i.

c. Each player i who received a complaint from player j broadcasts the values s_{ij}, s'_{ij}. Otherwise, player i is disqualified.

d. Each player i marks as disqualified any player j that either received more than $t - 1$ complaints in Step 1 or answered a complaint in Step 1 with invalid values.

e. Each player i then builds the same set of non-disqualified players $\text{QUAL}_{\text{player}}$ and sets his/her user secret key share as $x_i = \sum_{j \in QUAL_{player}} s_{ji} \bmod p$. The distributed user secret key x is not explicitly computed by any player, but it equals $\sum_{i \in QUAL_{player}} z_i \bmod p$.

2. Players generate the user public key $\mathsf{upk}_{\mathsf{ID}}(= \hat{e}(g_2, g_1)^x)$ and the second verification key share $svk_i(= \hat{e}(g_2, g_1)^{x_i})$, where $i \in QUAL_{player}$, interactively as follows:

   a. Each player i broadcasts $A_{il} = Y^{a_{il}} = \hat{e}(g_2, g_1)^{a_{il}} \bmod p$ for $l = 0, \ldots, t - 1$.

   b. Player j verifies the values broadcast by the other players; player j checks if $Y^{s_{ij}} = \prod_{l=0}^{t-1}(A_{il})^{j^l} \bmod p$ for $i \in QUAL_{player}$. If the check fails for an index i, player j complains against player i by broadcasting the values s_{ij}, s'_{ij}.

   c. Each player i can compute and publish user public key $\mathsf{upk}_{\mathsf{ID}} = \prod_{j \in QUAL_{player}} A_{j0} \bmod p$ and $svk_i = \hat{e}(g_2, g_1)^{x_i} = \prod_{j \in QUAL_{player}} \prod_{l=0}^{t-1}(A_{jl})^{i^l} \bmod p$.

Sign: Let m be a bit string representing a message and $\mathcal{M} \subset \{1, \ldots, n_m\}$ be the set of indices j such that $m[j] = 1$, where $m[j]$ is the j-th bit of m.

1. Each player i picks $r_\pi^i, r_m^i \leftarrow_R \mathbb{Z}_p$, computes $U = u' \prod_{i \in \mathcal{U}} u_i$, and broadcasts

$$\sigma'_i = \left(\mathsf{psk}_{\mathsf{ID}1}^i(U)^{r_\pi^i}\left(m' \prod_{j \in \mathcal{M}} m_j\right)^{r_m^i}, \mathsf{psk}_{\mathsf{ID}2}^i g^{r_\pi^i}, g^{r_m^i}\right) = (V'_i, R'_{\pi i}, R'_{mi})$$

2. On input of $\sigma'_i = (V'_i, R'_{\pi i}, R'_{mi})$ and first verification key fvk_i, each member j checks if the following equation holds:

$$\hat{e}(V'_i, g) = fvk_i \cdot \hat{e}(U, R'_{\pi i})\hat{e}\left(m' \prod_{i \in \mathcal{M}} m_i, R'_{mi}\right)$$

for $i \neq j$. If the check fails, member j broadcasts a complaint against player i.

3. Let $\lambda'_1, \ldots, \lambda'_t \in \mathbb{Z}_p$ be the Lagrange coefficients so that $\alpha = \sum_{i=1}^{t} \lambda'_i \alpha_i$. Without loss of generality we assume that player $i = 1, \ldots, t$ were used to generate the shares. Each member j computes and publishes the partial signature as follows:

$$\sigma' = \left(\prod_{i=1}^{t}(V_i)^{\lambda'_i}, \prod_{i=1}^{t}(R_{\pi i})^{\lambda'_i}, \prod_{i=1}^{t}(R_{mi})^{\lambda'_i}\right) = (V', R'_\pi, R'_m)$$

4. On input of the partial signature $\sigma' = (V', R'_\pi, R'_m)$, player i computes and publishes the complete signature share as follows:

$$\sigma_i = ((V')^{x_i}, (R'_\pi)^{x_i}, (R'_m)^{x_i}) = (V_i, R_{\pi i}, R_{mi})$$

5. On input of $\sigma_i = (V_i, R_{\pi i}, R_{mi})$ and second verification key svk_i, each player j checks if the following equation holds:

$$\hat{e}(V_i, g) = svk_i \cdot \hat{e}(U, R_{\pi i})\hat{e}\left(m' \prod_{i \in \mathcal{M}} m_i, R_{mi}\right)$$

If the check fails, player j broadcasts a complaint against player i.

6. Let $\lambda_1, \ldots, \lambda_t \in \mathbb{Z}_p$ be the Lagrange coefficients so that $x = \sum_{i=1}^{t} \lambda_i x_i$. The signature of u on message m can be computed as follows:

$$\sigma = \left(\prod_{i=1}^{t}(V_i)^{\lambda_i}, \prod_{i=1}^{t}(R_{\pi i})^{\lambda_i}, \prod_{i=1}^{t}(R_{mi})^{\lambda_i}\right) = (V, R_\pi, R_m)$$

Verify: Given a signature $\sigma = (V, R_\pi, R_m)$ on message m of ID, the verifier checks if the following equation holds:

$$\hat{e}(V, g) = \mathsf{upk} \cdot \hat{e}(U, R_\pi)\hat{e}\left(m' \prod_{i \in \mathcal{M}} m_i, R_m\right)$$

It outputs 1 if it is valid. Otherwise, it outputs 0.

9.5.4   Analysis

We will prove that Xiong et al.'s certificateless signature scheme is existentially unforgeable against type I and II adversaries, in the standard model, given that the CDH problem is hard.

Wang et al. [313] defined the simulatability of a certificateless threshold signature and proved the relationship between the security of a certificateless threshold signature and that of the corresponding underlying nonthreshold ID-based signature. From these results, we can obtain Theorem 9.8.

Definition 9.6 [313] *A certificateless threshold signature scheme is said to be simulatable if the following conditions hold:*

1. *The partial private key distribution is simulatable: given the system parameters* params *and the identity* ID, *there exists a simulator* SIM_p *that can simulate the view of the adversary on an execution of partial private key distribution.*

2. *The user secret key distribution is simulatable: given the system parameters* params *and the identity* ID, *there exists a simulator* SIM_u *that can simulate the view of the adversary on an execution of user secret key distribution.*

3. *The threshold signature generation is simulatable: given the system parameters* params, *the identity* ID, *the message* m, *the corresponding signature* σ, $t - 1$ *shares of the partial private key and user secret key that matches to* u *of the corrupted members, and the corresponding verification keys, there is a simulator* SIM_s *that can simulate the view of the adversary on an execution of threshold signature generation.*

Definition 9.7 (Robustness) *A certificateless threshold signature scheme is said to be robust if it computes a correct output even in the presence of a malicious attacker that makes the corrupted PKGs and the corrupted signature generation players deviate from the normal execution.*

Theorem 9.6 [313] *If a certificateless threshold signature scheme is simulatable and the corresponding ID-based signature scheme is EUF-IDS-CMA2 secure, then the certificateless threshold signature scheme is EUF-CLTS-CMA2 secure. More precisely, we have*

$$\mathrm{Succ}_{\mathrm{CLTS}}^{\mathrm{EUF\text{-}CLTS\text{-}CMA2}}(t, q_C, q_S) \leq \mathrm{Succ}_{\mathrm{IDS}}^{\mathrm{EUF\text{-}IDS\text{-}CMA2}}(t', q_C', q_S')$$
$$t' = t + t_{SIM_p} + t_{SIM_u} + t_{SIM_s}, \; q_C = q_C', \; q_S = 1$$

where $\mathrm{Succ}_{\mathrm{IDS}}^{\mathrm{EUF\text{-}IDS\text{-}CMA2}}(t', q_C', q_S')$ *is the maximum of the attacker* $\mathcal{A}_{IDS}$*'s success over all attackers having running time* t' *and making at most* q_C' *partial private key extraction and user secret key extraction queries and at most* q_S' *signature generation queries. Here,* t_{SIM_p}, t_{SIM_u}, *and* t_{SIM_s} *denote the running time of the simulators* SIM_p, SIM_u, *and* SIM_s, *respectively.*

As mentioned in [148], Paterson and Schuldts' scheme was proven in the standard model and rested on the hardness of the CDH problem.

Lemma 9.6 *The process of partial private key distribution of the proposed scheme is simulatable.*

Proof 9.7 *Without loss of generality, we assume that the PKGs corrupted by the adversary are PKG_i, where $1 \leq i \leq t-1$. Given the system parameters* params *and the identity* ID, *the adversary picks $\alpha_1, \ldots, \alpha_{t-1}$ at random from $\mathbb{Z}_p$ and computes $fvk_i = \hat{e}(g_2, g^{\alpha_i})$ for $i = 1, \ldots, t-1$. Note that $Y = \hat{e}(g_2, g)^{\alpha} = \hat{e}(g_2, g)^{\sum_{i=1}^{t} \lambda_i \alpha_i}$, where $\lambda_1, \ldots, \lambda_t$ are the Lagrange coefficients. So the adversary can compute $fvk_t = \hat{e}(g_2, g)^{\alpha_t}$ and the simulated value is correct and identical to the PKG_t as the real execution of "partial private key distribution."*

Lemma 9.7 *The process of user secret key distribution of the proposed scheme is simulatable.*

Proof 9.8 *Without loss of generality, the players indexed $1, \ldots, t-1$ have been corrupted by the adversary. Also, assume that the user public key* upk $= \hat{e}(g_1, g_2)^x$ *is provided as input to the adversary. First, we pick $x_1, \ldots, x_{t-1}$ at random from $\mathbb{Z}_p$ and compute $svk_i = Y^{x_i} = \hat{e}(g_2, g_1)^{x_i}$ for $i = 1, \ldots, t-1$. Due to* upk $= \hat{e}(g_1, g_2)^x = \hat{e}(g, g_2)^{\sum_{i=1}^{t} \lambda'_{ji} \cdot x_i}$ *(λ'_{ji} is the Lagrange interpolation coefficient), the adversary can compute $svk_t = \hat{e}(g_2, g_1)^{x_t}$. The simulated svk_t is correct and identically distributed to the one in the real execution of the "user secret key distribution."*

Lemma 9.8 *The process of signing of the proposed scheme is simulatable.*

Proof 9.9 *On input of the public parameters, the user identity* ID, *the message m, the corresponding signature σ, partial signature σ', $t-1$ partial private key shares $(\mathsf{psk}_{ID}^1, \ldots, \mathsf{psk}_{ID}^{t-1})$ and user secret key shares $(x_1, \ldots, x_{t-1})$ of the corrupted players, the adversary picks $r_\pi^i, r_m^i \leftarrow_R \mathbb{Z}_p$ and computes $\sigma'_i = (\mathsf{psk}_{ID1}^i (u' \prod_{i \in \mathcal{U}} u_i)^{r_\pi^i} (m' \prod_{j \in \mathcal{M}} m_j)^{r_m^i}, \mathsf{psk}_{ID2}^i g^{r_\pi^i}, g^{r_m^i}) = (V'_i, R'_{\pi i}, R'_{mi})$ for $1 \leq i \leq t-1$. From the partial signature $\sigma' = (V', R'_\pi, R'_m)$ and σ'_i for $1 \leq i \leq t-1$, the adversary generates $\sigma'_j = \sigma' / \prod_{i=1}^{t-1} (\sigma'_i)^{\lambda_{j,i}}$ for $j = t, \ldots, n$, with known Lagrange interpolation coefficients $\lambda_{j,i}$. Furthermore, the adversary computes $\sigma_i = ((V')^{x_i}, (R'_\pi)^{x_i}, (R'_m)^{x_i}) =$*

$(V_i, R_{\pi i}, R_{mi})$ *for* $1 \leq i \leq t - 1$. *Due to the signature* $\sigma = (\prod_{i=1}^{t}(V_i)^{\lambda'_{ji}}, \prod_{i=1}^{t}(R_{\pi i})^{\lambda'_{ji}}, \prod_{i=1}^{t}(R_{mi})^{\lambda'_{ji}})$ *(*λ'_{ji} *is the Lagrange interpolation coefficient), the adversary can compute* $\sigma_t = \sigma/\prod_{i=1}^{t-1}(\sigma_i)^{\lambda'_{ji}}$. *The simulated* $\sigma'_i, \sigma_i(t \leq i \leq n)$ *is correct and identically distributed to the one in the real execution of the "signing."*

Theorem 9.7 [313] *The proposed implementation of certificateless threshold signature is robust, that is, the scheme runs correctly even in the presence of a malicious adversary that makes the corrupted players deviate from their normal execution.*

Proof 9.10 *The robustness is evident. Combining Theorem 9.6, Lemmas 9.6, 9.7, and 9.8, the unforgeability of Paterson and Schuldts' scheme from [148], and corresponding robustness, we obtain the following theorem.*

Theorem 9.8 *Our proposed certificateless threshold signature is existentially unforgeable against adaptive chosen-message attacks in the standard model and its security rests on the hardness of the CDH problem.*

CHAPTER 10

Comparisons between CL-PKC, SGC-PKC, and CB-PKC

I N PARALLEL to certificateless public-key cryptography (CL-PKC), two alternative solutions, named certificate-based public-key cryptosystem (CB-PKC) [31,55] and self-certified public-key cryptosystem (SC-PKC) [32,318], have been introduced to enjoy the good aspects of identity-based public-key cryptography (ID-PKC) and traditional public-key cryptography (PKC) together. To some extent, these solutions are structurally similar to CL-PKC. As for CB-PKC, the public and private key pair of the user is calculated by the user himself/herself and a corresponding certificate of his/her public key is requested from a trusted certificate authority (CA). On one hand, the certificate can guarantee the connection between the user and his/her public key as in traditional PKC. On the other hand, this certificate in CB-PKC acts as part of the user's private key such that cryptographic operations such as signing or decrypting can only be performed by using the user's private key and certificate together. Featuring implicit certification, CB-PKC revokes the need for third-party queries in traditional PKC, and thus simplifies the complex certificate management. Also, CB-PKC does not inherit the key escrow problem from ID-PKC since the private key is generated and kept by the user himself/herself.

Similar to CL-PKC and CB-PKC, SC-PKC enables a user in the system to calculate his/her secret key and corresponding public key himself/herself. After that, the user's public key and identity will be

TABLE 10.1   Properties of Related Paradigms

	Implicit Certificates	Escrow Free	Secure Channel
Traditional PKI	×	✓	×
ID-PKC	✓	×	✓
CL-PKC	✓	✓	✓
CB-PKC	✓	✓	×
SC-PKC	✓	✓	×

sent to a trusted authority (TA), who in turn generates a witness to bind the user's public key and identity. Combining the witness from TA, the public parameters of TA, and the user's identity, the public key of the user can be easily recovered. In this way, the complex certificates in traditional PKC can also be simplified since SC-PKC offers the implicit certificate with the support of a witness and the identity. Furthermore, the key escrow problem has been avoided since the secret key is generated by the user himself/herself. The main difference between CL-PKC, CB-PKC, and SC-PKC rests on the fact that only a secure channel is needed during the distribution of the partial private key in CL-PKC, while the secure channel in CB-PKC and SC-PKC to deliver the certificate and witness is eliminated. A comparison between related paradigms can be found in Table 10.1. Due to the similarity between CL-PKC, CB-PKC, and SC-PKC, the transformation between these paradigms has received a lot of attention from the cryptographic community [52,55,319].

V

Future Directions

CHAPTER 11

Perspectives

I N THIS BOOK, the basic paradigms and principles of certificate-less cryptography are presented. We particularly discussed the formal definitions of certificateless encryption/certificateless signature (CLE/CLS) schemes followed by an examination and ranking of existing security models according to the adversaries' capabilities. After that, the design philosophy and the security proof of typical CLE, CLS, and certificateless authenticated key agreement (CL-AKA) schemes secure in the standard model and random oracle model have been analyzed, respectively, along with a brief introduction to the random oracle model. In addition, some applications of certificateless public-key encryption (CL-PKC) in scenarios such as anonymous communication, wireless body area networks (WBANs) and cloud computing, and extensions of CL-PKC have also been investigated. Moreover, we illustrated a comparison between the CL-PKC, certificate-based public-key cryptosystem (CB-PKC), and self-certified public-key cryptosystem (SC-PKC) paradigms.

The CL-PKC field contains a multitude of formal definitions and security models, which obscures a global view of CL-PKC. This book is a first attempt to cut through the obscurity and structure of the knowledge in this field. The proposed taxonomies are intended to help the community think about the open problems we face and possible future works. The proposed taxonomies are by no means complete and all-encompassing. New constructions, extensions, and applications will appear, some of which we cannot yet imagine. Innovative approaches to CL-PKC design will be discovered. They will also offer new design features carrying their share of benefits and weaknesses. We expect these taxonomies to offer a foundation for classifying design, analysis, and application in the CL-PKC field. As the field grows, the taxonomies will also grow and be refreshed.

Considering the problems existing in CL-PKC, some possible future work is summarized as follows:

Constructing efficient CLE, CLS, and CL-AKA schemes secure in the standard model still remains an interesting and challenging problem in the literature. Despite several constructions being given without resorting to the random oracle model, all of these schemes are impractical due to the following reasons: the security of these schemes rests on a relatively small set of strong complexity assumptions and the existing schemes secure in the standard model are currently regarded as not being efficient enough. Thus, it is interesting and challenging to design efficient CL-PKC schemes in the standard model.

Bearing quantum computing in the mind, it is natural to construct CL-PKC schemes provably secure against quantum attacks. Unfortunately omitted in the literature is any discussion of CL-PKC schemes based on specific, nonnumber-theoretic assumptions including those based on knapsacks, lattices, coding theory, or polynomial equations. To make matters worse, the only existing CLE scheme secure against quantum attack suffers from a long public parameters size [72]. Thus, one open problem is finding efficient CL-PKC schemes secure even for the postquantum world.

Identifying the relationships between the CL-PKC schemes and other primitives is regarded as another open problem. Until now, generic constructions of CLE schemes could be directly derived from any identity-based encryption (IBE) scheme and public-key encryption scheme or from an ID-based key agreement protocol. It is natural to identify whether CL-PKC schemes can be inherited from other existing primitives. In this way, the achievements in the other primitives can be enjoyed in the CL-PKC field.

Finding new applications for CL-PKC also is an interesting open problem. CL-PKC has been considered one of the most important primitives to reduce the trust on the private key generator (PKG) in the ID-PKC setting. Up to now, ID-PKC has been applied in different scenarios, for example, vehicular ad hoc networks, cloud computing, and the Internet of Things [320], due to its unique features. Therefore, it is desirable to apply CL-PKC in these environments where a fully trusted PKG is hard to find.

References

[1] A. J. Menezes, P. C. Oorschot, and S. A. Vanstone. *Handbook of Applied Cryptography*. CRC Press, Boca Raton, Florida, 1996.

[2] H. Delfs and H. Knebl. *Introduction to Cryptography: Principles and Applications*. Springer, Heidelberg, Germany, 2007.

[3] J. Katz. *Digital Signatures*. Springer, Heidelberg, Germany, 2010.

[4] W. Diffie and M. E. Hellman. New directions in cryptography. *IEEE Transactions on Information Theory*, 22(6):644–654, 1976.

[5] S. D. Galbraith. *Mathematics of Public Key Cryptography*. Cambridge University Press, Cambridge, UK, 2012.

[6] R. L. Rivest, A. Shamir, and L. Adleman. A method for obtaining digital signatures and public-key cryptosystems. *Communications of the ACM*, 21(2):120–126, 1978.

[7] P. Gutmann. PKI: It's not dead, just resting. *IEEE Computer*, 35(8):41–49, 2002.

[8] A. Shamir. Identity-based cryptosystems and signature schemes. In *Advances in Cryptology-Crypto '84*, pages 47–53. Springer Press, 1984.

[9] D. Boneh and M. Franklin. Identity-based encryption from the Weil pairing. In *Advances in Cryptology-CRYPTO 2001*, pages 213–229. Springer, 2001.

[10] C. Cocks. An identity based encryption scheme based on quadratic residues. In *B. Honary (Ed.): Cryptography and Coding 2001*, pages 360–363. Springer, 2001.

[11] S. Chatterjee and P. Sarkar. *Identity-Based Encryption.* Springer, Heidelberg, Germany, 2011.

[12] L. Martin. *Introduction to Identity-Based Encryption.* Artech House, Massachusetts, Norwood, Boston, 2008.

[13] A. Kate and I. Goldberg. Distributed private-key generators for identity-based cryptography. In *7th International Conference on Security and Cryptography for Networks-SCN 2010*, pages 436–453. Springer, 2010.

[14] V. Goyal. Reducing trust in the PKG in identity based cryptosystems. In *Advances in Cryptology-CRYPTO 2007*, pages 430–447. Springer, 2007.

[15] V. Goyal, S. Lu, A. Sahai, and B. Waters. Black-box accountable authority identity-based encryption. In *15th ACM Conference on Computer and Communications Security (CCS 2008)*, pages 427–436. ACM, 2008.

[16] S. S. M. Chow. Removing escrow from identity-based encryption. In *12th International Conference on Practice and Theory in Public Key Cryptography-PKC 2009*, pages 256–276. Springer, 2009.

[17] S.S. Al-Riyami and K.G. Paterson. Certificateless public key cryptography. In *Advances in Cryptology-ASIACRYPT 2003*, pages 452–473. Springer, 2003.

[18] A. W. Dent. A survey of certificateless encryption schemes and security models. *International Journal of Information Security*, 7(5):349–377, 2008.

[19] Z. Zhang, D. S. Wong, J. Xu, and D. Feng. Certificateless public-key signature: Security model and efficient construction. In *4th International Conference on Applied Cryptography and Network Security (ACNS 2006)*, pages 293–308. Springer Press, 2006.

[20] X. Huang, Y. Mu, W. Susilo, D. S. Wong, and W. Wu. Certificateless signatures: New schemes and security models. *The Computer Journal*, 55(4):457–474, 2012.

[21] L. Zhang, B. Qin, Q. Wu, and F. Zhang. Efficient many-to-one authentication with certificateless aggregate signatures. *Computer Networks*, 54(14):2482–2491, 2010.

[22] D. Catalano, D. Fiore, and R. Gennaro. Certificateless onion routing. In *Proceedings of the 16th ACM Conference on Computer and Communications Security (CCS 2009)*, pages 151–160. ACM Press, 2009.

[23] S. Heo, Z. Kim, and K. Kim. Certificateless authenticated group key agreement protocol for dynamic groups. In *Global Telecommunications Conference (GLOBECOM '07)*, pages 464–468. IEEE, 2007.

[24] J. Liu, Z. Zhang, X. Chen, and K. S. Kwak. Certificateless remote anonymous authentication schemes for wireless body area networks. *IEEE Transactions on Parallel and Distributed System*, 25(2):332–342, 2014.

[25] S. H. Seo, M. Nabeel, X. Ding, and E. Bertino. An efficient certificateless encryption for secure data sharing in public clouds. *IEEE Transactions on Knowledge and Data Engineering*, 26(9): 2107–2119, 2014.

[26] J. Song, Y. Zhuang, J. Pan, and L. Cai. Certificateless secure upload for drive-thru Internet. In *IEEE International Conference on Communications (ICC 2011)*, pages 1–6. IEEE Press, 2011.

[27] J. Teng and C. Wu. A provable authenticated certificateless group key agreement with constant rounds. *Journal of Communications and Networks*, 14(1):104–110, 2012.

[28] B. Wang, B. Li, H. Li, and F. Li. Certificateless public auditing for data integrity in the cloud. In *2013 IEEE Conference on Communications and Network Security (CNS 2013)*, pages 136–144. IEEE Press, 2013.

[29] Z. Zhang, W. Susilo, and R. Raad. Mobile ad-hoc network key management with certificateless cryptography. In *2nd International Conference on Signal Processing and Communication Systems (ICSPCS 2008)*, pages 1–10. IEEE Press, 2008.

[30] L. Zhang, Q. Wu, B. Qin, H. Deng, J. Liu, and W. Shi. Provably secure certificateless authenticated asymmetric group key agreement. In *10th International Conference on Information Security Practice and Experience (ISPEC 2014)*, pages 496–510. Springer Press, 2014.

[31] C. Gentry. Certificate-based encryption and the certificate revocation problem. In *Advances in Cryptology-EUROCRYPT 2003*, pages 272–293. Springer, 2003.

[32] M. Girault. Self-certified public keys. In *Advances in Cryptology-EUROCRYPT 1991*, pages 490–497. Springer, 1992.

[33] L. LeVeque. *Fundamentals of Number Theory*. New edition. Dover Publications, Mineola, New York, 1996.

[34] V. Shoup. *A Computational Introduction to Number Theory and Algebra*. Cambridge University Press, Cambridge, UK, 2008.

[35] D. Hankerson, A. Menezes, and S. Vanstone. *Guide to Elliptic Curve Cryptography*. Springer, Heidelberg, Germany, 2012.

[36] P. Barreto, H. Kim, B. Bynn, and M. Scott. Efficient algorithms for pairing-based cryptosystems. In *Advances in Cryptology-CRYPTO 2002*, pages 354–369. Springer, 2002.

[37] T. ElGamal. A public key cryptosystem and a signature scheme based on discrete logarithms. *IEEE Transactions on Information Theory*, 31(4):469–472, 1985.

[38] C. P. Schnorr. Efficient identification and signatures for smart cards. In *Advances in Cryptology-Crypto '89*, pages 239–252. Springer Press, 1984.

[39] NIST. Digital Signature Standard (DSS). In *Federal Information Processing Standards (FIPS PUB 186-4)*, National Institute of Standards and Technology, Gaithersburg, MD, 1993.

[40] J. C. Cha and J. H. Cheon. An identity-based signature from gap Diffie-Hellman groups. In *6th International Workshop on Theory and Practice in Public Key Cryptography (Public Key Cryptography-PKC 2003)*, pages 18–30. Springer Press, 2003.

[41] M. Bellare, C. Namprempre, and G. Neven. Security proofs for identity-based identification and signature schemes. In *Advances in Cryptology-EuroCrypt 2004*, pages 268–286. Springer, 2004.

[42] J. Katz and Y. Lindell. *Introduction to Modern Cryptography*. CRC Press, Boca Raton, Florida, 2007.

[43] J. Stern. Why provable security matters? In *Advances in Cryptology-EUROCRYPT*, pages 449–461. Springer Press, 2003.

[44] S. Goldwasser and S. Micali. Probabilistic encryption. *Journal of Computer and System Sciences*, 28(2):270–299, 1984.

[45] R. Cramer and V. Shoup. A practical public key cryptosystem provably secure against adaptive chosen ciphertext attack. In *Advances in Cryptology-CRYPTO*, pages 13–25. Springer, 1998.

[46] M. Naor and M. Yung. Public-key cryptosystems provably secure against chosen ciphertext attacks. In *Proceedings of the 22nd Annual ACM Symposium on Theory of Computing (STOC 1990)*, pages 427–437, 1990.

[47] S. Goldwasser, S. Micali, and R. L. Rivest. A digital signature scheme secure against adaptive chosen-message attacks. *SIAM Journal on Computing*, 17(2):281–308, 1988.

[48] S.S. Al-Riyami. Cryptographic schemes based on elliptic curve pairings. Ph.D. thesis, Royal Holloway, University of London, pages 1–277. www.isg.rhul.ac.uk/kp/theses/SARthesis.pdf, 2004.

[49] Q. Huang and D. S. Wong. On the relation among various security models for certificateless cryptography. *International Journal of Applied Cryptography*, 1(2):108–119, 2008.

[50] B. C. Hu, D. S. Wong, Z. Zhang, and X. Deng. Key replacement attack against a generic construction of certificateless signature. In *11th Australasian Conference on Information Security and Privacy (ACISP 2006)*, pages 235–246. IEEE, 2006.

[51] J. Baek, R. Safavi-Naini, and W. Susilo. Certificateless public key encryption without pairing. In *8th International Conference on Information Security (ISC 2005)*, pages 134–148. Springer, 2005.

[52] S. S. Al-Riyami and K. G. Paterson. CBE from CL-PKE: A generic construction and efficient schemes. In *8th International Workshop on Theory and Practice in Public Key Cryptography-PKC 2005*, pages 398–415. Springer, 2005.

[53] K. Bentahar, P. Farshim, J. Malone-Lee, and N. P. Smart. Generic constructions of identity-based and certificateless KEMs. *Journal of Cryptology*, 21(2):178–199, 2008.

[54] A. W. Dent, B. Libert, and K. G. Paterson. Certificateless encryption schemes strongly secure in the standard model. In *The 11th International Workshop on Practice and Theory in Public Key Cryptography (PKC 2008)*, pages 344–359. Springer, 2008.

[55] W. Gao, G. Wang, X. Wang, and K. Chen. Generic construction of certificate-based encryption from certificateless encryption revisited. *The Computer Journal*, 58(10):2747–2757, 2015.

[56] Q. Huang and D. S. Wong. Generic certificateless encryption in the standard model. In *Advances in Information and Computer Security, Second International Workshop on Security (IWSEC 2007)*, pages 278–291. Springer, 2007.

[57] Q. Huang and D. S. Wong. Generic certificateless key encapsulation mechanism. In *12th Australasian Conference on Information Security and Privacy (ACISP 2007)*, pages 215–229. Springer, 2007.

[58] Q. Huang and D. S. Wong. Generic certificateless encryption secure against malicious-but-passive KGC attacks in the standard model. *Journal of Computer Science and Technology*, 25(4): 807–826, 2010.

[59] B. Libert and J. J. Quisquater. On constructing certificateless cryptosystems from identity based encryption. In *9th International Conference on Practice and Theory in Public-Key Cryptography (PKC 2006)*, pages 474–490. Springer, 2006.

[60] J. K. Liu, M. H. Au, and W. Susilo. Self-generated-certificate public key cryptography and certificateless signature/encryption scheme in the standard model. In *Proceedings of the 2nd ACM Symposium on Information, Computer and Communications Security (ASIACCS 2007)*, pages 273–283. ACM, 2007.

[61] D. H. Yum and P. J. Lee. Generic construction of certificateless encryption. In *International Conference on Computational Science and Its Applications (ICCSA 2004)*, pages 802–811. Springer Press, 2004.

[62] M. H. Au, J. Chen, J. K. Liu, Y. Mu, D. S. Wong, and G. Yang. Malicious KGC attacks in certificateless cryptography. In *Proceedings of the 2nd ACM Symposium on Information, Computer and Communications Security (ASIACCS 2007)*, pages 302–311. ACM, 2007.

[63] J. Lai and W. Kou. Self-generated-certificate public key encryption without pairing. In *10th International Conference on Practice and Theory in Public-Key Cryptography-PKC 2007*, pages 476–489. Springer, 2007.

[64] D. Galindo, P. Morillo, and C. Ràfols. Breaking Yum and Lee generic constructions of certificate-less and certificate-based encryption schemes. In *3rd European PKI Workshop: Theory and Practice, Public Key Infrastructure (EuroPKI 2006)*, pages 81–91. Springer, 2006.

[65] J. H. Park, K. Y. Choi, J. Y. Hwang, and D. H. Lee. Certificateless public key encryption in the selective-ID security model (without random oracles). In *1st International Conference on Pairing-Based Cryptography (Pairing 2007)*, pages 60–82. Springer, 2007.

[66] Z. Cheng, L. Chen, L. Ling, and R. Comley. General and efficient certificateless public key encryption constructions. In *1st International Conference on Pairing-Based Cryptography (Pairing 2007)*, pages 83–107. Springer, 2007.

[67] J. Lai, W. Kou, and K. Chen. Self-generated-certificate public key encryption without pairing and its application. *Information Sciences*, 181(11):2422–2435, 2011.

[68] J. Lai, R. H. Deng, S. Liu, and W. Kou. RSA-based certificateless public key encryption. In *5th International Conference on Information Security Practice and Experience (ISPEC 2009)*, pages 24–34. Springer, 2009.

[69] Y. H. Hwang, J. K. Liu, and S. S. M. Chow. Certificateless public key encryption secure against malicious KGC attacks in the standard model. *Journal of Universal Computer Science*, 14(3):463–480, 2008.

[70] Y. Sun, F. Zhang, and J. Baek. Strongly secure certificateless public key encryption without pairing. In *6th International*

Conference on Cryptology and Network Security (CANS 2007), pages 194–208. Springer, 2007.

[71] Y. Sun and H. Li. Short-ciphertext and BDH-based CCA2 secure certificateless encryption. *Science China Information Sciences*, 53(10):2005–2015, 2010.

[72] R. Sepahi, R. Steinfeld, and J. Pieprzyk. Lattice-based certificateless public-key encryption in the standard model. *International Journal of Information Security*, 13(4):315–333, 2014.

[73] G. Yang and C. H. Tan. Certificateless public key encryption: A new generic construction and two pairing-free schemes. *Theoretical Computer Science*, 412(8-10):662–674, 2011.

[74] D. Cash, E. Kiltz, and V. Shoup. The twin Diffie-Hellman problem and applications. *Journal of Cryptology*, 22(4):470–504, 2009.

[75] M. Bellare and P. Rogaway. Random oracles are practical: A paradigm for designing efficient protocols. In *Proceedings of the 1st ACM Conference on Computer and Communications Security (CCS '93)*, pages 62–73. ACM, 1993.

[76] M. Bellare, A. Boldyreva, and A. Palacio. An uninstantiable random-oracle-model scheme for a hybrid-encryption problem. In *Advances in Cryptology-EuroCrypt 2004*, pages 171–188. Springer, 2004.

[77] R. Canetti, O. Goldreich, and S. Halevi. The random oracle methodology, revisited. In *Proceedings of the 30th Annual ACM Symposium on the Theory of Computing (STOC 1998)*, pages 209–218. ACM, 1998.

[78] D. Cash, E. Kiltz, and V. Shoup. The random oracle methodology, revisited. *Journal of the ACM*, 51(4):557–594, 2004.

[79] B. Waters. Efficient identity-based encryption without random oracles. In *24th Annual International Conference on the Theory and Applications of Cryptographic Techniques (Advances in Cryptology-EUROCRYPT 2005)*, pages 114–127. Springer Press, 2005.

[80] X. Boyen, Q. Mei, and B. Waters. Direct chosen ciphertext security from identity-based techniques. In *Proceedings of the 12th ACM Conference on Computer and Communications Security (CCS 2005)*, pages 320–329. ACM, 2005.

[81] D. H. Yum and P. J. Lee. Identity-based cryptography in public key management. In *1st European PKIWorkshop: Research and Applications, Public Key Infrastructure (EuroPKI 2004)*, pages 71–84. Springer Press, 2004.

[82] D. Fiore, R. Gennaro, and N. P. Smart. Constructing certificateless encryption and ID-based encryption from ID-based key agreement. In *4th International Conference on Pairing-Based Cryptography (Pairing 2010)*, pages 167–186. Springer, 2010.

[83] D. Fiore, R. Gennaro, and N. P. Smart. Relations between the security models for certificateless encryption and ID-based key agreement. *International Journal of Information Security*, 11(1):1–22, 2012.

[84] M. Abe, Y. Cui, H. Imai, and E. Kiltz. Efficient hybrid encryption from ID-based encryption. *Designs, Codes and Cryptography*, 54(3):205–240, 2010.

[85] K. A. Shim, Y. R. Lee, and C. M. Park. S^2DRP: Secure implementations of distributed reprogramming protocol for wireless sensor networks. *Ad Hoc Networks*, 19(4):1–8, 2014.

[86] L. B. Oliveira, A. Kansal, B. Priyantha, M. Goraczko, and F. Zhao. Secure-TWS: authenticating node to multi-user communication in shared sensor networks. *The Computer Journal*, 55(4):384–396, 2012.

[87] J. Baek. Important note on certificateless public key encryption without pairing. *http://www1.i2r.a-star.edu.sg/jsbaek/publications/note.pdf*, 2007.

[88] D. Fiore and R. Gennaro. Making the Diffie-Hellman protocol identity-based. In *The Cryptographers' Track at the RSA Conference 2010 (Topics in Cryptology-CT-RSA 2010)*, pages 165–178. Springer, 2010.

[89] E. Okamoto and K. Tanaka. Key distribution system based on identification information. *IEEE Journal of Selected Areas in Communications*, 7(4):481–485, 1989.

[90] X. Yan, P. Gong, Z. Bai, J. Wang, and P. Li. New certificateless public key encryption scheme without pairing. *IET Information Security*, 7(4):271–276, 2013.

[91] Y. Dodis and J. Katz. Chosen-ciphertext security of multiple encryption. In *2nd Theory of Cryptography Conference on Theory of Cryptography (TCC 2005)*, pages 188–209. Springer, 2005.

[92] S. S. M. Chow, C. Boyd, and J. M. G. Nieto. Security-mediated certificateless cryptography. In *9th International Conference on Practice and Theory in Public Key Cryptography-PKC 2006*, pages 508–524. Springer, 2006.

[93] S. S. M. Chow, V. Roth, and E. G. Rieffel. General certificateless encryption and timed-release encryption. In *6th International Conference on Security and Cryptography for Networks (SCN 2008)*, pages 126–143. Springer, 2008.

[94] G. Ateniese, K. Fu, M. Green, and S. Hohenberger. Improved proxy re-encryption schemes with applications to secure distributed storage. *ACM Transactions on Information and System Security*, 9(1):1–30, 2006.

[95] X. Wu, L. Xu, and X. Zhang. Poster: A certificateless proxy re-encryption scheme for cloud-based data sharing. In *Proceedings of the 18th ACM Conference on Computer and Communications Security (CCS 2011)*, pages 869–872. ACM, 2011.

[96] C. Sur, C. D. Jung, Y. Park, and K. H. Rhee. Chosen-ciphertext secure certificateless proxy re-encryption. In *11th IFIP TC 6/TC 11 International Conference on Communications and Multimedia Securit (CMS 2010)*, pages 214–232. Springer, 2010.

[97] L. Xu, X. Wu, and X. Zhang. CL-PRE: A certificateless proxy re-encryption scheme for secure data sharing with public cloud. In *Proceedings of the 7th ACM Symposium on Information, Computer and Communications Security (ASIACCS 2012)*, pages 87–88. ACM, 2012.

[98] K. Yang, J. Xu, and Z. Zhang. Certificateless proxy re-encryption without pairings. In *16th International Conference on Information Security and Cryptology (ICISC 2013)*, pages 67–88. Springer, 2014.

[99] Z. Qin, S. Wu, and H. Xiong. Strongly secure and cost-effective certificateless proxy re-encryption scheme for data sharing in cloud computing. In *First International Conference on Big Data Computing and Communications (BigCom 2015)*, pages 205–216. Springer Press, 2015.

[100] T. T. Tsai and Y. M. Tseng. Revocable certificateless public key encryption. *IEEE Systems Journal*, 9(3):824–833, 2015.

[101] H. Xiong and Z. Qin. Revocable and scalable certificateless remote authentication protocol with anonymity for wireless body area networks. *IEEE Transactions on Information Forensics and Security*, 10(7):1442–1455, 2015.

[102] Y. Zheng. Digital signcryption or how to achieve cost (signature and encryption) $\ll$ cost (signature) + cost(encryption). In *Advances in Cryptology-CRYPTO'97*, pages 165–179. Springer Press, 2014.

[103] M. Barbosa and P. Farshim. Certificateless signcryption. In *Proceedings of the 2008 ACM Symposium on Information, Computer and Communications Security (ASIACCS 2008)*, pages 369–372. ACM, 2008.

[104] C. Wu and Z. X. Chen. A new efficient certificateless signcryption scheme. In *Proceedings of IEEE International Symposium on Information Science and Engineering (ISISE 2008)*, volume 1, pages 661–664. IEEE, 2008.

[105] W. Xie and Z. Zhang. Efficient and provably secure certificateless signcryption from bilinear maps. In *Proceedings of IEEE International Conference on Wireless Communications, Networking and Information Security (WCNIS 2010)*, pages 558–562. IEEE, 2010.

[106] Z. Liu, Y. Hu, X. Zhang, and H. Ma. Certificateless signcryption scheme in the standard model. *Information Sciences*, 180(3):452–464, 2010.

[107] H. Xiong, Z. Qin, and F. Li. An improved certificateless signature scheme secure in the standard model. *Fundamenta Informaticae*, 88(1-2):1–14, 2008.

[108] S. Miao, F. Zhang, S. Li, and Y. Mu. On security of a certificateless signcryption scheme. *Information Sciences*, 232(20):475–481, 2013.

[109] J. Weng, G. Yao, R. H. Deng, M. R. Chen, and X. Li. Cryptanalysis of a certificateless signcryption scheme in the standard model. *Information Sciences*, 181(3):661–667, 2011.

[110] Z. Jin, Q. Wen, and H. Zhang. A supplement to Liu et al.'s certificateless signcryption scheme in the standard model. *IACR Cryptology ePrint Archive*, 2010.

[111] H. Xiong. Toward certificateless signcryption scheme without random oracles. *IACR Cryptology ePrint Archive*, 162:1–13, 2014.

[112] M. Bellare and S. Shoup. Two-tier signatures, strongly unforgeable signatures, and fiat-shamir without random oracles. In *10th International Conference on Practice and Theory in Public-Key Cryptography, Public Key Cryptography (PKC 2007)*, pages 201–216. Springer, 2007.

[113] B. C. Hu, D. S. Wong, Z. Zhang, and X. Deng. Certificateless signature: A new security model and an improved generic construction. *Designs, Codes and Cryptography*, 42(2):109–126, 2007.

[114] X. Huang, Y. Mu, W. Susilo, D. S. Wong, and W. Wu. Certificateless signature revisited. In *12th Australasian Conference on Information Security and Privacy (ACISP 2007)*, pages 308–322. Springer, 2007.

[115] Y. C. Chena and R. Tso. A survey on security of certificateless signature schemes. *IETE Technical Review*, 1–7, 2015, doi: 10.1080/02564602.2015.1049223.

[116] X. Huang, W. Susilo, Y. Mu, and F. Zhang. On the security of certificateless signature schemes from Asiacrypt 2003. In *4th International Conference on Cryptology and Network Security (CANS 2005)*, pages 13–25. Springer, 2005.

[117] K. Y. Choi, J. H. Park, J. Y. Hwang, and D. H. Lee. Efficient certificateless signature schemes. In *5th International Conference on Applied Cryptography and Network Security (ACNS 2007)*, pages 443–458. Springer, 2007.

[118] K. Y. Choi, J. H. Park, and D. H. Lee. A new provably secure certificateless short signature scheme. *Computers and Mathematics with Applications*, 61(7):1760–1768, 2011.

[119] H. Du and Q. Wen. Security analysis of two certificateless short signature schemes. *IET Information Security*, 8(4):230–233, 2014.

[120] H. Du and Q. Wen. Efficient and provably-secure certificateless short signature scheme from bilinear pairings. *Computer Standards and Interfaces*, 31(2):390–394, 2009.

[121] M. C. Gorantla and A. Saxena. An efficient certificateless signature scheme. In *International Conference on Computational Intelligence and Security (CIS 2005)*, pages 110–116. Springer, 2005.

[122] X. Cao, K. G. Paterson, and W. Kou. An attack on a certificateless signature scheme. In *Cryptology ePrint Archive*, International Association for Cryptologic Research (IACR), https://eprint.iacr.org/2006/367.pdf, 2006.

[123] P. Gong and P. Li. Further improvement of a certificateless signature scheme without pairing. *International Journal of Communication Systems*, 27(10):2083–2091, 2014.

[124] D. He, J. Chen, and R. Zhang. An efficient and provably-secure certificateless signature scheme without bilinear pairings. *International Journal of Communication Systems*, 25(11):1432–1442, 2012.

[125] M. Tian and L. Huang. Cryptanalysis of a certificateless signature scheme without pairings. *International Journal of Communication Systems*, 26(11):1375–1381, 2013.

[126] J. L. Tsai, N. W. Lo, and T. C. Wu. Weaknesses and improvements of an efficient certificateless signature scheme without

using bilinear pairings. *International Journal of Communication Systems*, 27(7):1083–1090, 2014.

[127] R. Tso, X. Yi, and X. Huang. Efficient and short certificateless signature. In *7th International Conference on Cryptology and Network Security (CANS 2008)*, pages 64–79. Springer, 2008.

[128] R. Tso, X. Yi, and X. Huang. Efficient and short certificateless signatures secure against realistic adversaries. *The Journal of Supercomputing*, 55(2):173–191, 2011.

[129] R. Tso, W. Susilo, and X. Huang. Efficient and short certificateless signatures secure against realistic adversaries. *Journal of Systems and Software*, 85(6):1409–1417, 2012.

[130] K. A. Shim and Y. R. Lee. Security pitfalls of the certificateless signature and multi-receiver signcryption schemes. *Fundamenta Informaticae*, 112(4):365–376, 2011.

[131] W. S. Yap, S. H. Heng, and B. M. Goi. An efficient certificateless signature scheme. In *Emerging Directions in Embedded and Ubiquitous Computing (EUC 2006)*, pages 322–331. Springer, 2006.

[132] J. H. Park. An attack on the certificateless signature scheme from EUC Workshops 2006. In *IACR Cryptology ePrint Archive*, 2006.

[133] Z. Zhang and D. Feng. Key replacement attack on a certificateless signature scheme. In *Cryptology ePrint Archive*, International Association for Cryptologic Research (IACR), https://eprint. iacr.org/2006/453.pdf, 2006.

[134] Y. Yu, Y. Mu, G. Wang, Q. Xia, and B. Yang. Improved certificateless signature scheme provably secure in the standard model. *IET Information Security*, 6(2):102–110, 2012.

[135] Y. Yuan and C. Wang. Certificateless signature scheme with security enhanced in the standard model. *Information Processing Letters*, 114(9):492–499, 2014.

[136] C. Guan, J. Weng, R. H. Deng, M.-R. Chen, and D. Zhou. Unforgeability of an improved certificateless signature scheme in the standard model. *IET Information Security*, 8(5):273–276, 2014.

[137] D. H. Yum and P. J. Lee. Generic construction of certificateless signature. In *9th Australasian Conference on Information Security and Privacy (ACISP 2004)*, pages 200–211. Springer Press, 2004.

[138] L. Zhang and F. Zhang. A new provably secure certificateless signature scheme. In *Proceedings of IEEE International Conference on Communications (ICC 2008)*, pages 1685–1689. IEEE Press, 2008.

[139] J. Zhang and J. Mao. An efficient RSA-based certificateless signature scheme. *Journal of Systems and Software*, 85(3):638–642, 2012.

[140] D. He, M. K. Khan, and S. Wu. On the security of a RSA-based certificateless signature scheme. *International Journal of Network Security*, 16(1):78–80, 2014.

[141] R. Castro and R. Dahab. Two notes on the security of certificateless signatures. In *1st International Conference on Provable Security (ProvSec 2007)*, pages 85–102. Springer Press, 2007.

[142] K. A. Shim. Breaking the short certificateless signature scheme. *Information Sciences*, 179(3):303–306, 2009.

[143] K. C. Barr and K. Asanovic. Energy-aware lossless data compression. *ACM Transactions on Computer Systems*, 24(3):250–291, 2006.

[144] D. Boneh, B. Lynn, and H. Shacham. Short signatures from the Weil pairing. In *7th International Conference on the Theory and Application of Cryptology and Information Security (Advances in Cryptology-ASIACRYPT 2001)*, pages 514–532. Springer, 2001.

[145] D. Boneh, B. Lynn, and H. Shacham. Short Signatures from the Weil Pairing. *Journal of Cryptology*, 17(4):297–319, 2004.

[146] D. He, B. Huang, and J. Chen. New certificateless short signature scheme. *IET Information Security*, 7(2):113–117, 2013.

[147] G. Sharma, S. Bala, and A. K. Verma. On the security of a RSA-based certificateless signature scheme. *International Journal of Network Security*, 18(1):82–89, 2016.

[148] K. G. Paterson and J. C. N. Schuldt. Efficient identity-based signatures secure in the standard model. In *11th Australasian Conference on Information Security and Privacy (ACISP 2006)*, pages 207–222. Springer, 2006.

[149] J. S. Coron. On the exact security of full domain hash. In *Advances in Cryptology-CRYPTO 2000*, pages 229–235. Springer, 2000.

[150] A. Fiat and A. Shamir. How to prove yourself: Practical solutions to identification and signature problems. In *Advances in Cryptology-CRYPTO '86*, pages 186–194. Springer, 1986.

[151] N. Koblitz and A. J. Menezes. The random oracle model: A twenty-year retrospective. *Designs, Codes and Cryptography*, 77(2):587–610, 2015.

[152] E. Fujisaki and T. Okamoto. Secure integration of asymmetric and symmetric encryption schemes. *Journal of Cryptology*, 26(1):80–101, 2013.

[153] M. Bellare, C. Namprempre, and G. Neven. Security proofs for identity-based identification and signature schemes. *Journal of Cryptology*, 22(1):1–61, 2009.

[154] R. Dutta and R. Barua. Overview of key agreement protocols. In *Cryptology ePrint Archive*, International Association for Cryptologic Research (IACR), https://eprint.iacr.org/2005/289.ps, 2005.

[155] M. Luo, Y. Wen, and H. Zhao. An enhanced authentication and key agreement mechanism for SIP using certificateless public-key cryptography. In *9th International Conference for Young Computer Scientists (ICYCS 2008)*, pages 1577–1582. IEEE, 2008.

[156] T. K. Mandt and C. H. Tan. Certificateless authenticated two-party key agreement protocols. In *11th Asian Computing Science Conference on Secure Software and Related Issues (Advances in Computer Science-ASIAN 2006)*, pages 37–44. Springer, 2006.

[157] C. Swanson and D. Jao. A study of two-party certificateless authenticated key-agreement protocols. In *10th International*

Conference on Cryptology in India (Progress in Cryptology-INDOCRYPT 2009), pages 57–71. Springer, 2009.

[158] F. Wang and Y. Zhang. A new provably secure authentication and key agreement mechanism for SIP using certificateless public-key cryptography. *Computer Communications*, 31(10): 2142–2149, 2008.

[159] H. Yang, Y. Zhang, Y. Zhou, X. Fu, H. Liu, and A. V. Vasilakos. Provably secure three-party authenticated key agreement protocol using smart cards. *Computer Networks*, 58:29–38, 2014.

[160] L. Zhang. Provably secure certificateless one-way and two-party authenticated key agreement protocol. In *15th International Conference on Information Security and Cryptology (ICISC 2012)*, pages 217–230. Springer Press, 2012.

[161] L. Zhang. Certificateless one-pass and two-party authenticated key agreement protocol and its extensions. *Information Sciences*, 293:182–195, 2015.

[162] A. Menezes, T. Okamoto, and S. A. Vanstone. Reducing elliptic curve logarithms to logarithms in a finite field. *IEEE Transactions on Information Theory*, 39(5):1639–1646, 1993.

[163] G. Frey, M. Müller, and H. G. Rück. The Tate pairing and the discrete logarithm applied to elliptic curve cryptosystems. *IEEE Transactions on Information Theory*, 45(5):1717–1719, 1999.

[164] A. Joux. A one round protocol for tripartite Diffie-Hellman. In *4th International Symposium on Algorithmic Number Theory (ANTS 2000)*, pages 385–394, 2000.

[165] N. P. Smart. An identity based authenticated key agreement protocol based on the Weil pairing. *Electronics Letters*, 38(3): 630–632, 2002.

[166] X. Cao, X. Zeng, W. Kou, and L. Hu. Identity-based anonymous remote authentication for value-added services in mobile networks. *IEEE Transactions on Vehicular Technology*, 58(7):3508–3517, 2009.

[167] X. Cao, W. Kou, and X. Du. A pairing-free identity-based authenticated key agreement protocol with minimal message exchanges. *Information Sciences*, 180(15):2895–2903, 2010.

[168] K. A. Shim and C. M. Park. A secure data aggregation scheme based on appropriate cryptographic primitives in heterogeneous wireless sensor networks. *IEEE Transactions on Parallel and Distributed Systems*, 26(8):2128–2139, 2015.

[169] M. Geng and F. Zhang. Provably secure certificateless two-party authenticated key agreement protocol without pairing. In *International Conference on Computational Intelligence and Security (CIS 2009)*, pages 208–212. Springer, 2009.

[170] M. Hou and Q. Xu. A two-party certificateless authenticated key agreement protocol without pairing. In *2nd IEEE International Conference on Computer Science and Information Technology*, pages 412–416. Springer, 2009.

[171] D. He, J. Chen, and J. Hu. A pairing-free certificateless authenticated key agreement protocol. *International Journal of Communication Systems*, 25(2):221–230, 2012.

[172] H. Xiong, Q. Wu, and Z. Chen. Toward pairing-free certificateless authenticated key exchanges. In *14th Information Security Conference (ISC 2011)*, pages 79–94. Springer Press, 2011.

[173] W. Han. Breaking a certificateless key agreement protocol without bilinear pairing. In *Cryptology ePrint Archive*, International Association for Cryptologic Research (IACR), https://eprint.iacr.org/2011/249, 2011.

[174] H. Tu, N. Kumar, J. Kim, and J. Seo. A strongly secure pairing-free certificateless authenticated key agreement protocol suitable for smart media and mobile environments. *International Journal of Communication Systems*, 74(16):6365–6377, 2015.

[175] C. Kudla and K. G. Paterson. Modular security proofs for key agreement protocols. In *11th International Conference on the Theory and Application of Cryptology and Information Security (Advances in Cryptology-ASIACRYPT 2005)*, pages 549–565. Springer, 2005.

[176] L. Chen, Z. Cheng, and N. Smart. Identity-based key agreement protocols from pairings. *International Journal of Information Security*, 6(4):213–241, 2007.

[177] F. Bao, R. Deng, and H. Zhu. Variations of Diffie-Hellman problem. In *5th International Conference on Information and Communications Security (ICICS 2003)*, pages 301–312. Springer, 2003.

[178] B. S. Kaliski Jr. An unknown key-share attack on the MQV key agreement protocol. *ACM Transactions on Information and System Security*, 4(3):275–288, 2001.

[179] Shamus Software Ltd. Multiprecision integer and rational arithmetic cryptographic library (MIRACL). In *https://github.com/CertiVox/MIRACL*, Nov. 2015.

[180] H. R. Tseng. A secure and privacy-preserving communication protocol for V2G networks. In *2012 IEEE Wireless Communications and Networking Conference (WCNC 2012)*, pages 2706–2711. IEEE, 2012.

[181] F. Li, M. Shirase, and T. Takagi. Key management using certificateless public key cryptography in ad hoc networks. In *IFIP International Conference on Network and Parallel Computing (NPC 2008)*, pages 116–126. Springer, 2008.

[182] D. He, S. Zeadally, and L. Wu. Certificateless public auditing scheme for cloud-assisted wireless body area networks. *IEEE Systems Journal*, 10.1109/JSYST.2015.2428620:1–10, 2015.

[183] H. Xiong. Cost-effective scalable and anonymous certificateless remote authentication protocol. *IEEE Transactions on Information Forensics and Security*, 9(12):2327–2339, 2014.

[184] D. Chaum. Untraceable electronic mail, return addresses, and digital pseudonyms. *Communications of the ACM*, 24(2):84–88, 1981.

[185] M. G. Reed, P. F. Syverson, and D. M. Goldschlag. Anonymous connections and onion routing. *IEEE Journal on Selected Areas in Communications*, 16(4):482–494, 1998.

[186] P. F. Syverson, D. M. Goldschlag, and M. G. Reed. Anonymous connections and onion routing. In *IEEE Symposium on Security and Privacy (S&P 1997)*, pages 44–54. IEEE, 1997.

[187] D. Catalano, M. D. Raimondo, D. Fiore, R. Gennaro, and O. Puglisi. Fully non-interactive onion routing with forward-secrecy. In *9th International Conference on Applied Cryptography and Network Security (ACNS 2011)*, pages 255–273. ACM Press, 2011.

[188] D. Catalano, M. D. Raimondo, D. Fiore, R. Gennaro, and O. Puglisi. Fully non-interactive onion routing with forward secrecy. *International Journal of Information Security*, 12(1): 33–47, 2013.

[189] C. Chen, D. E. Asoni, D. Barrera, G. Danezis, and A. Perrig. Hornet: High-speed onion routing at the network layer. In *Proceedings of the 22th ACM Conference on Computer and Communications Security (CCS 2015)*, pages 1441–1454. ACM Press, 2015.

[190] A. Kate, G. M. Zaverucha, and I. Goldberg. Pairing-based onion routing with improved forward secrecy. In 7th *International Symposium on Privacy Enhancing Technologies (PET 2007)*, pages 95–112, 2007.

[191] A. Kate, G. M. Zaverucha, and I. Goldberg. Pairing-based onion routing with improved forward secrecy. *ACM Transactions on Information and System Security*, 13(4):1–29, 2010.

[192] R. Dingledine and N. Mathewson. Tor protocol specification. In *https://www.torproject.org/docs/documentation.html.en#UpToSpeed*, 2008.

[193] I. Goldberg. On the security of the Tor authentication protocol. In *6th International Workshop on Privacy Enhancing Technologies (PET 2006)*, pages 316–331. Springer, 2006.

[194] L. Øverlier and P. F. Syverson. Improving efficiency and simplicity of Tor circuit establishment and hidden services. In *7th International Workshop on Privacy Enhancing Technologies (PET 2007)*, pages 134–152. Springer, 2007.

[195] J. Camenisch and A. Lysyanskaya. A formal treatment of onion routing. In *Advances in Cryptology (CRYPTO 2005)*, pages 169–187. Springer, 2005.

[196] R. Canetti and H. Krawczyk. Analysis of key-exchange protocols and their use for building secure channels. In *Advances in Cryptology (EUROCRYPT 2001)*, pages 453–474. Springer, 2001.

[197] R. Canetti and H. Krawczyk. Universally composable notions of key exchange and secure channels. In *Advances in Cryptology (EUROCRYPT 2002)*, pages 337–351. Springer, 2002.

[198] T. G. Zimmerman. Personal area networks: Near-field intrabody communication. *IBM Systems Journal*, 35(3–4):609–617, 1996.

[199] WBAN standard group. *http://www.ieee802.org/15/pub/tg6.html*, 2011.

[200] H. Alemdar and C. Ersoy. Wireless sensor networks for healthcare: A survey. *Computer Networks*, 54(15):2688–2710, 2010.

[201] B. Latré, B. Braem, I. Moerman, C. Blondia, and P. Demeester. A survey on wireless body area networks. *Wireless Networks*, 17(1):1–18, 2011.

[202] H. Cao, V. Leung, C. Chow, and H. Chan. Enabling technologies for wireless body area networks: A survey and outlook. *IEEE Communications Magazine*, 47(12):84–93, 2009.

[203] S. Ullah, H. Higgins, B. Braem, B. Latre, C. Blondia, I. Moerman, S. Saleem, Z. Rahman, and K. S. Kwak. A comprehensive survey of wireless body area networks. *Journal of Medical Systems*, 36(3):1065–1094, 2012.

[204] M. Seyedi, B. Kibret, D. T. Lai, and M. Faulkner. A survey on intrabody communications for body area network applications. *IEEE Transactions on Biomedical Engineering*, 60(8):2067–2079, 2013.

[205] M. Chen, S. Gonzalez, A. Vasilakos, H. Cao, and V. C. Leung. Body area networks: A survey. *Mobile Networks and Applications*, 16(2):171–193, 2011.

[206] D. He, C. Chen, S. Chan, J. Bu, and A. V. Vasilakos. Retrust: Attack-resistant and lightweight trust management for medical sensor networks. *IEEE Transactions on Information Technology in Biomedicine*, 16(4):623–632, 2012.

[207] D. He, C. Chen, S. C. Chan, J. Bu, and A. V. Vasilakos. A distributed trust evaluation model and its application scenarios for medical sensor networks. *IEEE Transactions on Information Technology in Biomedicine*, 16(6):1164–1175, 2012.

[208] D. Malan, T. Fulford-Jones, M. Welsh, and S. Moulton. Code-blue: An ad hoc sensor network infrastructure for emergency medical care. In *MobiSys 2004 Workshop on Applications of Mobile Embedded Systems (WAMES 2004)*, volume 5, 2004.

[209] V. Shnayder, B. r. Chen, K. Lorincz, T. R. F. Jones, and M. Welsh. Sensor networks for medical care. In *Proceedings of the 3rd International Conference on Embedded Networked Sensor Systems (SenSys '05)*, volume 5, pages 314–314, 2005.

[210] T. Gao, T. Massey, and L. Selavo. The advanced health and disaster aid network: A light-weight wireless medical system for triage. *IEEE Transactions on Biomedical Circuits and Systems*, 1(3):203–216, 2007.

[211] J. Zhou, Z. Cao, X. Dong, N. Xiong, and A. Vasilakos. 4S: A secure and privacy-preserving key management scheme for cloud-assisted wireless body area network in m-healthcare social networks. *Information Sciences*, 314:255–276, 2015.

[212] R. Lu, X. Li, X. Liang, X. S. Shen, and X. Lin. GRS: The green, reliability, and security of emerging machine to machine communications. *IEEE Communications Magazine*, 49(4):28–35, 2011.

[213] The Health Information Trust Alliance (HITRUST). In *http://www.hitrustalliance.org*.

[214] M. Li, S. Yu, J. D. Guttman, W. Lou, and K. Ren. Secure ad hoc trust initialization and key management in wireless body area networks. *ACM Transactions on Sensor Networks (TOSN)*, 9(2):18, 2013.

[215] D. He, C. Chen, S. C. Chan, J. Bu, and P. Zhang. Secure and lightweight network admission and transmission protocol for body sensor networks. *IEEE Journal of Biomedical and Health Informatics*, 17(3):664–674, 2013.

[216] Z. Zhang, H. Wang, A. V. Vasilakos, and H. Fang. ECG-cryptography and authentication in body area networks. *IEEE Transactions on Information Technology in Biomedicine*, 16(6): 1070–1078, 2012.

[217] K. Malasri and L. Wang. Design and implementation of a securewireless mote-based medical sensor network. *Sensors*, 9(8): 6273–6297, 2009.

[218] C. C. Tan, H. Wang, S. Zhong, and Q. Li. IBE-lite: A lightweight identity-based cryptography for body sensor networks. *IEEE Transactions on Information Technology in Biomedicine*, 13(6):926–932, 2009.

[219] J. Liu, Z. Zhang, R. Sun, and K. S. Kwak. An efficient certificate-less remote anonymous authentication scheme for wireless body area networks. In *Proceedings of IEEE International Conference on Communications (ICC 2012)*, pages 3404–3408. IEEE, 2012.

[220] S. Wang, Z. Cao, Z. Cheng, and K. K. R. Choo. Perfect forward secure identity-based authenticated key agreement protocol in the escrow mode. *Science in China Series F: Information Sciences*, 52(8):1358–1370, 2009.

[221] A. C. Yao and Y. Zhao. Oake: A new family of implicitly authenticated Diffie-Hellman protocols. In *ACM Conference on Computer and Communications Security 2013 (CCS '2013)*, pages 1113–1128. ACM, 2013.

[222] S. Blake-Wilson and A. Menezes. Authenticated Diffe-Hellman key agreement protocols. In *6th Annual International Workshop on Selected Areas in Cryptography (SAC 1999)*, pages 339–361. Springer, 1999.

[223] A. Perrig, R. Canetti, J. D. Tygar, and D. Song. The TESLA broadcast authentication protocol. *RSA CryptoBytes*, 5, 2005.

[224] M. K. Reiter, K. P. Birman, and R. Van Renesse. A security architecture for fault-tolerant systems. *ACM Transactions on Computer Systems (TOCS)*, 12(4):340–371, 1994.

[225] X. Lin, X. Sun, X. Wang, C. Zhang, P. H. Ho, and X. S. Shen. TSVC: timed efficient and secure vehicular communications with privacy preserving. *IEEE Transactions on Wireless Communications*, 7(12):4987–4998, 2008.

[226] K. Ren, W. Lou, K. Zeng, and P. J. Moran. On broadcast authentication in wireless sensor networks. *IEEE Transactions on Wireless Communications*, 6(11):4136–4144, 2007.

[227] F. Hess. Efficient identity based signature schemes based on pairings. In *9th Annual International Workshop on Selected Areas in Cryptography (SAC 2002)*, pages 310–324. IEEE, 2002.

[228] MICAz datasheet Crossbow. Crossbow Technology Inc, *http:// bullseye.xbow.com:81/products/product_pdf_files/wireless_pdf/ micaz_datasheet.pdf*, 2016. Springer.

[229] X. Cao, W. Kou, L. Dang, and B. Zhao. IMBAS: Identity-based multi-user broadcast authentication in wireless sensor networks. *Computer Communications*, 31(14):659–667, 2008.

[230] S. Subashini and V. Kavitha. A survey on security issues in service delivery models of cloud computing. *Journal of Network and Computer Applications*, 34(1):1–11, 2011.

[231] L. Wei, H. Zhu, Z. Cao, W. Jia, and A. Vasilakos. SecCloud: Bridging secure storage and computation in cloud. In *2010 IEEE 30th International Conference on Distributed Computing Systems Workshops (ICDCSW)*, pages 52–61. IEEE, 2010.

[232] L. Wei, H. Zhu, Z. Cao, X. Dong, W. Jia, Y. Chen, and A. Vasilakos. Security and privacy for storage and computation in cloud computing. *Information Sciences*, 258:371–386, 2014.

[233] J. Zhou, X. Dong, Z. Cao, and A. V. Vasilakos. Secure and privacy preserving protocol for cloud-based vehicular DTNs, *IEEE Transactions on Information Forensics and Security*, 10(6):1299–1314, 2015.

[234] R. Canetti and S. Hohenberger. Chosen-ciphertext secure proxy re-encryption. In *Proceedings of the 14th ACM Conference on Computer and Communications Security (CCS 2007)*, pages 185–194. ACM, 2007.

[235] B. Libert and D. Vergnaud. Unidirectional chosen-ciphertext secure proxy re-encryption. In *Public Key Cryptography (PKC 2008)*, pages 360–379. Springer, 2008.

[236] S. S. M. Chow, J. Weng, Y. Yang, and R. H. Deng. Efficient unidirectional proxy re-encryption. In *Progress in Cryptology (AFRICACRYPT 2010)*, pages 316–332. Springer, 2010.

[237] M. Green and G. Ateniese. Identity-based proxy re-encryption. In *Proceedings of the 5th International Conference on Applied Cryptography and Network Security (ACNS 2007)*, pages 288–306. Springer, 2007.

[238] L. Wang, K. Chen, X. Mao, and Y. Wang. Efficient and provably-secure certificateless proxy re-encryption scheme for secure cloud data sharing. *Journal of Shanghai Jiaotong University (Science)*, 19:398–405, 2014.

[239] J. Baek, R. Steinfeld, and Y. Zheng. Formal proofs for the security of signcryption. In *Public Key Cryptography-PKC 2002*, pages 80–98. Springer, 2002.

[240] F. Bao and R. H. Deng. A signcryption scheme with signature directly verifiable by public key. In *Public Key Cryptography-PKC'98*, pages 55–59. Springer, 1998.

[241] Y. Zheng and H. Imai. How to construct efficient signcryption schemes on elliptic curves. *Information Processing Letters*, 68(5):227–233, 1998.

[242] C. Gamage, J. Leiwo, and Y. Zheng. Encrypted message authentication by firewalls. In *Public Key Cryptography-PKC'99*, pages 69–81. Springer, 1999.

[243] H. Y. Jung, D. H. Lee, J. I. Lim, and K. S. Chang. Signcryption schemes with forward secrecy. In *Proceedings of the Information Security Application (WISA 2001)*, pages 463–475, Seoul, Korea, 2001.

[244] D. H. Yum and P. J. Lee. New signcryption schemes based on KCDSA. In *4th International Conference on Information Security and Cryptology (ICISC 2001)*, pages 305–317. Springer, 2002.

[245] J. B. Shin, K. Lee, and K. Shim. New DSA-verifiable signcryption schemes. In *5th International Conference on Information Security and Cryptology (ICISC 2002)*, pages 35–47. Springer, 2002.

[246] J. Malone-Lee and W. Mao. Two birds one stone: Signcryption using RSA. In *The Cryptographers' Track at the RSA Conference 2003 (CT-RSA 2003)*, pages 211–226. Springer, 2003.

[247] J. K. Liu, M. H. Au, and W. Susilo. A new identity based signcryption schemes from pairings. In *2003 IEEE Information Theory Workshop*, pages 155–158. IEEE, 2003.

[248] X. Boyen. Multipurpose identity-based signcryption: A Swiss army knife for identity-based cryptography. In *Advances in Cryptology-CRYPTO 2003*, pages 383–399. Springer, 2003.

[249] L. Chen and J. Malone-Lee. Improved identity-based signcryption. In *Public Key Cryptography-PKC 2005*, pages 362–379. Springer, 2005.

[250] S. S. M. Chow, S. M. Yiu, L. C. K. Hui, and K. P. Chow. Efficient forward and provably secure ID-based signcryption scheme with public verifiability and public ciphertext authenticity. In *Information Security and Cryptology-ICISC 2003*, pages 352–369. Springer, 2004.

[251] P. S. L. M. Barreto, B. Libert, N. McCullagh, and J. J. Quisquater. Efficient and provably-secure identity-based signatures and signcryption from bilinear maps. In *Advances in Cryptology-ASIACRYPT 2005*, pages 515–532. Springer, 2005.

[252] B. Qin, H. Wang, Q. Wu, J. Liu, and J. Domingo-Ferrer. A new identity based signcryption scheme in the standard model. In *4th International Conference on Intelligent Networking and Collaborative Systems (InCoS 2012)*, pages 606–611. IEEE, 2012.

[253] D. Aranha, R. Castro, and J. Lopez. Efficient certificateless signcryption. *8o. Simpósio Brasileiro em Segurança da Informaçao e de Sistemas Computacionais*, pages 257–258, 2008.

[254] X. Li, H. Qian, J. Weng, and Y. Yu. Fully secure identity-based signcryption scheme with shorter signcryptext in the standard model. *Mathematical and Computer Modelling*, 57(3):503–511, 2013.

[255] D. Boneh, C. Gentry, B. Lynn, and H. Shacham. Aggregate and verifiably encrypted signatures from bilinear maps. In *Advances in Cryptology-EUROCRYPT 2003*, pages 416–432. Springer, 2003.

[256] J. H. Ahn, M. Green, and S. Hohenberger. Synchronized aggregate signatures: New definitions, constructions and applications. In *Proceedings of the 17th ACM Conference on Computer and Communications Security*, pages 473–484. ACM, 2010.

[257] A. Bagherzandi and S. Jarecki. Identity-based aggregate and multi-signature schemes based on RSA. In *Public Key Cryptography–PKC 2010*, pages 480–498. Springer, 2010.

[258] A. Boldyreva, C. Gentry, A. O'neill, and D. H. Yum. Ordered multisignatures and identity-based sequential aggregate signatures, with applications to secure routing. In *Proceedings of the 14th ACM Conference on Computer and Communications Security (CCS 2007)*, pages 276–285. ACM, 2007.

[259] S. Lu, R. Ostrovsky, A. Sahai, H. Shacham, and B. Waters. Sequential aggregate signatures and multisignatures without random oracles. In *Advances in Cryptology-EUROCRYPT 2006*, pages 465–485. Springer, 2006.

[260] A. Lysyanskaya, S. Micali, L. Reyzin, and H. Shacham. Sequential aggregate signatures from trapdoor permutations. In *Advances in Cryptology-Eurocrypt 2004*, pages 74–90. Springer, 2004.

[261] G. Neven. Efficient sequential aggregate signed data. In *Advances in Cryptology–EUROCRYPT 2008*, pages 52–69. Springer, 2008.

[262] X. Cheng, J. Liu, and X. Wang. Identity-based aggregate and verifiably encrypted signatures from bilinear pairing. In *Computational Science and Its Applications–ICCSA 2005*, pages 1046–1054. Springer, 2005.

[263] C. Gentry and Z. Ramzan. Identity-based aggregate signatures. In *Public Key Cryptography-PKC 2006*, pages 257–273. Springer, 2006.

[264] J. Herranz. Deterministic identity-based signatures for partial aggregation. *The Computer Journal*, 49(3):322–330, 2006.

[265] K. A. Shim. An ID-based aggregate signature scheme with constant pairing computations. *The Journal of Systems and Software*, 83(10):1873–1880, 2010.

[266] J. Xu, Z. Zhang, and D. Feng. ID-based aggregate signatures from bilinear pairings. In *Cryptology and Network Security*, pages 110–119. Springer, 2005.

[267] Z. Gong, Y. Long, X. Hong, and K. Chen. Two certificateless aggregate signatures from bilinear maps. In *Proceedings of the 8th International Conference on Software Engineering, Artificial Intelligence, Networking, and Parallel/Distributed Computing (SNPD)*, volume 3, pages 188–193. IEEE, 2007.

[268] L. Zhang and F. Zhang. A new certificateless aggregate signature scheme. *Computer Communications*, 32(6):1079–1085, 2009.

[269] H. Xiong, Q. Wu, and Z. Chen. Strong security enabled certificateless aggregate signatures applicable to mobile computation. In *3rd International Conference on Intelligent Networking and Collaborative Systems (INCoS-2011)*, pages 92–99. IEEE Press, 2011.

[270] H. Xiong, Q. Wu, and Z. Chen. An efficient provably secure certificateless aggregate signature applicable to mobile computation. *Control and Cybernetics*, 42(2):373–391, 2012.

[271] L. Shen and Y. Sun. On security of a certificateless aggregate signature scheme. In *Cryptology ePrint Archive*, 2012.

[272] H. Xiong, Z. Guan, Z. Chen, and F. Li. An efficient certificateless aggregate signature with constant pairing computations. *Information Sciences*, 219(10):225–235, 2013.

[273] D. He, M. Tian, and J. Chen. Insecurity of an efficient certificateless aggregate signature with constant pairing computations. *Information Sciences*, 268:458–462, 2014.

[274] L. Cheng, Q. Wen, Z. Jin, H. Zhang, and L. Zhou. Cryptanalysis and improvement of a certificateless aggregate signature scheme. *Information Sciences*, 295:337–346, 2015.

[275] S. J. Horng, S. F. Tzeng, P. H. Huang, X. Wang, T. Li, and M. K. Khan. An efficient certificateless aggregate signature with conditional privacy-preserving for vehicular sensor networks. *Information Sciences*, 317:48–66, 2015.

[276] R. L. Rivest, A. Shamir, and Y. Tauman. How to leak a secret. In *Advances in Cryptology-ASIACRYPT 2001*, pages 552–565. Springer, 2001.

[277] R. L. Rivest, A. Shamir, and Y. Tauman. How to leak a secret: Theory and applications of ring signatures. In *Essays in Theoretical Computer Science: In Memory of Shimon Even*, pages 164–186. Springer, 2006.

[278] J. Herranz and G. Saez. Forking lemmas for ring signature schemes. In *4th International Conference on Cryptology in India (Indocrypt 2003)*, pages 266–279. Springer, 2003.

[279] M. Abe, M. Ohkubo, and K. Suzuki. 1-out-of-n signatures from a variety of keys. In *Advances in Cryptology-Asiacrypt 2002*, pages 415–432. Springer, 2002.

[280] L. Dallot and D. Vergnaud. Provably secure code-based threshold ring signatures. In *12th IMA Conf. Cryptography and Coding 2009*, pages 222–235. Springer, 2009.

[281] C. A. Melchor, P. Cayrel, and P. Gaborit. A new efficient threshold ring signature scheme based on coding theory. *IEEE Transactions on Information Theory*, 57(7):4833–4842, 2011.

[282] P. L. Cayrel, R. Lindner, and M. Rückert. A lattice-based threshold ring signature scheme. In *Progress in Cryptology–LATINCRYPT 2010*, pages 255–272. Springer, 2010.

[283] S. Wang, R. Ma, Y. Zhang, and X. Wang. Ring signature scheme based on multivariate public key cryptosystems. *Computers and Mathematics with Applications*, 62(10):3973–3979, 2011.

[284] A. Bender, J. Katz, and R. Morselli. Ring signatures: Stronger definitions, and constructions without random oracles. In *Theory of Cryptography*, pages 60–79. Springer, 2006.

[285] J. Li, X. Chen, T.H. Yuen, and Y. Wang. Proxy ring signature: Formal definitions, efficient construction and new variant. In *International Conference on Computational Intelligence and Security*, volume 2, pages 1259–1264. IEEE, 2006.

[286] E. Bresson, J. Stern, and M. Szydlo. Threshold ring signatures and applications to ad-hoc groups. In *Advances in Cryptology-Crypto 2002*, pages 465–480. Springer, 2002.

[287] L. Chen, C. Kudla, and K. G. Paterson. Concurrent signatures. In *Advances in Cryptology-EUROCRYPT 2004*, pages 287–305. Springer, 2004.

[288] J. Liu, V. Wei, and D. Wong. Linkable spontaneous anonymous group signature for ad hoc groups. In *9th Australasian Conference on Information Security and Privacy (ACISP' 04)*, pages 325–335. Springer, 2004.

[289] F. Zhang and K. Kim. ID-based blind signature and ring signature from pairings. In *Advances in Cryptology-ASIACRYPT 2002*, pages 533–547. Springer, 2002.

[290] C. Y. Lin and T. C. Wu. An identity-based ring signature scheme from bilinear pairings. In *Advanced Information Networking and Applications (AINA 2004)*, pages 182–185. IEEE, 2004.

[291] J. Herranz and G. Sáez. New identity-based ring signature schemes. In *Information and Communications Security*, pages 27–39. Springer, 2004.

[292] S. S. M. Chow, S. M. Yiu, and L. C. K. Hui. Efficient identity based ring signature. In *3rd International Conference on Applied Cryptography and Network Security (ACNS 2005)*, pages 499–512. Springer, 2005.

[293] L. Nguyen. Accumulators from bilinear pairings and applications. In *The Cryptographers' Track at the RSA Conference (CT-RSA 2005)*, pages 275–292. Springer, 2005.

[294] M. H. Au, J. K. Liu, T. H. Yuen, and D. S. Wong. ID-based ring signature scheme secure in the standard model. In *1st International Workshop on Security (IWSEC 2006)*, pages 1–16. Springer, 2006.

[295] J. Herranz. Identity-based ring signatures from RSA. *Theoretical Computer Science*, 389(1):100–117, 2007.

[296] P. P. Tsang, M. H. Au, J. K. Liu, W. Susilo, and D. S. Wong. A suite of non-pairing ID-based threshold ring signature schemes with different levels of anonymity. In *4th International Conference on Provable Security (ProvSec 2010)*, pages 166–183. Springer, 2010.

[297] S. S. M. Chow, R. W. C. Lui, L. C. K. Hui, and S. M. Yiu. Identity based ring signature: Why, how and what next. In *2nd European PKI Workshop: Research and Applications (EuroPKI 2005)*, pages 144–161. Springer, 2005.

[298] L. Zhang, F. Zhang, and W. Wu. A provably secure ring signature scheme in certificateless cryptography. In *1st International Conference on Provable Security (ProvSec 2007)*, pages 103–121. Springer, 2007.

[299] S. Chang, D. S. Wong, and Y. Mu. Certificateless threshold ring signature. *Information Sciences*, 179(20):3685–3696, 2009.

[300] N. Li, Y. Mu, W. Susilo, and F. Guo. Self-certified ring signatures. In *Proceedings of the 6th ACM Symposium on Information, Computer and Communications Security (ASIACCS' 2011)*, pages 396–400. ACM, 2011.

[301] M. H. Au, J. K. Liu, W. Susilo, and T. H. Yuen. Certificate based (linkable) ring signature. In *3rd International Conference on Information Security Practice and Experience (ISPEC 2007)*, pages 79–92. Springer, 2007.

[302] Z. Qin, H. Xiong, G. Zhu, and Z. Chen. Certificate-free ad hoc anonymous authentication. *Information Sciences*, 268(1):447–457, 2014.

[303] C. T. Long. *Elementary Introduction to Number Theory*. Prentice Hall, 1987.

[304] D. Pointcheval and J. Stern. Security arguments for digital signatures and blind signatures. *Journal of Cryptology*, 13(3):361–396, 2000.

[305] A. Shamir. How to share a secret. *Communications of the ACM*, 22(11):612–613, 1979.

[306] G.R. Blakley. Safeguarding cryptographic keys. In *Proceedings of the National Computer Conference*, volume 48, pages 313–317, 1979.

[307] M. Cerccedo, M. Matsumoto, and H. Imai. Efficient and secure multiparty generation of digital signatures based on discrete logarithms. *IEICE Transactions on Fundamentals of Electronics, Communications and Computer Sciences*, 76(4):532–545, 1993.

[308] R. Gennaro, S. Jarecki, H. Krawczyk, and T. Rabin. Robust threshold DSS signatures. In *Advances in Cryptology-EUROCRYPT'96*, pages 354–371. Springer, 1996.

[309] D. R. Stinson and R. Strobl. Provably secure distributed Schnorr signatures and a (t, n) threshold scheme for implicit certificates. In *Proceedings of the 6th Australasian Conference on Information Security and Privacy (ACISP 2001)*, pages 417–434. Springer, 2001.

[310] J. Baek and Y. Zheng. Identity-based threshold decryption. In *Public Key Cryptography–PKC 2004*, pages 262–276. Springer, 2004.

[311] J. Baek and Y. Zheng. Identity-based threshold signature scheme from the bilinear pairings. In *Proceeding of the International Conference on Information and Technology: Coding and Computing (ITCC'04)*, volume 1, pages 124–128. IEEE, 2004.

[312] X. Chen, F. Zhang, and D.M. Konidala. New ID-based threshold signature scheme from bilinear pairings. In *Proceedings of the 5th International Conference on Cryptology in India*, pages 371–383. Springer-Verlag, 2004.

[313] L. Wang, Z. Cao, X. Li, and H. Qian. Simulatability and security of certificateless threshold signatures. *Information Sciences*, 177(6):1382–1394, 2007.

[314] H. Yuan, F. Zhang, X. Huang, Y. Mu, W. Susilo, and L. Zhang. Certificateless threshold signature scheme from bilinear maps. *Information Sciences*, 180(23):4714–4728, 2010.

[315] H. Xiong, F. Li, and Z. Qin. Certificateless threshold signature secure in the standard model. *Information Sciences*, 237(10):73–81, 2013.

[316] Y. Long and K. Chen. Certificateless threshold cryptosystem secure against chosen-ciphertext attack. *Information Sciences*, 177(24):5620–5637, 2007.

[317] Y. Long and K. Chen. Efficient chosen-ciphertext secure certificateless threshold key encapsulation mechanism. *Information Sciences*, 180(7):1167–1181, 2010.

[318] C.H.Tseng, S. H. Wang, and W. J. Tsaur. Hierarchical and dynamic elliptic curve cryptosystem based self-certified public key scheme for medical data protection. *IEEE Transactions on Reliability*, 64(3):1078–1085, 2015.

[319] W. Wu, Y. Mu, W. Susilo, X. Huang, and L. Xu. A provably secure construction of certificate-based encryption from certificateless encryption. *The Computer Journal*, 55(10):1157–1168, 2012.

[320] Q. Jing, A. V. Vasilakos, J. Wan, J. Lu, and D. Qiu. Security of the internet of things: Perspectives and challenges. *Wireless Networks*, 20(8):2481–2501, 2014.

Index